# Weekend Breaks
# from London

**www.timeout.com**

**Time Out Guides Ltd**
Universal House
251 Tottenham Court Road
London W1T 7AB
United Kingdom
Tel: +44 (0)20 7813 3000
Fax:+44 (0)20 7813 6001
Email: guides@timeout.com
www.timeout.com

**Published by Time Out Guides Ltd**, a wholly owned subsidiary of Time Out Group Ltd.
Time Out and the Time Out logo are trademarks of Time Out Group Ltd.

**Printer** Printed and bound by BGP, Chaucer Business Park, Launton Road, Bicester OX26 4QZ.

Time Out Group uses paper products that are environmentally friendly, from well managed forests and mills that use certified (PEFC) Chain of Custody pulp in their production.

**ISBN:** 978-1-905042-68-5

Distribution by Comag Specialist (01895 433 800). For further distribution details, see www.timeout.com.

MIX
Paper from
responsible sources
FSC™ C004592

**Published by**

**Time Out Guides Limited**
**Universal House**
**251 Tottenham Court Road**
**London W1T 7AB**
Tel +44 (0)20 7813 3000
Fax +44 (0)20 7813 6001
email guides@timeout.com
www.timeout.com

**Editorial**
**Editor** Chris Moss
**Deputy Editor** Anna Norman
**Proofreader** Tamsin Shelton
**Indexer/researcher** William Crow

**Editorial Director** Sarah Guy
**Series Editor** Cath Phillips
**Editorial Manager** Holly Pick
**Management Accountants** Margaret Wright, Clare Turner

**Design**
**Art Editor** Pinelope Kourmouzoglou
**Senior Designer** Kei Ishimaru
**Group Commercial Designer** Jodi Sher

**Picture Desk**
**Picture Editor** Jael Marschner
**Picture Desk Assistant/Researcher** Ben Rowe

**Advertising**
**New Business & Commercial Director** Mark Phillips
**International Advertising Manager** Kasimir Berger
**International Sales Executive** Charlie Sokol
**Advertising Sales** (UK) Richard Delooze, Media Sales Network; (Amsterdam)
Keeley Warren-Langford, Time Out Amsterdam; (Copenhagen) Hans Hermansen,
Ad-Made; (Marrakech) Aniko Boehler

**Marketing**
**Guides Marketing Manager** Colette Whitehouse
**Group Commercial Art Director** Anthony Huggins
**Circulation & Distribution Manager** Dan Collins

**Production**
**Group Production Manager** Brendan McKeown
**Production Controller** Katie Mulhern-Bhudia

**Time Out Group**
**Chairman & Founder** Tony Elliott
**Chief Executive Officer** David King
**Chief Operating Officer** Aksel Van der Wal
**Editor-in-Chief** Tim Arthur
**Chief Technical Officer** Remo Gettini
**Group Financial Director** Paul Rakkar
**Group General Manager/Director** Nichola Coulthard
**UK Chief Commercial Officer** David Pepper
**Time Out International Ltd MD** Cathy Runciman
**Cultural Development Director** Mark Elliott

**Contributors** Jessica Baldwin, Alex Berwick, David Clack, Alix Cuthbertson, Daniel Elkan, Rachael Getzels, Sarah Guy, Zoe Kamen, Johanna Kamradt, Kathryn Miller, Anna Norman, Russell Parton, Emily Ray, Shalinee Singh, Clara Tait, Time Out Amsterdam, Time Out Beirut, Time Out St Petersburg, Chris Waywell, Natalya Wells, Jon Wilks, Ben Williams, Yolanda Zappaterra

**The Editor would like to thank** Arriva Wales, First Great Western, Tourism Southeast, Virgin Trains, Visit Ireland, Visit Liverpool, Visit Manchester, Visit Wales, Visit Scotland

**Maps** Kei Ishimaru.

**Cover photography** Available Light/Prioy Bay Hotel, Elan Fleisher, Grayshott Spa Hotel, Hi Hotel, Island Images/ Prioy Bay Hotel, Karl Blackwell, Mama Shelter, Shutterstock.

**Photography by pages** 3, 91, 121 Kevin Eaves; 11 (top) 231, 234, 235 Lydia Evans; 11 (bottom), 26 (bottom), 30 (bottom), 33 (right and bottom), 37, 40 (bottom), 44 (top), 70, 76 (bottom), 77 (top), 83, 84 (bottom), 93, 98 (top), 107 (top), 110 (bottom), 111 (top right), 116, 117, 118 (top), 131, 147, 148 (top left), 163 (top right), 169 (top), 171, 176, 184, 190, 212 (top), 216 (right), 225 (top), 226, 228, 236 (bottom), 250 (top), 251, 259, 260 (bottom), 261 (top right), 263 (bottom), 264, 265 (top right), 266 (top), 267, 275, 279 (top right) Shutterstock; 12 (left), 65, 66 (top) Sam Robbins; 12 (top right) Biddenden Vinyard; 12 (bottom right), 78 (left) Jason Ingram; 13 (top left), 172, 208 (bottom right), 210, 211 (bottom left), 212 (middle), 214 (bottom), 215 (top), 216 Karl Blackwell; 13 (top right), 139, 140 (right), 164, 165, 200 (top), 202, 236 (right), 243 (bottom right), 247 (top) elan fleisher; 13 (bottom left), 126, 128, 129, 140 (left), 141, 146 (middle), 151, 194, 195 (right), 202 (middle), 242, 243, 245, 247 (bottom), 266 (middle) Olivia Rutherford; 13 (bottom right), 225 (middle left) Mountainpix; 16 (left) Paul Wishart; 15, 77 (bottom) www.fishyrob.co.uk; 17 (bottom) Paul Winch-Furness; 18 Coverdale Studios; 18 (bottom) Nigel Pepper; 20 (right) Ady Kerry ABIPP; 21, 57, 100, 101 (bottom left), 165 (top right), 166, 218, 219 Britta Jaschinski; 22 (bottom) Roy Kilcullen/rkp.uk.com; 23 (top right) Martin Daly; 24 (top right) Jane Rix; 24 (bottom right) Mariyana Misaleva; 25 Adam Edwards; 26 (top) James Spinney; 28 (top) Andrew Roland; 28 (bottom) Gordon Bell; 29 (top right) James Hudson; 32 (bottom) Matthew Cole; 34 Hazeelin Hassan; 38 (top), 62 (bottom), 63 (middle), 225 (bottom right), 227 (bottom right) Rob Greig; 38 (bottom) Michael Stokes; 42 (bottom right) Evgeny Karandaev; 43 (top) Bernd Juergens; 44 (bottom) Tom Davison; 45 (bottom right) Rob Scotcher; 47 Chris Harvey; 48 (top) Richard Rowland; 48 (bottom left) David Churchill; 50, 51 (middle and bottom right) Adam Monaghan; 51 (top) Daniel Nielson; 53 (bottom left) Alan Jeffery; 53 (bottom right) Richard Donovan/Shutterstock; 54, 55 (bottom right), 56 (bottom), 83 (top), 157 (top right), 205 (bottom middle) Jonathan Perugia; 55 (top left) Andy Poole; 55 (top right) Lance Bellers; 55 (bottom right) Mark Bowditch; 56 (top) Mike Caldwell; 56 (middle) Nick Hawkes; 57 (bottom), 58 (bottom), 60 (top) Marilyn Barbone; 59 (bottom) Nick Reynolds; 60, 64, 65 (top right) Alys Tomlinson; 60 (top right) Russ Witherington/Shutterstock; 62 (middle), 63 (top), 157 (middle left), 166 (top right) Jael Marschner; 63 (bottom left) Lance Bellers/Shutterstock; 63 (bottom right) Maribel Bennett; 66 (middle) Peter Brown; 66 (bottom) Chris Herring; 67 Laurence Gough; 68 David Hughes; 69 Leonard Smith; 72, 73 Sam Robbins; 77 (top left) James Boden; 79 Matt Wilson; 80 (top) R. Gino Santa Maria; 80 (left) Chris Pierre; 81 (middle) Kayros Studios; 81 (bottom) Alexander Raths; 82 (bottom) Delmas Lehman; 84 (top left), 85 Bela Struzkova; 85 (top right) Ian Trotter; 85 (bottom) Eric Isselee; 86 Stanislav Komogorov; 87 Gail Johnson; 89 Emily Goodwin; 94 Nathan Cox; 96, 191 (bottom right), 229 (right), 265 (bottom left), 278 Alamy; 98 (bottom left) David Young; 98 (bottom right) Andrew Lever; 99 (bottom) The Red Carnation Hotel Collection; 103 Ant Cluasen; 104 Sandra van der Steen; 105 (bottom) Mark McNulty; 109 Kevin Eaves; 110 (top) Tom Plesnik; 114, 115 (bottom left) Walter Weber; 115 (right) Rachael Lewington; 123 David Hughes; 132 (middle left), 133 James A Gordon; 132 (middle left) Josemaria Toscana; 135 (bottom left) Nathan Guinn; 141 (bottom right), 177, 179 (top), 181, 239 (bottom left) Heloise Bergman; 143 Disney; 144 DR; 145, 204, 205 (bottom right) Gianluca Moggi; 148 (bottom left) Rémi Villaggi-Metz Rémi Villaggi for Mudam; 149 Lazar Mihai-Bogdan; 153 www.hugoferan.com; 153 (top left) Gemma Day; 153 (bottom), 205 (bottom left) Michelle Grant; 154 (top) Daphne van Goeningen; 154 (middle) Luuk Kramer; 155 Matthew Lea; 157 Oliver Knight; 163 (bottom left) Andy Poole; 168 (right) Andre Goncalves; 169 (bottom and middle left), 170 Liechtenstein Tourism; 172 (middle right) Jonathan Cox; 172 (bottom left), 179 (bottom), 211, 213 (top), 214 Anna Norman; 174 Tom Plesnik; 175 (top) Souchon Yves; 179 (middle) Tyler Olson; 183 Carlos Neto/Shutterstock; 185, 189, 276 (right) Philip Lange; 185 (bottom left) Tupungato/Shutterstock.com; 187 (top right) Anibal Trejo; 193, 194 (bottom), 195 Tove K. Breitstein; 197 Igor Plotnikov; 198 (top) Marketa Mark; 199 Carsten Medom Madsen/Shutterstock.com; 200 (bottom), 201 (middle right), 203 (top) Greg Gladman; 201, 203 (bottom) Marc Goodwin; 201 (bottom right) Regien Paassen; 205 (top) Timur Kulgarin; 207 KölnTourismus GmbH/Dieter Jacobi; 208 (top right), 268, 269 (top) Grace Manurung; 209 (bottom) KölnTourismus GmbH/ Andreas Möltgen; 189 (bottom) www.antoniochaves.com; 191 (middle left) Grande Duc/Shutterstock; 191 (bottom left) Oleksiy Mark; 191 (top right) Joel Rosenberg/ Kuvataiteen keskusarkisto/ Centralarkivet för bildkonst/CAA; 212 (bottom), 213 (bottom) Jon Santa Cruz; 215 (bottom) © Enrico Dagnino/2eBureau HI HOTEL; 219 (bottom left) Matthias Straka; 220 Schloss Schönbrunn Kultur- und Betriebsges.m.b.H.; 221 Botond Horvath; 223 Ben Rowe; 224 www.swiss-image.ch/Christof Sondereger; 225 (top right) Leonardo Viti; 225 (bottom), 236 (top) Janie Airey; 229 (left) Yadid Levy/Robert Harding; 236 (bottom) Eric Dahier; 237 (top) visitfinland.com; 237 (bottom) Paul Hakimata; 238 Svetlana Larina; 239 Anders Gjengedal/visitnorway.com; 241 251, 253, 254 Claire Bobbyer; 248 Robert Rozbora; 249 (top left) Arnold van Wijk; 249 (top right) Pavel Svoboda; 249 (bottom left), 250 Chris Moss; 249 (bottom right) Frank Bach; 255, 256, 257, 258 (top) Fumie Suzuki; 260 (top left) Sergey Petrov/Shutterstock.com; 263 Fernando Batista; 264 (middle left) Frank Gaertner; 265 (right) Pedro Salaverria; 269 (middle) Mikael Damkier; 270 Ben Rosenzweig; 271, 272 Michael Kirby; 272 (top left) Ilenia Martini; 272 (top right) PHB.cz/Shutterstock.com; 273 (top) Noah Kalina; 273 (bottom) Sergio Ruiz; 279 (top left), 280, 281 TO Beirut; 279 (bottom) Styve Reineck.

The following images were supplied by the featured establishments/artists: pages 16 (right), 17 (top), 20 (bottom left), 22, 23, 24, 26 (middle), 27, 29, 30, 32, 33, 35, 36, 38, 39, 40 (top), 42, 43, 45, 48, 51 (middle and bottom right), 53 (top), 58, 59 (top), 62 (top), 65 (bottom right), 75, 76, 77 (bottom right), 78 (right), 80 (right), 81 (top), 82, 84 (right), 85 (bottom right), 88, 89, 99 (top), 101, 104, 105, 107, 108, 111, 112, 115 (top), 118, 119, 121, 122, 124, 125, 127, 132, 134, 135, 136, 137, 141 (top right), 146, 148, 154, 163, 169, 175, 184 (top), 185, 187, 189 (middle), 191 (top left and middle right), 195 (bottom left), 198, 208, 209, 211 (middle right), 222, 227, 229 (bottom left), 235 (bottom), 237 (middle), 239, 258 (bottom), 260 (top right), 261 (bottom left), 265 (top left), 266 (bottom), 269 (bottom), 271 (bottom right), 276, 277.

# EXPLORE FROM THE INSIDE OUT

Time Out Guides written by local experts

Our city guides are written from a unique insider perspective
by teams of local writers.

Covering 50 destinations, the range includes the official
London 2012 guide.

**visit timeout.com/shop**

'UNSURPASSABLE'
*The Times*

# About the guide

No tricks here. There are four sections of varying length in this guide, covering Easy Weekends, Best of Britain, European Hops and Big Weekends. The book runs, loosely, from places that are close in space and time for London residents (Chilterns, Kent's Low Weald, Brighton) to those that are further away (Berlin, Istanbul, New York). It's all relative, of course, as a south-west Londoner can be in the New Forest a hell of a lot quicker than someone who lives in Hackney. The same goes for the airports: Stansted will suit residents of Bethnal Green and Tottenham Hale but won't be so convenient for anyone who lives close to the train line to Gatwick or in West London. Thus, all journey times are approximate and the journey times we give in 'Fast facts' are the main journey time (that is, from a London rail terminal or airport to another or along a motorway or main road from A to B).

Don't expect waffle about the cities, towns, villages and landscapes. This book is intended to be partly an inspirational prompt and partly a practical guide, to provide you with the motivation to get off your sofa-arse, and the essential information to plan a weekend of fun, tasty food, interesting culture and entertainment (though not too much of any one thing) and to book a good hotel, B&B or campsite. Modes of transport depend on your likes and dislikes and carbon concerns, and we've tried to provide advice as to whether you need a car to get to and around certain places. Equally, once you've arrived, many of the destinations in the book are walkable or bike-friendly; where not, we try to make it clear that you'll need to get a hire car or taxi.

## Length matters

It's easy to throw away four or five weeks' holiday on a couple of fortnights at the beach. But why not steal some of those days back and add on a Friday and/or a Monday to your weekend so you can go to Granada, or Palermo, or even Abu Dhabi, and not have to rush things? Anyone who has joined the Friday evening exodus out of the capital or, even worse, found themselves gridlocked on an inbound motorway after 4pm on a Sunday, will know that being amid the hordes is not fun – and does not represent the kind of break from London life you probably need. So, while your boss, your bank account, the demands of your kids' school and general life pressures will determine how you spend your leisure time, we do recommend adding an extra day for those trips that involve airports or train journeys of more than three hours.

## Extras

For most of the destinations, we've suggested some festivals and events you might want to plan around – most of these are pretty major shows, so make sure you book travel and accommodation well in advance if you opt for these weekends. We've also given some 'cultural baggage' suggestions: books, films and records to read, watch and listen to before you go, while you travel or once you've arrived. Time Out has arts and culture in its DNA and we know our readers want more than food, drink and sights when they travel.

## Keep in touch

We'd love to know how you get on with your travels. Email us at travel@timeout.com or follow us on twitter @TimeOutTravel. We know listings change and venues too, so let us know what you liked and disliked, loved and loathed so that we can make our update of *Weekend Breaks from London* even better.

# Contents

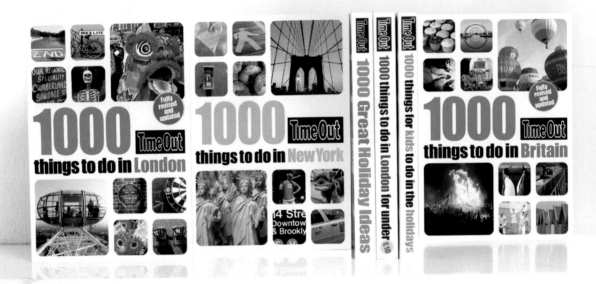

# EXPLORE FROM THE INSIDE OUT

## Time Out Guides written by local experts

Walk with a llama in Britain, discover a secret garden in London, get a rockabilly haircut in New York.

With original and inspirational ideas for both tourists and seen-it-all-before locals, there's always more to be uncovered.

## visit timeout.com/shop

1000's OF THINGS TO DO

# Introduction

What have Essex, Luxembourg, Reykjavik and New York got in common? The answer isn't dodgy bankers – well it is, but it's not the one we're after. The right answer is: weekends, and their belonging to the category of reachable, realistic breaks for anyone who wants to do something special on Saturday and Sunday.

It usually takes a few years of travelling before you realise that short breaks are more often than not better than long ones. Why? Three obvious reasons: one, you don't invest as much time, money or expectation-energy into them; two, it's human nature to make the most of a short-term experience – there's no time for wasting and worrying, not to mention missing home; three – and this is especially true for London – the variety of weekend experiences makes them feel like awakenings or little epiphanies, an easy, painless and neat way to ratchet up travel and your knowledge of the planet.

With so many London airports – bogus and otherwise – encircling the city, HS1 and the Channel Tunnel, fast and frequent intercity trains (including the only sleeper services in the country) a handful of major ports – as well as the great riches of the English countryside looping around

us in the south-east – we Londoners have it pretty easy. Think how tricky it is for someone in Leeds to get to northern France, or for someone in mid-Wales to fly to Barcelona. While travel often falls far short of Grand Tour-style fantasies, most of the no-frills airlines no longer treat passengers differently from the flag-flyers, and travelling in comfort is often a question of picking your weekend carefully (not bank holidays, not school holidays, not Christmas) and planning a clever exit strategy: a night drive, an off-peak train, a special deal for flying early or late.

'I don't have the time,' you protest. We have 104 weekend days in a year. That's a lot of time, especially if you multiply it by years in your adult life – from the ages of 20 to 70, for instance, that comes to more than 5,000 days (or 14 years) off.

While lots of Saturdays and Sundays can be happily given over to lying in at home, nursing hangovers, eating full breakfasts, sorting out the shopping and the kids and home life, it would be a bit insane to lose them all in a blur of recovering from work. Think of it like this: do you want to spend 15 years of your life watching *Saturday Kitchen* and *The X-Factor* and morosely daydreaming through an eternity of suburban Sundays.

After all, the French revolutionaries insisted on the right not to graft on Sundays and then our working-class forbears fought for an extra day to go to Blackpool or Brighton. Nowadays – as the spread of destinations in this guide indicates – we might go to rural Dorset or Iceland or even New York. Or we may opt for a dining experience

or luxurious spa treatment over distance. Or we may feel the inclination to work out and get some wind in our hair, in the Brecon Beacons, the Scottish Highlands or a campsite in Surrey. Or we may just go to Blackpool, and relive the nostalgia and (fairly) innocent freedoms of an English resort town. All in the name of the proletariat of course.

There you go – well, we hope you'll go, to Essex, Luxembourg, Reykjavik and New York, and to Belfast, Beirut, Berlin and Bognor. *Time Out*'s been doing weekend breaks for a couple of decades now, and we've kind of fallen in love with them. For a spell, it was all about rural retreats and walks. Then came the cheap short-haul flights to obscure but interesting airports. And we had a spell of flight-free European travel: trains, buses, bikes to Avignon and Scandinavia.

Fashions come and go, as do recessions and recoveries. For this guide, we've picked and chosen and tried to combine some classics with a few fresh ideas, and some cheap and easy options with some indulgent, splash-out, once-in-a-year trips. So, enjoy your travels – and if you work your way though this book you can consider your weekends well spent. You'll also appreciate the lie-ins and Saturdays and Sundays at home even more than you do now.

**Chris Moss**
Editor and *Time Out London* magazine's
Travel Editor

**Anna Norman**
Deputy Editor

NORTH NORFOLK
COAST
p64

NORFOLK BROADS
p67

SUFFOLK
p70

OXFORD
p44

ESSEX p16

THE CHILTERNS
p25

WHITSTABLE
p61

THE COTSWOLDS
p28

WINDSOR
p34

LONDON

HAMPTON COURT
p37

WILTSHIRE
p87

EAST SUSSEX
COAST
p50

WEST SUSSEX
COAST
p54

BRIGHTON
p47

LOW WEALD &
ROMNEY MARSH
p19

# UK Breaks:
# Easy Weekends

# Essex

Londoners flooding eastwards out of the city for the weekend usually snub Essex and speed towards further-flung destinations with reputations that promise more rural glamour and less bling. But Essex, unfairly caricatured in the media and in the snootier parts of London, offers some of the closest beaches to the capital along a coast that vies with Cornwall's for length. If it lacks the craggy drama of the Cornish cliffs, it offers instead a sublime, smooth landscape of sea walls and expansive tidal flats, tamed with sea-battered groynes and painted beach huts. Inland, the ornate turrets and finials of stately homes spike-wide open skies and offer sweeping vantage points from which to absorb the overwhelmingly pastoral landscape.

The easiest way to explore Essex is by car. Transport links to the main towns are good, but driving enables weekenders to delve into the winding back roads and smaller villages at a pace unrestricted by timetables.

## Fast facts

**Journey time** (Colchester) train 45 minutes; car around 1 hour 30 minutes
**Festivals & events** Essex Country Show (September, www.barleylands.co.uk) – the largest gathering of steam engines in the South-east with all the trappings of a country fair; Maldon Mud Race (April, www.maldonmudrace.com) – a yearly charity event that sees locals (often in fancy dress) run across the muddy River Blackwater at low tide; Burnham Art Trail (June, www.burnhamarttrail.co.uk) – a week-long annual event in the seaside town of Burnham, showcasing local artists
**Good for** Beaches, countryside, food, history, wildlife

LifeHouse Spa

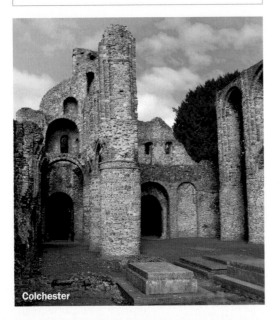

Colchester

Layer Marney Tower

Bull

## SEE & DO

**Colchester** is Britain's oldest recorded town, home to Colchester Castle and the site of scenic Roman ruins. The newly opened **FirstSite** art gallery (High Street, 01206 577067, www.firstsite.uk.net), with its golden alloy cladding, is strong on contemporary art – with collections on loan from the Tate – as well as ancient Roman artefacts including the Berryfield Mosaic. Another gallery worth a trip is the **Fry Art Gallery** in Saffron Walden (Castle Street, 01799 513779, www.fryartgallery.org), which features work by Edward Bawden, among other 20th-century artists.

Essex has over 14,000 listed buildings. **Layer Marney Tower** (near Colchester, 01206 330784, www.layermarney tower.co.uk) is a redbrick Tudor gatehouse, built in 1520 by Henry, 1st Lord Marney, to mimic Hampton Court. Exploring the maze of rooms that open off the precariously spiralling staircases can easily absorb a few rainy hours.

Of the many other beautiful buildings dotted all around the county, it's just a question of picking a period. Choose from Jacobean splendour at **Audley End House and Gardens** (Saffron Walden, 01799 522842, www.english-heritage.org.uk), or the Tudor pile of **Ingatestone Hall** (Ingatestone, 01277 353010, www.ingatestonehall.com); visit **Hedingham Castle** (Castle Hedingham, 01787 460261, www.hedinghamcastle.co.uk) for Norman severity or the softened ruins of **Hadleigh Castle** (near Southend, www.hadleighcastle.co.uk) out on the marshes for a more romantic view.

The county has some of the most diverse coastline in Britain. A labyrinth of meandering rivers, backwaters and tidal inlets opens out on to wide sandy beaches. The areas between Canvey Island in the Thames Estuary and Harwich to the north have seen a concerted push in recent years to conserve and regenerate natural wetlands and create reserves where visitors can witness the vast annual migrations of aquatic birds. The RSPB's most ambitious project, on **Wallasea Island**, encompasses an area two and a half times the size of London. Essex Marine Services offer regular seal-watching trips (01702 258666, www.ladyessex.com), out of **Burnham-on-Crouch**; on dry land, there are fossils to be found along the coast near **Walton-on-the-Naze**. The **Naze Tower** (www.nazetower.co.uk), built in 1720 and recently restored, provides a great view of the area and a tea house at the bottom provides sustenance for the 111-step climb.

Pheasant

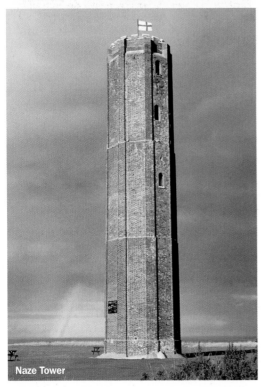

Naze Tower

Just over ten miles inland from Walton-on-the-Naze is the **Beth Chatto Garden** (01206 822007, www.bethchatto.co.uk), in Elmstead Market: one of several horticultural gems in the county, and a pioneering example of ecological gardening. There's a tearoom and garden centre attached.

## EAT & DRINK

The oysters of Essex have been famous for millennia. Colchester Natives were raised in the estuarine waters off the coast, and the succulent molluscs were shipped all the way to Rome when Romans ruled the shores. (Maldon's sea-salt flakes are the present-day global export.) Head to Mersea Island to slurp oysters and crack crustacean carapaces: the perennially popular **Company Shed** (129 Coast Road, West Mersea, 01206 382700, www.the-company-shed.co.uk) is a basic oyster shack where huge platters are served; diners bring their own bread and booze. Arrive early to chalk your name up on the board. Alternatively, the **West Mersea Oyster Bar** (Coast Road, West Mersea, 01206 381600, www.westmerseaoysterbar.co.uk), just along the quay, takes reservations and serves bread too.

Essex is still heavily devoted to pastoral pursuits and in the right season, the back roads are dotted with produce stands with honesty boxes for plums and other orchard fruits. Inland, the Wilkin family has been growing fruit and preserving history since 1885 on the **Tiptree Jam Estate**. Try some spread on scones at one of its three tearooms (Tiptree, 01621 814524, www.tiptree.com). Twenty miles north of Tiptree, the **Pheasant** pub in Gestingthorpe (01787 461196, www.thepheasant.net) has an on-site smokery, where they even waft smoke through the beer.

## STAY

Your appreciation of Essex's architectural heritage doesn't have to stop at the red ropes. **Hedingham Castle** (*see p17*), offers its Tudor lodge for hire and **Layer Marney** (*see p17*), has an Edwardian folly available for rent.

Offering something a little different, **Bouncers Farm** (01621 894112, www.operaintheorchard.co.uk) in Wickham Bishops has a gaggle of geese to greet your arrival, four restored gypsy caravans and a campsite in apple orchards. For a more traditional stay, the **Bull** at Great Totham (01621 89338, www.thebullatgreattotham.co.uk) has four en suite B&B rooms attached to a gastropub.

If you're looking to be pampered, the **LifeHouse Spa** (01255 860050, www.lifehouse.co.uk) in Thorpe-le-Stoken has 35 treatment rooms set amid 130 manicured acres.

## GETTING THERE & AROUND

Driving is the easiest way to get around Essex, but if you want to use public transport, there are plenty of trains from London and then an extensive network of local buses (www.travelinesoutheast.org.uk).

### Cultural baggage

**Book** *This Luminous Coast* (Jules Pretty, 2011)
**Film** *Starter for Ten* (Tom Vaughan, 2006)
**Album** *The Planets* (Gustav Holst, 1914-16)

# Low Weald & Romney Marsh

The historic seaside market towns of Rye in East Sussex and Hythe in Kent lie at either end of the Low Weald – the old Saxon name for the clay vales and low-slung woodlands between the chalk ridges of the North and South Downs. Inside its boundaries are the windswept wetlands of Romney Marsh as well as a trio of picture-perfect villages: Tenterden, Biddenden and Pluckley. Bleak-but-beautiful Dungeness, with its imposing skyline of two nuclear reactors, a 19th-century lighthouse and a miniature railway – all set in a national nature reserve – is an isolated outpost worth a visit in its own right.

## Fast facts

**Journey time** Train 1 hour 10 minutes; car 1 hour 50 minutes
**Festivals & events** New Romney Country Fayre (July, www.newromneycountryfayre.co.uk); Hythe Venetian Fete (August, www.venetian-fete.com) – takes place on the Royal Military Canal and features fireworks and floating tableaux; Rye Arts Festival (September, www.ryefestival.co.uk)
**Good for** Countryside, food, walking

## SEE & DO

Whatever you decide to do during a visit, walking through the countryside should feature. Undulating clay vales, patchwork fields and pockets of woodland that once covered the whole area make exploring on foot a pleasure. If you want to explore the coast and Romney Marsh, stay in Rye or Hythe, two historic market towns with easy access to the sea and Romney Marsh. Alternatively, if you would rather base yourself in the woodland-rich Lower Weald, a town like Tenterden is a great starting point for exploring the county's lush countryside. The weald is famous for being the genuinely horticultural bit of the 'Garden of England', and the prettiest of all Wealden gardens is at **Sissinghurst Castle** (Biddenden Road, near Cranbrook, 01580 710701, www.nationaltrust.org.uk), an Elizabethan manor house – the former home of Vita Sackville-West – with beautiful ornamental gardens set in acres of woodland.

A world away, in coastal hamlet Dungeness, at the edge of Romney Marsh, you can board the self-proclaimed 'world's smallest railway' (in reference to its 15-inch gauge), the **Romney, Hythe & Dymchurch Railway** (01797 362353, www.rhdr.org.uk), which chugs a 13.5-mile journey from Hythe to Dungeness's eerily beautiful nature reserve. The sparse, shingle landscape is home to a collection of privately owned, eclectic former-fishermen's huts that include film director Derek Jarman's **Prospect Cottage** (Dungeness Road) and Simon Conder Associates' modernist architectural masterpiece **Vista**, which won a RIBA award in 2004 for its innovative rubber cladding. For a breathtaking view of the sea and surrounding area (and nuclear power stations), climb the 169 steps of the **Old Lighthouse** (01797 321300, www.dungeness lighthouse.com).

Circumnavigating the vast, desolate Romney Marsh, the 28-mile **Royal Military Canal** follows the line of cliffs that used to mark the sea borders that have since silted up. It was built in 1809 as a bulwark against the expected invasion by Napoleon's navy, but never saw military action. Today, it's an important home for wildlife, including kingfishers, marsh frogs and dragonflies. It's also one of the best places for coarse fishing in the area: contact one of the local angling clubs for a day pass via www.royalmilitarycanal.com. If you'd like to traverse the waters at your own leisurely pace, hire a rowing boat for around £10 an hour from **Electric Boat Trips** (www.electricboathythe.co.uk, 07718 761236) at Ladies' Walk Bridge in Hythe.

Another highlight of Hythe is the ossuary or 'bonehouse' of **St Leonard's Church Crypt** (Oak Walk, 01303 262370, www.stleonardschurchhythekent.org), which contains some 2,000 skulls, all arranged on shelves so that you can get a good look at them. Their origins are somewhat of a mystery, but they are widely believed to be the remains of Hythe citizens exhumed in the 13th century so the church could be extended. For a small charge, a guide will point out skulls of specific interest.

For more medieval history, explore the battlements and spiral staircases of **Bodiam Castle** (Bodiam, near Robertsbridge, 01580 830196, www.nationaltrust.org.uk), which dates from 1385 and has the original portcullis still intact. The **Bodiam Ferry Company** (01797 253838, www.bodiam-ferry.co.uk) offers 90-minute return cruises three times a day between Newenden and Bodiam Castle.

A few miles away, you can get a hands-on taste of the good life at the **Rare Breeds Centre** (Woodchurch, 01233 861493, www.rarebreeds.org.uk). Daily 'meet the animals' sessions offer a chance to play with the piglets, or feed the hand-reared 'sock' lambs with a baby bottle of milk. There is also an aviary and a butterfly tunnel, as well as open

Bodiam Castle

West House

Quill House

Tenterden

'encounter paddocks' and tractor rides. Nearby, timber-framed **Smallhythe Place** (Smallhythe, Tenterden, 01580 762334, www.nationaltrust.org.uk), once home to actress Ellen Terry, houses an exhibition of her fabulous costume collection, and holds outdoor theatrical performances in the summer months.

## SHOP

If you like rummaging for vintage stuff, the smaller shops in Rye are a good place to start. Go to **Glass Etc** (18-22 Rope Walk, 01797 226600, www.decanterman.com), owned by *The Antiques Roadshow*'s glass specialist Andy McConnell, to pick up all kinds of antique glassware and bottles. **New 2 You Retro** (35 Cinque Ports Street, 01797 226379, www.new2youretrorye.vpweb.co.uk) specialises in mid-century homewares, from Ercol chairs to Midwinter china. **Classic Chaps** (9 Cinque Ports Street, 07918 664512, www.classicchaps.co.uk) – 'the home of sartorial elegance' – stocks a wide range of vintage attire for gentlemen, including one-off theatrical pieces and classic staples such as brogues and panama hats. **Rye Farmers' Market** (Wednesday mornings until 1pm, Strand Quay) has the usual home-made cakes and pies and fresh produce, as well as locally brewed beer and fresh fish. Stop by for a picnic lunch to take to the nearby dunes at **Camber Sands** (New Lydd Road, Camber, www.eastsussex.gov.uk), a wide stretch of sandy beach about a mile from Rye town centre.

Hythe also has a selection of interesting shops: **ArtWrite** (90A High Street, 01303 261925, www.artwritehythe.co.uk) has shelves stacked with all kinds of artists' materials, from brushes and charcoal to watercolours and art books. If you have somewhere to cook it, buy fish at **Griggs of Hythe** (Fisherman's Landing Beach, Range Road,

01303 266400, www.griggsofhythe.com), which supplies fish to many fine London restaurants.

Moving inland, the pretty market town of Tenterden has several smart antiques shops, including **Tenterden Antique & Silver Vaults** (66A High Street, Tenterden, 01580 765885), selling furniture, silver items, Victorian dolls and art deco-style jewellery. Handmade chocolates can be found further along the High Street at **Truffles@CoCo** (no.128, 01580 763501) and **Webb's of Tenterden** (www.webbsoftenterden.com) has three outlets on the High Street: the original hardware store and ironmonger at no.51 (01580 762132); a linen and gift shop at no.49; and a kitchen store at no.45 (01580 762133), selling high-end lines from Emma Bridgewater and Le Creuset.

## EAT & DRINK

Rye's the **George** (98 High Street, 01797 222114, www.thegeorgeinrye.com) has a wood charcoal grill that cooks fresh fish, local meats and vegetables in a flash; and local wines are served by the glass in the pub's cosy dining room. British food with a modern slant is **Landsgate Bistro**'s speciality (5-6 Landsgate, 01797 222829, www.landsgatebistro.co.uk), earning it the title of Rye's best restaurant in *The Good Food Guide 2012*. A new favourite with Rye locals is **Tuscan Kitchen Trattoria** (8 Lion Street, 01797 223269, www.tuscankitchenrye.co.uk). Florentine chef Franco offers traditional Tuscan dishes served with famous Tuscan wines.

In Hythe, the **Hythe Bay** (Stade Street, Marine Parade, 01303 233844, www.thehythebay.co.uk) restaurant and bar occupies a prime position on the seafront, and has a good selection of local seafood, from oysters to fried whitebait. **Everest Inn** (32-34 High Street, 01303 269898, www.everestinn.co.uk) serves authentic Nepalese and

Indian curries and counts Joanna Lumley among its loyal customers. The **White Hart** (71 High Street, 01303 238304, www.thewhiteharthythe.co.uk) is an 18th-century hotel, restaurant and freehouse serving British classics.

Away from the towns there are lots of small, local eating and drinking places. The Romney, Hythe & Dymchurch Railway's **Light Railway Café** (www.rhdr.org.uk) in Dungeness is a well-preserved slice of English caff culture. Formica tables and kitsch decorations make it a jolly spot to fill up – the fish and chips are eternally popular, as is the £8 Sunday-roast-plus-dessert deal. Lamb from Romney Marsh is a regular fixture on the menus of two of the best restaurants in the area: Michelin-starred **Apicius** (23 Stone Street, Cranbrook, 01580 714666, www.restaurant-apicius.co.uk) in Cranbrook and **West House** (28 High Street, Biddenden, 01580 291341, www.thewesthouserestaurant.co.uk) in Biddenden both serve seasonal Modern European dishes made with local produce. Reservations are essential, but excellent value three-course lunches (£25 at West House, £26 at Apicius) make it well worth the detour. Nearby, the village of Pluckley is famous for being Britain's most-haunted village, so fuel up for a night of ghostly encounters at the **Dering Arms** (The Grove, 01233 840371, www.deringarms.com), an atmospheric former hunting lodge serving local fish (try the soft herring roe or Sussex hot-smoked mackerel) as well as regional ales and ciders. If you're looking for the charms of a traditional Kentish pub, the **Three Chimneys** in Biddenden (Hareplain Road, 01580 291472, www.thethreechimneys.co.uk) will do nicely. Inky-black beams and small rooms interlinked by the main bar provide a cosy atmosphere to enjoy the extensive wine list and local strong ciders from nearby **Biddenden Vineyards** (Gribble Bridge Lane, Biddenden, 01580 291726, www.biddendenvineyards.com).

## STAY

Staying in Rye's historic town centre gives you the choice of a number of excellent B&Bs. **Rye Windmill B&B** (Ferry Road, 01797 224027, www.ryewindmill.co.uk) is conveniently placed just a few moments from the town centre and has ten rooms, two of which are situated in the windmill itself. The breakfast – a selection of fruit, local sausages, eggs and pancakes – is served in the granary

around a large oak table. More upmarket is the **George** (*see p20*), which has a number of chic rooms as well as a cosy bar and grill restaurant. The characterful **Mermaid Inn** (Mermaid Street, 01797 223065, www.mermaidinn.com), meanwhile, is one of the oldest and loveliest inns in the region, with oak-panelled rooms, carved beds, Caen stone fireplaces and lattice windows.

Self-catering cottages are better value for larger parties – and also mean you can cook with the local market produce. **Mulberry Cottages** (www.mulberrycottages.com, 01233 813087) has two cottages in Dungeness – with views of France on a clear day – and one in Hythe town centre, as well as several in neighbouring villages such as Saltwood and Wittersham. If you're looking to stay inland, **88 High Street B&B** (88 High Street, 07710 106280, www.88highstreet.com) in Tenterden is a Victorian property on the tree-lined broadway, and promises a perfect night's rest with orthopaedic mattresses and Egyptian cotton sheets. For a camping trip with pzazz, the fully furnished teepees at **Bloomsbury's at Biddenden** (Sissinghurst Road, Biddenden, 01580 292992, www.bloomsburysbiddenden.com) provide an all-round retreat. On-site therapies offered include Hawaiian Lomi-Lomi massages, and arts and crafts classes – such as ceramic painting and floristry – are also held.

## GETTING THERE & AROUND

Though easily accessible by train (South Eastern Railways will take you from St Pancras to Rye in 1 hour 10 minutes), public bus services in the area are infrequent and expensive. Driving into the area (or hiring a car from a local agency) is probably your best option. Rye is about 66 miles from London and the drive should take something short of two hours – and will free you up to explore, whatever the weather. Romney Marsh was made for cycling, thanks to its flat terrain and sheep-strewn fields leading to the sea. Plan your route to take in as many pub pitstops as you can manage: for inspiration, order the Romney Marsh Meanders, a pack of five circular rides from the **White Cliffs Countryside Partnership** (www.whitecliffscountryside.org.uk). Check public footpath routes online or, if you are a serious walker, pick up a walker's guide, such as the *Time Out Book of Country Walks*.

Dungeness

# Wine Tasting in England

In the past decade, wine production in the UK has tripled. Extreme snobs and Francophiles might still turn their nose up at the idea of 'serious' British wine, but most of us are learning to enjoy the fruits of perfect chalky soils in the south, and consistently good summer temperatures for ripening grapes. The fact that the climate is on the cool side of temperate has been particularly beneficial to sparkling wine producers; as the grapes don't get too sweet, the bubbly remains refreshingly acidic.

Chapel Down

## Chapel Down, Kent

This well-known winery owns two vineyards in Kent, the principal site being at Tenterden, and the other at Kit's Coty, off Bluebell Hill. At the main vineyard, landscaped grounds include over 22 acres of vines, as well as the Wine and Fine Food Store. This sells a full range of wines, plus quality English produce from chutney to ice-cream; there are also dedicated tasting areas. Collect a map here for a walking trail around the estate and vineyards, or take a hot air balloon flight from the vineyard (a glass of Chapel Down fizz is included in the price). Guided tours (01580 766111) of the vineyard and winery run daily, June to September, and on weekends in May and October. Nearby places to stay include Sissinghurst Castle Farmhouse (01580 720992, www.sissinghurst castlefarmhouse.com), a B&B on the National Trust estate, and Elvey Farm (01233 840442, www.elveyfarm.co.uk), which has 11 rooms in historic surroundings. The charming Three Chimneys (01580 291472, www.the threechimneys.co.uk) is the best foodie pub in the area.

**Chapel Down Winery** Tenterden (01580 763033, www.englishwinesgroup.com).

**Getting there** Trains run from Charing Cross to Headcorn, then 15 minutes by taxi.

## Denbies Estate, Surrey

Only 20 miles south-west of London, this is England's biggest single-estate vineyard (around 250 acres). The 2010 Chalk Ridge English rosé won gold at the International Wine Challenge in 2011, but sparkling wines are the speciality here; the soil on the North Downs – the North Downs Way passes directly above the higher slopes of the vineyards – is similar to that found in Champagne. Denbies is open all year (excluding Christmas Day, Boxing Day and New Year's Day). Tours (vineyard from £5.50, winery from £9.50) can be booked online (visit www.denbies.co.uk), or you can simply drop in for a light lunch at the estate's Conservatory restaurant, or something more substantial at the Gallery.

Denbies Farmhouse B&B (01306 876777) is situated at the edge of the vineyard and a double room costs from around £100. Otherwise, Blackbrook House (Blackbrook, Dorking, 01306 888898, www.blackbrookhouse.org.uk), not far away, is a grand Victorian pile with double rooms for around £85.

Ridgeview Wine Estate

Denbies Estate

Stanlake Park

**Denbies Wine Estate** London Road, Dorking (01306 876616, www.denbies.co.uk).
**Getting there** The vineyard is a 20-minute walk from Dorking or Box Hill & Westhumble stations. Trains to both stations run from Victoria and take 50 minutes; Dorking is also served by trains from Waterloo.

## Gusbourne Wines, Kent

This 200-acre estate dates back to 1410, and now holds 20 acres of vines; the three geese motif from the original crest is used on the vineyard's label. This is a family business, and one that takes pride in its sustainable methods. A tasting tour consists of a visit to the vineyards and winery, plus tastings of the estate's four wines: Brut Reserve, Blanc de Blancs, rosé and the still pinot noir. Stay nearby in High Halden in the Rectory Barn B&B (01233 850287, www.rectory barn-bedandbreakfast.co.uk), a converted medieval barn with a beautiful one-acre traditional English garden, or in Tenterden in the Tower House (www.tower-house.biz), a B&B in a Georgian house.
**Gusbourne Estate** Appledore (01233 758666, www.gusbourne.com).
**Getting there** Trains run from St Pancras to Appledore and take 1 hour 15 minutes, then 10 minutes by taxi (although Ashford, with its high-speed rail link to London, is only 10 minutes further away).

Olde Bell

**42 The Calls**

**Compleat Angler**

## Leventhorpe Vineyard, Yorkshire

Wine production in England now extends as far north as Yorkshire. This five-acre winery within Leeds' city boundaries is 25 years old, and has won praise from top chefs and wine critics for its delicate white Madeleine Angevine. The production building is more of a shed than a chateau, but its location is perfect, with its own microclimate in which vines are shielded from frost. It's open daily for visits and tastings (of wine and Yorkshire cheese). If you want to stay overnight, there are a number of boutique hotels in Leeds, including 42 The Calls (0113 244 0099, www.42thecalls.co.uk), converted from an 18th-century corn mill on the river.

**Leventhorpe Vineyard** Bullerthorpe Lane, Woodlesford, Leeds (0113 228 9088).

**Getting there** Woodlesford is less than 10 minutes on the train from Leeds station. There are regular trains from King's Cross to Leeds – the journey takes 2 hours 15 minutes.

## Ridgeview Wine Estate, East Sussex

This family-run winery in the South Downs was founded in 1994, and specialises in quality sparkling wines. The Grosvenor Blanc de Blancs 2007 won several awards in 2011. The vineyard is open 11am-4pm Mon-Sat (excluding October), and the tasting room is open throughout the year. Private tours (1.5 hours) cost £10 per person for a group of at least ten, and tasting events are held regularly. There's no food available, but the Bull Pub in Ditchling (a five-minute drive) serves seasonal dishes alongside roasts. If you want to stay in the area, Netherwood Lodge (near Lewes, 01825 872512, www.netherwoodlodge.co.uk) is a B&B in an old coach house with a lovely garden. It has two rooms from £45 per person per night including a home-made breakfast.

**Ridgeview Wine Estate** Ditchling Common (0845 345 7292, www.ridgeview.co.uk).

**Getting there** Trains run from London Bridge or Victoria to Wivelsfield and take 50 minutes, then 5 minutes by taxi.

## Stanlake Park, Berkshire

A small area of vines was planted on the estate in 1979, and this has now expanded to 25 acres with over 20,000 vines. Stanlake Park grows the largest number of grape varieties in England, and uses some unique trellising systems. Try the fruity but brightly acidic Bacchus from 2005. The vineyard is open all week; free tastings are offered for groups of up to four people. There is no restaurant on site, but the Olde Bell (01628 825939, www.theoldebell.co.uk) in Hurley is a minimally decorated but cosy inn with classic English grub and a pretty garden. A 20-minute drive away in Marlow, the Compleat Angler (08448 799128, www.macdonaldhotels.co.uk/compleatangler) is beautifully located on the Thames, and has a good restaurant.

**Stanlake Park Wine Estate** Twyford (01189 340176, www.stanlakepark.com).

**Getting there** The estate is a short walk or two-minute taxi ride from Twyford station, on the Paddington–Maidenhead–Reading line.

# The Chilterns

At the north-western end of both the Metropolitan tube and the Chiltern railway line, the Chiltern Hills in Buckinghamshire are an Area of Outstanding Natural Beauty as well as a popular, peaceful dormitory for commuters. As we go to press the rolling chalk hills are threatened by the government's HS2 scheme, which aims to build a high-speed rail line between London and Birmingham. Until that takes place, the Chilterns are one of London's closest genuine agricultural landscapes. Smart little towns such as Amersham, Chalfont St Giles, Great Missenden and Wendover allow easy access to hundreds of miles of way-marked walks, including sections of England's oldest footpath, the Ridgeway.

## Fast facts

**Journey time** Train from 50 minutes (Aylesbury); tube around 1 hour (Chesham); car around 1 hour (Aylesbury)

**Festivals & events** Chilterns Countryside Festival (September, www.chilternsaonb.org) – annual festival celebrating the crafts, industries and wildlife associated with the Chilterns countryside, with local produce stalls, craft displays, forestry demonstrations and children's activities in the meadow behind the AONB Visitor Centre; Roald Dahl Festival (July, www.aylesburyvaledc.gov.uk) – celebrations at Aylesbury's annual Roald Dahl Festival include a themed parade of giant Dahl characters, street theatre, competitions and free entrance to the Dahl Children's Gallery

**Good for** Countryside, food, walking

## SEE & DO

Welcome to Metroland, the name coined for the areas north-west of London served by the Metropolitan Railway. On the train (or tube) up to the area, read John Betjeman's poems 'Harrow-on-the-Hill' ('When melancholy autumn comes to Wembley/And electric trains are lighted after tea'), 'Middlesex' ('Gaily into Rusilip Gardens/Runs the red electric train') and 'The Metropolitan Railway' ('Early Electric! With what radiant hope/Men formed this many-branched electrolier'). By the time you get past Harrow-on-the-Hill you'll leave urban sprawl behind and start to see mock Tudor houses and leafy estates. Spend Saturday hopping on and off at stops on the Chiltern railway line to explore a handful of villages, before heading out to see the hills on Sunday.

**Great Missenden** is an excellent first stop. The town lay on a once major route between the Midlands and London; coaches were served by the George (94 High Street, 01494 862084, www.georgeinngreatmissenden.co.uk) and

**Roald Dahl Museum and Story Centre**

stretches where the hills are forested, with footpaths providing an easy ramble along the higher reaches. There are good paths from Wendover – the **Wendover Loop** is a great 14-mile stretch of the Chiltern Cycleway. See www.chilternsaonb.org for an interactive map with walks for all levels of difficulty. Look out for red kites wheeling overhead wherever you wander – between 1989 and 1993 90 birds were released into the Chilterns Area of Outstanding Natural Beauty, and the programme has been a huge success.

**Aylesbury**, the next stop on the line, is the county town of Buckinghamshire. It's not quite the quaint market town it would like to be, but it makes a handy base, and has a tourist information centre (Kings Head Passage, off Market Square, 01296 330559). The County Museum, which contains the **Roald Dahl Children's Gallery**, is housed in the old part of town (Church Street, 01296 331441, www.buckscc.gov.uk).

Just six miles to the west, overlooking the Vale of Aylesbury, is **Waddesdon Manor** (01296 653226, www.waddesdon.org.uk). Completed in 1889 and styled after a French château, it contains the Baron Ferdinand de Rothschild's collection of paintings, tapestries, furniture and ceramics as well as beautiful and extensive gardens.

All the above are possible by public transport. If you're driving, you could swing west to **Cookham**, not least to see the remarkable Stanley Spencer Gallery (High Street, 01628 471885, www.stanleyspencer.org.uk) and pretty **Henley-on-Thames**.

## EAT & DRINK

In Great Missenden, **Café Twit** at the Roald Dahl Museum (*see left*) serves good coffees, cakes and appetising lunches including child-friendly options. The town also has a clutch of decent pubs: the Fullers-owned **Cross Keys** (40 High Street, 01494 865373) is a 16th-century pub with real ales and a reliable restaurant. The 15th-century **Nag's Head** (London Road, 01494 862200, www.nagsheadbucks.com) was Roald Dahl's local; it's about a mile out of Great Missenden and serves excellent, if pricey, food. The former White Lion has been rebranded as **Origins at the White**

the Old Red Lion (now an estate agents). In the south-western corner of the village – reached by a bridge over the bypass – is the medieval parish church of St Peter and St Paul, the burial place of Roald Dahl.

Roald Dahl lived at Gipsy House (still the home of his widow Felicity and not open to the public) from 1954 until his death in 1990, and local scenes and characters are reflected in his work. In June 2005, the **Roald Dahl Museum and Story Centre** (81-83 High Street, 01494 892192, www.roalddahlmuseum.org) – housed in another old coaching inn – opened. On display are Dahl's manuscripts, 'Ideas books' and, from early in 2012, his original Writing Hut. There are interactive exhibits and a Story Centre where kids (and adults) are encouraged to dress up, invent words and stories and get messy in the craft room. There's also a Roald Dahl walking trail through the village – download it from the museum website.

**Wendover**, the next stop on the Marylebone–Aylesbury line, is charming in a rather nondescript way but is located at the foot of the **Chiltern Hills** and is useful for striking out into the **Vale of Aylesbury**. The steep, low Chiltern Hills – a chalk escarpment that's a remnant of the last ice age – extend all the way from Luton to the River Thames at Henley. In Buckinghamshire, there are several pretty

**Waddesdon Manor**

Royal Standard of England

Lion (57 High Street, 01494 863696, www.originswine bar.co.uk ) and is really a wine bar (serving great tapas).

Beaconsfield boasts the **Royal Standard of England** (Forty Green, 01494 673382, www.rsoe.co.uk), which claims to be England's oldest pub at 900 years old. The Sunday Vittals menu lists roasts and pies. In Chalfont St Giles, the **Ivy House** (London Road, 01494 872184, www.fullers hotels.com) is a beautiful old country inn with stunning views across the Misbourne Valley, with great food and well-appointed bedrooms – it also claims a ghost. The Farmers Bar at the National Trust-managed **King's Head** (Market Square, Aylesbury, 01296 381501, www.national trust.org.uk) is a 15th-century inn stocked with a selection of Chiltern Brewery's draught ales and bottled beers, a select wine list and locally sourced food. The **King and Queen** (17 South Street, 01296 623272) in Wendover offers home-cooked food and a great variety of ales, lager and wines.

## STAY

**Hartwell House & Spa** (Oxford Road, 01296 747444, www.hartwell-house.com), two miles outside Aylesbury, is a 17th-century mansion with an excellent restaurant and lavishly appointed bedrooms. Near Great Missenden, the **Nag's Head** (*see left*) has five rooms, all with modern decor and en suite bathrooms, plus flat screen TVs. The **Five Arrows** (01296 651727, www.waddesdon.org.uk/ five_arrows) is a charming Victorian hotel at the gates of Waddesdon Manor; antiques and original pieces from the Manor decorate the rooms.

For a more modern vibe, there's a branch of the **Hotel du Vin** chain (New Street, 01491 848400, www.hoteldu vin.com) in Henley-on-Thames; it's centrally located and has a bistro. The **Crown** (16 High Street, 01494 721541, www.thecrownamersham.com) in Old Amersham featured in *Four Weddings and a Funeral*, but since then has been styled by Ilse Crawford; rooms in the Main Inn are low-key rustic, with wool blankets and rocking chairs, Courtyard rooms have four-posters. The restaurant is modelled after a traditional British chop house, and serves grills, pies and sausage and mash.

## GETTING THERE & AROUND

The Metropolitan Line goes out as far as Chesham and Amersham, after which you can walk or take a local bus. Chiltern Railways runs fast, frequent services on the Marylebone–Aylesbury line between Marylebone and Great Missenden (35 minutes), Wendover and Aylesbury, and on the even faster main line between Marylebone, Beaconsfield and High Wycombe (22 minutes).

Hartwell House & Spa

THE CHILTERNS

# The Cotswolds

The Cotswolds is the fabled area that lies between Bath, Stratford-upon-Avon, Oxford and Cheltenham and is, as the calendars and chocolate boxes indicate, full of rolling hills, medieval churches and houses built with honey-coloured stone and topped by thatched roofs. 'Charming' is one of several clichés applied to the area, but it takes a real cynic to contest the claim. The Cotswolds, especially in the south, form an archetypal English landscape. To escape the tourist hordes, stay away from the place in summer. The south-west corner, between the Severn Valley and Wiltshire, is for the main part relatively low on coach parties and is also the easiest area for Londoners to access. Cotswolds cuisine is a cut above – there's money in these parts – so whenever you go you'll dine well.

Bibury

## Fast facts

**Journey time** Train and car from 1 hour 30 minutes; bus 3 hours
**Festivals & events** Stratford-upon-Avon Literary Festival (late April/early May, www.stratfordliterary festival.co.uk); Cheltenham International Jazz Festival (late April/early May, www.cheltenhamfestivals.co.uk); Cheltenham Food & Drink Festival (June, www.garden-events.com); Bath Christmas Market (Nov/Dec, www.bathchristmasmarket.co.uk); Cheltenham Racecourse (www.cheltenham.co.uk) has race meetings and events throughout the year
**Good for** Countryside, food, walking, wildlife

## SEE & DO

In Gloucestershire, ten miles north-east of Cirencester, is **Bibury**, dubbed 'the most beautiful village in England' by no less than aesthete William Morris. It's almost entirely empty, bar the locals, out of season. **Bibury Trout Farm** (in Bibury, next to Arlington Mill, 01285 740215, www. biburytroutfarm.co.uk) is great for kids, especially during feeding time. Have a look at nearby **Arlington Row** – it's a

Blenheim Palace

Barnsley House

Le Manoir aux Quat'Saisons

collection of Cotswold cottages that are so charming Henry Ford wanted to take them back home with him in the 1920s. Finish with a walk along the river to **Coln St Aldwyns**.

History buffs should check out both **Cirencester** (Roman Corinium) and the **Roman villa at Chedworth**. The **Corinium Museum** (Park Street, 01285 655611, www.cirencester.co.uk/coriniummuseum) has a fine display on why Corinium was one of Roman Britain's most vital settlements, and if you head to the western edge of Cirencester you can see the remains of the local amphitheatre. Yanworth near Chedworth, a bit further north, houses one of the biggest Roman villas in Britain (01242 890256, www.nationaltrust.org.uk).

Also in Gloucestershire is the 55-acre **Batsford Arboretum** (Batsford Park, Moreton-in-Marsh, 01386 701441, www.batsarb.co.uk), which houses one of the

biggest private collections of trees in the country. It's open daily (except for Christmas Day) from 9am.

Water sports fans can easily spend an entire day at the **Cotswolds Water Park** (01793 752413, www.water park.org), which is spread over 40 square miles across Gloucestershire and Wiltshire, and contains around 140 lakes. You can sail, canoe, jet-ski, windsurf or water-ski.

In Oxfordshire, **Blenheim Palace** (Woodstock, 0870 060 2080, www.blenheimpalace.com) is the only non-royal residence in England that's still named 'palace'. The library, state rooms, paintings and tapestries are all splendid; the permanent exhibition on Winston Churchill (who was born here) is interesting too. Also in Oxfordshire is **Burford** (www.burfordcotswolds.co.uk). Its high street is lined with Tudor buildings, and the entire village has an historical film-set atmosphere.

Bell at Sapperton

Bull at Burford

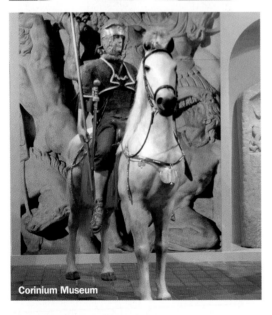

Corinium Museum

William Henry Fox Talbot is celebrated for his contribution to the development of photography. The earliest paper negative is on display at ancient **Lacock Abbey** in Wiltshire (01249 730459, www.nationaltrust. org.uk), which houses the Fox Talbot Museum.

## EAT & DRINK

Burford, as well as being gorgeous, is a perfect town for foodies. The **Bull at Burford** (105 High Street, 01993 822220, www.bullatburford.co.uk) is a anglo-french restaurant (which also doubles as a hotel), and does a great taster menu at dinner for £50.

French chef and BBC cooking show darling Raymond Blanc's **Le Manoir aux Quat'Saisons** (Church Road, Great Milton, 01844 278881, www.manoir.com) is a cookery school as well as a great restaurant. One-, two- or four-day courses are offered. The one-day Seasonal Dinner Party course costs £335 (lunch is included).

The **Seven Tuns** in Chedworth (Queen's Street, 01285 720242) is a 17th-century pub with a family feel. The bar menu is good, but the food in the restaurant at the back is even better. In summer, the South African barbecue is an unmissable treat.

The **Bell at Sapperton** (01285 760298, www.foodatthe bell.co.uk) has had a good reputation for years now, and rightfully so – try the locally sourced pan-fried calf's liver with smoked bacon or the Cotswold lamb with mint and pea risotto. If you're only popping in for lunch, the four-cheese ploughman's platter is a must-try.

## STAY

Boutique B&B **No.12** (12 Park Street, Cirencester, 01285 640232, www.no12cirencester.co.uk) occupies a Grade II-listed Georgian townhouse right in the middle of town, and has enticements such as extra long beds and Molton Brown-laden bathrooms. The **Swan Hotel** (Bibury, 01285 740695, www.cotswold-inns-hotels.co.uk) is right by the River Coln, which makes for great views and walks, plus it has its own spring water, a spa and five (out of 20) bedrooms sport jacuzzis. The **Bay Tree** in Burford (Sheep Street, 01993 822791, www.cotswold-inns-hotels.co.uk), won the 2011 Enjoy England Gold Award for the Best Small Hotel.

At the luxury end of the market is **Cowley Manor** (Cowley, 01242 870900, www.cowleymanor.com). It's a grand building tastefully modernised, with a relaxed, unstuffy atmosphere. The restaurant serves bistro food and there's also a spa on the premises. Alternatively, **Barnsley House** (Barnsley, 01285 740000, www.barnsleyhouse.com) is smaller in scale, but is also housed in an updated historic building, and has a spa. The bedrooms are contemporary and luxurious, with Egyptian cotton sheets, and LCD TVs in the bathrooms.

## GETTING THERE & AROUND

Having a car is the easiest way to explore, but you can also catch a train or bus from London. The train ride to stations such as Gloucester, Chippenham and Moreton-in-Marsh takes around 90 minutes from Paddington. The main coach route from London is via Victoria Station, and there are services to Bath, Gloucester and Oxford operated by National Express (www.nationalexpress.com/coach).

THE COTSWOLDS

# Spa Breaks

Cowley Manor

## Be king or queen for a weekend in Royal Berkshire

Coworth Park is a 240-acre estate, with a striking 17th-century mansion that provides a period backdrop for pampering and country pursuits. Book a relaxed hack around the estate or test yourself with an introductory polo lesson (April-September), and then soothe your muscles with a massage at the luxurious eco spa. The modern spa, built using natural materials, has a swimming pool, steam room, gym and eight treatment rooms.
**Coworth Park** Blacknest Road, Ascot, Berkshire (01344 876600, www.coworthpark.com). Doubles from £282 B&B.
**Getting there** Train from Waterloo to Sunningdale (50 minutes), then five minutes by taxi.

## Bling and bubbly in West Sussex

Bailiffscourt Hotel & Spa has a prime location close to the South Downs, a short walk from the sea and a hop away from the historic town of Arundel. After exploring the latter's medieval castle and antiques shops make your way to the spa where floor-to-ceiling windows flood the area with light and offer pleasant views of the woodland outside; there are indoor and outdoor swimming pools. One of the more luxurious treatments is the champagne and truffle deluxe facial, during which you get to drink a glass of bubbly while your therapist slathers you in lotions and potions. The hotel is a delightful collection of faux-medieval buildings, and some of the rooms have four-poster beds.
**Bailiffscourt Hotel & Spa** Climping, West Sussex (01903 723511, www.hshotels.co.uk). Doubles from £215 per night B&B.
**Getting there** Train from Victoria to Arundel (1 hour 20 minutes), then five minutes by taxi.

## Sort your life out in Essex

Opened in 2010, Lifehouse Country Spa Resort offers a more rounded approach to health and wellness than your average spa. As well as the usual preening and pampering treatments the expert team also offers nutritional advice, spiritual healing and even life coaching. The shiny new complex has weekends tailored to everything from relaxing retreats to weight loss classes and detox sessions. Resident life coach Pete Cohen offers motivational talks and a 'sort your life out' workshop. If you want a less intense stay, spend your weekend in the spa's 18-metre pool, sauna, steam room, plunge pool, jacuzzi or gym. For fresh air and a sneaky bar of chocolate out of sight, there are 130 acres of manicured countryside, including 12 acres of immaculate Grade II-listed gardens.
**Lifehouse Country Spa Resort** Frinton Road, Thorpe-le-Soken, Essex (01255 860050, www.lifehouse.co.uk). Spa breaks including a massage start from £175 per person per double room.
**Getting there** Train from Liverpool Street to Thorpe-le-Soken (1 hour 20 minutes), then a complimentary transfer.

## Pretend you're a WAG in Hertfordshire

Just 30 minutes from London, the Grove is one of the most convenient – as well as one of the most luxurious – semi-rural spa destinations for city dwellers. The estate's Grade II-listed mansion offers fine dining, an 18-hole golf course and 300 acres to explore (no surprise the England football team chose it as their training base). Head to the Sequoia Spa for the pricey 'Signature Ritual' (£340): during the three-and-a-half-hour treatment your body will be gently exfoliated, enveloped in a warm marine mud and honey (from the Grove estate) body wrap and treated to a relaxing Balinese massage and a full-on facial. For those on a tighter budget there's a selection of body massages, wraps and exfoliation treatments for under £100.
**The Grove** Chandler's Cross, Hertfordshire (01923 296010, www.thegrove.co.uk). Doubles from £310 B&B.
**Getting there** Train from Euston to Watford Junction (17 minutes), then ten minutes by taxi.

## Soho and serenity in Somerset

Despite its popularity with media folk, Soho House's rural outpost, Babington House, has an

Babington House

The Grove

easygoing atmosphere and is surprisingly affordable. The Cowshed spa offers an extensive range of mini-treatments that start from £40. It's divided into two distinct areas: Cowshed Active has pools, heat experience rooms and a techno-gym, while Cowshed Relax offers deep cleansing facials, reflexology and hot stone massages. Those after a romantic weekend should book one of the three walled garden rooms that come complete with private steam rooms, outdoor hot tubs for two and in-room treatments on request. Babington House also has an on-site crèche, cinema and even its own church.

**Babington House** Babington, near Frome, Somerset (01373 812266, www.babingtonhouse.co.uk). Doubles from £190 per night (members from £165).
**Getting there** Train from Paddington to Bath Spa (1 hour 20 minutes), then 30 minutes by taxi.

### Shed pounds, and sterling, in Surrey

With 36 treatment rooms, Grayshott is a very serious kind of spa. The country house, once the home of Tennyson, is set in 47 acres of gardens, woods and sweeping lawns, which segue into the neighbouring National Trust land and Surrey Hills. The spa offers lots of pampering but health is the main focus here, with portion-controlled meals, in-house nutritionists, health talks and a fitness centre led by a former Olympian. If the intense exercise routines feel too much like hard work, escape to the cinema or tennis courts, or – in summer – sunbathe beside the lake. Request a ground-floor room so you can step out of your bedroom into the aromatic gardens.
**Grayshott Spa** Headley Road, Grayshott, Surrey (, 01428 60202, www.grayshottspa.com).

Two nights from £420 per couple including two treatments.
**Getting there** Train from Waterloo to Haslemere (55 minutes), then 15 minutes by taxi.

### Break the rules in the Cotswolds

Forget body boot camps and juice fasts, Cowley Manor encourages guests to relax, unwind and indulge. Surrounded by 55 acres of gardens and meadows, the contemporary-style country house is awash with pop art and bespoke furniture and even has a funky cocktail bar. The bedrooms all come with free Wi-Fi, flatscreen TVs, rainforest showers and baths big enough for two. The on-site C.Side Spa is small but smartly designed, with a striking black slate indoor pool, a heated outdoor pool and the stylish new Pool.Side area – where you can sunbathe and enjoy mini-treatments, all with waiter service.

**Cowley Manor** Cowley, near Cheltenham, Gloucestershire (01242 870900, www.cowley manor.com). Doubles from £175 per night B&B.
**Getting there** Train from Paddington to Cheltenham (2 hours 15 minutes), then ten minutes by taxi.

**Grayshott Spa**

room, salt inhalation room, foot spas, ice fountain, sauna and hot tub, allow plenty of time. The restaurant offers a five-course tasting menu, or order from the 'Do Not Disturb' menu and eat in your room while watching a DVD from the extensive library.

**Feversham Arms Hotel** Helmsley, North Yorkshire (01439 770766, www.fevershamarmshotel.com). From £218 per person sharing a double room.

**Getting there** Train from King's Cross to York (2 hours), then 25 minutes by taxi.

### Play lady of the manor in Hampshire

With croquet, clay-pigeon shooting and horse riding on offer, the Four Seasons Hampshire provides a certain kind of quintessentially English experience. The enormous Georgian manor house is set in 500 acres of manicured gardens; the bedrooms have velvet drapes and marble bathrooms. ESPA treatments are provided in a Grade II-listed 18th-century stable block that still has its turrets and many original features. Activities include tennis or a gentle yoga class; if you're a swimmer, the elegant glass-covered conservatory pool leads into the outdoor heated pool.

**Four Seasons Hampshire** Dogmersfield Park, Chalky Lane, Dogmersfield, Hook, Hampshire (01252 853000, www.fourseasons.com/hampshire). Doubles from £210 per night.

**Getting there** Train from Waterloo to Fleet (45 minutes), then 15 minutes by taxi.

### Forage in the New Forest

Deep inside the New Forest, the Herb House Spa at Lime Wood Hotel applies a natural, holistic approach to its beauty treatments. There's a gym, steam room, sauna, hot tub, meditation area, an indoor pool and a rooftop herb garden, as well as the treatment rooms. The hotel has mountain bikes available to explore the woodland, while foodies can take part in foraging trips. Back at the hotel, the head chef will help you to cook up a feast with your findings.

**Herb House Spa** Lime Wood Hotel, Beaulieu Road, Lyndhurst, Hampshire (02380 286998, www.limewood hotel.co.uk). Doubles from £245 per night.

**Getting there** Train from Clapham Junction to Brockenhurst (1 hour 30 minutes), then ten minutes by taxi.

### Disrobe like a Roman in Bath

Set in a World Heritage Site, Bath Thermae Spa is the only place in Britain where you can bathe in natural mineral-rich thermal waters. After experiencing the heat treatment rooms (all treatments should be pre-booked), go to the steaming rooftop pool for fantastic views over the city and its Georgian buildings. It's a day spa only, so sleep at the Queensberry; a boutique hotel occupying three 18th-century townhouses just ten minutes' walk away. The plush rooms feature flatscreen TVs and comfortable beds stacked high with pillows.

**Thermae Bath Spa** Hetling Pump Room, Hot Bath Street, Bath (0844 888 0844, www.thermaebathspa.com).

**Queensberry Hotel** Russell Street, Bath (01225 447928, www.thequeensberry.co.uk). Doubles from £130.

**Getting there** Train from Paddington to Bath (1 hour 25 minutes), then five minutes by taxi.

### Get hot and steamy in Yorkshire

The log fire and heated outdoor pool make the Feversham Arms a good choice for a wintertime spa break. The old coaching inn's country decor blends traditional features with high-tech mod-cons. Take a hike across the Yorkshire Moors, kick your boots off and head to the Verbena Spa to warm up in the heat experience area. With a range of options including monsoon shower, aromatherapy steam

# Windsor & Around

Minimise travel and maximise sightseeing with a trip to Windsor, one of England's most beautiful towns – and just half an hour away from London by train. Cobbled streets and alleyways wind around the oldest and largest occupied castle in the world, an official residence of the Queen. The 7,600-acre Royal Estate is, if anything, even more of a draw, and there are plenty of opportunities to be beside the river. As well as this historic focal point, the Berkshire town has a brewery, good shopping and a lively nightlife. Though it wins no prizes for originality as a tourist destination, at touching distance from London there's no excuse not to visit Windsor at least once.

Windsor Castle

Queen Elizabeth statue, Windsor Great Park

## Fast facts

**Journey time** Train 30 minutes; car 45 minutes
**Festivals & events** Windsor Festival (September, www.windsorfestival.com) – the annual autumn festival lasts a fortnight and features music, theatre, art exhibitions and literary events; Royal Ascot (June, www.ascot.co.uk) – there are 18 races over five days , with £4 million in prize money up for grabs; Royal Windsor Horse Show (May, www.rwhs.co.uk) – the largest equestrian show in the UK with 3,000 horses and ponies taking part
**Good for** History, walking

## SEE & DO

If it's your first visit, take a tour of **Windsor Castle** (020 7766 7304, www.royalcollection.org.uk) – best to do it early in the day, before daytrippers flood in on the first off-peak trains. The State Apartments house the cream of artworks from the Royal Collection, including paintings by

Rembrandt, Rubens, Canaletto and Gainsborough, while St George's Chapel, apart from being a fine example of Gothic architecture, holds the tombs of ten monarchs, including Henry VIII and Charles I. From October to March the private apartments of George IV – considered to contain the castle's most rich and indulgently decorated interiors – are open to the public.

Afterwards, head down the three-mile Long Walk, past the historical Copper Horse monument, and you'll find yourself in the so-called Royal Landscape, aka **Windsor Great Park** (01753 860222, www.theroyallandscape.co.uk), an expanse of fields and forests that used to be the castle's private hunting grounds. Take in immaculate Savill Garden and keep walking until you reach Virginia Water Lake, one of the largest man-made bodies of water in the UK. Curios include a 19th-century 'Roman temple' and an incongruous 100-foot totem pole (a gift from the government of British Columbia).

Alternatively, a sightseeing tour on one of Windsor's open-top tourist buses (www.city-sightseeing.com) is an affordable and effective way of getting to know the town. Tours last 45 minutes and continue throughout the day.

For evening entertainment, the **Theatre Royal Windsor** (Thames Street, 01753 853888, www.theatreroyalwindsor.co.uk) runs a varied schedule of plays and musicals, most of which are suitable for families. There's also the **Firestation Centre** (St Leonard's Road, 01753 866865, www.firestationarts centre.com), which hosts stand-up comedy, music acts and art exhibitions.

Memorials to John F Kennedy and the Magna Carta are located a few miles away at **Runnymede**. Catch the no.71 bus or hop in a taxi. It's another green area and there's a nice walk up a gentle hill to another memorial, this time to the Allied Air Forces; there are also amazing views of Heathrow's runways. For a child-friendly option there's **Legoland** (www.legolandwindsor.co.uk), where you can walk among models of the London Eye, pan for buried treasure, and gain your very own Lego driving licence. For those who like a flutter, Ascot Racecourse (www. ascot.co.uk) is close by.

# EAT & DRINK

Refresh yourself after a walk through the Great Park with a local ale at the **Barley Mow** (Englefield Green, Egham, 01784 431857, www.thebarleymow.com). It's only a hop away from the Savill Garden, and the kitchen is open all day

Sir Christopher Wren Hotel

Fat Duck

serving traditional pub food. The inn is famous as the site where the last ever duel in England was fought.

Afternoon tea at the **Crooked House** (51 High Street, Windsor, 01753 857534, www.crooked-house.com) is a quintessentially English indulgence. The building was constructed in 1592, and since then has developed its trademark tilt, making it Windsor's very own leaning tower. There's a secret passage in the basement, rumoured to have been used by King Charles II for illicit trysts. These days it's more famous for its selection of cakes, scones and loose-leaf teas.

For those prepared to book well in advance, Heston Blumenthal's Michelin-starred restaurant, the **Fat Duck**, lies in the nearby village of Bray (High Street, 01628 580333, www.thefatduck.co.uk).

## SHOP

The high street may be a grim gauntlet of souvenir stalls, but scratch the surface and there are some gems. Designer clothing stores and the odd independent shop sit under the roof of the old railway station: **Havana House** (52 Windsor Royal Station, www.havanahouse.co.uk) is a cigar retailer, while **Vom Fass** (48 Royal Station Parade, 01753 832173, www.vomfassuk.com) stocks a variety of liqueurs and cooking oils that can be poured into a glass bottle of your choosing.

## STAY

Located in the centre of town, **Barbara's B&B** (16 Maidenhead Road, 01753 840273, www.bbandbwindsor. com) is a family-run establishment just 15 minutes' walk from Windsor Castle. **Park Farm B&B** is on the outskirts of the town centre (St Leonard's Road, 01753 866823, www.parkfarm.com). Some rooms are en suite, and there are family bedrooms that sleep up to four people. The **Sir Christopher Wren** hotel and spa (Thames Street, 01753 442400, www.sirchristopherwren.co.uk) is in a listed building overlooking the Thames at Eton Bridge, a two-minute walk from Windsor and Eton Riverside train station and close to Windsor Castle and the Old Town.

Slightly further away, options include camping at the **Hurley Village Riverside Park** (Hurley, 01628 824493, www.hurleyriversidepark.co.uk), 20 minutes from Windsor by car. Also in Hurley is the **Olde Belle** (High Street, 01628 703504, www.theoldebell.co.uk), an ancient inn updated with contemporary flair. Food is locally sourced where possible.

## GETTING THERE & AROUND

Taking the train to Windsor is by far the easiest option. Trains to Windsor & Eton Riverside leave from Waterloo Station, with the journey taking around 55 minutes. From Paddington there's a fast train to Slough with connections to Windsor & Eton Central – this journey takes half an hour.

Driving from central London takes around 45 minutes (but driving back on, say, a Sunday evening can be tediously slow). Once there, most sights are well within walking distance, but a car will allow access to the outlying areas. For Legoland there is a frequent shuttle bus service running from Windsor town centre.

# Hampton Court & Around

While a day trip to Hampton Court might feel too much like a commute – in the company of the legions of foreign tourists who take the slow train from Waterloo every morning from May to September – a weekend break is a relaxed and potentially inexpensive little holiday. Magnificent Hampton Court Palace is the obvious focal point of the area, but you can use the surrounding suburbs as a base for riverboat excursions and walks, either along the Thames or into the two nearby royal parks. There's a handful of good restaurants in the area and a number of traditional inns and, as you're sleeping over, you can get to play Henry VIII for a night.

Hampton Court Palace

## Fast facts

**Journey time** Train 40 minutes; car 40 minutes; boat 3 hours 30 minutes
**Festivals & events** Hampton Court Palace Flower Show (July, www.rhs.org.uk) – run by the Royal Horticultural Society, there are show gardens, floral marquees, talks and demonstrations; Hampton Court Palace Festival (June, www.hamptoncourtpalacefestival.com) – an annual music event, which has featured the likes of Eric Clapton, Van Morrison and the Buena Vista Social Club; Jolly Day Out Festival (August, www.jollydayout. com) – a new festival set over four days on Hampton Court Green, featuring music, a funfair, craft workshops and shows for children
**Good for** Culture, history, walking

## SEE & DO

If you've never been out here before you'll want to look around beautiful **Hampton Court Palace** (East Molesey, 0844 482 7777, www.hrp.org.uk). Henry VIII had many residences, but this one positively oozes historical drama. Shakespeare performed here and Cromwell made it his home after the Civil War. The ghost of Henry's fifth wife, Catherine Howard, who was executed for adultery at the Tower of London, is said to shriek in the Haunted Gallery (there are ghost tours of the palace, but they sell out quickly, so book ahead).

In Henry's time, there were tournaments and feasts, musical entertainment, plays, dances and more. The world-famous gardens are wonderful, with the maze taking centre stage in any child's itinerary. It's the oldest in the country, having been planted between 1689 and 1694. Themed activities are plentiful during the school holidays, and on

Tudor Kitchen, Hampton Court Palace

Privy Garden, Hampton Court Palace

The Georgian House

some bank holidays and weekends Tudor cookery demonstrations take place in the huge kitchens; children love the bubbling cauldrons and game bird carcasses.

The Palace easily takes up a long morning. After grabbing a snack or at one of the many cafés along Bridge Road – opposite Hampton Court railway station, on the other side of the Thames – you should wander alongside the river. There are easy, flat walks in all directions and buses back to Hampton Court from Walton-on-Thames, Surbiton or Kingston. If you want to go faster and further, Evans Cycles (www.evanscycles.com) in Kingston-upon-Thames hires out bikes for £25 per bike per day. The **Thames Cycle Path** allows you to do a seven-mile loop up to the palace and back, or you could head into **Bushy Park**, **Richmond Park** or quieter **Home Park**. There are some so-so eateries around Kingston but cycle a few minutes towards Richmond and you'll come to the **Boaters Inn** (Canonbury Gardens, 8541 4672, www.capitalpubcompany.com/the-boaters-inn), serving modern Mediterranean cuisine and a decent selection of wines and real ales.

From the bank of the river at Hampton Court are **riverboats** running to Kingston (25 minutes) and Richmond (45 minutes). Sights along the route include **Thames Ditton Ait**, **Teddington Lock** and **Eel Pie Island**. There's also a seasonal service running from April to October that goes all the way to Westminster (3 hours 30 minutes), passing by the **Royal Botanic Gardens** at Kew.

If you don't mind negotiating the river traffic along this stretch of the Thames, rent a day boat. They're surprisingly easy to handle, and allow you to explore the Thames at your own pace, stopping off at riverside pubs along the way. **Hampton Ferry Boathouse** (Thames Street, 8979 7471, www.hamptonferryboathouse.co.uk) offers boats that seat up to six adults and two children, available from March to October for full- and half-day hire.

The **London Loop** (www.walklondon.org.uk) is the 152-mile path circling London that's sometimes referred to as the M25 for walkers. You could attempt the ten-mile stretch of the walk starting at Kingston Bridge and running through Bushy Park and Crane Park, before finishing at Hatton Cross Station. There are several buses back to Hampton Court and Kingston from here.

## EAT & DRINK

What's now the **Tiltyard Café** was built on the Hampton Court Palace estate in 1537, and used for jousting tournaments and other sports competitions. The café serves a robust take on English grub: Suffolk pork and mustard sausage roll, beef and King's Ale pie and giant jammy dodger biscuits. There are also themed Tudor lunches – sample authentic Tudor cuisine on the first weekend of every month. **Le Petit Nantais** (41 Bridge Road, 07595 303866, www.lepetitnantais.co.uk) is a fine-dining alternative to the palace's English fare. Family-owned and run, this French restaurant specialises in seafood and classic dishes, and there's also a stall on Saturdays selling oysters and fish. Opposite the palace, on the Thames Ditton side of the river, is the **Albany** (Queens Road, 8972 9163, www.the-albany.co.uk), a stylish riverside pub known for its thin-base pizzas.

## STAY

There are two places in which to spend the night at Hampton Court Palace: **Fish Court** and the **Georgian House**. In Fish Court there's an apartment that sleeps up to six people (two single bedrooms, one twin and one double) and looks over Bushy Park. Originally built by Cardinal Wolsey, it was enlarged by Henry VIII, who added new kitchens, one of which was for the sole purpose of baking pies. The Georgian House sleeps up to eight people and has five rooms: two single, two twin and one double. It was built as a kitchen in the early 18th century for Prince George. For more information on staying at either, contact the Landmark Trust (01628 825925, www.landmarktrust.org).

The **Riverine** (Taggs Island, 8979 2266, www.feedtheducks.com) in Hampton is a houseboat with three bedrooms, all of which can sleep two people. (No under-12s allowed.)

The **Liongate Hotel** (Hampton Court Road, 8977 8121, www.theliongatehotel.com) is possibly the most straightforward option. Its location, near the entrance to Bushy Park, makes sightseeing a cinch. Rooms range from boltholes to suites with four-poster beds, all of which come with en-suite bathrooms.

## GETTING THERE & AROUND

The direct, slow train from Waterloo to Hampton Court takes less than 40 minutes; if you miss it, hop on the fast train to Surbiton and you might well catch up with it there. South West Trains offer a combined ticket to Hampton Court Palace, saving visitors a couple of quid. Cyclists can take their bikes on the London Overground as far as Richmond, before joining the Thames Path at Richmond Bridge. There are also buses to Hampton Court from Kingston (no.411) and Richmond (no.R68).

**Fish Court**

# Luxury Weekends

Sometimes you just need (and deserve) a treat. Whether the luxury is time, peace and quiet, food cooked by someone else, or top-notch surroundings, these easy-to-access breaks should do the trick.

**Old Thatch**

## Do nothing in Northamptonshire

This is a place to come and do very little, in style. Fawsley Hall has Tudor, Georgian and Victorian elements, and an air of sophisticated decadence. It's sumptuously furnished, has an on-site spa, and the gardens, designed by Capability Brown, wend their scenic way around three ornamental lakes. Bedrooms range from simple and modern to luxurious Tudor-style opulence; if you book a suite you also get a four-poster bed. Dining options include a Modern British restaurant, Equilibrium, and Bess's Brasserie.
**Fawsley Hall** Fawsley, near Daventry, Northamptonshire (01327 892000, www.fawsleyhall.com).
**Getting there** 55 minutes by train from Euston to Northampton, then a 15-mile taxi ride.

## Watch the river flow in Berkshire

Yards from the river and dating back to 1135, the Olde Bell at Hurley is both inn and restaurant. Reinvented as a modern and luxurious rural retreat, there are bedrooms spread across separate buildings. All are simply and stylishly furnished, and some have deep clawfoot baths. The bar has low beams, an open fire and local ales and the restaurant serves delicious seasonal and locally sourced food, much of it from the kitchen gardens round the back. The Thames that flows through Hurley is a much less murky prospect than the one in London. The clear waters and grassy, willow-draped banks meandering past Hurley, Marlowe and Cookham Dean offer riverside rambling that will nudge you back to a simpler time. (Overnight guests can borrow mountain bikes and zz to aid their explorations.) These stretches of river were the regular haunts and inspiration for authors Kenneth

Grahame (*Wind in the Willows*) and Enid Blyton; her home in Bourne End (Old Thatch, Coldmoorholme Lane, 01628 527518, www.oldthatchgardens.co.uk) is open to the public (May-August).
**Olde Bell** High Street, Hurley, Berkshire (01628 703510, www.theoldebell.co.uk).
**Getting there** from 18 minutes by train from Paddington to Maidenhead, then a ten-minute taxi ride.

## Stay at the birthplace of the English country garden, in West Sussex

In 1884, gardener and botanist William Robinson moved to Gravetye Manor and put his ideas about wild gardening into practice. His naturalised plantings, with tumbling borders of roses and wild flowers, influenced gardens all over the world. Nowadays the manor is a very English hotel with 17 well-appointed bedrooms, all named after trees growing on the estate. Food is first class too. Four miles away, Wakehurst Place (Ardingly, 01444 894066, www.kew.org), the country outpost of Kew Gardens, offers another horticultural idyll to explore.
**Gravetye Manor** Vowels Lane, West Hoathly, West Sussex (01342 810567, www.gravetyemanor.co.uk).
**Getting there** 54 minutes by train from Victoria to East Grinstead, then an 8-minute taxi ride.

## Retreat to another era on the Isle of Wight

The charm of the Isle of Wight is that it's stuck in a bit of a timewarp – the lovely scenery, sandy beaches, rolling hills and cute villages come with an old-fashioned vibe and, in general, a less frenetic atmosphere than the rest of the

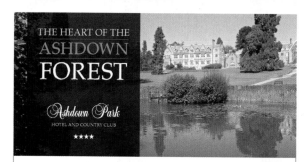

## THE HEART OF THE ASHDOWN FOREST

### Ashdown Park
HOTEL AND COUNTRY CLUB
★★★★

Ashdown Park Hotel and Country Club sits proudly within 186 acres of the Ashdown Forest in East Sussex, home of Pooh Bear. Boasting 106 bedrooms and suites, gourmet restaurant and elegant lounges it is the prefect place to relax and unwind. The extensive leisure facilities include pool, gymnasium, outdoor tennis courts, spa treatment rooms and 18-hole par 3 golf course.

ASHDOWN PARK HOTEL & COUNTRY CLUB,
WYCH CROSS, NR FOREST ROW, EAST SUSSEX, RH18 5JR
TEL: +44 (0)1342 824988  FAX: +44 (0)1342 826206
EMAIL: RESERVATIONS@ASHDOWNPARK.COM
WEB: WWW.ASHDOWNPARK.COM

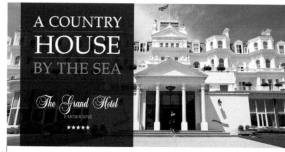

## A COUNTRY HOUSE BY THE SEA

### The Grand Hotel
EASTBOURNE
★★★★★

Standing majestically along the Eastbourne seafront, The Grand Hotel is England's only 5-star coastal hotel. The grandeur inside is typified by the breathtaking great hall, 152 bedrooms/suites and two award winning restaurants. A favourite with families, quality and service is paramount whether you are taking a dip in the outside pool, having afternoon tea or indulging in a spa treatment.

THE GRAND HOTEL, KING EDWARDS PARADE,
EASTBOURNE, EAST SUSSEX, BN21 4EQ
TEL: +44 (0)1323 412345  FAX: +44 (0)1323 412233
EMAIL: RESERVATIONS@GRANDEASTBOURNE.COM
WEB: WWW.GRANDEASTBOURNE.COM

## INIMITABLE LUXURY IN 1,065 ACRES

### Luton Hoo
HOTEL, GOLF & SPA
★★★★★

Set within 1,065 acres of countryside, Luton Hoo is the quintessential English country house hotel. Befitting a location of such historical importance, a stay at the hotel will live long in the memory. It boasts 144 unique bedrooms and suites, award winning cuisine, luxury spa with its own organic products, 18-hole par 73 golf course and much more.

LUTON HOO HOTEL, GOLF & SPA, THE MANSION HOUSE,
LUTON, BEDFORDSHIRE, LU1 3TQ
TEL: +44 (0)1582 734437  FAX: +44 (0)1582 485438
E-MAIL: RESERVATIONS@LUTONHOO.COM
WEB: WWW.LUTONHOO.COM

## HAMPSHIRE'S ORIGINAL COUNTRY RETREAT

### Tylney Hall
HOTEL, HAMPSHIRE
★★★★

Tylney Hall sits romantically in 66 acres of rolling Hampshire countryside. The palatial lounges and gourmet restaurant enjoy views of the tree lined vista, lake and formal gardens. Luxury and style greets you throughout the hotel and in the 112 bedrooms and suites, some of which contain four poster beds and spa baths. Indoor and outdoor pools, gymnasium and health spa complete the indulgent experience.

TYLNEY HALL HOTEL, ROTHERWICK,
HOOK, HAMPSHIRE, RG27 9AZ
TEL: +44 (0)1256 764881 FAX: +44 (0)1256 768141
E-MAIL: RESERVATIONS@TYLNEYHALL.COM
WEB: WWW.TYLNEYHALL.COM

*Family Celebrations* | *Gourmet Breaks* | *Romantic Retreats* | *Spa Days*

Gravetye Manor

country. Ventnor, a former fishing village turned resort, in the south of the island, is a good base. It has a botanic garden, coastal walks and the charmingly old-school Blackgang Chine theme park. Food offers a more contemporary pleasure – the Hambrough, a restaurant with rooms, has Michelin-starred chef Robert Thompson at the helm. The seven bedrooms are individually decorated and furnished and have Wi-Fi, flatscreen TVs, DVD/CD players and Illy espresso machines. **Hambrough** Hambrough Road, Ventnor, Isle of Wight (01983 856333, www.robert-thompson.com). **Getting there** 1 hour 30 minutes by train from Waterloo to Portsmouth Harbour, then 22 minutes by Fast Cat ferry from Portsmouth to Ryde pier.

## Stay in a country hut in West Sussex

A lazy, super-cosy option for couples, the Shepherd's Return is a traditionally styled shepherd's hut (it looks a bit like a gypsy caravan) with lovely countryside views. Snuggle up under the merino wool blankets and keep warm by the wood-burning stove if it's chilly out. Breakfast is a hamper full of organic goodies that includes yoghurt, fruit compote, muesli, soda bread and owner Lizzie Staples's hens' eggs. If you do decide to leave the hut, get your boots on and stroll across the South Downs, or hire a bike. Posh Pedalers will deliver (May-October only – 07720 080918). Or visit

Goodwood, just over ten miles away, and stop off en route at the Fox Goes Free (Charlton, 01243 811461, www.thefoxgoes free.com); the pub brews its own beer and serves gastropub fare. The 350-year-old Horse Guard Inn is just five miles away (Upperton Road, Tillington, 01798 342332, www.the horseguardsinn.co.uk) and has a short but excellent menu using local produce. Try own-made black pudding with duck egg or just a simple ploughman's with own-made chutney.

**Shepherd's Return** 1 The Hollow, Sutton End, Sutton, Pulborough, West Sussex (07989 976726, www.theshepherdsreturn.com). **Getting there** 1 hour 15 minutes by train from Waterloo to Pulborough, then it's a 15-minute taxi ride.

## Revel in Pugin's House in Kent

Ramsgate was one of the great Victorian seaside destinations and still has the residual, faded glamour of many British coastal towns. Augustus Pugin sought out Ramsgate for the 'delight of the sea' and made his family home at the Grange. It's now a Landmark Trust property, restored to Pugin's exacting Gothic detail, with bright detailed interiors and wooded panelling. The Grange sleeps eight in four bedrooms and has an open fire, and access to a small beach. Eat out at Age & Sons (Charlotte Court, 01843 851515, www.ageandsons.co.uk), just off the main drag on the harbour. Accomplished Modern British cooking emphasises local ingredients, with fish from day boats and foraged ingredients. Little details make a meal here feel special and the funky bar in the basement beckons for post dinner drinks.

**The Grange** (01628 825925, www.landmarktrust.org.uk).

**Getting there** 1 hour 17 minutes by fast train from St Pancras to Ramsgate.

## Live well in the Chilterns

Hartwell House – a 17th-century, hybrid Jacobean-Georgian mansion managed by the National Trust – is everything your London flat is not: lofty ceilings, a Gothic hall, massive bedrooms, antiques and fine art, with views of parkland. There are 30 bedrooms, all splendid, and some with four-poster beds. There's an on-site spa with a pool too. Local produce is used in the haute cuisine meals; for decent pub grub and real ales, go to the Bugle Horn (www.vintageinn.co.uk/the buglehornhartwell) across from Hartwell's main entrance. Close by are rambling tracks along the Midshires and North Bucks Ways (and Bicester Shopping Village is also within easy striking distance).

**Hartwell House & Spa** Oxford Road, near Aylesbury, Buckinghamshire (01296 747444, www.hartwell-house.com).

**Getting there** 54 minutes by train from Marylebone to Aylesbury, then a two-mile taxi ride.

## Go glamping in East Sussex

The Moroccan Yurt is set in secluded ancient woodland. Inside it's super cosy: lots of wood furniture, rugs, plush fabrics and a big round bed. There's a wood-burning stove too. If you need a reminder that you're sleeping in a tent you can open the yurt's skylight and gaze up at the night sky. Explore locally with a trip to Bodiam Castle (01580 830196, www.nationaltrust.org.uk), a couple of miles north. Michelin-starred restaurant the Curlew (Junction Road, Bodiam, 01580 861394, www.thecurlew restaurant.co.uk) is within an archer's shot of the castle and offers Modern British bistro food in an informal setting. The George Inn (High Street, 01580 880315, www.thegeorge robertsbridge.co.uk) in Robertsbridge sources food from within a 30-mile radius, while the White Horse (Silverhill, Hurst Green, Etchingham, 01580 860235, www.thewhite horsehurstgreen.com) serves posh pub grub.

**Moroccan Yurt** Woodside B&B, Junction Road, Staplecross, near Cripps Corner, East Sussex (01580 830903, www.yurt andbreakfast.co.uk).

**Getting there** 1 hour 15 minutes by train from Charing Cross or Canon Street to Hastings, then an 8-minute taxi ride.

Age & Sons

The Grange

# Oxford

Let's get the 'dreaming spires' out of the way first. Yes, they're everywhere, as are students, dons and, of course, the tourists, desperate to gawp at a 'typical' English gent or gentess on a vintage bike. It's hard to escape the clichés associated with the birthplace of Britain's oldest university – if it's not the Uni, it's *Brideshead Revisited* or *Inspector Morse* – but Oxford has much more to offer than all this. Some of its attractions are ancillary to the colleges, such as the revamped Ashmolean Museum and the Jacqueline du Pré Music Building. But, with a strong 'town and gown' schism among locals, there are pockets of the city that feel miles away from the quadrangles. Its position at a point where the Thames splits into several streams means there are plenty of riverside walks too, with proper pubs along the way.

Radcliffe Camera

## Fast facts

**Journey time** Train 1 hour; car 1.5 hours
**Festivals & events** Cowley Road Carnival (www.cowleyroadcarnival.co.uk, July) – born in 2000 to revive the Cowley area, this multicultural community event offers processions, outdoor music and food stalls; Oxford Jazz Festival (www.oxfordjazzfestival.co.uk, late April) – four days of jazz hosted in some of the city's most prestigious venues, such as the Ashmolean or the Town Hall; OxFringe (oxfringe.com, May/June) – running alongside the Oxford Literary Festival, the programme has artistic, musical and theatrical events in spaces all around the city
**Good for** Culture, food, history, shopping

## SEE & DO

On a first visit, it would be silly not to peek into a few of the University buildings, as they are steeped in history and – in the main – immaculately kept. **Keble College** (Parks

Museum of Natural History

Old Parsonage

Old Bank

Casa Rose

Road, 01865 272727, www.keble.ox.ac.uk), founded in 1870, is notable for its red and yellow patterned brickwork, and **Christ Church** college (St Aldates, 01865 276150, www.chch.ox.ac.uk), founded 1545, is one of the largest and richest, housing Oxford's cathedral. It's also home to **Christ Church Picture Gallery** (01865 276172, www.chch.ox.ac.uk/gallery), which owns a serious collection of Renaissance drawings, including Dürers and Da Vincis. The University's **Bodleian Library** (Broad Street, 01865 277000), which has a truly immense collection of books – second only to the British Library – hosts exhibitions and tours. Of its many annexes, the **Radcliffe Camera** (Radcliffe Square) is especially worth looking at – built in the style of Palladio, it was the country's first circular library.

The **Pitt Rivers Museum** (South Parks Road, 01865 270927, www.prm.ox.ac.uk) is a place to get lost in. Accessible through the **Museum of Natural History** (Parks Road, 01865 272950, www.oum.ox.ac.uk – also worth a look for the stuffed dodo and the swifts nesting in the tower of this 'Cathedral to science'), it resembles a posh attic, with treasures from around the world occupying every inch of space, from shrunken heads to magic charms to lethal weapons. Nearby, the University Parks is a great picnic spot, but the city is also home to Britain's oldest **Botanic Garden** (Rose Lane, 01865 286690, www.botanic-garden.ox.ac.uk), on one side of the historic **Magdalen Bridge** (from which students traditionally jumped during May Morning celebrations). To escape the obvious sights, take a walk through pretty Iffley village – to the south of the city – and come back into town along the river, passing the various University boat houses along the way and stopping in the beer garden of the **Isis** (01865 243854).

Like all British cities, Oxford has a bog-standard centre too – with the usual shops and banks, but here culture is hidden among the chains: you'll find the **Modern Art Oxford** gallery (30 Pembroke Street, 01865 722733, www.modernartoxford.org.uk) behind an M&S.

## EAT & DRINK

The Covered Market is a great place to stop after you're done walking the town centre. **Georgina's Café** (103 The Market, 01865 249527), a low-ceilinged coffee shop, serves cakes, bagels and salads. Go to the original **Ben's Cookies** (108-109 The Market, 01865 247407, www.benscookies.com) for afters. For picnic supplies, the best place is **David John Butchers** (96 The Market, 01865 200922), whose 'pantry' specialises in cold meats, pies and pastries.

The **Yard Café and Bar** (30 Pembroke Street, 01865 722733, www.modernartoxford.org.uk) is attached to the city's Modern Art Oxford gallery but is an innovative space in its own right. Monmouth coffee is served alongside the usual soups and panini. Around the corner, the second of the three **G&D's Ice Cream Cafés** (94 St Aldates, 01865 245952, www.gdcafe.com) offers its additive-free ice-cream in a huge range of flavours. The family-run **Edamame** (15 Holywell Street, 01865 246916, www.edamame.co.uk) serves authentic Japanese dishes, while **Sojo** (8-9 Hythe Bridge Street, 01865 202888) is a cut above the average Chinese restaurant. The newly opened **Ashmolean Dining Room** (Ashmolean Museum, Beaumont Street, 01865 553823, www.ashmoleandiningroom.com) has a smart, rooftop setting and an interesting menu featuring small plates of European dishes.

Jericho – in the north-west – is a hub for bars and eateries, with options varying from the vegetarian **Gardeners Arms** (39 Plantation Road, 01865 559814, www.thegarden-oxford.co.uk) to the decent Greek restaurant **Manos** (105 Walton Street, 01865 311782, www.manosfoodbar.com).

In the evening, you can't go wrong with a walk up the Cowley Road – Oxford's Hackney – stopping off at various independent drinking dens: **Kazbar** (nos.25-27, 01865 202920, www.kazbar.co.uk) and its sister **Café Baba** (no.240, 01865 203011) have Moroccan decor, and serve tapas. **Atomic Burgers** (no.96, 01865 790855,

www.atomicburger.co.uk) is a retro-styled diner. Halfway up, on Magdalen Road, is the **Rusty Bicycle** (no.28, 01865 204 842). On the Iffley Road, the **Magdalen Arms** (no.243, 01865 243159, www.magdalenarms.com) is a made-over old boozer that now has excellent food.

## SHOP

Avoid the pedestrianised Cornmarket – which is chock-a-block with chains and gets very crowded – and the endless souvenir shops stocking University-themed tat, and focus on the plentiful independent boutiques. From the team behind Truck music festival, **Truck Store** (101 Cowley Road, 01865 793866) opened in 2011 and is a real haven for music junkies, selling most genres and some rare vinyl. **Casa Rose** (74A Walton Street, 01865 510191, www.casaroseoxford.co.uk) and **Aspire Style** (21 High Street, 01865 202600, www.aspirestyle.co.uk) sell gifts and dresses from brands such as Avoca and Orla Kiely. **Reign Wear** (134 Cowley Road, 01865 250004) and **Unicorn** (5 Ship Street, no phone) supply vintage clothing to both sexes. The showroom at **Liscious Interiors** (12 South Parade, 01865 553111, www.liscious.co.uk) is also worth a look for its quality antiques.

## STAY

The quirkiest of the high-end options is **Malmaison** (3 New Road, 01865 268400, www.malmaison.com), which occupies the old prison. Rooms are in converted jail cells, though, thankfully, the parts of the prison associated with capital punishment are used as offices. Another converted building houses the **Old Bank** hotel (91-94 High Street, 01865 799599, www.oldbank-hotel.co.uk). Flanked by Merton, Oriel, University, Christ Church and All Soul's colleges, this Georgian edifice houses a collection of 20th-century art as well as a good restaurant. Slightly outside the centre near trendy Jericho, the **Old Parsonage** (1 Banbury Road, 01865 310210, www.oldparsonage-hotel.co.uk) has the air of an English country house, with open fires and 17th-century features. If you're visiting out of term time and are on a budget, consider renting a college room (www.universityrooms.co.uk). Although some are small, they often have spectacular views.

## GETTING THERE & AROUND

The Oxford Tube – a bus – runs every ten minutes from either Victoria, Marble Arch, Shepherd's Bush or Notting Hill Gate (from £14 return), and takes about 1 hour 40 minutes. The Oxford Express 'X90' bus takes the same amount of time, but also runs from Baker Street. These are comfortable, with free Wi-Fi, but Megabus often offers cheaper fares for the same journey. Trains from Paddington take approximately 1 hour, and the rail station is a short walk from the centre of Oxford. Once there, the city is easy to walk around, and there is a simple bus system too.

Punting is the best and most entertaining option for a trip out of the city, such as to Old Marston for a stop at the **Victoria Arms** (Mill Lane, 01865 241382, www.victoria arms.co.uk). Pick one up from the **Cherwell Boathouse** (50 Bardwell Road, 01865 552746, www.cherwellboathouse. co.uk) – which also has a fantastic restaurant. First-timers can hire a student to do the hard work.

OXFORD

# Brighton

Brighton, neither trading hub nor political epicentre nor of military significance, was born to be a place of pleasure and whimsy. In the mid 18th century, the fashion among the upper classes to retreat from 'Town' to the south coast for the 'summer season' led to the birth of a seaside resort – complete with amusement arcades and bathing huts. Notorious reveller the Prince of Wales (future King George IV) blazed the trail in 1783 when he first arrived for a holiday and gave Brighton its first architectural landmarks. Somehow, the Royal Pavilion marries well with both the kitsch of the fairground backdrop and the rainbow-striped flags flapping to let visitors know they're in the UK's gay capital. There is also a well-established hippie-cum-hipster community (that runs – and shops in – the town's many organic produce shops), which was the seedbed for the election of Britain's first Green Party MP in 2010. In the early 20th century, Brighton enjoyed some notoriety as a capital of lowlife crime and in the 1950s there were famous battles between Mods and Rockers. Fun in Brighton, while mainly for the family, has long had an element of decadence and debauchery.

## Fast facts

**Journey time** Train from 50 minutes; car 1.5 hours; bus 2 hours
**Festivals & events** Brighton Festival (May, www.brightonfestival.org) – the largest multimedia festival in England (second only to Edinburgh in the UK) sees the city buzzing with events, including Artists Open House; Great Escape Festival (May, www.escapegreat.com) – three days of new bands playing impromptu street gigs as well as big performances; Brighton Pride (August, www.brighton pride.org) – a week-long party celebrating everything LGBT that culminates in a carnival parade in Preston Park; White Night (October, www.whitenight nuitblanche.com) – this unique, and free, cultural festival takes place all night, on the weekend that marks the end of British Summer Time
**Good for** Beaches, food, nightlife, shopping

## SEE & DO

The first stop on a tour of Brighton should be the **Royal Pavilion** (Pavilion Buildings, 03000 290900, www.royal pavilion.org.uk), designed by John Nash between 1815 and 1822 to be a party mansion – and oriental fantasy – for the royal whose first visit sparked public interest in the seaside town. The **Brighton Museum & Art Gallery** (03000 290900, www.brighton-hove-rpml.org.uk) next door should be the second, not least for the galleries focused on the city itself, which provide a fascinating insight into local stories and changing history. Wander through the **Lanes**, one of the most historic areas, which is crammed with boutiques and specialist art spaces, such as the innovative **Fabrica** (01273 778646, www.fabrica.org.uk), set inside a Regency-period church.

The other obvious stretch for a stroll is the seafront, starting at **Brighton Pier** (www.brightonpier.co.uk). As well as the modern Super Booster rollercoaster, you can have your palm or tarot cards read and tuck into candyfloss. In the evening, watch hen-partying hordes warm up for a night out,

Kemp Townhouse

Terre à Terre

Snooze Guest House

while the sun sets over the crumbling shell of the **West Pier** (www.westpier.co.uk). The dance of starlings over the water – there are thought to be as many as 40,000 birds, moving together like a cloud of motes – draws people who wouldn't normally call themselves birdwatchers. For a nostalgic night out, visit the **Duke of York's Picturehouse** (Preston Circus, 0871 902 5728, www.picturehouses.co.uk), one of the oldest cinemas in England, which shows a selection of indie and arthouse films.

Sporty types should bring a swimsuit and take a dip in the water first thing in the morning. Otherwise, spend your energy at **Yellowave Beachsports** (299 Madeira Drive, 01273 672222, www.yellowave.co.uk), Britain's first dedicated beach volleyball court. For a day trip out of the city, the dramatic walk to Devil's Dyke from Ditchling Beacon offers fantastic views, rightly admired by Constable.

For a more leftfield outing, Southern Water (01903 272606, www.southernwater.co.uk) hosts tours of **Brighton's Victorian sewers** (which start under the Palace Pier and emerge through a manhole in the Old Steine Gardens), from May to September every year. Or, for less than £100 per person, you can go on a 20-30 minute private **helicopter tour of Brighton** from Shoreham Airport (www.helifly.co.uk). A helicopter ride and afternoon tea package costs £400-£529 for two people; £539-£569 for a group of four.

## Cultural baggage

**Book** *Brighton Rock* (Graham Greene, 1938)
**Film** *Oh! What a Lovely War* (Richard Attenborough, 1969)
**Album** *You've Come a Long Way, Baby* (Norman Cook aka Fatboy Slim, 1998)

# EAT & DRINK

Brighton's dining scene is expansive and established, covering a variety of cuisines and trends. The full-English breakfast is legendary at **Bill's Produce Store** (The Depot, 100 North Road, 01273 692894), a colourful restaurant-cum-deli with floor-to-ceiling shelves stocked with homemade fare. The indy café culture that has swept through London has made its way down south, with shops such as **Coffee@33** (33 Trafalgar Street, 01273 462460) aping the utilitarian-chic prominent in the capital. **Marwood Coffee Shop** (52 Ship Street, 01273 382063) is another example, with an antipodean influence and particularly delicious brownies. For ice-cream, **Scoop & Crumb** (5-6 East Street, 01273 202563, www.scoopandcrumb.com) is the pastel-coloured retro option.

With Brighton's green credentials, the disproportionate number of vegetarian restaurants isn't surprising, but **Terre à Terre** (71 East Street, 01273 729051, www.terreaterre.co.uk) consistently ranks as one of the best in the country. Residential Hove is not to be ignored, with high-end options such as **Meadow** (64 Western Road, 01273 721182, www.themeadowrestaurant.co.uk) and perfect local restaurant **Tin Drum** (10 Victoria Grove, 01273 747755, www.tindrum.co.uk), which sources much of its produce from nearby.

For an evening by the seafront, **Ohso Social** (250A Kings Road Arches, 01273 746067, www.ohsosocial.co.uk) is a great stopping point, while traditional fishy options can be found at **Regency Restaurant** (131 King's Road, 01273 325024, www.theregencyrestaurant.co.uk). **Jamie's Italian** (11 Black Lion Street, 01273 915480, www.jamieoliver.com/italian/brighton) serves good bloody marys. Somewhat more hidden in the Lanes is **Rasa** (2-3 Little East Street, 01273 771661, www.rasarestaurants.com), an authentic South Asian with commendable fish curries. End the evening in decadent fashion at a burlesque bar such as **Madame Geisha** (75-79 East Street, 01273 770847, www.madamegeisha.com).

Best of the chippies is **Bardsley's** (22-23A Baker Street, 01273 681256, www.bardsleys-fishandchips.co.uk). It's been going since 1926 and as well as serving battered cod or haddock and chips, the family-run restaurant cooks sustainably sourced fish such as Cornish Blue shark steak and fresh-dressed Scarborough crab.

# SHOP

A short hop from the railway station is **North Laine**, where a handful of roads hold a large number of independent shops selling a mix of contemporary and antique goods, with few chains in sight. On Saturdays, the **Brighton Street Market** (Upper Gardner Street, www.brightonstreetmarket.co.uk) adds to the retail possibilities. **Hope & Harlequin** (31 Sydney Street, 01273 675222, www.hopeandharlequin.com) offers quality vintage wear and style tips, while second-hand junkies could spend hours in **Snoopers Paradise** (7-8 Kensington Gardens, 01273 602558), filled with everything from buttons to wardrobes.

For dresses that haven't been worn before, ladies should seek out **Tribeca** (21 Bond Street, 01273 673755, www.tribeca-brighton.co.uk), full of sleek designer pieces, or friendly **Sirene** (37 Trafalgar Street, 01273 818061, www.sirene-boutique.com). The **Vegetarian Shoe Shop** (12 Gardner Street, 01273 691913, www.vegetarian-shoes.co.uk) is a bit of an institution. Music-lovers should not miss **Resident** (28 Kensington Gardens, 01273 606312, www.resident-music.com), with dedicated staff and gig tickets on sale. **City Books** (23 Western Road, 01273 725306, www.city-books.co.uk) in next-door Hove, now 25 years old, is similarly celebrated.

# STAY

**Drakes** (43-44 Marine Parade, 01273 696934, www.drakesofbrighton.com) is a popular high-end option, thanks to its fabulous views and excellent restaurant. However, with regular DJ nights and a decent bar, **Hotel Pelirocco** (10 Regency Square, 01273 327055, www.hotelpelirocco.co.uk) is perhaps a trendier option. There's also a branch of the popular **Hotel du Vin** (2-6 Ship Street, 01273 718588).

For local knowledge and a warm welcome, the boutique B&Bs of Kemp Town are highly regarded. **Snooze Guest House** (25 St George's Terrace, 01273 605797, www.snoozebrighton.com) and **Paskins Town House** (18-19 Charlotte Street, 01273 601203, www.paskins.co.uk) are mid-range, while **Kemp Townhouse** (21 Atlingworth Street, 01273 681400, www.kemptownhouse.com) is more luxurious.

**Seadragon** (36 Waterloo Street, 01273 711854, www.seadragonbackpackers.co.uk) is a hostel in a pleasantly quiet area, whereas both branches of **Grapevine** (75-76 Middle Street, 01273 777717; 29-30 North Road, 01273 703985, www.grapevinewebsite.co.uk) are great if you prefer to be more central.

Few cities offer as many themed hotels as Brighton, with rooms given names such as 'Titanic' and 'Rock and Roll'. **Sea Spray** (26 New Steine, 01273 680332, www.seaspraybrighton.co.uk) has 17 bespoke bedrooms, including the Marrakesh, Elvis, New York Penthouse and Brighton rooms (the latter has its own private courtyard).

# GETTING THERE & AROUND

Driving to Brighton is straightforward – the A23 goes all the way from London (Stockwell) to the centre of Brighton – and only takes an hour and a half from central London, but finding places to park and driving around the city are almost always a nightmare. A coach trip costs from £2.50 with National Express (depending on time of booking) and saves the hassle of driving your own car around: the journey time is 2 hours.

Most Londoners prefer to use the train. Choose between Southern trains from London Victoria and First Capital Connect from St Pancras or London Bridge – the journey takes from 50 minutes to 1 hour 15 minutes. Brighton station is just to the north of the centre of town, and most places you'd want to visit are easily walkable. For longer distances, Brighton & Hove Bus Company operates routes round the region, most journeys costing £1.80, half price for children. Taxis are also easy to find: look for white cars with turquoise bonnets. Because of the short distances, these are also inexpensive, with most short hops costing around £5.

# East Sussex Coast

The East Sussex Coast has some of the most spectacular landscapes and windswept sea views in the south-east. The chalk cliffs of Beachy Head and Seven Sisters, and the seaside joys of Hastings, Eastbourne and Bexhill, are only a couple of hours away from London. (For Brighton, *see pp47-49*.) Hastings Old Town is a delight, while neighbouring St Leonards-on-Sea has its own arty vibe. Just to the west, Bexhill boasts the De La Warr Pavilion, a handsomely restored modernist masterpiece. A few miles on, Eastbourne has a great contemporary gallery, the Towner, and a beautiful pier; just outside town is magnificent Beachy Head. Further inland is Lewes, an independently minded town with a fiercesome Bonfire Night.

Lewes

## Fast facts

**Journey time** Train and car 1 hour 45 minutes
**Festivals & events** Hastings Seafood and Wine Festival (September, www.visit1066country.com) – has stalls piled up with the best of local seafood and displays from Kent and Sussex vineyards; Lewes Bonfire Night (November, www.lewesbonfirecouncil.org.uk) – this wild evening attracts thousands of revellers with its firework displays and giant bonfire
**Good for** Beaches, countryside, food, history, walking

## SEE & DO

Start with a wander round **Hastings Old Town**. It's an atmospheric place: distinctive black fishermen's net shops line the seafront and behind them the town wanders in higgledy-piggledy fashion up the hill. Get a cliff-top view of the town and sea from **Hastings Country Park** – walk up, or hitch a lift on one of the town's two funicular railways, **East Hill Lift** (01424 451111). It opened in 1903 and was originally powered by an ingenious water balancing system, but was converted to electricity in the 1970s.

Hastings has a long artistic heritage, and the latest addition is the **Jerwood Gallery** (www.jerwoodgallery.org) on the Stade. One of the area's most talked-about developments, it's due to open in early 2012 and will feature major works by Augustus John, Walter Sickert, LS Lowry and Stanley Spencer.

For many people, Hastings means 1066 and the Battle of Hastings. This actually took place in Battle, some eight miles inland, and **Battle Abbey & Battlefield** (0870 333 1181, www.english-heritage.org.uk/1066) is definitely worth a visit; there's an audio tour of the site packed with details and vivid anecdotes as well as on-site falconry displays.

Head west out of Hastings and you'll soon come to **Bexhill**. A once-popular holiday destination that has lost some of its lustre, Bexhill is famous primarily for the spectacular 1935 modernist masterpiece the **De La Warr Pavilion** (Marina, 01424 229111, www.dlwp.co.uk). The light-filled structure houses a small but splendid permanent collection of classic design drawings, twin gallery spaces, a theatre and a café.

The drive west takes you past **Eastbourne** – Brighton's sleepier cousin. Attractions include the pier and the three-and-a-half-mile seafront promenade, which makes for an excellent, scenic stroll. There's also the town's contemporary art museum, the **Towner** (College Road, 01323 415470, www.townereastbourne.org.uk), a gleaming white building that opened in 2009. The collection began life in the 1920s as a modest 22 paintings but now numbers 4,000 pieces and features the largest and most significant body of work by Eric Ravilious (1903-42).

Nearby, the **Eastbourne Miniature Steam Railway Adventure Park** (Lottbridge Drive, 01323 520229, www. emsr.co.uk) has miniature locomotives running a mile-long track in a beautiful country park. There's a lake too; an angling day pass costs £6.

The rolling cliffs of **Beachy Head** and the **Seven Sisters**, which stretch west from Eastbourne to the

Beachy Head

Bexhill

Eastbourne

SWAN HOUSE

Swan House, Hastings

Cuckmere River, are the finest examples of chalk downland in Britain and make an excellent walk. Beachy Head itself is a vertical drop of 530 feet to the sea and offers magnificent views; it's also sadly famous as the most popular place in England for suicides. The area is one of the locations for monthly fossil hunts organised by **Discovering Fossils** (www.discoveringfossils.co.uk). For £12, hard hats, goggles, hammers and chisels are provided, and if you're lucky you might find a turtle shell or shark's tooth.

Finally, **Lewes**, to the north-west, is a handsome Regency town with a fiercely independent community: in 2008 retailers produced their own currency, the 'Lewes Pound', with the aim of getting people to spend their money locally. Lewes is also known for the raucous festivities of its **Bonfire Night**, which attract thousands of revellers each year. Great views of the town can be reached by climbing the tower of **Lewes Castle** (169 High Street, 01273 486290, www.sussexpast.co.uk), a motte-and-bailey relic from the 11th century. Four miles away is Firle, home to **Charleston Manor** (01323 811265, www.charleston. org.uk), a farmhouse that once belonged to artists Vanessa Bell and Duncan Grant, who covered the interior with a gorgeous explosion of colour and creativity.

## EAT & DRINK

In Hastings, there are few more welcoming pubs than the **First In Last Out** (14-15 High Street, 01424 425079, www.thefilo.co.uk), which has a central fire, snug booths and its own microbrewery (producing superb ales such as Ginger Tom and Cardinal). It also serves top-notch pub food. For fish and chips, head for the **Blue Dolphin**

(61B High Street, 01424 425778), which has a small restaurant as well as a takeaway counter. In St Leonards' up-and-coming Norman Road area, unpretentious **St Clement's** (3 Mercatoria, 01424 200355, www.stclements restaurant.co.uk) has gained a stellar reputation, thanks to dishes such as fish stew with chorizo, chickpeas and tomato.

The star of Eastbourne's seafront is **Beachouse** (Lower Promenade, between Wish Tower and bandstand, 07526 930625, www.thegreenhousebar.com), with a relaxed vibe and a brasserie menu; its prime location means it's always packed in the summer. Have a pint in the town's oldest inn, the **Lamb** (36 High Street, 01323 720545, http://thelamb.eu) – the beers are good; the pub is supplied by Harveys, the Lewes brewery. The **Gardener's Arms** (46 Cliffe High Street, 01273 474808) in Lewes also sells its beers. It's a tiny boozer with tasty bar snacks (hot pasties, sandwiches) and a superb choice of real ales and cider. Also in Lewes, **Bill's** (56 Cliffe High Street, 01273 476918, www.bills-website.co.uk) is an upmarket produce store and café, popular for wholesome comfort food from breakfast to teatime.

## STAY

Hastings has some of the best accommodation in the area. **Swan House** (1 Hill Street, 01424 430014, www.swanhouse hastings.co.uk) was built in 1490 and has been beautifully updated: muted colours, an open fire and wooden floors covered in rugs. There is a small courtyard where breakfasts are served in warm weather. **Lavender Lace 1066** (106 All Saints Street, 01424 422709, www.lavenderlace 1066.co.uk) is a B&B in a Grade II-listed building, and is traditional and utterly charming; breakfasts sometimes include produce from the owner's allotment.

In Eastbourne, top drawer accommodation comes in the form of the five-star **Grand Hotel** (King Edward's Parade, 01323 412345, www.grandeastbourne.com) on the seafront. Opened in 1875, hotel guests have included Charlie Chaplin, Winston Churchill and Edward Elgar. Nowadays there are 152 rooms and two restaurants. **Guesthouse East** (13 Hartington Place, 01323 722774, www.theguesthouse east.co.uk) offers seven stylish suites in a Grade II-listed Regency property, all with their own kitchens (though there is also the option of a cooked breakfast). For a traditional B&B near the town centre, try the **Manse** (7 Ditton's Road, 01323 737851, www.themansebandb.co.uk), an Arts and Crafts-style building with three ensuite rooms.

Beachy Head is home to the **Belle Tout Lighthouse** (Beachy Head, 01323 423185, www.belletout.org.uk), a former lighthouse decommissioned in 1902 and now a B&B. There are six modern rooms: the Keepers Loft is a tiny, circular space with the original stepladder to reach the double bed, while the Lantern Room at the top has stunning 360-degree views.

Lewes is curiously lacking in accommodation options. **Berkeley House B&B** (2 Albion Street, 01273 476057, www.berkeleyhouselewes.co.uk) offers three en suite rooms in a Georgian terraced townhouse, with a fine cooked breakfast.

## SHOP

A wander around the Old Town in Hastings (particularly along the High Street and George Street) reveals plenty of second-hand and gift shops, plus charming one-offs such as **Made in Hastings** (82 High Street, 01797 344655, www.madeinhastings.co.uk), selling handmade goods from

Grand Hotel, Eastbourne

Charleston Manor

Hastings

De La Warr Pavilion

delicate ceramics to hand-printed tea towels, and **Warp & Weft** (68A George Street, 07947 225424), which has a carefully edited selection of clothes and accessories. It's also home to organic store **Judges Bakery** (51 High Street, 01424 722588, www.judgesbakery.com).

Next door St Leonards-on-Sea has a burgeoning art scene, and **Norman Road** (www.thenormanroad.co.uk) – once home to boarded-up shops – is now packed with art galleries and independent shops. Photography specialist the **Lucy Bell Gallery** (46 Norman Road, 01424 434828, www.lucy-bell.com) is worth a visit, while nearby **McCarron's of Mercatoria** (no.68, 01424 428929) has a charming range of furnishings and gifts, and **Skylon** (no.64, 01424 445691, www.skyloninteriors.co.uk) is retro heaven.

Near Eastbourne, Alfriston is an almost unbearably quaint village on the South Downs Way that's home to **Much Ado About Books** (8 West Street, 01323 871222, www.muchadoaboutbooks.com). Stock is a mixture of carefully selected new releases and rare books on antique bookshelves; there's a special collection of works by the Bloomsbury Group, and some hard-to-find editions. Eastbourne has **Penelope's Portmanteau** (47 South Street, 01323 649982, www.penelopesportmanteau.com), which specialises in vintage jewellery, handbags and accessories.

## GETTING THERE & AROUND

Trains to Eastbourne depart from Victoria Station and take around 90 minutes. Trains to Hastings leave from both Charing Cross and Victoria, and take from 90 minutes to 2 hours. Eastbourne Buses runs a service along the coast from the Sovereign Centre in Eastbourne to Beachy Head. By car, it takes about 1 hour 50 minutes to drive from London to the East Sussex coast.

# West Sussex Coast

West Sussex offers a heady mixture of seaside fun, glorious countryside and charming towns and villages. By the sea there's the choice of wild West Wittering or resorts such as Littlehampton, Bognor Regis and Worthing. There are South Downs villages with timber-framed, rose-clad cottages and pretty churches, and history-packed towns such as Arundel and Chichester, the latter home to the lovely Pallant House Gallery. One-offs include magnificent Goodwood House and the fascinating Weald & Downland Open Air Museum.

Littlehampton

## Fast facts

**Journey Time** Train from 1 hour 30 minutes; car 2 hours
**Festivals & events** Sands of Time Festival (July/August, www.sandsoftime.co.uk) – a jamboree featuring sandcastle building, donkey rides, Punch & Judy and a cavalcade of vintage cars in Bognor Regis; Arundel Festival (August, www.arundelfestival.co.uk) – a ten-day celebration of music, art and drama with Shakespeare performances in the castle grounds, open-air film screenings and gigs; Goodwood Revival (September, www.goodwood.co.uk) – vintage car motor racing and attendees dressed up in vintage fineries; Arundel Food Festival (October, www.arundelfoodfestival.org.uk)
**Good for** Beaches, countryside, food, history, walking

## SEE & DO

**Worthing**, once a thriving seaside resort, is slowly becoming popular again, but doesn't get too crowded; go to enjoy the beach, the pier and **Worthing Museum & Art Gallery** (Chapel Road, 01903 221447, www.worthingmuseum.co.uk), which has an impressive stash of costumes (with pieces dating from the 17th century to the present day) as well as a vast collection of teddy bears, toys and more than 1,000 dolls.

Further west, **Littlehampton** was once the resort of choice for Coleridge, Byron and Constable. Nowadays it exudes a ramshackle, down-to-earth charm, and its **East Beach Café** (*see p55*) has been lauded for its architectural elegance and good cooking. The beach has been awarded a Blue Flag, and is perfect for a dip. Towards the western end, the beach becomes more rugged, with dunes and no sign of crazy golf or amusement arcades.

Inland, **Arundel** has lovely 11th-century **Arundel Castle** (High Street, 01903 882173, www.arundelcastle.org), which contains a collection of paintings by Van Dyck, Gainsborough and Reynolds, as well as tapestries, furniture and the 14th-century FitzAlan Chapel. The town also boasts Georgian townhouses, Tudor dwellings, a ruined medieval priory and the River Arun, and is an attractive place to explore.

Further west along the coast, **Bognor Regis** (officially the sunniest place in Britain) has long traded on its clement climate. The five miles of sand and shingle beach are backed by amusements galore and the Butlins' flagship resort (www.butlins.com). Relive the town's 18th-century heyday at the **Bognor Regis Museum** (25-27 West Street, 01243 865636, www.sussexmuseums.co.uk).

North-west of Bognor, **Chichester** is a historic city that makes a perfect base for exploring the area. **Pallant House Gallery** (9 North Pallant, 01243 774557, www.pallant.org.uk) houses a fine collection of 20th-century British art and also has an exciting line-up of temporary exhibitions. More 20th-century gems can be found at **Chichester Cathedral** (West Street, 01243 782595, www.chichestercathedral.co.uk), where there's a window by Marc Chagall, a tapestry by John Piper and paintings by Graham Sutherland. More antique treasures, such as the 12th-century Lazarus reliefs (stone carvings), are also on show here.

Seven miles north of Chichester is the **Weald & Downland Open Air Musuem** (Singleton, 01243 811363, www.wealddown.co.uk). It's more a village of rescued historic buildings from the 13th to 19th centuries than a

Bognor

East Beach Café, Littlehampton

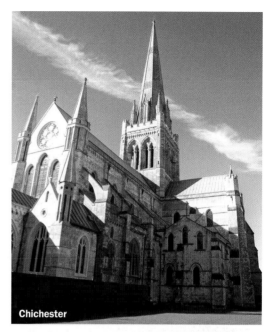
Chichester

Richmond House, Chichester

regular museum, and includes a water mill, a school and farm cottages, as well as animals and livestock, period gardens and orchards, all set in 40 acres of countryside. There is also a lakeside picnic spot with a café.

There are dozens of historic houses and stately homes in the area, but the oldest residence in this region is **Fishbourne Roman Palace** (Roman Way Road, Fishbourne, 01243 789829, www.sussexpast.co.uk), a mile and a half from the centre of Chichester. Only discovered in 1960, the 100-room palace was built in the first century AD and boasts some marvellous mosaics. The foundations of a quarter of the rooms can still be seen, and there are 3-D reconstructions. Ten minutes' drive from Chichester brings you to immaculately restored **Goodwood House**, a Regency mansion on a 12,000-acre estate, with a glorious collection of paintings, a sculpture park, a motor circuit and a racecourse.

In the other direction, the sea is just a few moments' drive away. **West Wittering**'s long, sandy beach is known as 'God's pocket', sheltered by the Isle of Wight and the swell of the South Downs. It's refreshingly undeveloped, and at low tide the beach is peppered with shallow tidal pools. Avoid the queue for the car park (especially treacherous on weekends) by catching the no.53 bus from Chichester, or by cycling the 11-mile **Salterns Way Cycle Path** (www.conservancy.co.uk), which runs through some beautiful countryside.

## EAT & DRINK

Bognor Regis has plenty of chippies – otherwise try the **Dolphin Café** (5 Waterloo Square, 07929 597561), which has a good selection of roasts, jacket potatoes and traditional puddings for an inexpensive and filling lunch. Worthing has classic ice-cream parlour **Macari's** (24-25 Marine Promenade, 01903 532753, www.macarisrestaurant.co.uk), which opened in 1959 and is situated next to the Edwardian Dome cinema. Flavours change daily, but mainstays include honeycomb, turkish delight, and maple and walnut, as well as chocolate sauce-covered sundaes. Macari's also serves fry-ups, sandwiches and classic pasta dishes.

Littlehampton's **East Beach Café** (Sea Road, 01903 731903, www.eastbeachcafe.co.uk) has attracted national interest for its architecture: the organic curves of this low-lying, steel-framed building have a sculptural quality, like a piece of driftwood or an upturned shell. Inside, the boutiquey restaurant serves simple classics (soup of the day, welsh rarebit and watercress, fish and chips) and more ambitious Modern British offerings: warm rabbit and chestnut salad, or mussel, gurnard and salmon chowder with saffron.

Chichester has several options: **Comme Ça** (67 Broyle Road, 01243 788724, www.commeca.co.uk) has an authentically Gallic menu (think smoked duck, foie gras and chateaubriand) with a cleverly British twist: stilton soufflé, for example. There is outdoor seating in the summer. Located in the Pallant House Gallery, **Field and Fork** (9 North Pallant, 01243 770827, www.fieldandfork.co.uk) is a small restaurant

Goodwood House Racecourse

Arundel Castle

Arundel

with a big reputation for its Modern British menu (slow-cooked cheek of beef, celeriac and horseradish purée with shallots, or pea, feta and chickpea fritters with toasted pumpkin seed salad); afternoon tea is served from 3pm.

Around Goodwood, the 18th-century **Star & Garter** (01243 811318) in East Dean prides itself on its food: the seafood platter features sweet-fleshed Selsey crab and lobster. In nearby Singleton the 16th-century **Partridge Inn** (Singleton Lane, 01243 811251, www.thepartridgeinn.co.uk) offers well-executed pub classics (ploughman's lunches, steak and mushroom pie, deep-fried whitebait).

## STAY

Worthing is packed with old-school B&Bs, but there are also a few places being updated in a more modern style, such as the **Ardington Hotel** (Steyne Gardens, 01903 230451, www.ardingtonhotel.co.uk), which also has a restaurant.

Arundel's standout place to stay is **Arundel House** (11 High Street, 01903 882136, www.arundelhouseonline.com), a Georgian merchant's house that holds a quality restaurant and five handsome bedrooms. Chichester offers more choice, including **Richmond House** (230 Oving Road, 01243 771464, www.richmondhousechichester.co.uk), a stylish B&B with Wi-Fi, Molton Brown toiletries and excellent breakfasts. A more central option is **Trents** (50 South Street, 01243 773714, www.trentschichester.co.uk) with five understated but comfortable rooms above a lively wine bar and restaurant.

Budget options are **Littlehampton Youth Hostel** (63 Surrey Street, 0845 371 9670, www.yha.org.uk); it has plenty of family rooms, a TV lounge and a cycle store, and the beach is four minutes away. Not far from West Wittering beach is **Wick's Farm Holiday Park** (Redlands Lane, 01243 513116, www.wicksfarm.co.uk), a campsite and winner of a gold David Bellamy Conservation Award.

## SHOP

Arundel offers good browsing opportunites. On the High Street, **Spencer Swaffer Antiques** (no.30, 01903 882132, www.spencerswaffer.co.uk) is an Arundel institution, with an impressive array of furniture and lighting, while **Kim's Bookshop** (no.10, 01903 882680, www.kimsbookshop. co.uk) stocks more than 30,000 new, second-hand and antiquarian books. In Chichester, although high-street chains dominate many of the main shopping streets, there is an outpost of Sussex-based chocolatier **Montezuma's** (29 East Street, 01243 537385, www.montezumas.co.uk), which specialises in unusual flavour combinations. For one-off gifts, **Pretty Scruffy** (1 Coopers Street, 01243 779715, www.prettyscruffy.com) should satisfy: it is a delightful mix of jewellery, ceramics, furnishings and arty bits and bobs.

## GETTING THERE & AROUND

Trains to Bognor Regis and Chichester depart from Victoria Station and take between 1 hour 30 minutes and 1 hour 50 minutes. By car from London the journey takes about 2 hours. Local buses are operated by Stagecoach (www.stagecoach bus.com) – the no.700 runs from Bognor Regis through Worthing, Chichester, Littlehampton and on to Brighton; the no.60 serves the Weald & Downland Open Air Museum, as well as Chichester, Bognor Regis and Midhurst.

# Autumn Breaks: Deep in the Woods

Sometimes a handsome stand of beech trees in one of London's parks just isn't enough, and more serious woods are called for. Fortunately, the south-east has some pretty substantial swathes of protected woodland and many of these forested areas have hotels or campsites buried within them. Autumn is, of course, the time of year when the sunlight, the leaf fall and the whole seasonal metamorphosis make a weekend in the woods special, but the following places can be visited year-round. Here are ten suggestions close to home and a further five that involve a little more travel. For more information see www.visitwoods.org.uk.

Burnham Beeches

## CLOSE TO LONDON

### Ashdown Forest
The largest free public space in the south-east and an Area of Outstanding Natural Beauty, Ashdown Forest is also the inspiration for the adventures and 'expotitions' of Winnie-the-Pooh. Wander the 6,500-acre wood on one of the 'Pooh Walk' routes, quoting AA Milne and his bear of little brain.
**Ashdown Forest Centre** Wych Cross, Forest Row, East Sussex (01342 823583, www.ashdownforest.org). East Grinstead rail.
**Stay** In a yurt or tepee at Wowo (www.wowo.co.uk), a family-friendly campsite with a brook running through it, six miles from the forest.

### Ashridge Woods
At the northern end of the Chilterns, the Ashridge Estate is a Site of Special Scientific Interest and home to the ancient Frithsden Beeches. These pollarded trees featured in the Harry Potter films as the Forbidden Forest. Lady's Walk is the place to see the autumn colour roll in, or join an organised deer walk to watch the fallow deer rut. Taste the last of the summer sun at nearby Frithsden Vineyard.

**Ashridge Estate Visitor Centre** Moneybury Hill, Berkhamsted, Hertfordshire (01494 755557, www.national trust.org.uk, www.friendsofashridge.org.uk). Tring rail.
**Stay** Lord it up at Pendley Manor (www.pendley-manor.co.uk), just outside Tring.

### Bedgebury National Pinetum
The most complete conifer collection in the world makes for a beautiful woodland area, interspersed with open spaces and water. Test your aim at archery (www.archeryatbedgebury.co.uk), hire a bicycle (www.quenchuk.co.uk) or have a treetop adventure (www.goape.co.uk).
**Bedgebury National Pinetum** Bedgebury Road, Goudhurst, Kent (01580 879820, www.bedgebury pinetum.org.uk). Open from 8am daily, weather permitting. £8.50 car parking charge. Etchingham rail.
**Stay** Beckett's B&B (www.becketts-bandb.co.uk) has four rooms in a converted barn with vaulted ceilings and exposed beams. Or there's the more contemporary Slides Farm (www.slides farm.com).

### Box Hill
A Londoners' day trip for generations. Box Hill's panoramic views over the North Downs inspired Keats

Stour Wood

and Austen. Graham Simmonds, trustee of the Trees for Cities charity (www.treesforcities.org), says, 'My favourite forest to escape to near London is the woodlands at Box Hill near Dorking in Surrey, which has got some great beech and oak woods and even wild cherry on the top of the hill; plus there's amazing views, and a very nice pub too!'

**Box Hill** Tadworth, Surrey (www.nationaltrust.org.uk). Box Hill rail.

**Stay** A little further out in Shadow Woods near Billingshurst with Woodland Yurting (www.woodland yurting.com). Accommodation is in yurts and a cottage; bushcraft courses are offered.

## Brede High Woods

Six miles north of Hastings, along the B2089, Brede is the largest ancient woodland managed by the Woodland Trust. Part of the High Weald Area of Outstanding Natural Beauty, it's been exploited since Roman times for its deposits of iron ore, and is now proving to be a focus of archeological interest. The furnaces and bellows have given way to mossy trails that weave through peaceful woods. Local ecologist Patrick Roper (www. patrickroper.co.uk) runs nature walks in the woods.

**Brede High Woods** Cripps Corner, near Battle, East Sussex (www.woodlandtrust.org.uk). Doleham rail.

**Stay** At Hawthbush Farm (www.hawthbushfarm.co.uk), on the campsite or in accommodation such as the Piggery (sleeps two) or the Cowshed (sleeps eight).

## Burnham Beeches

The ancient pollarded oaks and beeches of Burnham wood were saved from encroaching development in 1880 by prescient City of London bankers. The 'very reverend vegetables', as the poet Thomas Gray put it, were filmed in *Robin Hood: Prince of Thieves* as a stand-in for Sherwood. Volunteers play an important role in the management and upkeep of the woodland. Pitch in and help out with heathland restoration or birch cutting.

**Burnham Beeches** Hawthorn Lane, Farnham Common, Buckinghamshire (01753 647358, www.cityoflondon. gov.uk/burnham). Open 8am-5pm Mon-Fri. Burnham rail.

**Stay** Chequers Inn is a family-run, 17th-century coaching inn with 17 classic rooms (www. chequers-inn.com).

## Epping Forest

Epping Forest (6,000 acres) remains the largest area of ancient forest around London, and is reachable by tube. It was dedicated to the people by Queen Victoria in 1882 and the forest is considered a Site of Special Scientific Interest and Special Area of Conservation.

**Epping Forest** High Beach, Loughton, Essex (8508 0028, www.cityoflondon.gov.uk/www.epping forest.co.uk). Chingford rail or Loughton tube.

**Stay** Within the forest, the Elms Caravan and Camping Park (www.theelmscampsite.co.uk) has log cabins, cottages and pre-pitched tents.

## Grovely Wood

Walk the ancient Ridgeway in Wiltshire through Grovely Wood – another AONB – along a path that has been used to travel the downland for centuries. In the spring you can see purple emperor butterflies here, while the autumn is the season for rutting deer, fungi, sloes and, after the first frost, wild plums, blackberries, cobnuts and chestnuts.
**Grovely Wood** Grovely Road, Wilton, Salisbury, Wiltshire (www.visitwiltshire.co.uk). Salisbury rail.
**Stay** In the Compasses Inn (www.thecompassesinn.com), a 14th-century thatched freehouse.

## Savernake Forest

Europe's oldest planted woodland has been owned by a single family, incredibly, for 31 generations. At 4,500 acres, Savernake Estate has the ordered grace of landscape architect Lancelot 'Capability' Brown's 'Grand Avenue' of beeches (planted in the 1790s) and the gnarly majesty of ancient oaks in groves carpeted with fallen leaves. A few miles further west, explore Neolithic Avebury, which includes the largest stone circle in the world.
**Savernake Forest** Marlborough, Wiltshire (01672 512161, www.savernakeestate.co.uk). Great Bedwin rail.
**Stay** The White House B&B (01672 870321, www.the-white-house-b-and-b.co.uk) has two rooms in Little Bedwyn, Wiltshire.

## Stour Wood

Deep in Constable country, and managed by the RSPB, Stour Wood is a place to gather sweet chestnuts for roasting or join a fungal foray. Native trees with spectacular colours give way to estuary saltmarshes where wading birds congregate on their winter migrations.
**Stour Wood** Harwich Road, Wrabness, Harwich, Essex (www.woodlandtrust.org.uk). Wrabness rail.
**Stay** In luxurious canvas tents at Layer Marney Tower (www.countryhousehideout.co.uk) 25 miles away.

# FURTHER AFIELD

## Forest of Dean

Where the wild boar roam: the Dean's mixed conifer and broad-leaf forest stretches along the River Severn up to Gloucester and has been a haven for wildlife since before the Normans. Swing through the treetops at the GoApe adventure park (www.goape.co.uk) or learn how to capture the scene in a forest photography course (www.djs photography.co.uk). Join a Winter Owl evening (www.icbp.org) on Friday and Saturday nights in November and December.
**Dean Heritage Centre** Camp Mill, Soudley, Gloucestershire (01594 822170, www.visitforestofdean.co.uk). Lydney rail.
**Stay** Nestled in the Forest of Dean in a private 'tree-house' log cabin (www.forestholidays.co.uk) or at Abbey Home Farm (www.theorganicfarmshop.co.uk) in Cirencester, an organic farm with yurts, cabins and camping.

Chequers Inn

Epping Forest

## Grizedale Forest Park

In the heart of the Lake Country, Grizedale (meaning 'valley of the pigs') has meandering trails leading to over 90 forest sculptures by Andy Goldsworthy, David Nash and others. If that sounds a little slow, there's always the aerial assault course of GoApe (www.goape.co.uk).
**Grizedale Forest Park** Hawkshead, Ambleside, Cumbria (01229 860010, www.forestry.gov.uk/grizedalehome, www.grizedalesculpture.org). Windermere rail, then bus or taxi.
**Stay** Grizedale Lodge B&B (015394 36532, www.grizedale-lodge.com) on the edge of the forest has four-poster bedrooms from £50.

## Mortimer Forest

A remnant of the Saxon hunting forests of Mocktree, Deerfold and Bringewood, Mortimer is the largest block of forest in the Marches – an area stretching from Shrewsbury to Leominster. Take in the geology trails and ridge walks on horseback and cover a lot more ground (www.north farmludlow.co.uk).

**Mortimer Forest** Whitcliffe, Ludlow, Shropshire (www.forestry.gov.uk). Ludlow rail.
  **Stay** In a log cabin (www.ludlowecologcabins.co.uk) inspired by the owner's stay in Idaho.

## Sherwood Forest

Home to the legend of Robin Hood and dominated by native species, Sherwood has some of the oldest oaks in Britain: the 'Major Oak' is estimated at 800 years. Join a hawk walk or learn to string a bow at the Adrenalin Jungle activity park (www.adrenalinjungle.com).
**Sherwood Forest** Edwinstowe, Mansfield, Nottinghamshire (www.naturalengland.org.uk). Mansfield rail.
**Stay** In the forest's new log cabins (www.forestholidays.co.uk).

## Thetford Forest Park

Britain's largest lowland pine forest was created after World War I and is now a centre for activities of all sorts. Glide through the forest trails on a Segway or a bicycle (www.goape.co.uk). In December, walk through illuminated woods (www.theelectricforest.co.uk).
**Thetford Forest Park** near Brandon, Norfolk (01842 815434, www.forestry.gov.uk/thetfordforestpark). Brandon rail.
**Stay** On the edge of the forest at Peddars Way B&B (www.farmholidaysnorfolk.co.uk).

Thetford Forest Park

# Whitstable

It's hard for any coastal town within an easy two hours of the capital to withstand the middle-class bolthole effect of London gentrification, but Whitstable has managed it with ease, thanks to a buoyant fishing industry and the refusal of locals to simply cash in and ship out to the 'burbs. Stroll along the seafront – past the pretty cottages of Island Row – with a bag of fish and chips, and take in the sea and sky views made famous by a certain William Turner, and you won't think of London at all. Whitstable is fully Kentish, with a far slower rhythm than the capital and a more down-to-earth sensibility all round. And when you need respite from the occasional biting wind, there are plenty of great pubs and, of course, fish restaurants – many of them serving oysters from local beds given royal protection by Elizabeth I.

## Fast facts

**Journey time** Train 1.5 hours
**Festivals & events** The Whitstable Oyster Festival (July, www.whitstableoysterfestival.co.uk) spans nine days in July. As well as oyster processions and fish dances, there's the Whitstable Regatta, on the festival's second weekend
**Good for** Beaches, food

## SEE & DO

Whitstable has smartened itself up for visitors over the past decade, with many of the old fishermen's huts on the seafront being fashioned into holiday retreats. Yet much of the town looks as it always has, from the **Island Wall**, with its mid 19th-century cottages, to the little alleyways once used by fishermen to cut through the town to the sea (Squeeze Gut Alley is so narrow that many people have to walk through it sideways). The main streets, running north from Oxford Street to High Street to Harbour Street, all lead towards the seafront and harbour. Here you'll find a selection of small shops, galleries and cafés. To learn about the town's history, pop into **Whitstable Museum & Gallery** (Oxford Street, 01227 276998, www.whitstable-museum.co.uk). Exhibits include a display devoted to the town's most famous fan, Peter Cushing, who bought a seafront house here in 1959. It includes film stills, props and examples of the actor-turned-painter's art. There are also interesting artefacts and photographs depicting the town's fishing and oyster-catching heritage.

Continuing north from Harbour Street to Tower Hill, **Whitstable Castle & Gardens** (The Gate House, Tower Hill, 01227 281174) sits on the border of Whitstable and the suburb of Tankerton. The newly restored castle and grounds has become a centre for community activities and is a good place to take in some sea air. If you climb to the top of the hill you'll come out opposite **Tower Hill Tea Gardens** (07780 662543), an idyllic and often peaceful spot with sea views.

Running parallel to the shingle beach is **Island Row**, lined with pretty cottages; walk east to reach the harbour. Stand facing the sea and you'll see some of the 30 or so turbines of the **Kentish Flats Wind Farm**. Low tide reveals a natural

spit of shingle on a clay bank, known as the **Street**. You can walk it for about half a mile, on the last of the town's land to the north, the rest having been eroded and swallowed by the sea. Keep an eye on the rising tide, though.

Keen cyclists can enjoy the **Crab & Winkle Way** (www.crabandwinkle.org) while in town – a seven-mile bike and foot path (14 miles round trip) between Whitstable and Canterbury, which follows the route of a railway line that was shut down in 1952. It passes through some lovely farmland and woodland glades, with only a couple of thigh-toning hills en route. In Canterbury itself, you can take a tour of the famous cathedral, and peruse the city's historic backstreets.

## EAT & DRINK

Whitstable has been praised for its oysters since Juvenal shucked a few here a couple of thousand years ago. These days, the oyster beds granted royal protection by Elizabeth I are no secret. The Royal Native Oyster Company, one of the earliest commercial ventures in Europe, was reconstituted as the **Whitstable Oyster Fishery Company** in 1896. A combination of overfishing and disease almost finished off the industry in the 1920s, but it was revived in the 1980s. These days, the WOFC runs many of the businesses in town and spearheaded Whitstable's gentrification. Native oysters (from Whitstable, as well as Colchester and Helford) will cost you about £15 per half dozen. If you're paying about a fiver, chances are you're eating the less expensive pacific (also known as rock or gigas) oysters, which have larger, longer shells.

The main restaurant of the Whitstable Oyster Fishery Company is in a handsome building on the beach (Royal Native Oyster Stores, Horsebridge, 01227 276856, www.oysterfishery.co.uk). The nautical-looking dining room is the setting for a meal that might run from half a dozen native oysters to a whole roast local wild seabass with garlic and rosemary. The more casual sister establishment, the **Lobster Shack** (01227 772157, www.thelobstershack.co.uk), is located at the end of the East Quay.

Another key spot for seafood is the tiny **Wheelers Oyster Bar** (8 High Street, 01227 273311), which has been serving local oysters since 1856. It's a quirky place, bright pink on the outside and simply decorated; book well in advance to avoid disappointment as there are limited tables.

At **JoJo's** (209 Tankerton Road, 01227 274591, www.jojosrestaurant.co.uk), chef Nikki Billington produces mouthwatering Mediterranean tapas in her tiny open-plan kitchen, using organic ingredients. The place is unlicensed, but you can bring your own booze. The equally relaxed **Samphire** (4 High Street, 01227 770075, www.samphirerestaurant.co.uk) provides a plump brunch menu (eggs benedict and the like), alongside lunch and supper, which might feature slow-braised lamb, venison sausages or Rye Bay scallops.

Further out of town, near the sea wall on the old coastal road west of Whitstable, sits renowned gastropub the **Sportsman** (Faversham Road, Seasalter, 01227 273370, www.thesportsmanseasalter.co.uk). It's in a rather remote, somewhat bleak location, but the food is so good that people flock here from afar.

Back in Whitstable proper, the **Crab & Winkle** (South Quay, 01227 779377, www.crabandwinklerestaurant.co.uk), the **Pearson's Arms** (Sea Wall, 01227 272005, www.pearsonsarms.com) and **Williams & Brown Tapas** (48 Harbour Street, 01227 273373, www.thetapas.co.uk) are all reliable places for fish and seafood. And there are plenty of takeaway options too – try the fish market on **South Quay** (01227 771245; there are barbecues here in summer). For fish and chips, **VC Jones** is a favourite (25 Harbour Street, 01227 272703, www.vcjones.co.uk). Note that many of the aforementioned places are closed on Mondays.

Lastly, for evening drinks, don't miss the atmospheric **Old Neptune** pub (Marine Terrace, 01227 272262, www.neppy.co.uk), on the beach. In winter, cosy up with a pint and listen to live music, surrounded by whiskery dogs and fishermen; in summer, take advantage of the outdoor seating.

Sportsman

## SHOP

Whitstable has a good number of small, independently run shops and boutiques, many of which are on Harbour Street. **Mosaic** (30 Harbour Street, 01227 276779) sells handmade jewellery, pewter designs, wraps and pashminas. **Buttercup** (16 Harbour Street, 01227 265978) sells a range of gifts and cards, including a variety of twee children's toys. Fans of antiques should pop into **L'Image** (44 Oxford

Old Neptune

Street, 01227 366288), which is full of gorgeous 18th-century-style French furniture. On the same street is **Oxford Street Books** (01227 281727, www.oxfordstreet books.com), where every nook and cranny is stuffed with second-hand books.

## STAY

The **Front Rooms** (9 Tower Parade, 01227 282132, www. thefrontrooms.co.uk) is a stylish and homely B&B in a Victorian townhouse, with just two double rooms (which share a bathroom); both rooms have comfy cast-iron double beds and a stock of books and DVDs.

More than 300 years old, the **Duke of Cumberland** (High Street, CT5 1AP, 01227 280617, www.thedukein whitstable.co.uk) hotel and Shepherd Neame boozer originally took in the local oyster and dredger men after a hard day's work fishing. Now it's a well-priced hotel with nine simply furnished, ensuite guest rooms.

**Belmont House** (74 Oxford Street, CT5 1DA, 01227 266911, www.belmonthousewhitstable.co.uk) on the high street, has one double and two single rooms, all with ensuites.

The **Hotel Continental** (29 Beach Walk, 01227 280280, www.hotelcontinental.co.uk) is a large 1930s hotel on the seafront, refurbished in 1998 by the Whitstable Oyster Fishery Company. As well as 23 nicely decorated rooms, there's a brasserie and a bar, both offering lovely views and a relaxed atmosphere. The Continental also owns ten delightful fishermen's huts on the seafront, which have been transformed into upmarket and very popular holiday accommodation. All (except hut 6) have great sea views, and are right on the beach.

## GETTING THERE & AROUND

There's a direct train from London Victoria to Whitstable, which takes just under an hour and a half, and a slightly quicker service from St Pancras that involves a change at Rochester. Travelling by car from south-east London would take around the same amount of time. You will only need your feet to get around the town and beach areas, and a bike if you want to go to Herne Bay or Canterbury. Bike hire is available at Whitstable Cycle Hire (Captain's House, 56 Harbour Street, CT5 01227 275156, www.whitstable cyclehire.com).

# North Norfolk Coast

The north Norfolk coast encompasses marsh, dunes and huge expanses of sand, as well as windswept brick and flint villages and lively seaside towns. There are pine woods fringing Holkham's vast sandy beach, miles of salt marshes at Stiffkey and sloping dunes on Blakeney point – it's no wonder artists and writers flock to the county for inspiration. Check out the sunset from Hunstanton, the only west-facing resort on this coast. The area is also known for its produce, in particular Cromer crabs, Morston mussels and fresh samphire, all of which are shipped to London's best restaurants. Here they're sold along the roadside at a fraction of the price seen in the capital.

Cromer beach

## Fast facts

**Journey time** Train 1 hour 35 minutes; car 3 hours
**Festivals & events** Norfolk & Norwich Festival (May, www.nnfestival.org.uk) – an Arts Council-funded celebration of art, performance and culture; Norfolk Open Studios (May-June, www.norfolkopen studios.org.uk); Royal Norfolk Show (June, www.royal norfolkshow.co.uk) – the largest two-day agricultural show in the country; Cromer Carnival (Aug, www.cromercarnival.co.uk)
**Good for** Beaches, countryside, food, walking, wildlife

## SEE & DO

Pine-fringed **Holkham beach** is a must-see; its miles of sand are a knockout, even on the dullest day. **Burnham Market**, just inland, is a smart village with plenty of spending and eating options; be aware that thanks to the influx of affluent second-homers and visitors, it may feel a little too like London for some weekenders. Further along the coast is picturesque **Blakeney Harbour**, popular with families who go crabbing off the harbour wall. There are also seal-spotting excursions, departing from both Blakeney Harbour (01263 740753) and Morston Quay (01263 740038, www.beansboattrips.co.uk).

Blakeney and Cley marshes are good for birdwatching. Many twitchers regard the Norfolk Wildlife Trust's **Cley Marshes** reserve (01263 740008, www.norfolkwildlife trust.org.uk) as one of the best in the UK. Its shingle beach, saline lagoons and reed beds support a huge variety of local and migrating birdlife. The new eco centre shop has some superb viewing areas and a great café overlooking the reserve. The creeks and salt marshes give way to crumbling cliffs and sandy shingle shores as the coast curves round to the popular Victorian seaside towns of **Sheringham** and **Cromer**. The former is well preserved, with narrow winding streets, gift shops and ice-cream opportunities; the Poppy Line steam train runs from here inland to the handsome market town of **Holt**. Cromer is famous for its pier (01263 512495, www.cromer-pier.com). The Pavilion Theatre, perched at the end of the pier, plays host to the traditional end-of-pier show as well as a year-round calendar of theatre, music and comedy. From here, those with cars can continue down the coast to see Trimingham's golden shores and Happisburgh's candy-striped lighthouse.

More strenuous activities than walking or birdwatching are possible: you can sign up for a day's kitesurfing course in Hunstanton (01485 534455, www.hunstantonwater sports.com), try your hand at sailing or powerboating in Morston (01263 740704, www.norfolketc.co.uk) or take surf lessons at Cromer (07966 392227, www.glide surfschool.co.uk).

Cromer Pier

Blakeney Point

Holkham beach

## EAT & DRINK

As well as good local produce, Norfolk has some great pubs, cafés and restaurants. A few miles from Hunstanton, the **Lifeboat Inn** (Ship Lane, Thornham, 01485 512236, www.lifeboatinnthornham.com) is at its best in winter when there's a warming fire and mussels are in season.

The hub of upmarket Burnham Market is the **Hoste Arms** (The Green, 01328 738777, www.hostearms.co.uk), a 17th-century coaching inn serving quality local fare, including Holkham Estate venison. A few miles away, the Stiffkey **Red Lion** (44 Wells Road, 01328 830552, www.stiffkey.com) offers a warm welcome, with four log fires and dishes such as fresh local lobster and Stiffkey fish pie. In Morston the **Anchor Inn** (The Street, 01263 741392) serves top-notch fish and chips.

In and around Holkham there's a range of options. For a romantic dinner, book a table at the Grade II-listed **Cley Windmill** (01263 740209, www.cleywindmill.co.uk), which sits among the reed beds and serves three-course meals by candlelight. In the picturesque village of Salthouse, right on

Byfords

Sheringham

Cley Windmill

Blakeney

the tiny village green, the **Dun Cow** (Purdy Street, 01263 740467) serves pub grub and has views over the salt marshes. **Cookies Crab Shop** (The Green, 01263 740352, www.salthouse.org.uk) next door sells super-fresh shellfish and sandwiches. Inland, **Byfords** (1-3 Shirehall Plain, Holt, 01263 711400, www.byfords.org.uk) is ideal for light lunches and elevenses. Try a slice of the coffee cake.

## SHOP

For the best independent shops head to Burnham Market and Holt (where the cobbled streets and hidden yards are crammed with art galleries, jewellery shops, bric-a-brac and cafés). In the former, **Anna** (Market Place, 01328 730325, www.shopatanna.co.uk) is a popular boutique that opened here before opening branches on the King's Road and in Primrose Hill. Sixteen years on, it stocks a selection of designer clothes as well as its own-label clothes. Andrew Ruffhead's coastal art studio, **Fish and Ships** (19 Ulph Place, 01328 738621, www.fish-and-ships.com), sells his sea-themed drawings, prints, cards and sculptures.

If you're in a car, check out **Alby Crafts** (Cromer Road, Erpingham, 01263 761590, www.albycrafts.co.uk) just inland from Cromer, where potters, painters and furniture makers work and sell their wares.

## STAY

As well as a restaurant and a deli, **Byfords** (*see above*) in Holt also has 16 stylish bedrooms, featuring traditional local brick and flint and photos of the surrounding coast. For boho opulence, the **Victoria at Holkham** (Park Road, 01328 711008, www.victoriaatholkham.co.uk) provides the warmest of welcomes after a windswept walk. **Cley Windmill** (*see p65*) is a unique property, with wooden floorboards, exposed beams and stunning views out to sea.

If you're on a budget or in a group – and keen to cook those Cromer crabs – consider hiring a cottage. **Blakeney Cottages** (01263 741777; www.blakeneycottagecompany. co.uk) has a range of properties from one-bed cottages to an enormous barn conversion complete with swimming pool that sleeps 17. **Norfolk Country Cottages** is also a great choice and offers accommodation throughout the county (01603 871872, www.norfolkcottages.co.uk).

## GETTING THERE & AROUND

Having a car means a lot more freedom to explore. However, the area has reasonable rail links with London. First Capital Connect (www.firstcapitalconnect.co.uk) runs a regular train service between King's Cross and Kings Lynn that takes just over an hour and a half, and from there operates bus services to Hunstanton and Wells-next-the-Sea. Trains also run from Liverpool Street Station to Norwich on National Express East Anglia (www.nationalexpresseast anglia.com) and take 2 hours. From Norwich there's a connection through to Cromer (45 minutes) and Sheringham (1 hour) on the Bittern Line (www.bitternline.com). The Coasthopper buses (01553 776980, www.coasthopper.co.uk) also operate from Kings Lynn, connecting the coastal towns for 45 miles down to Cromer.

To explore inland using public transport take a 20-minute nostalgia trip on the Poppy Line from Sheringham to Holt (Sheringham Station, 01263 820800, www.nnrailway.co.uk).

# Norfolk Broads

Norfolk's network of rivers and lakes was created by the large-scale excavation of peat during the Middle Ages. Over the centuries, rising sea levels created 117 square miles of wetland that, since their discovery by Victorian sailing enthusiasts, have become one of England's most popular 'natural' wonders. The combination of water, trees, marsh, sky and wildlife make for a distinctive landscape that feels very far from civilisation, whether you're sitting on a boat travelling at four miles an hour or walking around the edge of the wetlands. Medieval stone bridges, flint churches and picturesque draining pumps are the noteworthy man-made elements of the landscape – and while a car is very handy for exploring a region dotted with villages and teeming with almost as many back roads as watercourses, the generally flat terrain makes the Broads bike-friendly.

## Fast facts

**Journey time** Train 1 hour 50 minutes; car 2 hours 30 minutes
**Festivals & events** The Broads Outdoor Festival (May, (www.outdoorsfestival.co.uk), now in its second year, celebrates all things outdoorsy, with archery, rambling, cycle tours, canoeing and treasure hunts, as well as art workshops and paddle boat sailing; World Wetlands Day (February, www.norfolkwildlife trust.org) events are held throughout the Broads to mark the 1971 signing of the Convention on Wetlands; the annual Barton Broad Regatta (August Bank Holiday, www.bartonbroadopenregatta.co.uk) sees a flotilla of yachts take to the waters to battle for boating supremacy.
**Good for** Countryside, wildlife

## SEE & DO

Many people think of the Broads as one of those old Hoseasons adverts – all sleepy barges, smiling grandparents and coarse fishermen catching nothing. But adventure tourism has livened up some areas and if you can't cope with an entire weekend of slow-traveller tranquillity you'll find plenty to get you up and about.

Outdoor fun of the 'soft' family-friendly kind can be found at **Bewilderwood** (Horning Road, near Horning, 01603 783900, www.bewilderwood.co.uk.), an adventure park packed with tree houses, zipwires, jungle bridges and marsh walks. Parents are encouraged to join in the antics, and there are snack bars and restaurants, as well as picnic areas. With the priciest admission at £11, it's a relatively inexpensive day out.

For adult daredevils, the **Anglian Air Centre** (Norwich International Airport, 01603 410866, www. anglianaircentre.co.uk) offers flying lessons for absolute

beginners lasting either 30 minutes or an hour. There's the potential for bird's eye views of the Broads if you dare take your eyes off the controls. The trial lessons cost £75 to £175, depending on whether you opt for a two- or a four-seater aircraft.

A boat trip of some description is the main reason most visitors travel to the Broads. Moored outside the Swan Hotel in Horning, Mississippi-style paddle boat the **Southern Comfort** (www.southern-comfort.co.uk) makes three to four excursions daily lasting one and a half to two hours. The upper deck affords panoramic views and there's a fully stocked bar. An alternative is to climb aboard the solar-powered catamaran **Ra** (01603 782281) for a 75-minute trip around Barton Broad, leaving from Gay's Staithe at Neatshead. A one-hour guided cruise of the peaceful waters of Horsey Mere is provided by **Ross' River Trips** (01692 598135, www.rossrivertrips.co.uk) aboard the *Lady Ann*, a wooden vessel that seats 12.

You can hire canoes and kayaks for day or weekend trips with **Canoe Man** (01603 499177, www.thecanoeman.com), based in Wroxham, which will allow you to explore those tiny channels off the main waterways and see more wildlife than you ever would on a larger craft. The Broads habitat can be split into two main areas: the fens and open water (the Broads themselves) and the drained grazing marshes. The former are the home of swallowtail butterfly, breeding bittern and marsh harrier, while the grazing marshes with their drainage ditches harbour water voles and a wide variety of ducks and geese.

Motorboats of all sizes are available to hire from **Norfolk Broads Direct** (01602 670711, www.broads. co.uk), operating out of Wroxham and Potter Heigham or, for a low-tech and eco-friendly alternative, you can book a 1930s wooden yacht from half a day to a week at **Hunter's Yard** (01692 68263, www.huntersyard.co.uk)

Bikes for adults and children are available to hire from **Broadland Cycle Hire** (07887 480331), and for a close-up look at the vegetation, the boardwalk nature trail is set up at many of the main Broads, including Barton, Ranworth, Hickling and Upton, and is managed by the **Norfolk Wildlife Trust** (01603 270479, www.norfolk wildlifetrust.org.uk)

Learn more about the history of the Broads at the award-winning **Museum of the Broads** (The Staithe, Stalham, 01692 581681, www.norfolk.org/museumofthebroads).

There's also the unofficial cathedral of the Broads, **St Helen's Church** (Ranworth, 01603 270769), which, after climbing its '89 uneven steps, two ladders', and 'one trap-door', boasts far-reaching views across the Broads including, on a clear day, the spire of Norwich Cathedral.

## EAT & DRINK

Picturesque pubs, often located by the water's edge, serving reliable and hearty grub, are what you're most likely to find in this region. The **Crown Inn** (41 The Street, Catfield, 01692 580128) is a mile from Catfield Staithe, and is a proper village pub with decent food and a good selection of ales. The bar is cosy and there's a garden outside. In the area around Wroxham lies the **Kings Head** (26 Wroxham Road, 01603 737426), which has a raised wooden deck from which you can enjoy some of the best pub food in the area. **Staithe 'N' Willow** (16 Lower Street, Horning, 01692 630915) is a thatched cottage that, even if the food wasn't great, would make a lovely lunch spot. **Bure River Cottage** restaurant (27 Lower Street, Horning, 01692 631421) specialises in Modern European fish and seafood dishes. The service is excellent and many of the ingredients locally sourced. In the Trinity Broads area lies the **Riverside Tea Rooms & Stores** (The Green, Stokesby, 01493 750470), which offers takeaway home-made pies and cakes, plus breakfasts and light lunches, which you can munch while relaxing on the banks of the nearby river.

## SHOP

While not renowned for its shopping, there are many farm outlets and independent shops selling arts and crafts in the market towns around the Broads. Near Wroxham, **Sutton Pottery** (Church Road, Sutton, 01692 580595, www.suttonpottery.com) is an open studio workshop where you can buy handmade kitchen and tableware. You can also watch pottery being made and even have a go yourself on one of its courses. In Wroxham lies the self-proclaimed 'biggest village store in the world'. **Roys** (01603 782131, www.roys.co.uk) is a department store that stocks everything from food and clothing to hardware and electrical appliances. Otherwise, nearby Norwich will cater for all your shopping needs, high street and otherwise.

## STAY

In most trips to the Broads, the water plays a significant role, and hiring a cruiser takes that up a level, with the added excitement that you'll wake up in a different location each day. Try **Waterway Holidays** (0845 127 1020, www.waterwayholidays.com) – boats usually sleep around three to six people and cost on average £500 to £700 for a week's hire.

If you plan to spend a lot of time on the water, but would prefer accommodation on dry land, Wroxham is a good base. Its reliable B&B options include the **Coach House** (96 Norwich Road, 01603 784376, www.coachhouse wroxham.co.uk) while the **Wroxham Hotel** (The Bridge, 01603 782061, www.arlingtonhotelgroup.co.uk) is slighly more plush and has 18 rooms, plus a bar and restaurant.

Nearby Coltishall also has good accommodation options. **Bridge House** (1 High Street, 01603 737323, www. bridgehouse-coltishall.co.uk) offers rooms in a 300-year-old ex-coaching inn, while **Norfolk Mead Hotel** (01603 737531, www.norfolkmead.co.uk) is an elegant,

creeper-covered country mansion with a homely vibe, located on a quiet stretch of the Bure, with moorings available for boats.

For weekend breakers who want their trip to combine bucolic scenery with the hubbub of a city, elegant **St Giles House Hotel** (41-45 St Giles Street, 01603 275180, www.stgileshousehotel.com), located in the heart of Norwich, is an attractive option. Facilities include a restaurant, a cocktail bar and a spa, and rooms come equipped with flat screen TVs and DVD players, minibars and Wi-Fi.

## GETTING THERE & AROUND

Trains run regularly to Norwich from Liverpool Street Station, taking around two hours. An off-peak return ticket usually costs around £45, though if booked well in advance can be as little as £15. Both National Express and Megabus run reliably inexpensive coach services. Driving from north-east London should take around 2.5 hours.

**Hickling Broad**

# Suffolk

Though its western fringes lie within the London commuter belt, Suffolk is a predominantly rural county and if you spread your weekend between Bury St Edmunds and the coast you'll see a glorious variety of countryside. Start at this medieval market town, after which you can make your way through a series of lovely villages to the coast. Take in the sandy beaches and charm of Southwold before going down the coast towards Aldeburgh, home of the world-renowned Aldeburgh Music Festival. There are walks and cycle trails galore across the region, as well as numerous wildlife and nature reserves. Expect spectacular scenery all the way – from open heath to wild marshland to shingle spits and dune-backed sands – and tiny, isolated inns. What's more, Suffolk's restaurants get better every year, with local produce increasingly standard on most menus.

## Fast facts

**Journey time** Train 1 hour 10 minutes to 2 hours 45 minutes; car 2 hours 30 minutes
**Festivals & events** Aldeburgh Festival (June, www.aldeburgh.co.uk) – launched by Benjamin Britten, Peter Pears and Eric Crozier in 1948, this two-week festival attracts top performers from around the world, filling the area's churches and public halls with a variety of music, poetry, literature and drama; Aldeburgh Food & Drink Festival (September, www.aldeburghfoodanddrink.co.uk) – a ten-day gourmet foodathon; Theatre in the Forest (August, www.redrose chain.com) – theatre and film company Red Rose Chain holds performances in Rendlesham Forest
**Good for** Beaches, countryside, food, walking

## SEE & DO

The bustling market town of **Bury St Edmunds** was founded in the seventh century and grew exponentially during the Industrial Revolution. Its side streets are full of architectural curiosities; it's most beautiful heading south from the market square, where Georgian façades give way to unadorned medieval buildings. Fans of architect Sir John Soane will want to look at the house he designed at 81 Guildford Street, now owned by a firm of solicitors. At the bottom of Abbeygate Street is a huge 14th-century gatehouse, leading to the flint ruins of what used to be one of the largest and wealthiest Benedictine monasteries in Europe.

Just outside Bury lies **West Stow Anglo-Saxon Village** (Icklingham Road, 01284 728718, www.westow.org). In the 1960s, a test for gravel and sand extraction here led to the discovery of an Anglo-Saxon village of considerable size.

Bury St Edmunds

Southwold

It's now a top tourist draw to the area, and you can visit a weaver's house, a workshop and several other buildings.

Further north lie the open expanses of the Brecks, 370 square miles of sparsely populated heathland. The region contains Thetford Forest, which has become a major recreation space for outdoor pursuits. Here you can take a picnic, hire bicycles (Bike-Art, High Lodge Forest Centre, 01842 810090, www.bike-art.com) or explore **Lynford Arboretum**, which protects a great variety of tree species.

However, Suffolk is all about villages, many quaint to the point of cliché. Try the cluster east of the A140 that includes **Fressingfield** – it's a lively and community-focused place boasting a pottery and a village shop, with the 16th-century Fox & Goose pub at its centre, and is a pleasure to stroll around. Nearby **Hoxne** is famous for two separate archaeological discoveries; further south there's **Brundish**, home to Lane Farm (01379 384593, www.lanefarm.co.uk), where air-dried Suffolk salami is made. **Debenham** is another gem, being both pretty and historically interesting; there are several circular walks around the village or into the surrounding countryside. But **Eye** takes the prize for architectural

sophistication, with many handsome houses, civic buildings and the striking St Peter & St Paul's church.

It's only 20 miles or so from this clutch of villages to the north Suffolk coast. The big-hitter here is **Southwold**, a small, picture-postcard town, with sandy beaches, a tastefully refurbished pier, higgledy-piggledy streets and lots of greenery around the edges. Independent shops include an old-fashioned sweet shop selling sugar mice and fudge. Visit the social history-focused **Southwold Museum** (Victoria Street, 01502 726097, www.southwoldmuseum.org) and climb the 92 steps of **Southwold Lighthouse** (Shadbroke Road, 01502 722576) for the views. Don't miss the **Under the Pier Show** (www.southwoldpier.co.uk), the most eccentric amusement arcade in England.

Down the coast, **Walberswick** is so pretty that artists such as Charles Rennie Mackintosh and Philip Wilson – and his circle of Impressionists – came here to capture its beauty. The pristine village green and chocolate-box houses are a great starting point for a walk along the coast. Next along is the tiny seaside settlement of **Dunwich**, which in the 13th century was the sixth most important town in England. It's being steadily consumed by the sea, and now all that's left is a pebble beach, some tearooms and a few

Dunwich

Maggi Hambling sculpture, Aldeburgh

lonely-looking buildings. The desolate shingle beach backs on to a heath teeming with wildlife, a major draw for nature-lovers. From the beach it's a pleasant hour's walk to the RSPB reserve at **Minsmere** (Westleton, 01728 648281, www.rspb.org/uk/minsmere).

A few miles south of the Sizewell B nuclear reactor – its white dome is visible for miles – lies quirky **Thorpeness**. The village was built in the 1920s, taking inspiration from Tudor and Jacobean styles, by an Edwardian barrister who wanted to create a seaside resort for his friends and their families. The Haven nature reserve, with its wild flowers and nesting birds in season, lies between Thorpeness and Aldeburgh to the south, and provides a lovely walk between the two.

**Aldeburgh** feels positively well-to-do, a result of decades of gentrification. The town oozes culture, with the world-famous **Aldeburgh Festival** a highlight of the year's cultural calendar. Benjamin Britten lived here for many years with Peter Pears and there are guided tours of their abode, **Red House** (Golf Lane, 01728 451700). The High Street offers plenty of browsing opportunities, and the little **Aldeburgh Cinema** (51 High Street, 01728 452996, www.aldeburghcinema.co.uk) is charming.

## EAT & DRINK

Half of the **Old Cannon Brewery** (86 Cannon Street, 01284 768769, www.oldcannonbrewery.co.uk) in Bury St Edmunds is a pub, where drinkers sample tipples brewed on the premises (try Old Cannon Best Bitter or one of the seasonal ales), with the other half given over to diners. The kitchen uses Old Cannon's brews wherever possible, so expect steak and ale pie, beer-battered fish and a range of beery sausage recipes. On warm days there's seating on the cobbled courtyard outside. The **Elveden Estate Café Restaurant** (Elveden, 01842 890223, www.elveden.com) outside Bury serves local food (from soups and sandwiches to shepherd's pie) at reasonable prices. The **Fox & Goose** (Church Road, 01379 586247, www.foxandgoose.net) in Fressingfield serves a menu of seasonal Suffolk classics, from Metfield pork belly to asparagus and line-caught fish. The food is fancier than most pub fare, with the kitchen even making its own ice-creams and sorbets. The menu doesn't deviate from pub classics at the **Swan Inn** (Low Street, Hoxne, 01379 668275, www.hoxneswan.co.uk), but they're done well. There's a lengthy vegetarian menu, cosy log fires in winter and spacious picnic benches outside.

Good food in Southwold is plentiful, though dining out can be expensive. On the pier there are fish and chips and ice-creams. Take your own bread and wine to accompany a huge and varied seafood platter at the **Sole Bay Fish Company** (Shed 22E, Blackshore, 01502 724241, www.solebayfishco.co.uk). The **Lord Nelson** (56 High Street, 01502 722079, www.thelordnelsonsouthwold.co.uk) is located bang on the seafront, and has friendly staff, outdoor seating in the summer and huge portions of cod and chips. **Tilly's** is the best tearoom in town (51A High Street, 01502 725677, www.tillysofsouthwold.co.uk), dispensing English breakfasts, light lunches, cakes and ice-cream sundaes.

In Aldeburgh, both the **Golden Galleon** (01728 454685) and **Aldeburgh Fish & Chips** (01728 454685) – at opposite ends of the High Street but under the same ownership – serve splendid portions of glistening fish and chips. Queues at peak times are out of the door. The Golden Galleon has a first-floor restaurant. Fish is also the star at Modern European restaurant the **Lighthouse** (77 High Street, 01728 453377, www.lighthouserestaurant.co.uk).

## SHOP

The **Butter Market** in Bury St Edmunds on Wednesday and Saturday is the liveliest provisions market for miles around, and has existed in some form since medieval times. The town is clinging on to its independent shops in the face of competition from chains and the new ARC shopping centre. **Cavern 4** (4 Whiting Street, 01284 700009) is worth a look. It's run by a charity that teaches skills to people who have suffered mental illness and sells furniture, lamps, pottery and accessories and has a gallery downstairs showing the work of local artists. **Wibbling Wools** (Angel Hill, 01284 749555, www.wibblingwools.co.uk) has a lovely selection of hand-dyed yarns, other wools and buttons.

Southwold has a butcher, a greengrocer, several delis and the **Adnams Shop** (Victoria Street, 01502 727244, www.adnams.com). Market days are Monday and Thursday, and antiques and craft fairs often appear in the Town Hall on the High Street.

Aldeburgh has good browsing opportunities along the High Street. The **Aldeburgh Book Shop** (no.42, 01728 452389, www.aldeburghbookshop.co.uk) is a delightful independent bookshop whose owners run the annual Aldeburgh Literary Festival.

## STAY

Set in gorgeous countryside, **Tuddenham Mill** (High Street, Tuddenham, 01638 713552, www.tuddenhammill.co.uk) is an 18th-century former watermill with 15 striking minimalist-chic rooms with soaring ceilings, bespoke furniture and great views. Whether you're in the mill itself or one of the two extensions, you get luxurious bathrooms, vast beds and all mod cons. Just outside Mildenhall, the **Olde Bull Inn** (Barton Mills, 01638 711001, www.bullinn-bartonmills.com) is an old coaching inn that's been given a revamp without destroying any of its charm. Bright wallpaper in bold colours and statement furniture give a stylish feel to the 14 rooms. The **Bildeston Crown** (High Street, Bildeston, 01449 740510, www.thebildestoncrown.com) is a combination of slick hotel and restaurant, housed in a Grade II-listed former coaching inn. The 12 luxury ensuite rooms are boldly decorated with some dramatic colour schemes and distinctive features; the restaurant serves quality, locally sourced dishes.

Over on the coast, **House in the Clouds** (020 7224 3615, www.houseintheclouds.co.uk) is the iconic place to stay in Thorpeness. This extraordinary folly seems straight out of an Enid Blyton book, a cottage lodged 70 feet in the air. It was originally intended to provide water to the village, but now has room for a dozen people over five bedrooms and three bathrooms. The top-most chamber, which used to house the water tank, is a galleried games room with spectacular views over the countryside and sea.

Aldeburgh's **Martello Tower** (Slaughden Road, 01628 825925, www.landmarktrust.org.uk), a sea-facing, quatrefoil-shaped brick monolith, is the most striking place to stay in Aldeburgh. Originally designed to keep out Napoleon, it has sail-like canopies overhead, a teak floor and two bedrooms.

## GETTING THERE & AROUND

For weekenders, exploring Suffolk by car is the most practical option; the journey from London to Suffolk by car takes around 2 hours 30 minutes. Otherwise, trains run to Bury St Edmunds from Liverpool Street or King's Cross and take 1 hour 30 minutes to 2 hours; usually you have to change at Cambridge. Alternatively, take the train from Liverpool Street to Ipswich (1 hour 10 minutes).

**House in the Clouds**

# Weekend Breaks for Foodies

Food has become something of a national obsession, and for Londoners in particular – who tend to be critical shoppers and seasoned diners-out – food is a key part of a weekend break. The following are our ten current favourites close to London.

Abbey Home Farm

Daylesford Organics

## Back to foodie basics at Abbey Home Farm, Gloucestershire

Abbey Home Farm (Burford Road, Cirencester, 01285 640441, www.theorganicfarmshop.co.uk) is a working farm that is perfect for a one-stop rural, foodie break. It's entirely organic and is owned by Hillary and Will Chester-Master; they run cheesemaking courses, half-day cookery workshops – where you can learn to make cheese, pastry and cakes – and workshops for children. There's also a farm shop and a café, plus tractor farm tours.

The farm produces its own dairy, vegetables, fruit, meat and bread (made from its own wheat). So you can either buy ingredients to create your own locavore feast, opt for the farm-made ready meals, or just eat in the café. There is even a tiny museum with local archeological finds.

### Stay

From Easter to October turn up unannounced (during shop hours) to camp out in the Green Field or Magical Glade. This is a place with strong eco-credentials, so expect compost loos and heat-your-own shower water over braziers.

If you're seeking a few more home comforts and year-round accommodation, the Shepherd's Hut and Hut by the Pond (each sleeping two) have wood-burning stoves and hot showers. There is also a holiday cottage that sleeps four.

### Getting there

Trains run from Paddington to Kemble station (via Swindon) and take about one and a half hours.

## Perry Pilgrimage in Herefordshire

Perry is an alcoholic drink similar to cider but made from pears. Two perry pear varieties sum up the possible imbibing effects well: Mumblehead and Merrylegs. For some, the thought of perry and cider conjures up sickly memories of teenage inebriation that are best forgotten. For others, the gentle fizz brings to mind happy thoughts of crisp countryside and evenings of mellow fruitfulness. If you fall into the latter category, a trip to the source might appeal.

There are three main perry producing counties: Herefordshire, Worcestershire and Gloucestershire. The circular Herefordshire Cider Route (www.ciderroute.co.uk) takes in a variety of museums, pubs, cider mills and perry producers, from Ross-on-Wye to Leominster. Exploring on two wheels (be warned, this is hilly country) works up a thirst and avoids the legalities of operating machinery while under the influence. There are two recommended routes, starting out from Ledbury or Pembridge, depending on your level of commitment.

### Stay

The Wilton Court Hotel (Wilton Lane, Ross-on-Wye, Herefordshire, 01989 562569, www.wiltoncourthotel.com) is a smart option. Hire bikes to explore at Pedal a Bike Away (01594 860065, www.pedalabikeaway.co.uk), five miles away over the Gloucestershire border. Wheely Wonderful Cycling (01568 770755, www.wheelywonderful cycling.co.uk) has exploration packages (from two days, £175) that include cycle hire and accommodation.

### Getting there

Trains run from Paddington to Hereford and take about three hours.

## My Farm, Cambridgeshire

Londoners often dream of upping sticks and moving to a countryside farm. Fortunately, you can test the experience before flogging your flat. My Farm is a National Trust experiment near Cambridge on the Wimpole Estate, where subscribing online 'farmers' play a role in the management of a working farm. It is Farmville come to life with live webcams, but more than that, it is a chance for 10,000

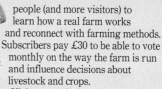

people (and more visitors) to learn how a real farm works and reconnect with farming methods. Subscribers pay £30 to be able to vote monthly on the way the farm is run and influence decisions about livestock and crops.

Visitors get the benefits without having to offer opinions. On a day out at the farm stride through the fields to inspect crops, and eye-up rare breed pigs, poultry and cattle: Wimpole Estate, Old Wimpole Road, Royston, Cambridgeshire, 01223 206000, www.my-farm.org.uk.

After exploring the farm, eat at the tearoom, or retreat to the luxury of Michelin-starred Midsummer House in central Cambridge (Midsummer Common, 01223 369299, www.midsummerhouse.co.uk).

### Stay

Hotel Du Vin (15-19 Trumpington Street, 01223 227330, www.hotelduvin.com) is within walking distance of Midsummer House and has some of the best rooms in the city.

### Getting there

Trains run from King's Cross to Cambridge and take about 45 minutes; a slower stopping service runs to Royston.

## Bray: A Glutton's Town

The Thameside village of Bray was originally put on the culinary map in 1972 by the Roux brothers when they opened the Waterside Inn (www.waterside-inn.co.uk). An exquisitely refined anglo-french experience, the Waterside Inn has the record for the longest-held three Michelin Stars of any restaurant in Britain. The 11 bedrooms upstairs mean that impeccable service and elegant hospitality can continue throughout the night and into breakfast the following morning.

Fat Hen

Fishy Rob

The Pig Hotel

In 1995, a very different type of chef came to Bray. Heston Blumenthal opened the Fat Duck (www.thefatduck.co.uk) and garnered the town another three Michelin Stars with his distinctive dining experience.

If you want a taste of Heston's expertise but without the wait for a reservation or quite such a hefty bill, try the Crown or the Hind's Head. Both are historic village pubs, serving polished British fare (www.hindsheadbray.com or www.thecrownatbray.com).

You could also try a meal or a cookery course at Italian restaurant Caldesi in Campagna (www.caldesi.com).

**Stay**

At the Waterside Inn (*see pxx*) or in self-catering cottages in Bray (www.braycottages.com).

**Getting there**

Trains run from Paddington to Maidenhead and take 40 minutes; from there it's a short taxi ride to Bray.

## National Fruit Collection at Brogdale Farm, Kent

The National Fruit Collection at Brogdale Farm (Brogdale Road, Faversham, 01795 536250, www.brogdale collections.co.uk) has nearly 4,000 varieties of fruit in its orchards. The collection is beautiful at any time of the year, but check the events calendar for dates of fruit festivals and blossom walks. There are also regular courses on how to grow, prune and compost. The orchards can be explored with a guide, or by following one of the self-guided walks.

**Stay**

Read's restaurant with rooms (Macknade Manor, Canterbury Road, Faversham, 01795 535344, www. reads.co.uk) is based in a Georgian house, within walking distance of the fruit collection.

**Getting there**

Trains run from St Pancras to Faversham and take just over an hour.

My Farm

King's Head Inn

## Guided fishing with Fishy Rob

These classes are available on beaches from Brighton to Dorset, depending on the season. Robin (www.fishy rob.co.uk) provides the tackle and the expertise for those who really want to know where their fish comes from. Days out can take a variety of formats, depending on the group size (up to four), the tides and the species you'll be targeting: perhaps with catching bait in rockpools, or mussel collecting before the rods come out. Contact Rob to find out what he recommends for your trip.

**Stay**

Stay in self-catering accommodation on Brighton Marina (www.watersideholidaylets.com) so you can cook your catch. Or stay the night before the trip in Drakes (43-44 Marine Parade, Brighton, 01273 696934, www.drakesof brighton.com), a boutique hotel with a restaurant and a swish cocktail bar.

**Getting there**

Trains run from London Bridge to Brighton and take about an hour by train; trains also run from St Pancras (and take slightly longer).

## Go the whole hog in the New Forest

The New Forest's mix of trees and woodland means that a wide variety of mushroom species can be found. Fungi forays have become so popular that some groups are booked up years in advance. Operators that are worth checking for availability include mycologist John Wright (www.wild-food.net), who has written three handbooks for River Cottage on wild food and how to find it. He runs popular foraging courses in the New Forest (and Devon). The Forestry Commission (www.forestry.gov.uk) runs several foraging courses; New Forest keeper Maarten Ledeboer also introduces groups to the culinary aspects of deer management. New Forest Mushrooms (www.newforestmushrooms.co.uk) supplies restaurants and home kitchens with mushrooms and takes groups out on fungi walks into the woods from Ringwood.

**Stay**

The Pig Hotel (Beaulieu Road, Brockenhurst, Hampshire, 01590 622354, www.thepighotel.co.uk) is a boutique hotel that prides itself on its local food, with both a forager and a kitchen gardener on the team.

**Getting there**

Trains run from Waterloo to Brockenhurst and take about one and a half hours.

## Foraging in Cornwall

Fat Hen (01736 810156, www.fathen.org) runs foraging courses around Land's End that will take you through field, forest and shore in search of edible morsels. The courses run from a morning's ramble and lunch to entire weekends revolving around found foodstuffs. Any of the options will change the way you look at the natural world and make you appreciate the snacking opportunities at your feet.

**Stay**

There are a variety of self-catering cottages (along with camping fields) at the Fat Hen headquarters (Gwenmenhir, Boscawen-noon Farm, St Buryan, Cornwall, 01736 810156, www.fathen.org). The nearby Gurnard's Head (near Zennor, 01736 796928, www.gurnardshead.co.uk) restaurant and hotel at St Ives has a menu filled with locally produced food and comfortable beds.

**Getting there**

Trains run from Paddington to Penzance and take about five and a half hours.

## Cotswold Organics

Daylesford Organics (near Kingham, Gloucestershire, 01608 731703, www.daylesfordorganic.com) has farm shop outlets in London but is based in the Cotswolds. On the organic farm, visitors can sign up to one- or two-day cookery courses or learn about keeping bees and hens at the Farm School. Cookery school classes cover artisanal breads, head to tail butchery, fish, pastries and dairy. There are even classes for kids.

**Stay**

There are self-catering cottages on and near the farm. Or stay in nearby Bledington at the King's Head Inn (The Green, Bledington, Oxfordshire, 01608 658365, www.thekingsheadinn.net), where meals are sourced as locally as possible.

**Getting there**

Trains run from Paddington to Kingham and take about an hour and a half.

## Game in Berkshire

One way to get close to the source of your food is to stalk, shoot and prepare the animal for the table yourself. At Frilsham in Berkshire, game gourmet Mike Robinson runs the Pot Kiln (www.potkiln.org), a pub where the lines between plate and field blur. Menus feature several varieties of locally dispatched game, the game cookery school (www.gamecookeryschool.co.uk) teaches you how to cook it, and there are deer stalking courses for those who want to go the whole hog (www.wherewisemenshoot.com). If you've never held a gun before, the Royal County of Berkshire Shooting School (Pangbourne, 01491 672900, www.rbss.co.uk) can provide tuition and guns and clays to practise on.

**Stay**

The Royal Oak pub (01635 201325, www.royaloak yattendon.co.uk) in picturesque Yattendon has rooms and prides itself on a locally sourced menu.

**Getting there**

Trains run from Paddington to Theale (or Pangbourne with one change) and take from 45 minutes.

# Food festivals

**January**
Wassailing (Sussex), late January, www.middlefarm.com

**February**
Rye Bay Scallop Festival, 11-19 February, www.ryebayscallops.co.uk

**March**
Brighton & Hove Food Festival, 30 March-9 April, www.brightonfoodfestival.com

**April**
British Asparagus Festival (Evesham, Worcestershire), 23 April-21 June, www.britishasparagusfestival.org

**May**
English Wine Week, 29 May-6 June, www.englishwineweek.co.uk
Cromer and Sheringham Crab and Lobster Festival, mid-May, www.crabandlobsterfestival.co.uk

**June**
Taste of London, 16-19 June, www.tastefestivals.com

**July**
Whitstable Oyster Festival, late July, www.whitstableoysterfestival.com

**August**
Isle of Wight Garlic Festival, 20-21 August, www.garlic-festival.co.uk

**September**
Ludlow Marches Food and Drink Festival, 7-9 September, www.foodfestival.co.uk

**October**
Falmouth Oyster Festival, 11-14 October, www.falmouthoysterfestival.co.uk
Apple Day, late October, www.commonground.org.uk

**November**
Clovelly Herring Festival, 20 November, www.clovelly.co.uk

**December**
Taste of Christmas (ExCeL London), 2-4 December, www.tasteofchristmas.com

# Camping in the Home Counties

If you want to keep travelling time down to a minimum, head for the Home Counties. Between the conurbations there are national parks, and plenty of woodland, vineyards and vales, fertile farmland and the kind of gently rolling fields even northerners go soft about. Try a weekend of camping instead of booking into a hotel or B&B and you can easily feel you're many miles from London. Note that all prices below are per night, unless otherwise stated.

## BUCKINGHAMSHIRE

### Home Farm Radnage

Despite its commuter belt location, Home Farm – in the chalky Chilterns – is remarkably quiet. The set-up is very simple: two camping fields on a hillside, with great views of the valleys below. Red kites, reintroduced to the area in 1989 after almost dying out in England, have thrived and now you'll almost certainly see them circling overhead. The essentials are all here, including bathrooms with under-floor heating, a laundry room with coin-operated machines, and chickens that provide campers with fresh eggs. There's no food shop but there's a supermarket in nearby Stokenchurch if you're not planning on living on omelettes.

### The facts

City Road, Radnage, High Wycombe, 01494 484136, www.homefarmradnage.co.uk.

There are pitches for 20 tents, 12 caravans and four motorhomes. Prices range from £12.50 to £17.50; though campfires aren't allowed, dogs (on leads) are. Open all year round, booking is done via the website, with a minimum stay of two nights. It's certainly not party central, with no groups of under-25s allowed and 'no noise' after 10.30pm. The easiest way to get there by road is the A40, between High Wycombe and Stokenchurch, and by rail via Saunderton train station, which is five miles from the campsite (a taxi costs around £13 one way).

## ESSEX

### Debden House

The obvious appeal of this campsite is that it's only a half-hour tube journey from Liverpool Street, and within walking distance of two tube stops. Because of its size, evenings at Debden House are a bit Glastonbury, minus the loud music. The clientele is diverse – everything from

Home Farm Radnage

Roundhill

tweens in flashy tops to hen dos and laid-back families, while chickens, goats and pigs frolic in the animal enclosure. There are seven fields spread over 50 acres, and the facilities are more than adequate, with a shop, a café and free firewood. If the acreage isn't large enough for you, Epping Forest starts at the back of the campsite.

**The facts**
Debden Green, Loughton, 020 8508 3008, www.debdenhouse.com. There are 350 tent/caravan and/or motorhome pitches. Open between May and September, the average price is £7.50, half price for children. Campfires and dogs (on leads) are allowed, with single-sex groups having to be pre-arranged and no noise after 10.30pm. If you're getting there by road, the route goes via the A406 to the M11, ending up at the A121. The nearest tube stops are Debden (1.5 miles away) and Loughton (2 miles), both on the Central line.

## KENT

### Welsummer

Named after a breed of chicken, Welsummer is a small site, with two fields, some woodland and stands of apple and plum trees. The atmosphere is relaxed, with fewer rules than most campsites and thoughtful touches sprinkled across the site, such as hand basins placed at the right height for kids. Most of the woodland is wild-looking so it's a pleasure to walk through. Respect for the environment is one of the site's concerns, which translates as basic showers and toilets. There's also ten per cent off for campers who don't arrive by car. The campsite shop sells

fresh eggs, apples and plums straight from the trees, basic groceries and great bacon butties.

**The facts**
Chalk House, Lenham Road, Harrietsham, 01622 844048, www.welsummercamping.co.uk. There are 30 pitches for tents, but none for caravans or motorhomes. Open between April and October, pitches cost £12 (small and £20 (large), with a £3 surcharge for adults and £1 for children. Campfires are allowed, at an extra charge, and dogs have to be 'booked' beforehand. No noise after 10.30pm. Getting there by road is easiest via the A20 from Maidstone to Harrietsham, or via Harrietsham or Lenham rail stations plus a cab ride under £10.

## WEST SUSSEX

### Stubcroft Farm

Set on a family-run sheep farm, Stubcroft Farm is ideal for family camping, with a peaceful vibe. The five-acre field is within walking distance of sandy beaches, and it's totally flat, which means you can pitch your tent anywhere. The farm offers cycle hire (£10 per day), has facilities for the disabled and even two B&B rooms for camping grumps. The atmosphere is welcoming and informal, meaning that many people stay on the grounds during the day despite the fact that the beach is less than a mile away.

**The facts**
Stubcroft Lane, East Wittering, Chichester, 01243 671469, www.stubcroft.com.

Woodland Yurting

There are pitches for 60 tents and five caravans/motorhomes, plus two B&B rooms. Open all year, minimum stays are two nights (three nights on Bank Holiday weekends), with prices from £5 for adults, £2.50 for children and £70 for B&B rooms. Both campfires and dogs (on leads) are allowed, with no noise after 11pm, which is half an hour longer than most campsites. You can get there by road via the A286 from Chichester towards Witterings, or via Chichester train station, after which you can get the 52 or 53 bus to East Wittering, getting off at Bracklesham Corner, which takes about 15 minutes.

### Woodland Yurting

Since its opening in spring 2009, Woodland Yurting has been pretty much constantly booked up. The five Chinese-made yurts are tucked away in trees next to a large meadow; on arrival, campers receive a gas stove, a lantern and a cooler box with ice packs. There are alfresco, solar-heated showers and 'treebogs' (controlled compost heaps with mounted seating platforms that use no water) with open windows. There are pubs all around the area, none more than half a mile away from the site. When in season, the bluebell fields are a delight, and despite being only an hour from either London or Brighton, the site feels pleasingly isolated.

**The facts**
Keepers Barn, Tittlesford, The Haven, Billingshurst, 01403 824057, www.woodlandyurting.com.
There are five yurts, sleeping two or four. Open between April and mid-October, with booking (of a minimum stay of two nights) essential. Yurts start at £60 per night (plus £20 supplements during High Season), with all bedding included. Dogs and amplified music

Welsummer

aren't allowed, but campfires are. Get there by road on the A29 and A281, or via Billingshurst train station, which is four miles away from the site, with taxis costing under £10.

## EAST SUSSEX

### Wowo Campsite

Originally a strawberry farm, Wowo was turned into a campsite in the late 2000s, and is one of very few sites that actively encourage campfires, with each pitch having its own fire pit. Family groups dominate, though it's possible to book pitches along the 'tipi trail' (at a £10 supplement), which are more secluded. Bread, eggs, milk and tea are sold on site, so you won't starve, and a greater variety of produce is available from the numerous farm shops in the area.

**The facts**

Wapsbourne Manor Farm, Sheffield Park, TN22 3QT, 01825 723414, www.wowo.co.uk.
There are pitches for 48 tents, three yurts (which sleep two, four and six), but no caravans or motorhomes, though campervans can be booked by arrangement. It's open all year, with a minimum stay of two nights, and a £5 a day charge for cars. Prices ranging from £10 for tents (£5 for children), and £104 for two nights in a yurt for two people. Campfires and dogs are allowed, but single-sex groups and unsupervised teenagers aren't, with a midnight curfew in place. Wowo is accessible by road via the A275 (Lewes to Wych Cross Road) or Haywards Heath station, from which the campsite can collect you for £12.

## Blackberry Wood

Don't let the romantic name fool you – Blackberry Wood is quirky rather than quaint. There are only 20 pitches in small clearings around the site, and each has a different name – Fruity, Humpty Dumpty, Eden and so on. You can also rent a London double-decker bus, a 1963 retro caravan or a traditional gypsy caravan to sleep in. The site is on the flight path into Gatwick, but there's a hum rather than the sort of hell-scream you get in Hounslow. Once in your tent, it's easy to feel as though you're on your lonesome, and in your own private forest. Do bring wellies, as the site can get very muddy when it rains.

**The facts**

Streat Lane, near Ditchling, 01273 890035, www.blackberrywood.com.
No caravans/motorhomes, but pitches for 20 tents (£5), plus a double-decker bus (£70), gypsy caravan (£35) or retro caravan (£20) to choose from, all plus surcharges for adults (£5-£9) and children half price for under-12s, under-3s free. Campfires and dogs are allowed, unsupervised under-18s only by arrangement. Take the B2116 between Ditchling and the A275 to get there by road, or take the train to Plumpton followed by a 25-minute walk or £12 taxi.

# HAMPSHIRE

## Manor Farm

One of 23 campsites run by Feather Down Farms in the UK, Manor Farm is really 'glamping', as campers need not bring any gear at all and the accommodation laid on is spacious and well appointed. Tents with beds, a wood-burning stove and candles are all set up for you to make yourself at home as soon as you arrive. They even have interior wooden walls and raised floors. Barnyard animals, to pet and to feed, are kept on the working farm, with the site clearly designed with children in mind. There's a small shop on site that sells basics, plus portable barbecues for hire and even home-made frozen meals.

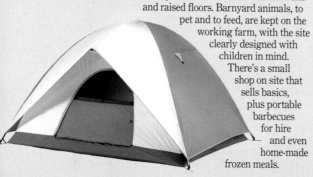

**The facts**

Blanket Street, West Worldham, Alton, 01420 80804, www. featherdown.co.uk.
Seven tents (sleeping five adults) are available between Easter and October, with prices starting at £318 for a three night midweek stay and £279 for a weekend. Campfires and dogs are allowed, though large groups are only permitted if they rent the entire site. You can get there by road from the A31 to Alton, turning on to the B3006 by Selborne Road, or via public transport with a fast train from Waterloo to Alton, plus a five-minute taxi ride at £6.

## Roundhill

Roundhill is set within the ancient woodland of the New Forest National Park, which makes it a remarkable site. It's well run and family-oriented (and popular with groups), but not really a site for hardcore campers. The site covers a large area and isn't very remote-feeling; staff are friendly and efficient. The free-roaming ponies are one of the site's largest plusses, though beware, they may well wake you up early in the mornings if they're sniffing around your tent.

**The facts**

Beaulieu Road, Brockenhurst, SO42 7QH, 0845 130 8224, www.forestholidays.co.uk.
The site is considerably larger than many others in the South-east, with 500 pitches for tents, caravans or motorhomes. Open between the end of March and September, typical costs range between £9.50 to £18.50 for two people, with surcharges for extra adults/children. Campfires aren't allowed but dogs are, and groups of under-18s are only allowed by arrangement. Take the A35 (Southampton to Bournemouth road) and A337 (towards Lymington) to get there by road, or get out at Brockenhurst rail station if you're arriving via public transport, plus a five-minute taxi ride at £7.

# OXFORDSHIRE

## Britchcombe Countryside Holidays

Set a mile's walk from the 3,000-year-old White Horse, the four camping fields of Britchcombe have no allocated pitches. The facilities are basic and clean, with each field having a Portacabin loo and cold-water taps. Charmingly, the campsite's owner serves cream teas at weekends, and the Oxfordshire countryside views are glorious, with excellent stargazing opportunities come nightfall.

**The facts**

Britchcombe Farm, Uffington, Faringdon, SN7 7QJ, 01637 821022.
Open all year, pitches are available for 80 tents/caravans/motorhomes, costing £8 for adults and £3 for kids. Campfires and dogs are allowed, single-sex groups and unsupervised under-18s only by arrangement, with an 11pm curfew. If you're getting there by road, take the A420 (Swindon to Oxford Road), turning on to the B4000 towards Lambourn; by public transport, get the train to Swindon, followed by a £25 taxi ride (buses are infrequent).

# Walks Close to London

City life can be pretty sedentary. Most people's London walks are limited, and, while some of the bigger parks succeed as *rus in urbe* spaces, they offer only shortish circular walks or linear hikes between roads – with the faint music of traffic almost impossible to escape.

Fortunately, it doesn't take too much effort to get away for a proper countryside amble, and these can be combined with a stay overnight so you can hike on, back or elsewhere – or just have a well-deserved lie-in – on Sunday. Most of the walks listed here can be done in around five hours straight, but it's best to allow the whole day, so a pub lunch, tea break or picnic can be integrated. Because the routes go from one place to another, it's more convenient to travel by train rather than car.

Detailed route instructions and walk updates can be found by following the links given to the website of the Saturday Walkers Club. Further walks and, again, detailed route instructions for these walks can be found in Time Out's *Country Walks Volume 1*.

Winchelsea to Hastings

Sun Inn

## Winchelsea to Hastings

Although once a coastal port, Winchelsea now sits inland after silting of the harbour. This walk follows the River Brede and its canals towards Icklesham, where it passes the part-Norman All Saints Church. The Queens Head (Parsonage Lane, Icklesham, 01424 814552, www.queenshead.com) is hard to miss, with its name emblazoned in white paint on the roof tiles; it's an old timber-framed pub with a real fireplace and a peaceful garden. After crossing the streams of Pannel Sewer and Marsham Sewer, you continue to reach the channel at Cliff End.

The walk along the coast goes through Hastings Country Park, with steep uphill climbs at some points. Doing the walk in the summer allows a dip in the sea at Fairlight Glen and a walk along the beach all the way to Hastings. However, in spring the woodland floor is a beautiful sight, covered in bluebells and wild flowers. Rye is also nearby, with cobbled streets and medieval buildings and some excellent restaurants. The town hosts an annual Scallop Festival (www.rye bayscallops.co.uk) in February, but Webbe's Fish Café (17 Tower Street, 01797 222226, www.webbes restaurants.co.uk) and the Ship Inn (The Strand, 01797 222233, www.theshipinnrye.co.uk) are open year-round.

Stay at the Rye Windmill (01797 224027, www.rye windmill.co.uk), a converted Grade-II listed white smock windmill on the banks of the River Tillingham or boutique hotel the George (01797 222114, www.the georgeinrye.com).

**Getting there** Take the train from Charing Cross to Winchelsea, changing at Ashford International or Hastings, journey time 1 hour 50 minutes to 2 hours
**Length** 20.3km (12.6 miles)
**Toughness** 9/10
**Details** www.walkingclub.org.uk/book_1/walk_25/index.shtml

**Hever to Leigh**

**Tring to Wendover**

**Olde Bell**

**Cookham to Maidenhead**

## Manningtree Circular

Walking through the Stour Valley, it's easy to see how the landscape inspired Constable for so many of his paintings. East Bergholt is where he was born, and the area between Dedham and Manningtree is home to the scenes portrayed in *The Hay Wain*, *Flatford Mill* and *The Cornfield*, and is now acknowledged as an Area of Outstanding Natural Beauty.

The pretty village of Dedham makes for a good lunch stop, with the Sun Inn (High Street, 01206 323351, www.thesuninndedham.com) serving Italian-influenced, seasonal food. For afternoon tea, the Essex Rose Tea House (High Street, 01206 323101, www.trooms.com) showcases the famous local Wilkin & Sons Tiptree jam. The walk carries on from Essex into Suffolk, where you can see the 4000 BC circular sanctuary henge at Stratford St Mary, and explore the village of East Bergholt, with its unusual church. There's another cracking tearoom in the form of the National Trust's Bridge Cottage (Flatford, 01206 298260, www.nationaltrust.org.uk).

**Getting there** Take the train from Liverpool Street to Manningtree, journey time 1 hour
**Length** 17.3 km (10.7 miles)
**Toughness** 4/10
**Details** www.walkingclub.org.uk/book_1/walk_39/ index.shtml

## Hanborough to Charlbury

The soft hills and lush countryside around the River Evenlode provided inspiration for Tolkien's Shire, homeland of the hobbits. A walk from Hanborough begins with over 2,100 acres of the Great Park, leading to Blenheim Palace (01993 810500, www.blenheimpalace.com), built for the Duke of Marlborough in recognition of his victory over the French at the Battle of Blenheim. It's also the birthplace of Winston Churchill.

Following the route along the old Roman road from Alchester to Cirencester, some of the original stone slabs are still visible. The meadows by Stonesfield Ford near the old slate quarries are great for picnics in summer, and you can even take a dip in the river. Another option is the White Horse (The Ridings, 01993 891063), which has reinvented itself as a bistro-cum-gastropub with both formal and informal dining rooms. After passing through Finstock, walk alongside Lord Rotherwick's deer park, Cornbury Park – this was carved from Wychwood Forest, originally a vast area of royal hunting ground, which in pre-Norman times stretched as far as London. On arriving in Charlbury, head for the Bull Inn (Sheep Street, 01608 810689, www.bullinn-charlbury.com), a 16th-century pub with four bedrooms and a good restaurant.

**Getting there** Take the train from Paddington to Hanborough, journey time 1 hour 10 minutes. Trains from Charlbury to Paddinton run hourly, journey time 1 hour 20 minutes
**Length** 20.5 km (12.7 miles)
**Toughness** 6/10
**Details** www.walkingclub. org.uk/book_1/ walk_38

## Kent Castles: Hever to Leigh

Less than an hour away from London, this walk incorporates two castles, a stately home, rivers, hills and a National Trust village. Hever Castle (01732 865224, www.hevercastle.co.uk) was where Anne Boleyn lived as a child, and where she was courted by Henry VIII. Pass through the hamlet of Hill Hoath to get to the entrance of Chiddingstone Castle (01892 870347, www.chiddingstonecastle.org.uk). More of a country squire's house than a castle, it dates from the 17th century and now houses a collection of art and curiosities left by Denis Eyre Bower, as well as having a decent tearoom. The handsome Castle Inn (01892 870247, www.castleinn-kent.co.uk) is the best lunch option. Cross the River Eden and stroll through the gardens of Penshurst Place (01892 870307, www.penshurstplace.com), a perfectly preserved manor house that has been home to the Sidney family since 1554. For an overnight stop, try Charcott Farmhouse (Charcott, Leigh, Tonbridge, 01892 870024), a family home as well as a B&B, where breakfasts are eaten communally in an Aga-warmed kitchen.

**Getting there** Take the train from London Bridge to Hever, journey time 40 minutes (on Sundays change at East Croydon and/or Oxted). Returning from Leigh, the journey is 1 hour. You can either travel to London Bridge via Edenbridge and Redhill, or Charing Cross via Tonbridge

**Length** 14.2km (8.8 miles)
**Toughness** 2/10
**Details** www.walkingclub.org.uk/book_1/walk_19

## Tring to Wendover

This walk starts along the banks of the Grand Union Canal, and passes the Tring Reservoirs, which were opened at the turn of the 19th century to provide water for the canal. Take your binoculars along, as Wilstone Reservoir is also a nature reserve – birds to look out for include widgeon (with their signature whistling call) and the rarer 'pintail' Hertfordshire duck.

After passing through the village of Drayton Beauchamp and under the A41 bypass, visit the 13th-century church of All Saints in Buckland. Through farms and meadows, you will get to Aston Clinton where the Oak (119 Green End Street, 01296 630466) serves real ale and hearty lunches.

The public footpath passes along a Ministry of Defence airfield on the grounds of what was Halton House Estate, where the Rothschild family used to have teams of zebras to escort them to their picnic spots. Walk through Wendover Woods and reach one of the highest points in the Chilterns before arriving at Wendover for tea at Le Petit Café (South Street, 01296 624601) or a treat at Rumsey's Chocolaterie (26 High Street, 01296 625060, www.rumseys.co.uk). Stay at Long Crendon Manor (Frogmore Lane, Long Crendon, 01844 201647, www.longcrendonmanor.co.uk) in Aylesbury, a 15-minute taxi journey away. This is an amazing medieval house (recognisable from numerous period dramas) with a maze, croquet lawn and ancient yew trees.

**Getting there** Take the train from Euston to Tring, journey time 40 minutes. The train from Wendover to London takes 55 minutes

**Length** 21 km (13 miles)
**Toughness** 6/10
**Details** www.walkingclub.org.uk/book_1/walk_11

## Netley to Botley

From Netley station, follow signs for Royal Victoria Country Park, which is on the site of the British Army's first purpose-built hospital from 1863. Netley Chapel (02380 455157) was at the centre of the building that has since been demolished. After heading towards Southampton Water you can walk along the stony beach, enjoying a view of the huge Fawley oil refineries. Head through the woods towards the village of Hamble, and hop on the distinctive pink-painted Warsash Ferry (02380 454512, www.hamble-warsashferry.co.uk), which runs on request across the River Hamble.

Spot grey herons and kingfishers as you walk past marinas and mudflats all the way to Lower Swanwick. Stop for lunch at the Spinnaker Inn (Bridge Road, 01489 572123, www.thespinnakerinn.co.uk), which has 23 rooms (doubles from £50) if you wish to split the walk over two days. Ater crossing the bridge over the A27, walk through woodlands and fields towards Manor Farm (01489 787055), which has a tearoom. Finally, follow Lovers Lane across a stream and into Botley. For an overnight stop, head into Southampton to the revived old seafarer's hotel the White Star Tavern (28 Oxford Street, Southampton, 023 8082 1990, www.whitestartavern.co.uk).

**Getting there** Take the train from Waterloo to Netley, changing at Southampton Central. Journey time 2 hours. Direct trains from Botley to London take 1 hour 35 minutes

**Length** 14.5 km (9 miles)
**Toughness** 1/10
**Details** www.walkingclub.org.uk/book_1/walk_03/index.shtml

## Cookham to Maidenhead

Starting with a circuit around Cookham through Cookham Dean, Bisham Woods and Winter Hill, walk along the river inhabited by Mole and Ratty of *Wind in the Willows* fame. Kenneth Grahame lived nearby, and used the peaceful waters as the model for the fictional backdrop.

The artist Stanley Spencer was born on Cookham High Street, and lived and worked on High Road; today the Stanley Spencer Gallery (High Street, 01628 471885, www.stanleyspencer.org.uk) is housed in what used to be the Wesleyan Chapel, where Spencer attended services.

After lunch at the Kings Arms (High Street, 01628 530667, www.thekingsarmscookham.co.uk) head south on the Thames Path and stop at Boulter's Lock to watch the river traffic before arriving in Maidenhead. Dinner options include the trendy Olde Bell (High Street, 01628 703509, www.theoldebell.co.uk), a 15-minute taxi ride away in Hurley, which also has rooms – perfect if you wish to extend the walk the next day. A short taxi ride to Bray brings the possibility of dinner at one of Heston Blumenthal's more casual dining options, either the Crown (www.thecrownatbray.com) or the Hinds Head (High Street, 01628 626151, www.hindsheadbray.com).

**Getting there** Take the train from Paddington to Cookham, changing at Maidenhead, journey time around 55 minutes. There are four trains an hour from Maidenhead to London. Bray has no train station

**Length** 17 km (10.6 miles)
**Toughness** 3/10
**Details** www.walkingclub.org.uk/book_1/walk_24

# Wiltshire

This chapter is unashamedly a car-focused one, and the sights that follow are all within striking distance of the A303. This road forms a direct route to the nicest parts of Wiltshire, avoiding the M4 and M5 – and what's more, it goes past Stonehenge. It runs through some lovely rolling open country in the shape of the West Wiltshire Downs before splintering off into a network of small roads that lead to charming villages such as Tisbury, Fonthill Bishop and Barford St Martin as well as the neolithic site of Avebury and the Iron Age hill fort of Old Sarum. This part of the world is also notable for having some great places to eat and drink.

Stone Circle, Avebury

## Fast facts

**Journey time** Train 1 hour 30 minutes; car 1.5 to 3 hours
**Festivals & events** Swindon Festival of Literature (May, www.swindonfestivalofliterature.co.uk); Summer Solstice at Stonehenge (21 June, www.english-heritage. org.uk); Larmer Tree Festival (July, www.larmertree festival.co.uk) – family-friendly folk festival; Salisbury Food and Drink Festival (September, www.salisbury festival.co.uk)
**Good for** Countryside, food, history, walking, wildlife

## SEE & DO

This chapter assumes you've seen the big sights (Stonehenge, Salisbury Cathedral, Longleat Safari Park) and are more interested in discovering the villages and countryside. Wiltshire has more than its fair share of mystics, myths and mysteries, from the moonrakers (smugglers who hid contraband booze in ponds) to pagan rituals galore. As well as the stone circle at **Avebury** (www.nationaltrust.org.uk) and hill fort of **Old Sarum** (www.english-heritage.org.uk), look out for the many hillside etchings of white horses (www.wiltshirewhitehorses.org.uk), long barrow burial sites and, in summer, crop circles (if you want to know more, book a guided tour through www.wccsg.com).

Almost every village sports stone and flint cottages with neatly trimmed thatch. If you are looking for rural idylls,

the cluster of hamlets and villages between the A303 and the A30, in the Wyle and Nadder Valleys, make for particularly scenic detours. The untamed ancient majesty of Grovely Wood near Wilton, or the area around Fonthill Lake just south of Fonthill Bishop, offer scenic places to wander. The romantic ruins of **Old Wardour Castle** (www.english-heritage.org.uk) are near to the village of Tisbury, which has a teashop (*see p88*).

Further west, just a few miles north of the A303, the grand Palladian mansion of **Stourhead** (01747 841152, www.nationaltrust.org.uk/stourhead) is a splendid edifice, and the extensive 18th-century landscaped gardens are a must-see. They're crossed by pathways circling a lake, dotted with follies, grottos, temples and an icehouse.

For child-friendly animal encounters, visit the **Bush Farm Bison Centre** (West Knoyle, 01747 830263, www. bisonfarm.co.uk) to see herds of imported American bison roaming, as well as raccoons and chipmunks. **Bentley Wood** (West Dean Road, West Tytherly), a large stretch of mixed woodland, is the place to see butterflies and moths, as well as fritillaries carpeting the floor. Towards the end of June and into July, the car park here is one of the best places in the country to spot the protected Purple Emperor butterfly – there's something about the smell of rubber tyres that they find attractive. The **Hawk Conservancy** (Weyhill, 01264 773850, www.hawk-conservancy.org), just over the Hampshire border, has the only aviary of great bustards in the UK. The great bustard features on the Wiltshire coat of arms and is currently being reintroduced to Salisbury Plain.

Howard's House Hotel

Lamb at Hindon

Hawk Conservancy

Chisenbury, 01980 671124, www.redlionfreehouse.com)
is a thatched pub with exceptional food (much of which
is grown or made in-house, right down to the bread and
butter). From summer 2012 there will be five B&B rooms
available too. Further south, in Donhead St Andrew, the
**Forester** (Lower Street, 01747 828038, www.theforester
donheadstandrew.co.uk) has a menu with a focus on
fresh day-boat fish.

The **Potting Shed Café** (West Hatch, Tisbury, 01747
870444, www.pythouse-farm.co.uk), in the 18th-century
walled Pythouse Kitchen Gardens, specialises in genteel
afternoon teas. Also in Tisbury, **Beatons Tearooms**
(The Square, 01747 871819, www.beatonstearooms.co.uk)
has particularly good toasted teacakes served with
blackcurrant jam, and doubles as a bookshop.

A little further afield, the **Harrow at Little Bedwyn**,
(Marlborough, 01672 870871, www.theharrowatlittle
bedwyn.co.uk) is known for its unfussy, modern take
on the classics, and has been awarded a Michelin Star
for the sixth year in a row.

Finally, on the journey there or back, don't overlook
the **Little Chef** at Popham (A303, Micheldever, http://
littlechef.co.uk/heston). This was the branch given a
makeover by Heston Blumenthal in 2009.

## STAY

The **Beckford Arms** is country house, hotel, pub
and restaurant rolled into one (Fonthill Gifford, near
Tisbury, 01747 870385, www.beckfordarms.com).
It ticks all the boxes for a country retreat – eight
bedrooms with comfortable beds, Bramble bath products
in the en suite bathrooms, a fire in the shared sitting
room and local ales such as Keystone Brewery's Phoenix
beer in the bar (and, on our visit, a giant freshly baked
sausage roll waiting to be sliced). The restaurant is
excellent, and even breakfast is a cut above: duck egg
on hash browns, for example, or waffles with butter
and maple syrup.

## EAT & DRINK

Local products to look out for include Keystone and
Ramsbury ales, North Wiltshire loaf and ashmore
farmhouse cheeses, and wine and brandy from Fonthill
Glebe Winery.

Many local pubs will feature one or several of the above
in their menu, but for top-end gastro grub there are a couple
of dead certs. Just north of the A303, the **Red Lion** (East

The **Compasses Inn** (Lower Chicksgrove, near Tisbury, 01722 714318, www.thecompassesinn.com) is a tiny thatched pub, with low beams. There are four bedrooms and a self-catering cottage, plus a highly praised restaurant. It's on a single track lane, behind the hamlet of Lower Chicksgrove.

The hospitable 12th-century **Lamb at Hindon** (Hindon, 01747 820573, www.boisdale.co.uk/lamb-at-hindon) is a taste of Scotland in the depths of Wiltshire. The Lamb has 19 rooms decked out in tartan, and big open fires in the stone-floored bar, from where you can nurse a dram or two of the fine whisky collection.

**Howard's House Hotel** (Teffont Evias, 01722 716392, www.howardshousehotel.co.uk) is a warm stone Grade II-listed hotel set amid rolling green fields. The in-house restaurant has a menu filled with local venison, pork, wild rabbit and cheese. Dogs are welcome.

## Local shopping

Bringing Wiltshire home in a shopping bag.
**Farmers' markets** www.wiltshirefarmersmarkets.org.uk
Devizes (9am-1pm, 1st Saturday of the month); Salisbury (9am-2pm, 1st and 3rd Wednesday of the month; Swindon (10am-4pm, every Sunday); Warminster (9am-1pm, 3rd Friday of every month).
**Ginger Piggery** Boyton Village, Warminster, 01985 850381, www.thegingerpiggery.co.uk. Own-reared Tamworth pork or Suffolk beef.
**Stourhead Farm Shop** High Street, Stourton, 01747 841164, www.stourhead-farm-shop.co.uk. Stourhead-raised organic beef and local cheeses.
**Pythouse Farm Shop** West Hatch, Tisbury, 01747 870444, www.pythouse-farm.co.uk.
Fresh garden vegetables brought in by wheelbarrow.
**Cholderton Farm Shop** Tidworth Road, Cholderton, 01980 629894, www.choldertonfarmshop.co.uk. Local eggs, meat and cheeses.

## GETTING THERE & AROUND

From London, drive along the A30 to meet the A303 just past Basingstoke. Most places in this chapter can be reached well within three hours' drive of London. Direct trains run from Waterloo Station to Salisbury and take about an hour and a half.

**Beckford Arms**

THE HIGHLANDS
p131

GLASGOW
p126

EDINBURGH
p128

BELFAST
p134

THE LAKE DISTRICT
p120

YORKSHIRE
p109

BLACKPOOL
p117

MANCHESTER
p93

LIVERPOOL
p103

BRECON BEACONS
p100

LONDON

DORSET
p96

SOUTH DEVON
p114

FOWEY
p123

ISLE OF WIGHT
p106

# UK Breaks:
# Best of Britain

**Hard Rock CAFE**

**SEE THE SHOW** MANCHESTER

EXCHANGE SQUARE • MANCHESTER
0161 831 6700 • HARDROCK.COM

facebook.com/hardrockcafemanchester
twitter.com/hardrockcafemanchester

# Manchester

While grand civic buildings, Victorian pubs, canals and (repurposed) cotton mills and factories point to its starring role in the Industrial Revolution, modern-day Manchester is a shiny kind of city. Football zillionaires and pop music magnates are the brasher face of this, but a weekend trip will reveal a thriving retail, business and media hub that also likes to party in some style. Manchester's museums and art galleries house some of the UK's finest collections, and the daring and dashing biennial Manchester International Festival is a sort of mission statement for a city that works hard to keep up with the likes of London and Berlin. If it's not the prettiest city in provincial England, Manchester makes up for this with heaps of energy and attitude. Put in a little effort, put aside your prejudices – and pack a brolly – and Manchester will reward you with a weekend as memorable as any in more obviously glamorous cities.

## Fast facts

**Journey time** Train 2 hours; car 4-5 hours
**Festivals & events** The Warehouse Project (September-New Year's Day, www.thewarehouse project.com) – three months of underground raves with the biggest names in dance and electronica; Manchester International Festival (June-July 2013, www.mif.co.uk) – launched in 2007, the ambitious – and often audacious – biennial arts bonanza prides itself on original work and cross-platform concepts; Manchester Christmas Markets (November-December) – stocking-fillers, glühwein and festive food at the north-west's biggest, oldest and best Christmas market
**Good for** Culture, nightlife, shopping

Urbis Building

## SEE & DO

Manchester has an untidy, sprawling layout and it can take a while to get the hang of navigating its sidestreets. One way to get oriented is to ride up in the lift of the 168-metre **Beetham Tower** (303 Deansgate, 0161 870 1600, www.beethamtower.org) – and take in the sweeping views from Cloud 23, the café-bar on the 23rd floor. You'll still be able to see Manchester and Salford and the Pennines beyond and the two football powerhouses: to the west, **Old Trafford**, and to the east, the **Etihad Stadium**. On a clear day you may even see Blackpool Tower. Beetham Tower's architect, Ian Simpson, lives on the top floor, from where he can see all the way to the mountains of Snowdonia.

Down at street level, the massive regeneration project that followed the 1996 IRA bombings has seen public squares and glass-sheathed buildings shoot up next to soot-stained warehouses. Manchester also has some splendid civic buildings. An old fave is the glorious neo-Gothic **Town Hall** (Albert Square, 0161 234 5000), which speaks volumes about Manchester's sense of self and is a fine introduction to the industrious city. Unless there's a special event the public are allowed to visit the ground-floor Sculpture Hall and, on the first floor, the Great Hall, which features a noted series of 12 Ford Madox Brown murals.

Even where gentrification and regeneration have changed the look of the city, Manchester's history lives on in place names. Heading north along Deansgate will take you past the **Spinningfields** complex (all steel and glass façades and top-name designer outlets) before it opens out on to the smaller, older charms of St Ann's Square, home to the **Royal Exchange Theatre**. Further north lies Exchange Square and the retail delights of **Selfridges** and nearby **Harvey Nichols**; the square's benches make it a pleasant place to

MANCHESTER

Sankeys

Royal Exchange Theatre

rest if it's sunny. It's also home to the the **Urbis Building**, opened in 2002 as a museum dedicated to the city and urban living, rebranded in 2004 as a museum of popular culture, and now – controversially – in the process of being turned into the National Football Museum (see www.urbis.org.uk for updates). The striking building's vertiginous glass façade opens directly on to the undulating green slopes of Cathedral Gardens, often colonised by skateboarders and emo tribes.

Slotted between Victoria Station and the **Triangle** shopping centre, a corner of medieval Manchester lives on in the form of **Chetham's Library** (Long Millgate, 0161 834 7961, www.chethams.org.uk), a vestige of the 15th century that has survived more or less intact and which is open to visitors. Within its impressive walls Karl Marx and adopted Mancunian Friedrich Engels met in the reading room to research their radical economic theories. It's still a functioning library, so phone to check that all rooms are open.

Looping through the city will take you to the **Northern Quarter**, Manchester's self-styled creative centre. The record shops, vintage boutiques and galleries exemplify the 'independent' ideal. It's defiantly chain-free – even the pubs are fiercely singular. Part of the Northern Quarter's charm comes from its architecture – a slightly ramshackle collection of 18th- and 19th-century warehouses. Some have been beautifully restored, such as the building housing the **Buddhist Centre** (16-20 Turner Street, 0161 834 9232, www.manchesterbuddhistcentre.org.uk); many are falling into a state of terminal dilapidation.

If you walk back towards the city centre, you'll arrive at the neoclassical **Manchester Art Gallery** (Mosley Street, 0161 235 8888, www.manchestergalleries.org), which is home to some stunning Pre-Raphaelite art. Highlights of the permanent collection include Rossetti's *Astarte Syriaca*, and there are notable pieces by Turner and Modigliani.

If industry is Manchester's grand old narrative, its newest story is perhaps music. The **Manchester Free Trade Hall** (Peter Street) is a city landmark with a long musical history. Now a Radisson hotel, it was the venue where, in May 1966, Bob Dylan first used an electric guitar, causing an audience member to cry out 'Judas!' mid-concert. Behind Great Bridgewater Street is the former site of the legendary Fac51 Haçienda, better known simply as the Hacienda (Whitworth Street West). It first opened in 1982, sparking off the so-called 'Madchester' years that laid the foundations of the UK rave scene. Although the club closed in 1997 to make way for luxury apartments, carved into the back wall

of the building is a timeline of the many bands that made Manchester a '24-hour party' city, for a while. On Little Peter Street, a minute's walk south, was the Boardwalk, most famous as the venue where Oasis first played live. If you love this sort of stuff, check out **Manchester Music Tours** (07958 246917, www.manchestermusic.com), which offers tours of the city's musical hotspots.

## EAT & DRINK

As you'd expect, a city with a proud northern heart still has places where you can eat traditional grub. **Sam's Chop House** (Chapel Walks, 0161 834 3210, www.samschop house.co.uk) might be a beautiful old pub, but you don't go there just for the Victorian tiles. Menu highlights include brown onion soup, dumplings, roast beef and corned beef hash. Spurred by the appetite for sustainable sustenance, **Albert's Shed** (20 Castle Street, 0161 839 9818, www. albertsshed.com) and **Mark Addy** (Stanley Street, 0161 832 4080, www.markaddy.co.uk) use regionally sourced ingredients in reinterpretations of classic dishes.

Out of town, in Didsbury, is **Greens** (43 Lapwing Lane, 0161 434 4359, www.greensdidsbury.co.uk) where it's become more or less compulsory for carnivores to declare: 'I loved it, and I'm not even vegetarian.' Owned by TV chef Simon Rimmer, the short set menu is brilliant value for money.

Cosmopolitan Manchester has some good foreign eateries. At **Sapporra Teppenyaki** (91-93 Manchester Road, 0161 831 9888, www.sappora.co.uk), 'show chefs' throw, dice and grill dinner delights before your eyes. Manchester also has a sprawling Chinatown, which welcomes visitors in with a multi-tiered **Imperial Arch**, followed by streets of top-class Asian eats and juicy street bites. The glamorous **Yang Sing** (34 Princess Street, 0161 236 2200, www.yangsing.co.uk) Chinese restaurant has had a colourful 34-year history. Don't bother with the menu: simply explain to your waiter what you like and don't like, agree a price per head, and a banquet will be devised for you. Meanwhile, **EastZEast** (Princess Street, 0161 244 5353, www.eastzeast.com) serves one of the best chicken tikka masalas in town; the menu also offers an extensive breakdown of curry by type. If you can't make your mind up which country to eat, go for the fusion food at **Michael Caines** restaurant (107 Piccadilly, 0161 247 7744, www.michaelcaines.com) at the Abode hotel; try partridge served with cumin purée and lentils. At the even more eclectic **Chaophraya** (19 Chapel Walks, 0161 832 8342, www.chaophraya.co.uk), you can order *penang nua yang*, a delicious if slightly genre-bending dish that combines beef steak, Yorkshire pudding, red chilli and kaffir lime.

The Northern Quarter is the heart of the city-centre bar scene. **Odd** (30-32 Thomas Street, 0161 833 0070, www.odd bar.co.uk), **Night & Day** (26 Oldham Street, 0161 236 1822, www.nightnday.org) and **Dry Bar** (28 Oldham Street, 0161 236 9840, www.drybar.co.uk) are places long favoured among creative types for their fine selections of rare beers.

As well as fancy places such as **Cloud 23** (0161 870 1600, www.cloud23bar.com), the city is also home to plenty of smoke-stained (inside and out) traditional pubs: **Peveril of the Peak** (126 Great Bridgewater Street, 0161 236 6346), largely unchanged since World War II, is a tiled corner wedge with a warm atmosphere and an antique table-football game.

Strolling down **Canal Street** in the Gay Village can feel like walking on to the set of *Queer as Folk*, the late-'90s TV show that propelled the street into national consciousness. Bars, clubs and restaurants cluster along the canal, and it's a great place to people-watch. **Tribeca** (50 Sackville Street, 0161 236 8300, www.tribeca-bar.co.uk), **Taurus** (1 Canal Street, 0161 236 4593, www.taurus-bar.co.uk) and **Manto** (46 Canal Street, 0161 236 2337, www.mantobar.com) are good places to start the night, while the large choice of clubs means you don't have to stop until sunrise. Canal Street is also the focal point of **Manchester Pride** (www.manchesterpride.com) – ten days of parades, picnics, sport, comedy, music and partying that culminate in the Gay Pride Parade (17-27 August 2012).

# NIGHTLIFE

Two decades after 'Madchester' and the baggy revolution that made the city the club capital of Europe, Manchester still has a living Factory outlet: **FAC251** (112-118 Princess Walk, 0161 272 7251, www.factorymanchester.com). Far from being a rehashing of Factory branded offerings, its musical menu is refreshingly varied. Three floors open six nights a week to the sounds of dubstep, Motown, tropical, hip hop, indie, experimental, disco and more.

Mancunian institution **Sankeys** (Beehive Mill, Radium Street, 0161 236 5444, www.sankeys.info) is proof that serious clubbing in Manchester is not solely about the mega-club experience, while nearby **Corridor** (Barlow's Croft, 0161 832 6699, www.corridorbar.co.uk), set down an obscure back alleyway, boasts an even more intimate experience, with leather booths, low lights and sparse decoration.

The **Deaf Institute** (135 Grosvenor Street, 0161 276 9350, www.thedeafinstitute.co.uk), a Grade II-listed building that was once an institute for the deaf and dumb, has been converted into a cavernous café-bar and music hall to rival the best of the central music venues. **Islington Mill** (James Street, 0161 278 6404, www.islingtonmill.com), a converted cotton warehouse, has led something akin to a cultural revolution in Salford over the past decade. The building, just a few minutes' walk from the city centre, houses 50 artists'

studios, a gallery and art school, a recording studio, gig space, a B&B and more. **Manchester Apollo** (Stockport Road, 0870 401 8000, www.manchesterapollo.co.uk), a staple of the Manchester gig circuit, is a great place to catch up-and-coming bands, as well as more well-known names.

# SHOP

**Market Street** is Manchester's main shopping area, with high-street names lining up inside and around the looming **Arndale** centre (www.manchesterarndale.com). Flagship stores from the likes of Mulberry, DKNY and Armani gleam out from **Spinningfields**, in the western part of the city. For independent shops, follow the stream of skinny jean-clad kids heading to **Oldham Street**, in the Northern Quarter, with its vintage boutiques, galleries and record shops. The famous – and famously ramshackle – flea market, **Afflecks**, formerly Affleck's Palace (52 Church Street, 0161 839 0718, www.afflecks.com), and enduring **Piccadilly Records** (53 Oldham Street, 0161 839 8008, www.piccadillyrecords.com) are good places to start. For the pick of the best vintage clothes, check out **Retro Rehab** (91 Oldham Street, 0161 839 2050), which has a lavish spread of clothing dating back to the 1950s.

# STAY

Manchester's hotel scene has undergone a radical overhaul in recent years. Since the arrival, in 2006, of the landmark **Hilton** hotel in Beetham Tower (303 Deansgate, 0161 870 1600, www.hilton.co.uk), with its swanky rooms and impressive views, a rash of high-spec hotels have sprung up, and older establishments have been treated to makeovers. The **Abode** chain (107 Piccadilly, 0161 247 7744, www. abodehotels.co.uk) has successfully made its modern mark on this Grade-II listed warehouse while retaining many original features, including the walnut and wrought-iron staircase. **Arora International** (18-24 Princess Street, 0161 236 8999, www.arorahotels.com) has sleek, modern rooms and funky furniture. Gay-friendly boutique hotel **Velvet** (2 Canal Street, 0161 236 9003. www.velvetmanchester.com) offers 19 unique rooms, including a penthouse suite and three 'King Balcony Rooms', which overlook the throng of Canal Street.

Budget chains have also smartened up their their acts. The **Hilton Chambers** (15 Hilton Street, 0161 236 4414, www.hattersgroup.com) offers the best rooms in the Northern Quarter, so book in advance. Gastropub the **Ox** (71 Liverpool Road, 0161 839 7760, www.theox.co.uk) is the place for *Coronation Street* star-spotting; it also has nine comfy rooms.

# GETTING THERE & AROUND

There are frequent rail services from Euston Station to Manchester Piccadilly, taking around two hours. National Express coaches travel between Victoria Coach Station and Manchester Central. The journey takes five hours.

The city itself has good public transport, though it always seems to be being upgraded. Daysaver tickets, which allow you to use buses, trains and the Metrolink services can be bought at stations or on buses. Metroshuttle, the brilliant free city-centre service, runs from Manchester Piccadilly and visitors can hop on and off at stops all around the city. The Metrolink service is a modern tram system running through the centre of Manchester and out to the suburbs.

## Cultural baggage

**Book** *Love on the Dole* (Walter Greenwood, 1933)
**Film** *There's Only One Jimmy Grimble* (John Hay, 2000)
**Album** *The Smiths* (The Smiths 1984)

MANCHESTER

# Dorset: Hardy Country and Beyond

Londoners often overlook Dorset, a county full of babbling brooks, cute cottages, dramatic coastlines and, of course, Thomas Hardy. Beyond fictional Wessex, Dorset abounds with alternative ways into its ancient heritage, from the Roman villa at Dorchester to the Jurassic Coast and the beaches of Bournemouth. The county is arguably the closest bit of rural England to London that doesn't feel like part of the tamed commuter belt. Dorset is best suited to a road trip – a car will free you up to explore – but you could also opt to see the highlights and main hubs using the train and buses (and a bike and your legs) if you are patient and plan your itinerary carefully.

**Max Gate**

## SEE & DO

**Dorchester**, the county town, is the natural point of entry for Dorset if coming by train, and is also a compact primer on what you can see and experience around the county. Begin your weekend with a walk around the town and see the **Roman Town House** (Colliton Park, 01305 228241, www.romantownhouse.org), parts of which date from the fourth century. Stop off, too, at the Thomas Hardy Society (www.hardysociety.org), which has its home at the **Dorset County Museum** (High West Street, 01305 262735, www.dorsetcountymuseum.org), to see a reconstruction of Hardy's study (from his home in Max Gate), as well as books and possessions such as the pen he used to write *Tess of the d'Urbervilles*. The main museum also has fossils from the Jurassic Coast and

| Fast facts |
| --- |
| **Journey time** Train 2 hours; car 2 hours 30 minutes (Poole), 3 hours (Swanage) |
| **Festivals & events** Swanage Railway Diesel Gala & Dorset Beer Festival (May, www.swanagerailway.co.uk) – trains and beer, what more could you want?; Swanage Jazz Festival (July, www.swanagejazz.org) – a mixture of up-and-coming and well-known British jazz artists; Bridport Literary Festival (November, www.bridlit.com) – debates, talks and the chance to hear from some of the most influential literary minds of the year |
| **Good for** Beaches, countryside, walking |

Roman mosaics. Drop in for a pint of ale at the **King's Arms** (30 High East Street, 01305 265353, www.kings armsdorchester.com), which featured in *The Mayor of Casterbridge*.

Hardy's home, **Max Gate** (Alington Avenue, 01297 489481, www.maxgate.co.uk), is just south of the river and a 20-minute walk from the museum; designed by the author in 1885, it still contains original pieces of furniture. If you want to take the Hardy theme further, pick up a Tess tour pamphlet at the society headquarters. The scene-by-scene walk takes pilgrims east towards **West Stratford** and along the banks of the **Frome** to a river crossing (where Angel carries Tess over the floodwater), **Woolbridge Manor** (where their wedding night is spent) and **Marnhull** (Marlott in the book, Tess's home town).

From Dorchester, head south-east to **Lulworth Cove**; part of the Jurassic Coast, it is a geologist's dream. The beach is packed in summer, but still worth visiting. Climb on to the narrow cliff on the west side of the cove and you can see Stair Hole, a perfect display of the 'Lulworth Crumple', complete with sea caves and a blowhole. Take a pleasant walk along the coastal path over the rolling cliffs to the west and you come to one of the most stunning natural arches in Britain, and a geological wonder: **Durdle Door**.

Bournemouth

From Lulworth Cove, continue your journey along the Jurassic Coast to **Swanage**. On your way, stop off at impressive **Corfe Castle** (The Square, East Street, 01929 481294, www.nationaltrust.org.uk). Just below the castle is the **Swanage Railway** (Station Road, 01929 425800, www.swanagerailway.co.uk) where you can visit the railway museum and take a steam train through beautiful scenery towards Swanage. A traditional seaside town that feels delightfully 1950s, it has a multitude of quaint shops and no amusements on the pier. Visit the **Swanage Museum & Heritage Centre** (The Square, High Street, 01929 425800, www.swanagemuseum.co.uk) to find out more about the Jurassic Coast's landforms and Swanage's pioneering radar technology role in World War II. It's

also home to the UK's oldest scuba school, **Divers Down** (01929 423565, www.diversdownswanage.co.uk).

Continue along the Jurassic Coast to **Studland Bay**, to walk the one and a half miles to Old Harry Rocks and/or the 3.3 miles along the South West Coast Path from Swanage to Old Harry. Studland Bay itself is a natural wonder, with a National Nature Reserve at the back of a four-mile stretch of golden sandy beach, attracting birdwatchers and pleasure-seekers. In summer, the gentle shelves at South Beach are perfect for swimming and Knoll Beach is set up for water sports, from banana boats and wakeboarding to windsurfing – check **Studland Watersports** (Ferry Road, 01929 554492, www.studlandwatersports.co.uk) for details. Knoll Beach is also home to one of the most popular naturist beaches in the UK; non-naturists can avoid the stretch by using the Heather Walk trail to get to other parts of the beach.

From Studland, the best way to get to Bournemouth is the chain ferry (01929 450203, www.sandbanksferry.co.uk) from Shell Bay to swanky Sandbanks and then drive the five miles to Poole. It's only a short drive from Poole Harbour to Bournemouth.

On your way, visit the ten-acre historic gardens of **Compton Acres** (164 Canford Cliffs Road, 01202 700778, www.comptonacres.co.uk), three and a half miles before you get to the city centre. The tranquil gardens were laid out in

1924 and feature seven different styles, including Japanese and Italian. In **Bournemouth**, the sandy beaches stretch for seven miles. If you fancy an aerial view, check out the **Bournemouth Balloon** (The Lower Gardens, 01202 314539, www.bournemouthballoon.com), a spectacular ride that takes you along the beaches from above.

## EAT & DRINK

The **Martyrs Inn** (Tolpuddle, Dorchester, 01305 848249, www.themartyrsinn.co.uk) serves a selection of real ales alongside locally sourced dishes. The **Acorn Inn** (*see below*) is another good choice, with a menu that features the likes of slow roast pork belly. North of Dorchester – 20 minutes by car – is the **Brace of Pheasants** (Plush, 01300 348357, www.braceofpheasants.co.uk), a fabulously cosy gastropub and B&B – try West Bay scallops with black pudding and garlic. At the **Wild Garlic** in Beaminster (4 The Square, 01308 861446, www.thewildgarlic.co.uk), ten minutes' drive north-east of Dorchester, *Masterchef* winner 2009 Mat Follas serves food sourced from within a ten-mile radius.

In Lulworth, head to the **Weld Arms** (01929 400211, www.weldarms.co.uk) for a traditional seaside pub, with tankards above the bar and a model yacht on the mantelpiece, and good food too. **Olivers** (5 West Street, 01929 477111, www.oliversofcorefecastle.co.uk), just down from Corfe Castle, has gourmet sandwiches and a wide range of salads at lunch, plus a more substantial evening menu. There's an open fire in winter. Go to **Ocean Bay** (2 Ulwell Road, 01929 422222, www.oceanbayrestaurant.com), on the beach in Swanage, for dishes such as Swanage Bay dressed crab, superior fish and chips or lobster ravioli.

The views from **Bistro on the Beach** (Southbourne Coast Road, Bournemouth, 01202 431473, www.bistro onthebeach.co.uk) are its first selling point; the rack of lamb its second. Also in Bournemouth, the **Goat and Tricycle** (27-29 Westhill Road, 01202 314220, www.goat andtricycle.co.uk) is, despite its name, a traditional pub that serves real ales and home-made dishes.

## STAY

You can continue the Thomas Hardy theme at the 16th-century **Acorn Inn** (28 Fore Street, Evershot, 01935 83228,

Wild Garlic

www.acorn-inn.co.uk) near Dorchester – it's mentioned in *Tess of the d'Urbervilles* as the Sow and Acorn. The ten rooms are named after Hardy's locations and characters, and while Tess avoided it (staying instead in a little cottage by the village church), you shouldn't. The four-posters are comfortable and the food is good. **Burngate Farmhouse** (West Lulworth, 01929 400783, www.burngatefarm.co.uk) is perfect for a secluded getaway. Not too far from Durdle Door, this old stone farmhouse is very comfortable, with a large sitting room and wood-burning stove. Lifts to the pub are part of the service and the breakfasts are exceptional, with home-made bread and Dorset porridge oats. Dogs are welcome to join the owners' pointer, Guinness. In Swanage, the **Swanage Youth Hostel** (Cluny Crescent, 0845 3719346, www.yha.org.uk) is just a few minutes' walk from the town centre, in a beautiful old building. In Bournemouth, boutique hotel **Urban Beach** (23 Argyll Road, 01202 301509, www.urbanbeach.co.uk) is just five minutes' walk from the beach, and has a bar and a bistro.

Acorn Inn

DORSET: HARDY COUNTRY AND BEYOND

# The Black Mountains & Brecon Beacons National Park

The Brecon Beacons National Park is about the size of London and is home to just 33,000 people. In place of towns and cities it packs in an amazing diversity of scenery, from waterfalls and sandstone escarpments to sculpted cliffs and fertile valleys, dense forests, glacial lakes, springy moorland and miles of caves. With more than half of the area 1,000 feet or more above sea level, it's very easy to get up high and enjoy the wildlife, adventure activities and, of course, walking – there are more than 620 miles of public footpath criss-crossing the 519 square miles that make up the park, and pretty much every inch of them is worth covering. For a weekend visit, base yourself in the east, in the attractive gateway town of Abergavenny, and from there explore the small mountains in the vicinity (part of the Black Mountains range) or drive to the west to explore the central Brecon Beacons and perhaps climb Pen-y-Fan, the highest peak in southern Britain.

## Fast facts

**Journey time** Train 2 hours 15 minutes; car from 3 hours
**Festivals & events** Abergavenny Food Festival (September, www.abergavennyfoodfestival.com) – the annual showcase for the outstanding local produce, with talks, tastings, masterclasses and markets; Hay Festival (May/June, www.hayfestival.com) – Hay-on-Wye's annual literary love-in is hell or heaven, depending on how much you value peace/press; Brecon Jazz Festival (August, www.hayfestival.com/ breconjazz) – run since 2009 by the Hay Festival organisers, this three-day music festival has an international flavour
**Good for** Countryside, food, walking

Crickhowell

## SEE & DO

**Abergavenny**'s Welsh name, Y Fenni, was originally the name given to a stream that empties into the River Usk here – it dates from pre-Roman times and means 'place of the smiths', in reference to the town's importance in the iron-smelting industry. This was later anglicised to Gavenny (Abergavenny means 'mouth of the Gavenny'). The town has also had importance as a border fortress (the ruins of a Norman castle lie to the south-east of the town centre), as a market town and as a centre for tanning and weaving. Have a walk around the main street, and you'll be struck by the looming market hall and its striking clock tower, and note, too, the number of handsome Georgian buildings; there's always been money round these parts and Abergavenny has been built to impress the English ever since merchants travelled the old London–Pembroke road for the ships to Ireland. The town's retail, accommodation and eating options make it something of a regional magnet – on Friday and Saturday evenings people come up from the valleys to the south for drinks and fun – but it's a compact little place and as you walk you keep catching glimpses of the surrounding fields and hills.

The town is a great base for a weekend break – convenient for climbs up the 1,955-foot **Sugar Loaf** or up 1,595-foot **Skirrid Fawr**. The former is either a ten-minute drive to a car park at the foot of the peak followed by less than an hour of steep climbing, or a two- to three-hour hike all the way from Abergavenny up through the bracken-swathed moors and to the summit. The latter, thought to be a holy mountain (and shrouded in myths as well as mists) is a two-to three-hour round trip and ideal for a morning climb.

You can also make excursions further afield to the magical 12th-century **Llanthony Priory**, where atmospheric ruins cling to a lovely little pub and a walk up to the ridge affords stunning views back across the valley. For a gentle outing, head across the Usk into **Llanfoist** and walk towards the west along the former railway line for around half an hour, until you see a zig-zagging incline that rises to the side of the **Monmouthshire and Brecon Canal** (www.mon-brec-canal-trust.org.uk), built at the turn of the 18th century to move coal, iron ore and limestone between Brecon, Abergavenny and Newport. Either head back to Llanfoist to do a short round trip or do a longer walk on the dead flat canal towpath to the historic villages of **Govilon** or **Gilwern**. Between March and October, you can hire a narrowboat at **Beacon Park Boats** (The Boathouse, Llanfoist, 01873 858277, www.beaconparkboats.com); the weekend hire runs from 2.30pm on Friday to 9am on Monday.

Beyond the Abergavenny area, the **Black Mountains** are a very special introduction to the **Brecon Beacons National Park**. The rural landscape – sheep and cattle are raised here, as well as Welsh Mountain ponies – is itself bleakly beautiful, rising to rugged hills, flat-topped mountains and deep valleys that stretch from Hay-on-Wye in the north to the River Usk in the west and the Vale of

Gliffaes Country House Hotel

Walnut Tree

Angel Hotel

Ewyas on the Welsh/English border in the east. Across the region there are lots of opportunities for walking, horse riding, climbing, mountain biking, paragliding, canoeing and sailing.

If you have a car (or a road bike and good legs), take the A40 to visit little **Crickhowell**, with its curious 17th-century bridge (with 13 arches visible from one side and only 12 from the other), castle ruins, pretty high street and impressive medieval church of St Edmund. From here, it's a fairly gentle five-mile hike to the top of **Table Mountain**, whose brown cone provides a spectacular backdrop to the small town. The 1,480-foot summit, complete with Iron Age fort, has good views over the Usk Valley.

Head north on the A479 and A438 if you want to visit **Hay-on-Wye** and from here turn to go south-east on the Stanton road through the Gospel Pass on a super-curvy road that reaches its highest point at Hay Bluff, within striking distance of fabulous walks along dramatic sections of the 182-mile **Offa's Dyke Path National Trail**.

If you want to tick off a moderate-to-tough climb during your weekend, climb **Pen-y-Fan**, which, at 2,907 feet, is the highest mountain in South Wales (and southern Britain). If you're attempting this and staying out in the National Park for a long weekend, you might want to consider spending one night in little **Brecon**: you can choose to approach the peak on a five-mile ascent – and its near neighbour, **Corn Du** – from here or set out on a ten-and-a-half-mile alternative from **Llanfrynach** village, which first summits the lower peak of Fan-y-Big (a name Dylan Thomas would have approved of).

## EAT & DRINK

Abergavenny is the foodie capital of Wales, now rivalling neighbour Ludlow for ambition, artisanal know-how and sheer range of produce. In the region you'll find everything from home-grown whisky (at the **Penderyn Distillery** – www.welsh-whisky.co.uk) to wine (**Sugarloaf Vineyard**, www.sugarloafvineyard.co.uk) to venison (**Welsh Venison Centre**, www.welshvenisoncentre.com) to several smokeries. As a result, local pub food is a cut above and there's increasingly a fine-dining scene on offer too – see www.visitabergavenny.go.uk and click on a list of restaurants; if you really want to indulge, time your trip to coincide with the annual **Abergavenny Food Festival** (*see p100*).

In town, the best dining option is the **Angel Hotel** (15 Cross Street, 01873 857121, www.angelabergavenny.com); service and food are top quality, and the Tea Guild named the Angel as the best place for afternoon tea outside London. On the dinner menu, the cured meat platter is a massive and delicious starter, while the lamb and game dishes are sublime. The owner of the hotel is part-owner of the **Walnut Tree** (Llanddewi Skirrid, 01873 852797, www.thewalnuttreeinn.com), three miles north-east of Abergavenny, where Shaun Hill serves Michelin-starred food: mains are rich and hearty (pigeon, venison, fowl, in buttery French rural cuisine-style sauces) or delicate (monkfish, sea bass, lemon sole) and the wine list is London-standard but Wales-priced. As you'll want to indulge in the latter, walk there (30 minutes max) and catch a taxi back (the roads are too dark for walking after nightfall). Alternatively, stay in one of the cottages at the end of the Walnut Tree's garden.

For pub food, the **Hen & Chickens** (5-7 Flannel Street, 01873 853613, www.sabrain.com/henandchickens) is one of the cosier and more relaxed places in town, hosting folk and poetry evenings and serving good Welsh pork dishes and a Penderyn whisky chicken. For after-dinner music or, occasionally, comedy aim for the **King's Arms** (29 Nevill Street, 01873 855074, www.kingsarmsabergavenny.co.uk); the pub has its own microbrewery and art gallery.

Delightful B&B **Gentle Jane** in Grosmont (01981 241655, www.gentlejane.co.uk) is perfect for light lunches or tea and cakes, and is well placed on the 20-mile Three Castles Walk that takes in Grosmont, Skenfrith and White Castle in the Welsh Marches.

In Crickhowell, the **Gliffaes Country House Hotel** (01874 730371, www.gliffaeshotel.com) is big on local produce and modern classic dishes such as scallops on black pudding, and pork tenderloin with lentils and bacon in a cider and thyme sauce. The **Nantyffin Cider Mill Inn** (Brecon Road, 01873 810775, www.cidermill.co.uk), near Tretower on the Crickhowell–Brecon road, is a sprawling 16th-century drovers' inn with a confident, creative menu: shoulder of home-reared mountain lamb and Welsh goat's cheese toasts are highly recommended.

## STAY

There's no shortage of friendly B&Bs in the Brecon Beacons, but when it comes to hotels, especially those with a dash of style, choices are limited. Plan well ahead for the Hay Festival (late May to early June), and the Brecon Jazz Festival (August), as accommodation gets snapped up months in advance.

The **Angel Hotel** (15 Cross Street, 01873 857121, www.angelabergavenny.com) in Abergavenny is by far the smartest place in town. The 35 rooms at this former Georgian coaching inn have undergone a stylish refurb and, in addition to the main hotel building, there are rooms in the former stables, a 16th-century cottage and a Victorian lodge in the adjacent castle grounds. All have comfortable beds and ultra-modern bathrooms featuring powerful showers. The superb full English is first class and ideal preparation for a hiking excursion.

In Brecon, **Cantre Selyf** (5 Lion Street, 01874 622904, www.cantreselyf.co.uk) is a 17th-century townhouse with mainly 18th-century interiors and heaps of original features, including moulded ceilings, elegant fireplaces and oak beams. The three double rooms are furnished in country house style and owner Helen Roberts does great breakfasts of smoked salmon and scrambled eggs, veggie cheese-and-leek sausages or a full Welsh. A lovely walled garden and comfortable sitting rooms provide spaces to rest your limbs after Pen-y-Fan.

## GETTING THERE & AROUND

Take the First Great Western train from Paddington to Newport and change for Abergavenny. The journey takes around 2 hours 15 minutes. By car, the trip will take at least three hours, depending on the M4 traffic and the time you arrive in South Wales: there's heavy traffic in Newport from 4pm to 6pm on Fridays. Of course, if you want to explore several areas of the National Park, you'll need a car or bike to get around, but a few carefully booked taxis can also open up the area beyond Abergavenny. See www.travelbeacons.info for information about local buses and trains.

# Liverpool

The maritime grandee and political miscreant of the north-west celebrated its 800th birthday in 2007 and was European Capital of Culture in 2008. Huge investment has changed the look of the city, especially along Strand and Wapping, the main north–south dock road. If the headline openings have been the £1billion Liverpool One retail space and new Museum of Liverpool, housed in a flash, futuristic building beside the Mersey, other notable events have been the revamping of the Bluecoat, high-profile shows (Rothko, Magritte and Alice in Wonderland) at Tate Liverpool and a major new concert and conference venue in the shape of the Echo Arena. But Liverpool finds a lot of its energy away from the civic schemes, and the social and entertainment hubs around Hope Street, Ropewalks and the Baltic Triangle have reinvigorated Liverpool's cultural life.

Unlike its north-western rival, Manchester, this is a city on the water and a walk along the cobbled prom behind the Albert Dock is a must. After dark, the city throbs like few others, with an appetite for drinking, talking and dancing that London can only envy.

## Fast facts

**Journey time** Train 2 hours 10 minutes; car 4-5 hours
**Festivals & events** Mathew Street Festival (August, www.mathewstreetfestival.org) – the city's biggest music festival, with an international slant and an associated 'fringe' festival at local studios and and small venues; Liverpool Irish Festival (October, www.liverpoolirishfestival.com) – celebrating the city's cultural ties with the Emerald Isle, with the requisite céilidh dancing, plangent pipe and penny whistle solos and improv folk sessions; Liverpool Beer Festival (February, www.liverpoolcamra.org.uk) – try 200-odd organic beers, perries, ciders and real ales, including the tasty tipples made at the local Liverpool Organic Brewery, an event sponsor
**Good for** Nightlife, shopping

## SEE & DO

Visitors leaving Lime Street Station are plunged into the mainly Georgian political and cultural heart of the city. If you've come by train and are travelling light, you can view some art and sculpture before you even check in. The **Walker Art Gallery** (William Brown Street, 0151 478 4199, www.liverpoolmuseums.org.uk/walker) is home to one of the UK's most important collections of art – with works by Rembrandt, Monet, Turner and Hockney – and next door is the **World Museum** (William Brown Street, 0151 478 4393, www.liverpoolmuseums.org.uk/wml), a combination of archaeology, natural history and science museum that has a lot of child-friendly exhibitions and hands-on spaces. But the most celebrated sight in this area is arguably the Grade I-listed neoclassical **St George's Hall** (St George's Place, 0151 225 6911, www.stgeorgesliverpool.co.uk): a Heritage Centre is open to the public Tue-Sat but to see the Minton mosaic floor, fabulous brick arch and immense vaulted ceiling, book a guided tour.

After you've checked in to your hotel, you can get stuck into the hectic city centre. At first glance – and especially

on a Saturday – it might appear that the whole city is taken over by shoppers, hawkers, buskers and stalls selling LFC and EFC scarves. But just off the retail strip of Church Street and Lord Street is the **Bluecoat** arts centre (School Lane, 0151 702 5324, www.thebluecoat.org.uk), formerly the Bluecoat Gallery. Dating from the 18th century – though extensively refurbished in 2008 – the handsome former school building is home to more than a dozen exhibitions at any one time, with an emphasis on craft and design, and it also hosts music, dance and avant-garde multimedia events.

After a wander and perhaps a coffee at the Bluecoat's Espresso caff, walk up Bold Street and head for the gargantuan neo-Gothic building on the horizon. **Liverpool Cathedral** (St James' Mount, 0151 709 6271, www.liverpoolcathedral.org.uk), the Anglican cathedral, was built between 1904 and 1978 (and mainly designed by Sir Giles Gilbert Scott, who died in 1960). It's the longest cathedral in the world and home to the biggest pipe organ in the UK; it's cavernous and rarely crowded. This is a city of two Christian congregations, so head north up Hope Street to see the Roman Catholic **Metropolitan Cathedral of Christ the King** (Mount Pleasant, 0151 709 9222,

Hard Days Night Hotel

Tate Liverpool

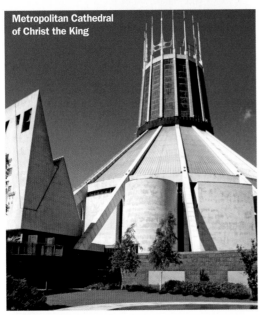

Metropolitan Cathedral
of Christ the King

www.liverpoolmetrocathedral.org.uk), aka 'Paddy's Wigwam', a striking modernist structure completed in 1967. Around the cathedral is the university district and rows of elegant Georgian houses. Hope Street (*see below*) is a good spot for lunch; alongside a selection of smart bistros, there's the **Everyman Theatre** (www.everyman playhouse.com), which has a good basement restaurant as well as an eclectic programme.

To get to the front, either take a path through the ultra-slick **Liverpool One** shopping area or go via the old city – Dale Street goes right down to the river and the **Three Graces** – the UNESCO-listed Royal Liver Building, the Cunard Building and the Port of Liverpool Building – that stand proudly on the Pier Head.

It's only a short walk from here to the **Albert Dock**, site of the new **Museum of Liverpool** (Pier Head, 0151 478 4545, www.liverpoolmuseums.org.uk/mol; opened in stages between July and September 2011 and with a price tag of £72 million), which celebrates the history of the city; the **Maritime Museum** (Albert Dock, 0151 478 4499, www.liverpoolmuseums.org.uk/maritime); and the **Beatles Story** (Albert Dock, 0151 709 1963, www.beatlesstory.com). Wrap up your exploration with an hour or two at **Tate Liverpool** (Albert Dock, 0151 702 7400, www.tate.org.uk/ liverpool), which has a permanent display as well as rotating major exhibitions, and does decent coffee and cake too.

If you have any free time left, take a stroll down to **Cavern Walks** centre (www.cavern-walks.co.uk) – famous for that club – or head out to glorious **Princes Park** – used as the model for New York's Central Park – in Toxteth; or perhaps take the famed **ferry** over to the Wirral.

## EAT & DRINK

During the 1990s, Hope Street, a row of Georgian townhouses, evolved into a meeting and eating district. **60 Hope Street** (60 Hope Street, 0151 707 6060, www.60hopestreet.com) is a smart, serene establishment that serves Modern British food using regional produce such as Cumbrian lamb and Goosnargh chicken. If you fancy a pre-dinner pint or just want to ogle a beautiful pub, check out the **Philharmonic Dining Rooms** (36 Hope Street, 0151 707 2837, www.nicholsonspubs.co.uk/the philharmonicdiningroomsliverpool). Housed in a former RC church, **Alma de Cuba** (45 Seel Street, 0151 702 7394, www.alma-de-cuba.com) offers classy Latin American and Caribbean fusion dishes, steaks and seafood, and segues into a carnivalesque club after dinner. It sounds cheesy but Liverpudlians are supreme partiers and the atmosphere is riotous verging on anarchic once the music gets going.

Liverpool's Chinatown dates back to the late 1800s and is often said to be the oldest in Britain. **Yuet Ben** (1 Upper Duke Street, 0151 709 5772, www.yuetben.co.uk), established in 1968, does great Northern Chinese food; see the neighbourhood's website (www.liverpool chinatown.co.uk) for a full list of restaurants.

## NIGHTLIFE

Liverpool has a thriving weekend nightlife, while the two big universities (Liverpool and John Moores) and a handful of smaller FE institutions mean there are a few busy gig venues waiting for the next Echo or Julian Cope to come along. **Concert Square** and the surrounding streets are

60 Hope Street

Liverpool One

Museum of Liverpool

mad-busy Friday and Saturday evenings and the mix of flashy bars and old pubs is a safe onestop shop for meeting locals. **Mathew Street** has a lot of pubs and bars – see www.mathew.st. Clubbers may also want to check out Nation, the home of **Cream** (www.cream.co.uk).

## SHOP

The hype is all about **Liverpool One** (www.liverpool-one.com), the city's smart new shopping (and residential) district. Built between 2004 and 2009 at a cost of £1 billion, it's home to a humungous John Lewis, several mega-brand flagships and loads of places to buy tracksuits. For more interesting options, skip the main drag of Church and Lord streets and head to the friendlier shopping hubs of **Bold Street**, **Mathew Street** (home to Cavern Walks boutique arcade) and upmarket mall **Metquarter**, off Whitechapel.

## STAY

Despite the name, the **Hard Days Night Hotel** (Central Buildings, North John Street, 0151 236 1964, www. harddaysnighthotel.com) is actually very cool. Rooms have pop art and old rock 'n' roll photographs on the walls and the main bar is a beaut. On the waterfront, the chic, party-loving **Malmaison** (7 William Jessop Way, Princes Dock, 0151 229 5000, www.malmaison.com) was reopened in autumn 2011 after extensive redecoration. The **Britannia Adelphi** (Ranelagh Place, 0871 222 0029, www.britannia hotels.com) opened in 1826 and is a popular (and tranquil) place for afternoon tea; the rooms are elegant and airy. In the Ropewalks area, the **Parr Street** hotel (33-45 Parr Street, 0151 707 1050, www.parrstreet.co.uk) has 12 minimal, modern rooms and a very good bar; the three recording studios here are fully operational so you might trip over a rock chick/chap on the way to your room.

## GETTING THERE & AROUND

Virgin trains from Euston Station to Lime Street take just 2 hours to cover 220 miles. Driving takes 4 to 5 hours on the M1 and M6; the coach takes a little longer still.

### Cultural baggage

**Film** *Of Time and the City* (Terence Davies, 2008)
**Book** *The Mersey Sound* (Roger McGough, Brian Patten and Adrian Henri, 1967)
**Album** *Back in the DHSS* (Half Man Half Biscuit, 1985)

# Isle Of Wight

England's largest island has a mixed reputation. While it holds rock 'n' roll credentials as the location of the opening and closing of the summer festival season (the Isle of Wight festival and Bestival), the Isle of Wight is often imagined as being stuck in the 1950s. Also, where much of Hampshire feels very much part of the south-western London commuter belt, the short hop across the Solent is akin to passing through a bit of a cultural and geographical portal. For Londoners, it's certainly a shock to the system to find pubs where mobiles are frowned upon and where a landmass smaller than the Big Smoke is home to a single, coherent community. But with the time-warp element comes a peacefulness that makes it worthy of at least one weekend in your year, especially if you like walking. With more footpaths per square mile than anywhere else in Britain, it's possible to plan a long weekend around a circular coastal trail (four days at a leisurely pace) and see the variety in the landscape, from estuary marshland to unspoilt beaches and chalky cliffs, not to mention the views out to sea.

## SEE & DO

While rockpooling and paddling along the beaches at **Bembridge** might tick the usual seaside break boxes, the island has more to offer. Tiny **Yarmouth**, despite having few destination attractions, is a charming town to while away a few hours and is a good starting point for a walk along the coastal path to Alum Bay. There you should pay a visit to the **Needles Old & New Batteries** (West High Down, Alum

**Fast facts**

**Journey time** Train 3 hours; car 3 hours
**Festivals & events** Bestival (September, www.bestival.net) – organised by well-known DJ Rob da Bank, Bestival has gone from strength to strength since its initial crowd of 10,000; known for its fancy-dress themes, it is also very family-friendly; Isle of Wight Garlic Festival (August, www.garlic-festival.co.uk) – firmly established as one of the UK's top food festivals, this has been going for 25 years. Although the garlic marquee is the highlight, there are plenty more attractions for foodies and families; Isle of Wight Walking Festival (May, www.isleofwightwalkingfestival.co.uk) – over 300 walks to suit all ages and abilities, including round the island walks
**Good for** Beaches, countryside, food, walking

Bay, 01983 754772, www.theneedlesbattery.org.uk), the former being a 19th-century fort built to guard against the French, and the latter a site for secret rocket-testing during the Cold War. An underground tunnel leads to dramatic sea views, particularly of the famous **Needles**, three prominent stacks of chalk at the island's westernmost point. **Needles Park** (www.theneedles.co.uk) has various attractions including traditional rides for children, a sweet factory, and a chair lift from the beach to the cliffs. A ten-minute drive inland, the **Dimbola Lodge Museum** (Terrace Lane, Freshwater Bay, 01983 756814, www.dimbola.co.uk) was the home of pioneering Victorian photographer Julia Margaret Cameron, whose work is permanently displayed.

On the south side of the island, **Ventnor** is arguably the least British town on the island, with tall, Italianate buildings adorning the steep cliffs and a microclimate that allows tropical plants to grow. Some 22 acres here are taken up by the **Botanic Garden** (Undercliff Drive, 01983 855397, www.botanic.co.uk), located on the site of an old sanatorium for chest diseases. West along the coast, **Blackgang Chine** (01983 730330, www.blackgangchine.com) is a theme park

Needles

Hambrough

Botanic Garden

Priory Bay

that claims to be the oldest in the UK. Established as a pleasure garden in the 1840s, it's a series of paths along the cliffs linking themed rides, mazes and fibreglass fantasy figurines. Test the nerves at the nearby **Whale Chine**, a 140-foot-deep ravine that cuts through the sandstone to the beach, where a now very rickety staircase with warnings to 'Keep Off' will put off all but the most reckless.

Inland, **Newport** is at the head of the Medina estuary. Once a busy port, the quay has been developed – among many converted buildings is **Quay Arts** (Sea Street, Newport Harbour, 01983 822490, www.quayarts.org), a gallery with a theatre named after the late Anthony Minghella.

Quay Arts

## EAT & DRINK

The Isle of Wight is fast becoming a destination for culinary adventures, with many chefs making the most of local, seasonal produce. Two hotel restaurants provide the fine dining: the **Hambrough** hotel (Hambrough Road, 01983 856333, www.robert-thompson.com) has won a Michelin Star for its seven-course tasting menu that features unusual flavour combinations such as smoked eel and foie gras, while the Island Room at the **Priory Bay** hotel (Priory Road, Seaview, 01983 613146, www.priorybay.com) offers locally foraged produce in its Regency dining room.

Less fancy but perhaps more fun are the island's many dining pubs. The **New Inn** (Mill Road, Shalfleet, 01983 531314, www.thenew-inn.co.uk) – which dates from 1743 – is renowned for its fish dishes, as is the **Crab & Lobster Inn** (32 Forelands Field Road, Bembridge, 01983 872244, www.crabandlobsterinn.co.uk), which has a prime clifftop location.

The timeless quality that pervades the island makes for particularly magical drinking pubs – the **Red Lion** (Church Place, 01983 754925) at Freshwater is wonderfully traditional; people are fined if their mobile rings (the money goes towards the local lifeboat appeal) and no young children are allowed. The **Buddle Inn** (St Catherine's Road, Niton, 01983 730243) has real ales, captain's chairs and walls hung with pewter mugs; the **Spyglass Inn** (Esplanade, Ventnor, 01983855338) is decked out with seafaring memorabilia and musicians play most nights.

New Inn

Seaview Hotel

## SHOP

There's an abundance of well-stocked charity shops around the island, but head to Newport for boutiques and high-street chains, as well as a **Farmers' Market** (01983 840798), which takes place every Friday in St Thomas' Square. To take home something unique to the island, visit the **Garlic Farm** (Mersley Lane, Newchurch, 01983 868732), where you can tour the crops and stock up on the many different varieties of garlic, as well as chutneys, mustards, beer and gadgets.

## STAY

On the east side of the island, the **Crab & Lobster Inn** (*see left*) has five rooms – two of which have sea views – from £40 per night for a double. The **Priory Bay** hotel (*see left*) is in between Nettlestone and the popular sailing village of Seaview. The old mansion has 18 rooms, plus the likes of a golf course and an oyster bar. There are also yurts on site, set in the glades. Also nearby is the **Seaview Hotel** (High Street, 01983 612711, www.seaviewhotel.co.uk), chic with white furnishings but welcoming to families, and with one of the best restaurants on the island.

Over on the west side, the **George** (Quay Street, Yarmouth, 01983 760331, www.thegeorge.co.uk) is one of the island's best hotels, with a brasserie-style restaurant serving seasonal food. The island's smartest destination is the **Hambrough** (*see left*) – a small, seven-bedroom property overlooking Ventnor Bay.

For something alternative, **Vintage Vacations** (07802 758113, www.vintagevacations.com) has a group of refurbished Airstream caravans (parked at Hazlegrove Farm near Ryde) from £175 for two nights. Larger groups will enjoy the **Mission**, a beautiful, classic tin tabernacle from around 1895. It sleeps eight (at £475 for two nights), and has a well-equipped kitchen and dining area for self-catering. 1960s and '70s furniture sits alongside Victorian kitsch, but there's also Wi-Fi and an iPod dock.

## GETTING THERE & AROUND

From Waterloo Station, it takes about 1.5 hours to reach both Portsmouth Harbour and Southampton. For the Portsmouth trip, you can buy a ticket that includes a foot-passenger crossing to Ryde on one of Wightlink's catamarans.

If you take the car, there are various ferry operators that sail across the Solent. Wightlink (0871 376 1000, www.wightlink.co.uk) runs a 24-hour shuttle service to Fishbourne. On Fridays, the service runs virtually 24 hours with the last departure at night being at 11pm and the first in the morning being at 1.30am. Wightlink also operates a slightly quicker service from Lymington to Yarmouth (35 minutes) with crossings between 3.45am and 11.59pm.

Red Funnel (0844 844 9988, www.redfunnel.co.uk) crosses from Southampton to Cowes, and takes around 40 minutes. Hovercrafts (Hovertravel, 01983 811000, www.hovertravel.co.uk) also cross speedily (to Ryde) but are for foot passengers only; catch them from a hoverport by Southsea Common in Portsmouth.

On the island, Island Line Trains runs between Ryde, Brading, Sandown, Lake and Shanklin, while Wightbus operates services across the island. Driving allows more freedom, and is very manageable as distances are small (for example, Yarmouth to Ventnor takes 40 minutes).

# North Yorkshire Moors & Coast

North Yorkshire, covering 3,340 square miles, is Britain's largest county and has enough sights, landscapes, towns and festivals to keep you busy for a year of weekends. But the triangle formed by Pickering, Scarborough and Whitby has the kind of topographical variety you need to shake off any urban fatigue, including dense forests, craggy coasts, expanses of golden beach, and moors that range from lush rolling valleys to elemental, heather-covered highlands. Pretty fishing town Whitby, famous as the home of Captain Cook, Bram Stoker's *Dracula* and the real-world 18th-century whalers of Melville's *Moby Dick*, is a delight. The North Yorkshire Moors Railway line links up villages and ambling walks that are easy on both eye and knees, and, for a bit of seaside fun, you won't go far wrong with Scarborough's stunning beaches.

## Fast facts

**Journey time** Train 2 hours (York), 3 hours (Scarborough)
**Festivals & events** Whitby Folk Week (August, www.whitbyfolk.co.uk); Whitby Regatta (August, www.whitbyregatta.co.uk); Scarborough Jazz Festival (September, http://scarboroughjazzfestival.co.uk); Railway in Wartime (October, www.nymr.co.uk) – a weekend of re-enactment and nostalgia, on the North Yorkshire Moors Railway
**Good for** Beaches, countryside, walking

Robin Hood's Bay

## SEE & DO

Get your walking boots on. The dramatic terrain of open moorland is easy to find along the A171 and A169 or the 109-mile Cleveland Way; download a route from www.yorkshire.com/nationaltrails or head for Ravenscar, 600-feet above sea level on the coast. For a more manicured view of the moors, the **North Yorkshire Moors Railway** (01751 472508, www.nymr.co.uk) plies an 18-mile route through picture-postcard villages such as **Goathland** (aka *Heartbeat* village Aidensfield and Hogsmeade in the Harry Potter movies). **Newtondale Halt** is a great point from which to access a glacial valley and woodland walks, while **Levisham** is the start point for the seven-mile round walk to the Hole of Horcum, a 400-foot natural hollow carved out of the moors by glacial ice flow. And a few miles south of here, **Dalby Forest** (car £7 Mar-Oct, £4 Nov-Feb, www.forestry.gov.uk/dalbyforest) has some fantastic walks and bike trails – hire bikes at the visitor centre (01751 460011).

On the coast, **Whitby** is by far the nicest of the resorts, with its colourful quayside overlooked by the atmospheric abbey ruins (01947 603568, www.english-heritage.org.uk); reach it via the 199 Church Street steps climbing up from the cobbled streets of the Eastcliff old town. If it's raining, the eclectic **Whitby Museum** (Pannett Park, 01947 602908, www.whitbymuseum.org.uk) is a good place to while away an hour; if it's not, the **Dracula Trail** (maps

Goathland

Scarborough

Scarborough Castle

available from the tourist office at Langbourne Road, 01723 383636, www.whitbyonline.co.uk) is a hoot. Either way, the local seafood, tiny pubs, narrow cobbled streets of Eastcliff and grand Victorian resort architecture of Westcliff make Whitby a great weekend base.

Six miles south of here, **Robin Hood's Bay** is a revelation. Backed by picturesque cottages that tumble down the gully to the harbour, this one-time smugglers' haven offers everything a day at the seaside should – lovely beach and clifftop walks, rock pooling, fossil hunting in 170-million-year-old rock beds and cliff faces and, back in the village, heaps of tearooms, gift shops and pubs with fine views. Raw and ancient, it's a far cry from **Scarborough**, where Georgian, Edwardian and Victorian villas back two stunning beaches offering old-school attractions such as donkey rides, seafood stalls, deckchair hire and ice-cream vans. Climb 300-feet up to the rocky promontory topped by **Scarborough Castle** (01723 372451, www.english-heritage.org.uk) for expansive views of it all. **St Martin on the Hill** (Albion Road, 01723 363828, www.st-martin-on-the-hill.org.uk) is the town's best church, housing a wealth of Pre-Raphaelite art and architecture by William Morris, Edward Burne-Jones and Ford Maddox Brown. For rainy days, the **Rotunda Museum** (Vernon Road, 01723 353665, www.rotundamuseum.org.uk) and **Art Gallery** (The Crescent, 01723 374753, www.scarboroughart gallery.org.uk) are dedicated respectively to geology and visual arts, and the **Stephen Joseph Theatre** (Westborough, 01723 370541, www.sjt.uk.com), sited in an old art deco cinema, has a better-than-you-might-expect programme of plays and films, including premières of all plays by local boy Alan Ayckbourn.

## EAT & DRINK

With its fishing heritage, Whitby is by far the best hub for food in the area. At **Greens of Whitby** (13 Bridge Street, 01947 600284, www.greensofwhitby.com), chef Rob Green imaginatively mixes local fish, shellfish, meat and game with spices to create unusual flavour combinations. The lively and friendly **Moon and Sixpence** (16 Marine Parade, 01947 604416, www.moon-and-sixpence.co.uk) serves good fish

dishes and a smattering of carnivore-pleasers such as steaks and burgers, while the **Magpie Café** (14 Pier Road, 01947 602058, www.magpiecafe.co.uk) and **Humble Pie n Mash** (163 Church Street, 07919 074954, www.humblepienmash. com) are famous for their fish and pies – the former's fish and chips sees queues outside year-round. The **Mad Hatter** tearoom in La Rosa hotel (*see p111*) lives up to its name, with colourful decor and irresistible cakes, while the **Duke of York** (Church Street, 01947 600324, www.dukeofyork.co.uk) and **Black Horse** (91 Church Street, 01947 602906, www. the-black-horse.com) are two superior old town pubs.

In Scarborough, the local fish dishes at the **Lanterna** (33 Queen Street, 01723 363616, www.lanterna-ristorante. co.uk) and always-reliable fish and chips at the **Golden Grid** (4 Sandside, 01723 360922, www.goldengrid.co.uk) are the best food choices, while the sweet **Gala Coffee Bar** (Museum Terrace, 07977 472016) makes a pretty tea stop next door to the Rotunda Museum (*see left*). Pubs-wise, the **Merchant** (27-29 Eastborough, 01723 351426), **Valley Bar** (51 Valley Road, 01723 372593, www.valleybar.co.uk), **Cellars** (35-37 Valley Road, 01723 379992) and **Golden Ball** by the harbour (31 Sandside, 01723 353899) are all safe bets. On the moors, Levisham's **Horseshoe Inn** (01751 460240) and the **Birch Hall Inn** (01947 896245, www.beck hole.info) in Beck Hole near Goathland are well worth the walks to reach them.

Crown Spa Hotel

Magpie Café

Whitby

Bensons

## SHOP

Food should be your first move when it comes to retail. Whether it's slabs of parkin from **Botham's of Whitby** (35-39 Skinner Street, 01947 602823) or whopping great fresh dressed crabs, food is the thing you'll most likely want to buy to take home. Unless you're a goth, in which case **Venus Trading** (4 Sandgate, 01947 601221) has local jet jewellery, chunky woollens and black lace galore. The **Sandgate Sweet Shop** next door does old-school sweets that make pretty gifts. Robin Hood's Bay is great for fans of junk and antiques shops, and also has two good second-hand bookshops. In Scarborough, the **Blandscliff Gallery and Studio** (9 Blands Cliff, 01723 367252, www.blandscliff gallery.com) has more substantial gift potential.

## STAY

Whitby's accommodation ranges from boutique B&Bs such as **Bensons** (20 Bagdale, 01947 820400, www.bensons ofwhitby.com) to the original rooms of the **Marine Hotel** (13 Marine Parade, 01947 605022, www.the-marine-hotel. co.uk) and the brilliantly eccentric **La Rosa** hotel (5 East Terrace, 01947 606981, www.larosa.co.uk), high up on Westcliff, whose owners also run the romantic La Rosa campsite, complete with vintage caravans, near Goathland in the North Yorkshire Moors National Park. **Greens of Whitby** (*see p110*) does a range of apartments available for weekend breaks. In Robin Hood's Bay, the **Bay Hotel** (The Dock, 01947 880278) has a great harbour location and wonderful views, though the views from the sumptuous fifth-floor rooms at Scarborough's **Crown Spa Hotel** (Esplanade, 01723 357400, www.crownspahotel.com) are even better, and the spa facilities, gym and heated indoor pool are tempting on a coast that often feels the full force of the North Sea's weather. Back in the old town, the **Windmill** (Mill Street, 01723 372735, www.windmill-hotel.co.uk) consists of nine rooms in a wonderfully incongruous windmill and cobbled courtyard, and the modern, comfortable **Helaina** (14 Blenheim Terrace, North Bay, 01723 375191, www.thehelaina.co.uk) perches on the cliffs near the castle.

## GETTING THERE & AROUND

From King's Cross Station, York is two hours by train on East Coast Trains (08457 225225, www.eastcoast.co.uk) and Grand Central trains (0844 811 0071, www.grand centralrail.com). From York, frequent trains run to Scarborough in an hour. During the summer, plus Sundays and Bank Holidays from April to October, the Moorsbus (01845 597000, www.northyorkmoors.org.uk/moorsbus) service links towns and villages throughout the entire coast and moors area. By car, the A64 links York with Scarborough, the A171 Scarborough with Whitby, and the A169 through the moors from Whitby back south to York; if you're only planning on a few out-of-town drives don't bother with a hire car; it's far more economical to take local taxis.

# Quirky Camping

Sometimes you want to be at one with nature, but a tent just won't do. You want to hear birds singing but not so loudly that you're wearing Bose NR headphones at dawn, and you'd like a few creature comforts. If this sounds familiar, try these for size – a selection of tepees, huts, yurts, retro caravans, domes and treehouses, all designed to make country living easy.

Dome Garden

Roulotte Retreat

Gypsy Caravan Breaks

Gypsy Camp

## TEPEES & YURTS

### Eco Retreats

These five tepees and one yurt offer get-away-from-it-all weekends deep in the heart of one of Wales's largest forests. They're in secluded spots, near Machynlleth, at the southern tip of the Snowdonia National Park. There's a spring-fed shower and a natural loo.

**The facts**
01654 781375, www.ecoretreats.co.uk.
Tepees cost from £279 for two adults per weekend, including bedding and towels. Children under four are free, children 5-15 are £7.50 each. The yurt (recommended for families or larger groups) is £299. A 'full' package, from £349, includes a healing session, twilight meditation and an organic welcome hamper.

### Tipi Adventure

These weekend trips are based around a Canadian canoe expedition along the Wye in Herefordshire (starting in Hampton Bishop), with an overnight stay in riverside tepees.

**The facts**
Whitehall Farm, Hampton Bishop, Hereford, Herefordshire, 01432 870700, www.tipiadventure.co.uk. The package costs from £270. Tepees sleep up to seven people and are equipped with bedding, cooking equipment and a table. There are toilets in close proximity, as well as picnic benches and barbecue pits.

# CARAVANS

### Gypsy Caravan Breaks

These beautifully restored gypsy wagons are nestled in a cider orchard in Somerset. Local eggs, sausages and a jug of farmhouse cider are provided to get you started, after which you have to forage (or go to the farm shop down the road).

**The facts**

Marsh Farm, Pitney, Langport, Somerset,
01458 270044, www.gypsycaravanbreaks.co.uk.
The bow tops sleep two in a traditional extending double bed, from £95 per night. Bed linen is provided, as well as basic kitchen utensils to use with the open fire (or gas cooker in a trailer nearby).

### Gypsy Camp

The two caravans at Bouncers Farm are also bow tops, and are also set within an orchard. Ann Bishop at the farm can deliver food, or cook with enough warning. There is also an excellent seafood restaurant nearby – the Company Shed, (Mersea Island, 01206 382700, www.the-company-shed.co.uk).

**The facts**

Bouncers Farm, Wickham Lane Hall, Wickham Bishops, Essex, www.canopyandstars.co.uk.
Sleeps four from £105 per night, including bedding and cooking equipment. A private loo and shower room is attached to the main house on the farm.

### Happy Days Retro Vacations

Head to the east Dorset countryside and you'll find Peggy, Dee Dee and Betsy, a trio of lovingly restored Airstream trailers, at a peaceful campsite beside a small lake. Each is kitted out with kitchen equipment, as well as heaters and blankets for winter weather, plus radios and small TVs with DVD players.

**The facts**

Meadow View Campsite, Wigbeth, Horton, Wimborne, Dorset, 01202 567606, www.happydaysrv.co.uk.
Dee Dee and Betsy sleep four and cost from £280 to £295 for three nights; Peggy sleeps five and costs £315 to £400.

### Roulotte Retreat

Sited in the Scottish Borders, just three miles from Melrose, Roulotte Retreat offers handcrafted Romany-style wooden caravans. Each roulotte is decorated Indian-, Moroccan-, or Orient Express-style, and has en suite facilities.

**The facts**

0845 094 9729, www.roulotteretreat.com.
Roulottes sleep two adults from £90 per night, and include bedding and towels, as well as various eco-gadgets.

### Trailerflash

These Airstream 'International 534' trailers, barely changed in iconic design since the 1930s, have central heating, hot water, an onboard toilet and wet room, plus a small kitchen. The best thing about them is that you choose the backdrop, so the mountains, coastlines or islands of Scottish countryside can be explored. The company can also arrange themed itineraries, from fine dining to luxury spas.

**The facts**

0800 756 7772, http://trailerflash.co.uk.
Low season rates start from £800 per week, high season rates from £975 per week.

# HUTS ETC

### Dome Garden

A cluster of geodesic domes in the Forest of Dean, two hours from London. During your stay, guests learn how to light a fire properly, and the owners promise a glass of wine to those who bring along an instrument for campfire singsongs. There's a pizza oven, which stays warm for bread in the mornings.

**The facts**

Edge End Road, Mile End, Coleford, Gloucestershire, 07974 685818, www.domegarden.co.uk.
Domes house four adults, or five people including children from £445 for three nights Friday to Monday. The price includes en-suite facilities, firewood, hot water and bedding.

### Frogwell Wigwams

These big, wooden structures are tent-shaped but comfortable – with central heating, a toaster, a kettle, a microwave and a fridge – and provide better shelter from the elements. Each pod has space for up to five people. The wigwams are sited on a farm, where ingredients for the campfire can be bought from the farm shop, and children can meet the animals.

**The facts**

West Frogwell Farm, Frogwell Road, Callington, Cornwall, 01579 382743, www.westfrogwellfarm.co.uk.
Wigwams cost from £17.50 per night per adult (from £5 per child). Kennels are supplied for dogs at £5 per night.

### Kocoons

Set in the grounds of Kirkhill Mansion (www.kirkhillmansion.com) near Edinburgh, these lockable wooden structures are more comfortable than tents and have cosy insulated interiors that protect guests from the Scottish elements. Each pod has bunks for two people, with bedside tables with a reading lamp. Loos and showers are in a shared block.

**The facts**

Book through Adventure in the Meadow (0131 240 0080, www.adventureinthemeadow.com).
Kocoons for two people cost from £15, with breakfast extra.

### Original Huts

Made largely of reclaimed and locally sourced materials, these huts are located in the woods on an East Sussex farm.

**The facts**

01580 831845, www.original-huts.co.uk.
Huts sleep four or five people, and cost from £75 per night (low season) to £295 per weekend (peak season) with a surcharge of £6 per person for water, gas and logs for the fire. There's a communal wash hut with two loos and two showers.

# TREEHOUSES

### Harptree Treehouse

A new addition to the grounds of country house B&B Harptree Court (www.harptreecourt.co.uk), the treehouse is set at the edge of a wood with views towards a lake. Walk up the beautifully constructed staircase to canopy level to access the round structure with attached veranda. Inside is a king-sized bed, a standalone copper bathtub and leather armchairs.

**The facts**

Book through Canopy and Stars (www.canopyandstars.co.uk).
The treehouse sleeps two adults, and costs from £175 per night. No children or pets allowed.

QUIRKY CAMPING

# South Devon: Totnes & Around

Totnes is a town teeming with liberal-leaning exiles from the capital – in Elizabethan times it was a flourishing market town, and 500 years later continues to thrive. The town's right-on radical agenda saw it become the first place in England to sign up to the Transition Town initiative, which aims to reduce our reliance on oil, and the town boasts a wealth of independent retailers and smarter restaurants than you get in the nearby seaside resorts. There are fêtes, markets and arts events running all year round, and generally quite a buzz around the place. For weekenders, Totnes is above all a useful hub, with some pleasant places to stay; the delights of the South Devon countryside lie a short bike, taxi or bus ride away.

## Fast facts

**Journey time** Train from 3 hours; car from 4 hours
**Festivals & events** South Devon Crab festival (August, www.visitsouthdevon.co.uk) – a week-long festival dedicated to all things crab-based (crabbing competitions, tastings, crab-cracking events and cooking demonstrations) held at various locations. Local restaurants, pubs and hotels show their solidarity by introducing special crab menus for the week; Dartmouth Food Festival (October, www.dartmouthfoodfestival.com) – the annual festival attracts around 10,000 visitors, and is a showcase for contemporary and traditional food and drink, inspired by Devon's farming, fishing and producing traditions. The main events take place on Dartmouth's Market Square, and include cookery demonstrations, kids' activities and wine tasting; Agatha Christie Festival (September, www.englishriviera.co.uk) – fans of the crime writer Agatha Christie are drawn every year to Torquay, the town of her birth, for a week-long celebration of her life and work. Throughout the week there are theatre productions, guided walks, a fireworks display and a guided tour of Greenway, her former home
**Good for** Countryside, food, walking

Totnes Castle

## SEE & DO

To get a quick rundown of Totnes's history as a very important (and, for a time, very rich) market town and as a centre for minting coins, visit the **Totnes Museum** (70 Fore Street, 01803 863821, www.devonmuseums.net), housed in an Elizabethan merchant's house that retains many of its original features. In its 12 galleries are collections going back as far as 5000 BC and there's a room dedicated to the Victorian mathematician Charles Babbage. Opposite the market square, along Butterwalk, you'll find the **Devonshire Collection of Period Costume** (43 High Street, 01803 862857), an array of costumes dating from the 18th century up until the end of the 20th century.

Close to the East Gate arch on Fore Street, look out for the **Brutus Stone**, a granite boulder set into the pavement, said to be the first stone that Brutus of Troy, the legendary founder of Britain, stepped on when he reached these shores. More ancient boulders can be found in the walls of **Totnes Castle** (Totnes, 01803 864406), a Norman motte-and-bailey fortress that was founded after the Conquest to overawe the then Saxon town. Situated on a steep mound, it provides impressive views of the town rooftops and the River Dart.

A 1,200-acre estate just outside Totnes, **Dartington Hall Estate** (01803 847000, www.dartington.org) was first established in the 1920s as a centre for progressive education. It now hosts a limited range of courses, but is still worth a visit – its Great Hall dates from 1388, while the spectacular gardens that sweep all the way down to the Dart feature a sculpture by Henry Moore. Trainspotters and steam locomotive lovers will be in their element aboard the **South Devon Railway** (0845 345 1420, www.southdevonrailway.co.uk) to Buckfastleigh from Totnes. The seven-mile stretch of the Great Western Railway branch line was built in 1872, and runs along the valley of the River Dart.

Malsters Arms

Vineyard Café

Totnes

You can feed red squirrels, watch the tiny pygmy goats and get within touching distance of endangered animals of the English countryside at **Totnes Rare Breeds Farm** (Littlehempston, 01803 840387, www.totnes rarebreeds.co.uk). You'll also be taught how hedgehogs use their spikes and other titbits of animal trivia. Arrive at the family-owned attraction on the South Devon Steam Railway.

Three miles south-west of Totnes lies the picturesque village of **Harburton**, containing a fine medieval church with a striking tower and a couple of decent village pubs. A mile south along the Harbourne River you'll find the smaller but equally charming village of **Harbertonford**, which once upon a time used to serve many water mills as the gradient of the river there is naturally steep. These days a flood defence dam has tamed the once wild waters.

## EAT & DRINK

In Totnes, the **Tangerine Tree Café** (50 High Street, 01803 840853) is part-gallery, part-brasserie, in a friendly, modern setting. There are plump sofas and chunky wooden chairs over two floors, and daily specials that include the likes of Brixham crab salad, and pork belly and butterbean stew.

The **Vineyard Café** (Sharpham Estate, near Totnes, 01803 732178, www.thevineyardcafe.co.uk) isn't exactly posh: the kitchen is in a trailer, and the tables occupy a marquee and outdoor decking area. But views over the Dart are splendid, as is the Modern British food. The restaurant is closed in winter, and even in the summer the hours are weather-dependent. Also just outside Totnes, the **Malsters Arms** (Tuckenhay, 01803 732350, www.tuckenhay.com) was once owned by the late Keith Floyd. Overlooking a creek, it offers gastopub style food, several ales and 15 wines by the glass.

You'll get a whole field-to-plate experience at the **Riverford Field Kitchen** (Wash Barn, Buckfastleigh, 01803 762074, www.riverford.co.uk). To eat here you'll first have to look around the farm, either on a guided tour or by way of a quick DIY potter around. Chef Jane Baxter dishes up five vegetable dishes and one meat dish in a canteen-style setting; organic ciders feature among the drinks.

Built in the 17th century, the **Watermans Arms** (Bow Bridge, Ashprington, 01803 732214) has served as a smithy, a brew house and a prison. Today it's a cosy waterside pub, where kids can play in the shallow creek while adults relax with a drink on the terrace. The menu has a strong local theme and there are 15 en suite bedrooms.

Riverford Field Kitchen

The **Church House Inn** (Harberton, 01803 863707, www.churchhouseharberton.co.uk) must be a contender for oldest pub in the area. It was built in the 13th century and contains beams, settles and pews. There's a savvy selection of wines and local ales, and some top-notch pub food dished up by the pub's long-serving Portuguese chef.

## STAY

Contemporary-styled B&B **Great Grubb** (Plymouth Road, Totnes, 01803 849071, www.thegreatgrubb.co.uk) displays work by local artists in the guests' lounge, dining room and bedrooms. All bedrooms have en suite bathrooms, Wi-Fi and DVD players, while breakfast features a wealth of Devon produce. The **Old Forge** (Seymour Place, 01803 862174, www.oldforgetotnes.com), just a few minutes' walk from the centre of town, is a friendly B&B housed in a 15th-century building that has a lovely garden.

**Dartington Hall** (01803 847000, www.dartington.org) offers B&B accommodation in a peaceful setting. The wooden-beamed rooms are tastefully furnished, and have views of the countryside. A stay at Dartington gives you access to the rolling farmland of its large estate, including the ancient deer park and the many walks along the River Dart.

## SHOP

The residents of Totnes have taken the 'shop local' concept to heart, with a number of standout independent shops making it a great town for gifts and artisan products. Ticklemore Street holds a number of fine food shops, including Country Cheeses, Annie's greengrocer and Ticklemore Fish. Up the hill along the High Street there's the superb Totnes Bookshop (01803 863273). The nearby Civic Square is home to a market on Fridays and Saturdays, while on Tuesday mornings from May to September there's an Elizabethan Market, packed with crafts and costumes. If you decide to go on a spree, don't be surprised to find some strange-looking coins in your change, for the non-conformist Totnes boasts its own local currency, the Totnes Pound, which a growing number of shops accept.

## GETTING THERE & AROUND

Trains run to Totnes from Paddington, and take from 3 hours. Driving from London is a long haul, taking 4 to 4.5 hours.

Dartington Hall

# Blackpool

Tea dances or stag dos? Seaside tat or old-fashioned coastal charm? Blackpool has a mixed reputation, but despite a drop in visitor numbers due to the rise of cheap air travel, the town remains the most popular seaside resort in the UK. Lancashire's largest town was a magnet for mill workers needing a break from the looms, and has long been a place where holidaymakers could combine family fun (the Pleasure Beach rides, the Illuminations) with grown-up entertainment (ballroom dancing and cabaret). The number and range of hotels is also thanks to its importance as a political nexus; the grand Winter Gardens complex has witnessed addresses from every British Prime Minister since World War II.

A few years ago, the candy floss-coated reputation was blighted by drunken stag and hen parties and tacky nightclubs. But tens of millions of pounds are being pumped into regenerating the Promenade, smartening up existing tourist hotspots and building brand new attractions with the hope of boosting the town's reputation and alluring Brits away from Tenerife. Meanwhile, Blackpool has put in a bid to be granted UNESCO World Heritage status.

## Fast facts

**Journey time** Train 3 hours; car 4.25 hours
**Festivals & events** Blackpool Dance Festival (late May-early June, www.blackpooldancefestival.com) – the world's oldest ballroom dancing competition, held in the Empress Ballroom at the Winter Gardens since the 1920s; Blackpool Fringe (ongoing, www.blackpool fringe.org.uk) – run by a community interests group, this provides a platform to bring Blackpool's arts scene to the public through workshops and events; Rebellion Festival (August, www.rebellionfestivals. com) – billed as 'the original punk and alternative festival', this features more than 200 bands playing over four days at the Winter Gardens
**Good for** Beaches, nightlife

## SEE & DO

Walk ten minutes from Blackpool North rail station and you're on the **Promenade** that looks out on to the Irish Sea – at some distance, notoriously – with the iconic spire of **Blackpool Tower** (www.theblackpooltower.com) rising above you. The 117-year-old crimson-coloured iron structure has reopened after a major revamp, with a new Skywalk and viewing room made entirely of glass, from which (on a clear day) you can see as far as Scotland. Unlike the Eiffel Tower, on which its design was modelled, Blackpool's beacon is not free-standing, but has a large base that houses other attractions, most famously the **Tower Ballroom** (www.blackpooltower.com/ballroom). Home to *Come Dancing* for many years, this 1894 dance hall still has its original Wurlitzer organ, with resident organist Phil Kelsall providing the tunes since 1977. The immaculately polished wooden dancefloor is open daily for tea dances, and although the original strict rules such as 'No gentlemen without a lady' have slackened, it's still wonderfully traditional.

Blackpool Tower

**Grundy Art Gallery**

**Kwizeen**

Below ground, the **Blackpool Dungeon** (01253 622242, www.the-dungeons.co.uk) opened in 2011, combining history with thrills. Further south along the Promenade is the famed **Pleasure Beach**, with three of the best roller coasters in Britain, of which the Pepsi Max Big One, at over 200 feet, is the highest. For youngsters, **Nickelodeon Land** (0871 222 1234, www.nick.co.uk/nickelodeonland) provides an opportunity to meet characters such as Spongebob Squarepants.

Blackpool isn't just a big theme park. The **Grundy Art Gallery** (01253 478170, Queen Street, www.grundy artgallery.com) has an exhibition programme that draws greatly from the city's heritage and culture. And if you need some peace and quiet, hop on to one of the double-decker trams to Starr Gate at the southern end of the line, where there are dunes and a wide stretch of beach to be found.

In the evening, visit the old Blackpool Odeon for a performance of **Funny Girls** (5 Dickson Road, 0844 247 3866, www.funnygirlsonline.co.uk), the notorious transvestite burlesque cabaret 16 years in the running, started by legendary local entrepreneur on the gay nightclub scene Basil Newby. Otherwise catch a show at the **Blackpool Grand Theatre** (33 Church Street, 01253 290190, www.blackpoolgrand.co.uk), if only to see inside the wonderfully-restored space designed in 1894.

## EAT & DRINK

For the real Blackpool experience, you have to go to at least one chippy. One of the best is the **Cottage** (31 Newhouse Road, 01253 674088, www.cottagefishand chips.co.uk), which is off the beaten track but serves superb hand-cut chips made from local maris pipers. **Seniors** (106 Normoss Road, 01253 393529, www.think seniors.com) is suitably brightly lit and simply furnished, **Thornton Fisheries** (11 Victoria Road East, 01253 858668, www.thorntonfisheries.co.uk) has won awards for its mushy peas, and **AJ's Bistro** (65 Topping Street, 01253 626111, www.ajs-bistro.co.uk) serves good fresh scampi. For a more upmarket meal, **Kwizeen** (47-49 King Street, 01253 290045, www.kwizeenrestaurant.co.uk) bistro serves Lancashire market food with a Mediterranean twist, and has a menu that changes seasonally. **Toast** (28 Corporation Street, 01253 749777, www.toast-cafe-bar.co.uk) is another Modern British restaurant that does excellent breakfasts.

After fish and chips, ice-cream is the other Blackpool staple. Try the secret ice-cream recipe at **Ashurst Café** (3 Red Bank Road, 01253 357020), or soak up the atmosphere at **Nottarianni's** (9-11 Waterloo Road, 01253

Funny Girls

Imperial Hotel

342510, www.notarianniicecreamblackpool.co.uk), the only original Italian ice-cream parlour left. For a drink, avoid the city centre-clubs and head up the coast to Blackpool Fylde, to family-run pub the **Pump & Truncheon** (13 Bonny Street, 01253 624099, www.thepumpandtruncheon) for some local Lytham Gold Ale.

## SHOP

Blackpool's not known for its boutiques, but you'd be wise to bring back some Blackpool rock and other tooth-rotting confections from **Caitlin's Traditional Sweet Shop** (219 Bispham Road, 07972 215561, www.caitlinssweet shop.co.uk). To take that vintage holiday vibe to the next level, **Brooks Collectables** (7 Waterloo Road, 01253 344478, www.donkeyrides.co.uk) sells miniature treasures from Betty Boop figurines to old army badges.

## STAY

For a bit of old-style luxury, the **Imperial Hotel** (North Promenade, 01253 623971, www.barcelo-hotels.co.uk) on the Promenade has all the glamour of 1867, complete with uniformed doormen and high ceilings. The **Big Blue Hotel** (0871 222 4000, www.bigbluehotel.com) on the Pleasure Beach is a more modern alternative, with spacious rooms and an in-house bar and restaurant. For a cosier experience, **Langtrys** (36 King Edward Avenue, 01253 352031, www.langtrysblackpool.co.uk) is a stylish B&B with generously appointed rooms.

## GETTING THERE & AROUND

Trains from London Euston to Blackpool North Station run hourly (around 3 hours, with a change at Preston). The easiest way to get around Blackpool is by bus, with most services running regularly on weekends. Going up and down the Promenade, you should take the tram. It's a novelty experience and is the best way to see the city all lit up. For timetables see www.blackpooltransport.co.uk.

# The Lake District: Ambleside and Waterhead

Ambleside is the hub of the Lake District, with plenty of accommodation options and transport links, and is a good base for easy lowland walks and excursions to Grasmere and beyond. It is also, for all the obvious impact of tourism, still a rather pretty town, with more restaurants and pubs than just about any other conurbation in the region. A mile south of the town is Waterhead, right on the north-east shore of Lake Windermere, where old steamers take visitors to notable places around the lake, in search of Wordsworth or Beatrix Potter's legacies.

## Fast facts

**Journey time** Train 3 hours 45 minutes; car 6 hours
**Festivals & events** Brathay Windermere Marathon (mid May, www.brathaywindermeremarathon.org.uk) – with just over 26 miles round Lake Windermere and Esthwaite Water, this is one of the most picturesque marathon routes in Britain; Rushbearing Ceremony (first Saturday in July) – a time-honoured ceremony where children parade through St Mary's Church, carrying flowers and rushes from the lakeside, followed by a children's sports day; Lake District Summer Music Festival (August, www.ldsm.org.uk) – one of the top classical music festivals in the country, this two-week event attracts world-class performers as well as rising young stars, with quite a few venues in Ambleside
**Good for** Countryside, food, walking

## SEE & DO

There's not that much to actually 'do' in **Ambleside** except eat, drink, and buy outdoor gear or souvenirs – but the stone houses are pretty enough (Bridge House is possibly the most photographed building in the Lakes) and it's worth an hour's wandering to get a sense of how Lakeland communities live. Wordsworth enthusiasts should head to 19th-century St Mary's Church on Vicarage Road where a side chapel is dedicated to the poet.

The one significant cultural pitstop is the **Armitt Collection** (Rydal Road, 015394 31212, www.armitt.com), which displays Beatrix Potter's watercolours of fungi, and findings from Ambleside's Roman fort. Upstairs is the impressive Lakeland literature library: check out the first guide to the Lakes and the original 19th-century Herbert Bell prints of the peaks.

Once you've got your bearings, it's time to explore the beautiful countryside beyond the town: don your walking boots and get ready to get active, sweaty and (probably) wet through. There's a lovely, easy walk to Wordsworth's Dove Cottage in **Grasmere**, along the old Coffin Road and past his house at Rydal Mount. Another fairly painless hike is up to **Stock Ghyll Force**, an impressive 70-foot waterfall east of the town, reached via a well-trodden route starting at the Old Market Hall. In spring, there's a carpet of daffodils that makes you realise why Wordsworth was so taken with the area. The waterfall tumbles down mossy rocks set among the trees and feeds the Stock Ghyll river that once powered 12 watermills. Both of these walks are suitable for inexperienced hikers.

If more serious hiking is your thing, then a four-and-a-half-mile climb of **Loughrigg** – with a jaunt to the caves of Loughrigg Quarry – will give you amazing views over Rydal Water, Grasmere and Lake Windermere, as well as a spectacular range of peaks to the west. It also gives you the chance to visit Rydal Mount, Wordsworth's home for 37 years.

There are numerous cycle trails around Ambleside. For a trip that includes lakes, woodland fells and lanes take the Loughrigg Fell circular mountain bike tour, just west of the town. Pick up a Town Trail leaflet for walks and cycle trails from the tourist office, in tiny, 17th-century **Bridge House**, so quaint that even Turner was impressed enough to paint it.

For water-based activities, it's a quick 15-minute walk to **Waterhead** where you can board a steamer cruise, bound for **Brockhole** for the Park Visitor Centre, or **Bowness**, where the **World of Beatrix Potter** (0844 504 1233, www.hop-skip-jump.com) attracts families and Peter Rabbit enthusiasts. There is also the option of doing a cruise of the entire lake – at just over 11 miles, **Lake Windermere** is Britain's longest natural lake and is 219 feet at its deepest point. In spring and summer, water sports from wakeboarding to dinghy sailing can be enjoyed at the **Low Wood Watersports Centre** (015394 39441, www.elh.co.uk/watersports).

Loughrigg Tarn

Lucy's on a Plate

Ambleside

## EAT & DRINK

Ambleside is the culinary heart of the Lake District, and the choice runs from cosy country pubs and tearooms to Thai, Indian and Chinese restaurants. The **Log House** (*see below*) – literally a log cabin – serves Modern European cuisine using local produce in dishes such as Cumbrian beef fillet with wild mushroom and blue cheese gratin. Easy-going café **Lucy's on a Plate** (Church Street, 015394 32288, www.lucysofambleside.co.uk) is open from breakfast through to dinner, and is incredibly popular at all hours of the day. The traditional afternoon tea is excellent. Sister venture **Lucy4** (St Mary's Lane, 015394 34666, www.lucysofambleside.co.uk) is a brightly painted wine bar and bistro serving tapas and an impressive 90 wines by the glass. **Zeffirellis** (Compston Road, 015394 33845, www.zeffirellis.com) incorporates a café and pizzeria,

Waterwheel

while sister restaurant **Fellinis** (Church Street, 015394 33845, www.fellinisambleside.com) serves ambitious Mediterranean-influenced vegetarian food. (Both are sited below Ambleside's independent cinema.) The **Rattle Gill Café** (2 Bridge Street, 015394 34403), good for morning coffee, veggie lunches and afternoon tea, is hidden away on a terrace right on the banks of Stock Ghyll. In Waterhead, the **Bay Restaurant** at the Waterhead Hotel (Lake Road, 015394 30708, www.elh.co.uk) features a gourmet menu including ostrich and Cumbrian beef in an up-to-date setting.

For a genuine Cumbrian pub off the tourist trail, go to **Golden Rule** (Smithy Brow, 015394 32257). Think beams and brass, old photos and period paintings, inside a rabbit warren of rooms where Cumbrian ales and bar snacks such as pork pies and filled rolls are served. Slightly further south is the **Churchill Inn** (Lake Road, 015394 33192, www.churchillinn.co.uk), which pays homage to Sir Winston himself, with memorabilia and photographs smattering the walls. Serving casks of ale from local brewers, decent pub grub and showing all major football matches, this pub is popular with visitors and families at lunchtime and locals and students in the evening. The **Lake Road Wine Bar** (12-14 Lake Road 015394 33175, www.lakeroadwinebar.co.uk) serves cocktails and has an early evening happy hour.

For picnic supplies, head to **Lucy's Specialist Grocer** (Compston Road, 015394 32223, www.lucysofambleside.co.uk) for delicious own-made pâtés, regional cheeses, bread, cakes and more. **Organico** (Fisherbeck Mill, Old Lake Road, 015394 31122, www.organi.co.uk) has more than 100 wines and claims to be Britain's first dedicated organic wine store.

## STAY

For simple luxury with views over the fells, the **Log House** (Lake Road, 015394 31077, www.loghouse.co.uk) has three attractive rooms. The 300-year-old, Grade II-listed **Waterwheel** (3 Bridge Street, LA22 9DU 015394 33286, www.waterwheelambleside.co.uk) is in an idyllic location, and is perfect for a romantic break. Perched above Stock Ghyll, this little B&B features Victorian baths and is the setting of many a marriage proposal, honeymoon and anniversary, not to mention a delicious Cumbrian breakfast. For those on more of a budget, the **Ambleside Youth Hostel** (Waterhead, 0845 371 9620, www.yha.org.uk) has possibly one of the finest views in Waterhead. Situated on the shores of Lake Windermere in an imposing building with a café-bar and self-catering facilities, it is one of the best hostels in the Lake District.

## GETTING THERE & AROUND

Virgin Trains operates fast, frequent services from Euston to Oxenholme, from which there is a timetabled connection to Windermere (3 hours 15 minutes for the whole journey). From here take the nos.555, 599 or 618 bus to Ambleside (around 25 minutes) or catch a cab (10 minutes).

# Fowey & the South East Coast of Cornwall

Don't attempt to see all of Cornwall in a weekend – it's huge and the roads are slow. The south-east corner of the county is a pocket of cultural activity, bolstered by the success of the Eden Project. Tagged as the Cornish Riviera, it's long been a favourite holiday destination for families because of the opportunities it offers for messing about on or beside the water. Every little coastal town has its regatta week, when bunting is put up, fireworks organised and flotillas of colourful sails take to the waves.

Beyond the busy tourist strongholds of Fowey, Looe and Mevagissey, the area is full of rural hideaways: sleepy creeks and tiny beaches, jungly gardens and stately homes. But perhaps it's the blustery heights that are most rewarding – head out on to the South West Coast Path for a scramble and great views over clear-watered bays. And don't forget Cornwall's 'forgotten corner': the stunningly scenic and vividly historic Rame Peninsula, right on the border with Devon.

Fowey

## Fast facts

**Journey time** Train 4 hours; car 5 hours
**Festivals & events** Port Eliot Festival (July, www.porteliotfestival.com) – held in the grounds of the Port Eliot estate, this fuses literature and music; St Austell Torchlight Carnival (November) – there's family entertainment during the day, and it all culminates in a torchlight procession; Eden Sessions (www.edenproject.com/sessions) – the futuristic venue often hosts musical performances from big names
**Good for** Beaches, countryside, food, walking

## SEE & DO

The best 'sights' in these parts don't cost a penny. For those prepared to explore, there's a beach for every taste: small, sheltered coves; wild and windy expanses; surf breaks; craggy bays, teeming with rockpools at low tide; or good old-fashioned stretches featuring sandcastles and cornets.

The waterside of **Fowey** estuary also offers some beautiful walks and picnic spots. Fowey Marine Adventures (35 Fore Street, Fowey, 01726 832300, www.fowey-marine-adventures.co.uk) organises boat trips along the coast and river where, if you're lucky, dolphins, whales or basking sharks might make an appearance. Above the water, the **South West Coast Path** (www.southwestcoastpath.com)

is the longest national walking trail in Britain. The whole length (630 miles from Minehead to Poole Harbour) would take weeks to cover, but plenty of stretches can be included in circular day walks: the jagged coastline between Polruan and Polperro is blissfully unspoilt, as it's owned almost entirely by the National Trust.

The **Shipwreck & Heritage Centre** (Quay Road, Charlestown, 01726 69897, www.shipwreckcharlestown. co.uk) is housed in old china clay-loading premises, and holds a fascinating mix of objects rescued from shipwrecks, and an intriguing collection of old diving equipment. It is worth braving the crowds at the **Eden Project** (Bodelva, 01726 811911, www.edenproject.com) to explore the largest greenhouses on earth. There are floral and arboreal wonders from every corner of the globe, and play structures for kids. The site is on three cycle routes including the **Clay Trails** (www.claytrails.co.uk), and if you arrive by bike there is a £4 discount. Tim Smit, the man behind the Eden Project, had previously worked on the restoration of the lovely **Lost Gardens of Heligan** (Pentewan, St Austell, 01726 845100, www.heligan.com).

The museum at **St Austell Brewery** (63 Trevarthian Road, 0845 241 1122, www.staustellbrewery.co.uk) tells stories of Cornish brewing families, and offers samples too. Inland from Looe Bay, children will enjoy the Amazonian woolly monkeys at **Wild Futures' Monkey Sanctuary** (Murrayton, 01503 262532, www.monkeysanctuary.org).

## EAT & DRINK

For better or worse, this area has not received the same Rick Stein treatment as Padstow and the north coast, but there are some gems – particularly in and around Fowey – from smart seafood restaurants to historic pubs. The **Rashleigh Inn** (Polkerris, 01726 813991, www.rashleigh innpolkerris.co.uk) is a good halfway point on a circular walk along the coastal path via Polkerris (on the east of St Austell Bay) and has excellent crab sandwiches, while the **Dwelling House** (6 Fore Street, Fowey, 01726 833662, www.thedwellinghouse.co.uk) along the main coastal road is a pretty Georgian tearoom, stocked with tiers of pastel-coloured creations and 25 varieties of tea. Shop for pork pies, cheese and other picnic supplies at **Kittow Bros** butcher and deli (1-3 South Street, 01726 832639, www.kittowsbutchers.co.uk).

In Lostwithiel at the top of the estuary, the reassuringly simple **Trewithen** (3 Fore Street, 01208 872373) restaurant tops the dining scene, but for local snacks **Bella Mama** deli (24 Fore Street, no phone) is the best bet. A farmers' market pops up in the community centre (01840 250586, www.cornishfood.org.uk/farmers_market) every other Friday lunchtime.

Further east in Polperro, the **Blue Peter** (Quay Road, 01503 272743, www.thebluepeter.co.uk) is an old,

Botelet

Rashleigh Inn

white-washed fisherman's pub lodged into the cliff, fitting in a town famous for its smugglers. If you get the urge for a pasty, **Sarah's Pasties** (Fore Street, 01503 263973) up the coast in Looe is reliably good.

On the Rame Peninsula, the **View** (Treninnow Cliff Road, 01752 822345, www.theview-restaurant.co.uk) in Millbrook offers superb, simply served fish and seafood. No prizes for guessing how the owner came up with the name; the panorama stretches as far as the Lizard. In Tideford, the **Rod & Line** (Church Road, 01752 851323) is a quirky, almost theatrical hideaway pub with excellent food.

## SHOP

Quieter and less touristy than Fowey, Lostwithiel has a number of interesting independent shops along its two main thoroughfares – this is the unofficial antiques capital of Cornwall. **Nanadobbie** (8 Fore Street, 01208 873063) is a good bet for 1950s-'80s retro pieces. **Watts Trading** (12 Fore Street, 01208 872304, www.wattstrading.co.uk) is the place to stock up on wholesome accessories, from bamboo towels to eco-friendly toilet cleaner.

## STAY

The inspiration for Toad Hall, **Fowey Hall** (Hanson Drive, 01726 833866, www.foweyhallhotel.co.uk) is as extravagant as you would expect, but with no old-world stuffiness. Babysitting and a crèche are available, as well as luxurious spa facilities for grown-ups. Also in Fowey, the **Golant Youth Hostel** (Penquite House, 01726 833507, www.yha. org.uk) houses families in one room in the large Georgian mansion. For an alternative retreat, **Pencalenick House** (Pont Hill, Lantelgos-by-Fowey, www.pencalenickhouse. com) is a stunning modernist property built into the banks of Pont Pill Creek (maximum 13 guests).

In St Austell, quality accommodation is scarce; **Lower Barn** (Bosue, St Ewe, 01726 844881, www.bosue.co.uk) is a luxury B&B near the Eden Project, but is only an option if you have a car. The best place to stay in Looe is **Barclay House** (St Martin's Road, 01503 262929,

www.barclayhouse.co.uk), which has views over the river and woodland. In the vicinity, **Botelet** (Herodsfoot, Liskeard, 01503 220225, www.botelet.com) is a 300-acre farm with a feel of a bygone era. Choose between self-catering or B&B accommodation; there's also camping in a yurt in the meadow for £5 a night.

Rame Peninsula offers quirky accommodation in the shape of a dinky old train carriage at the **Old Luggage Van** (Haparanda Station, Nut Tree Hill, St Germans, 01503 230783, www.railholiday.co.uk), right at St Germans station. For an organic experience, lodge at **Buttervilla Farm** (Polbathic, Torpoint, 01503 230315, www.buttervilla.com), whose produce has supplied Jamie Oliver's Cornish outpost. **Westcroft** (Market Street, Kingsand, 01752 823216, www.westcroftguesthouse.co.uk) is one of the best B&Bs around, with a husband and wife team maintaining exceptional standards, and where thoughtful touches include home-made cake and lavender-scented pillows.

## GETTING THERE & AROUND

Trains run from Paddington to St Austell and take around four hours. From here, the surrounding towns of Looe and Lostwithiel can be accessed by train, but hiring a car will make exploration easier. The Night Riviera, the sleeper service, is worth considering; you board around 11pm in Paddington, and wake up in to breakfast in Cornwall.

Watts Trading

# Glasgow

Over the last 30 years Glasgow has enjoyed a remarkable renaissance, thanks to some serious investment in cultural venues and blue riband events. The city's post-industrial reinvention continues apace: at the end of November 2011 the relocated Museum of Transport opened as the Riverside Museum, a striking, zinc-clad building designed by Zaha Hadid, while the Commonwealth Games is heading this way in 2014. Glasgow is Scotland's biggest centre for entertainment, nightlife and shopping, with a smart new generation of restaurants and café-bars, and a weekend here is enough time to appreciate its unique nature – it has the biggest heart of any Scottish city, and its industrial and working class heritage fathers a certain demeanour: bold, brash and allergic to fuss.

## Fast facts

**Journey time** Train 4-5 hours
**Festivals & events** Glasgow Film Festival (February, www.glasgowfilm.org/festival) – screenings, speakers, premières and retrospectives; Glasgow Comedy Festival (March, www.glasgowcomedyfestival.com) – hundreds of comics acoss 50 venues; West End Festival (June, www.westendfestival.co.uk) – two-week community festival complete with opening parade and a street party; Glasgow Jazz Festival (June, www.jazzfest.co.uk)
**Good for** Culture, food, nightlife, shopping

Café Gandolfi

## SEE & DO

The heart of modern Glasgow is 18th-century **George Square**, dominated by the impressive City Chambers (0141 287 4018, www.glasgow.gov.uk) building – the free tours of this Italianate marvel are well worth 45 minutes of anyone's time. The square itself is littered with statues commemorating the greats of empire and industry, along with the dynamic duo of Scottish literature, Robert Burns and Sir Walter Scott. The square also has its practical side, though, and is home to Queen Street railway station, Buchanan Street underground station and, at no.11, the main Tourist Information Office.

Round the corner in **Buchanan Street**, retail therapy is the order of the day, with a series of stand-alone stores and two major malls. Princes Square (nos.38-42, 0141 221 0324, www.princessquare.co.uk) is the more upmarket, while the Buchanan Galleries (no.220, 0141 333 9898, www.buchanangalleries.co.uk) is the biggest city centre mall in Scotland. If shopping leaves you cold, the **Royal Concert Hall** on Sauchiehall Street (no.2, 0141 353 8000, www.glasgowconcerthalls.com) offers a cultural alternative. Sauchiehall Street is also home to the **Willow Tea Rooms** at no.217 (0141 332 0521, www.willowtearooms.co.uk). It was designed by Charles Rennie Mackintosh, and remains a beautiful place for afternoon tea. At no.350, the eclectic **Centre for Contemporary Arts** (0141 352 4900, www.cca-glasgow.com) is housed in a building by Alexander 'Greek' Thomson, Glasgow's other noted architect (see www.greekthomson.org.uk for more on him).

Just north of here is **Glasgow School of Art** (167 Renfrew Street, 0141 353 4526, www.gsa.ac.uk), Mackintosh's acknowledged masterpiece. Completed in 1909, it still functions as a working art school, and houses a collection of Mackintosh's furniture, drawings and paintings, along with a shop; pop in for a guided tour. For anyone with an interest in architecture, the Charles Rennie Mackintosh Society (0141 946 6600, www.crmsociety.com) has a comprehensive website with information on Mackintosh buildings across Glasgow and downloadable walking tours. Head back to handsome Royal Exchange Square, with its optimistic abundance of café and restaurant terraces, for the **Gallery of Modern Art** (0141 287 3050, www.glasgowlife.org.uk).

South-east of George Square is an area branded the **Merchant City**, thanks to its associations with Glasgow's 18th-century tobacco and sugar lairds. Since the 1980s it has been promoted as a small but beautifully formed quartier with high-class shopping, restaurants, café-bars and entertainment. There is some fine old architecture, so casting your eyes above pavement level reaps rich rewards; try following the Merchant City Initiative's trail (www.glasgowmerchantcity.net).

The **East End** is where it all began. Before the great urban expansions of the 18th and 19th centuries, this essentially was Glasgow: around **Glasgow Cathedral** (Castle Street, 0141 552 6891, www.glasgowcathedral.org.uk) precincts, you can still get a sense of the old Glasgow; here, you'll find the 15th-century townhouse **Provand's Lordship** (Castle Street), the faux-medieval **St Mungo Museum of Religious Life & Art** (Castle Street, 0141

276 1625, www.glasgowlife.org.uk) and the **Necropolis** (0141 287 5064, www.glasgow.gov.uk), a Victorian cemetery modelled on Père Lachaise in Paris. Down by the Clyde you'll find the **People's Palace & Winter Gardens** (0141 276 0788, www.glasgowlife.org.uk). Built at the tail end of the 19th century, the Palace originally served as a cultural and municipal centre for the working classes. It now houses a cherished exhibition that covers all aspects of Glasgow life, with a particular focus on industrial and social history since the mid 18th century.

Out west lies the **Kelvingrove Art Gallery & Museum** (Argyle Street, 0141 287 2699, www.glasgow life.org.uk). More people come through its doors than visit Edinburgh Castle, making it Scotland's top tourist attraction. Surrounding the gallery are the open spaces of Kelvingrove Park, while the skyline is dominated by the Gothic tower and campus of the University of Glasgow. On the north side of the campus, off University Avenue, is the **Hunterian Museum & Art Gallery** (0141 330 4221, www.gla.ac.uk/hunterian), on two sites and covering art and science. Near here, down on the Clyde, is the city's latest pride and joy, the stunning **Riverside Museum** (100 Pointhouse Place, 0141 287 2720, www.glasgowlife.org.uk). Designed by architect Zaha Hadid – her first major public building in the UK – the museum displays Glasgow's industrial heritage in all its glory. Further south, but well worth the trip, are the art and artefacts of the **Burrell Collection** (Pollok Park, 0141 287 2550, www.glasgowlife.org.uk), .

## EAT & DRINK

The very central **Pot Still** (154 Hope Street, 0141 333 0980, http://thepotstill.co.uk) is a wonderful, unreconstructed city pub. It sells nearly 500 malts, doesn't do food and is staffed by friendly, larger-than-life owners. Another trad classic is seafood specialist **Rogano** (11 Exchange Place, 0141 248 4055, www.roganoglasgow.com) – try lunch at the bar or take a booth for dinner. **Fratelli Sarti** (133 Wellington Street, 0141 248 2228, www.sarti.co.uk) is another Glasgow institution, with three branches in the city; the deli-and-trat

in Wellington Street remains a welcoming place to stop for a plate of pasta or a pizza and a glass of wine.

In Merchant City, old stager **Café Gandolfi** (64 Albion Street, 0141 552 6813, www.cafegandolfi.com) has been serving standards such as smoked venison with gratin dauphinoise for over 30 years. Also here are the **Metropolitan** (60 Candleriggs, 0141 552 9402, www.metropolitan-bar.com), a lively, modern pre-club dinner and drinks venue that does excellent steaks, and the ostentatious **Corinthian** (191 Ingram Street, 0141 552 1101, www.thecorinthianclub.co.uk), a bar-restaurant-entertainment complex set in a grand old building.

The **Ubiquitous Chip** (12 Ashton Lane, 0141 334 5007, www.ubiquitouschip.co.uk) out in the West End (a ten-minute taxi ride from the centre) is a Glasgow classic that has evolved into an entire complex of venues (dining room, brasserie, pub and so on) since it opened in 1971. The signature dish is a starter of venison haggis.

## STAY

Of the many places to stay, the **Grand Central Hotel** (99 Gordon Street, 0141 240 3700, www.thegrandcentral hotel.co.uk), is a classic terminus hotel and was recently refurbed to the tune of £20 million. The buffet-style breakfast is impressive; rooms start from around £65. **ABode** (129 Bath Street, 0141 572 6000, www.abode hotels.co.uk) is more of a boutique hotel. The location couldn't be more central, while the 59 rooms are quietly chic and stellar chef Michael Caines is in charge of the dining options. **Hotel du Vin at One Devonshire Gardens** (1 Devonshire Gardens, Great Western Road, 0141 339 2001, www.hotelduvin.com) is one of Glasgow's most prestigious crashpads, with a bistro that serves polished fare in intimate, oak-panelled surrounds.

## GETTING THERE & AROUND

The train from Euston to Glasgow Central takes 4-5 hours, while Scotrail's Caledonian Sleeper service runs every night except Saturday.

Riverside Museum

# Edinburgh

Pulling into Waverly station, the first impression of the Scottish capital is a view dominated by the past. On one side of the valley that divides the city, the Old Town sprawls over multiple levels, with the medieval castle looming from the vantage point of the city's foundation 'rock'; on the other, Enlightenment aesthetics are epitomised in the Georgian elegance of the New Town's regimented grid. High-rise buildings are distinctly lacking, keeping the views from the seven hills free of modern eyesores and in tune with the natural surroundings.

Over the years, outlying villages have become incorporated into the city – but retain separate identities; Duddingston has a picturesque loch-side setting and Scotland's oldest pub, while shoreside Leith (made famous by Irvine Welsh's *Trainspotting* as a poor suburb, rife with drugs) has forged a new identity as a hub for young professionals, who occupy the warehouse conversions and trendy bars. Of course, the city is renowned for hosting the world's biggest cultural festival – during which the population doubles and all kinds of buildings are transformed into performance venues – but year-round, Edinburgh fuses small-town charm with international status.

## Fast facts

**Journey time** Train 4.5 hours
**Festivals & events** Hogmanay (31 December); Edinburgh International Festival (August, www.eif.co.uk) – the festival specialises in classical musical events, and draws performers from around the world; Edinburgh Fringe Festival (August, www.edfringe.com) – the largest performing arts festival in the world; St Andrew's Day (30 November) – find a restaurant serving haggis, recite some Burns and raise a glass to Scotland's patron saint
**Good for** Culture, food, history, nightlife, shopping

Edinburgh Castle

## SEE & DO

If you're lucky enough to start the weekend with a clear day, make the trek up extinct volcano **Arthur's Seat** (it takes around 40 minutes) for stunning views out over the Firth of Forth. Otherwise, you can trace the edge of the 'Crags' all the way to **Holyrood Palace** (0131 556 5100, www.royalcollection.org.uk), the Queen's official Scottish residence, where the Queen's Gallery hosts exhibitions from the royal collection. From here it's a short walk up to Calton Hill, with its Pantheon-lookalike the **National Monument**, left half-finished due to a lack of funds in the 1820s. Every year, **Beltane fire festival** (www.beltane.org) is held here at the end of April to revive the ancient Celtic Mayday celebrations. **Edinburgh Castle** (Castlehill, 0131 225 9846, www.edinburghcastle.gov.uk) is expensive to visit and has few exciting exhibits, but the view from the surrounding courtyard is impressive.

The **Scottish National Gallery** (The Mound, 0131 624 6200, www.nationalgalleries.org) boasts classic works by great masters such as Velázquez and Titian, while the **Scottish National Gallery of Modern Art** (75 Belford Road, 0131 624 6200, www.nationalgalleries.org)

Holyrood Palace

Dogs

Filmhouse

Hotel Missoni

21212

houses favourites from Matisse and Picasso up to Emin and Hirst, and has an impressive land-art display in the grounds.

From this area (known as Dean Village) you can walk along the Water of Leith to **Stockbridge**, a pretty residential area with Georgian buildings and some quirky boutiques and pubs. A walk around the **Royal Botanic Gardens** (20 Inverleith Row, 0131 552 7171, www.rbge. org.uk) is also a great way to spend an afternoon. For contemporary art, **Fruitmarket Gallery** (45 Market Street, 0131 225 2383, www.fruitmarket.co.uk) regularly has interesting thematic exhibitions and also boasts an excellent café, while **Ingleby Gallery** (15 Calton Road, 0131 556 4441, www.inglebygallery.com) is one of the country's leading commercial galleries. The **National Museum of Scotland** (Chambers Street, 0300 123 6789, www.nms.ac.uk) has recently undergone huge transformation, linking the Corbusian-style sandstone building with the Victorian Grand Gallery of the former Royal Museum.

Catch a film at one of the city's best independent cinemas – **Filmhouse** (88 Lothian Road, 0131 228 2688, www.filmhousecinema.com) hosts the Edinburgh International Film Festival, while **Cameo Picturehouse** (38 Home Street, 0871 902 5723, www.picturehouses. co.uk) is cosy, with themed double bills every Sunday.

To escape the city, get a bus to **Portobello** for a walk along the beach, or to **Cramond** in the west of the city, where at low tide (see www.britishbeaches.info for tide times) you can walk across to Cramond Island and explore its WW2 bunkers.

## EAT & DRINK

Tom Kitchin was the youngest chef to win a Michelin Star for his Leith restaurant the **Kitchin** (78 Commercial Street, 0131 555 1755, www.thekitchin.com), where the tasting menu might feature Orkney scallops, Arisaig razor clams, or Perthshire elderberries; Dominic Jack's **Castle Terrace** (33-35 Castle Terrace, 0131 229 1222, www.castleterrace restaurant.com) also has a Scottish-focused menu, while at **21212** (0845 222 1212, www.21212restaurant.co.uk), you'll find slick interior design to match the architecturally presented dishes. Eccentric restaurateur David Ramsden owns a trio of bistros seemingly in honour of his pets – the **Dogs** (110 Hanover Street, 0131 220 1208, www.thedogs online.co.uk) resembles a front room and serves hearty pies and offal, and **Seadogs** (43 Rose Street, 0131 225 8028, www.seadogsonline.co.uk) specialises in fish. The **Outsider** (15 George IV Bridge, 0131 226 3131) has great views out to the castle and serves inventive European fare; for vegetarians, **David Bann** (56-58 St Mary's Street, 0131 556 5888, www.davidbann.co.uk) is a must.

**Edinburgh Farmers' Market** (www.edinburgh farmersmarket) operates every Saturday from 9am to 2pm, complete with porridge bar from local brand Stoats. Coffee-wise, Scottish barista champion Jonathan Sharp has it covered with five shops around the city, the most central being **Wellington Coffee** (33A George Street, 0131 225 6857) and **Kilimanjaro Coffee** (104 Nicolson Street, 0131 662 0135), though the only place with its own roastery is **Artisan Roast** (57 Broughton Street, 07590 590667, www.artisanroast.co.uk), where you can either buy beans to take home or drink your brew in the 'snug' at the back. For cheap eats, **Kebab Mahal** (7 Nicolson Square, 0131 667 5214, www.kebab-mahal.co.uk) outperforms its dodgy takeaway façade with home-cooked Pakistani curries and enormous naans. **Kampong Ah Lee** (28 Clerk Street, 0131 662 9050) offers Malaysian specialities in a canteen-like setting.

## SHOP

Avoiding the chains and crowds of Princes Street, the best place for boutique browsing is around the Grassmarket in the Old Town. Follow the cobbles of Victoria Street down from George IV Bridge, sampling the best of the national cheeses at **IJ Mellis** (30 Victoria Street, 0131 226 6215, www.mellischeese.co.uk), whisky at the **Whisky Shop** (28 Victoria Street, 0131 225 4666, www.whiskyshop.com) and flavoured oils, vinegars or sherries at **Demijohn** (32 Victoria Street, 0131 225 3265, www.demijohn.co.uk).

Also in the area, **Red Door Gallery** (42 Victoria Street, 0131 477 3255, www.edinburghart.com) and **Hannah Zakari** (43 Candlemaker Row, 0131 516 3264, www.hannah zakari.co.uk) both sell artwork, stationery and gifts made by local artists. There are plenty of bookshops, notably **Analogue Books** (39 Candlemaker Row, 0131 220 0601, www.analoguebooks.co.uk), which supplies graphic design

and photography titles. Nearby West Port is famous for its cluster of independent second-hand and antique booksellers, the most eccentric being **Armchair Books** (72-74 West Port, 0131 229 5927).

**Armstrongs** (81-83 Grassmarket, 0131 220 5557, www.armstrongsvintage.co.uk) is the place to rummage for vintage clothes from all eras, but **Godiva** (39 West Port, 0131 221 9212, www.godivaboutique.co.uk) offers more upmarket second-hand pieces as well as collections from Edinburgh College of Art graduates. Avoiding the ubiquitous tartan and cashmere shops on the Royal Mile, head to **Anta** (93 West Bow, 0131 225 4616, www.anta.co.uk) where you'll find authentic *earasaids* (oversize scarves) as well as thick blankets woven from Shetland wool. For an alternative take on Scottish attire, **Joey D** (54 Broughton Street, 0131 557 6672, www.joey-d.co.uk) refashions kilts and old tweed with leather, buckles and studs. In the centre of town, **Goodstead** (76 Rose Street, 0131 228 2846, www.goodstead.co.uk) offers pieces from minimally chic brands such as APC and Folk.

**Avalanche Records** (5 Grassmarket, 0131 225 3939, www.avalancherecords.co.uk) is the city's indie music institution after 20 years on the scene, housing second-hand vinyl and CDs with a particular emphasis on Scottish talent. For the sound of bagpipes head to **Coda Music** (12 Bank Street, The Mound, 0131 622 7246, www.codamusic.co.uk), which holds Scotland's biggest selection of folk music.

## STAY

For a truly indulgent weekend, it's got to be the **Balmoral** (Princes Street, 0131 556 2414, www.balmoralhotel.com), established in 1902, and now sporting a spa and a Michelin-starred restaurant. The **Scotsman** (20 North Bridge, 0131 556 5565, www.theetoncollection.com) is housed in the vacated premises of the *Scotsman* newspaper, and is a smart, dependable hotel with a spa. Book well in advance for the **Witchery** (The Royal Mile, Castle Hill, 0131 225 5613, www.thewitchery.com), known mostly for its excellent restaurant but which also has eight suites with names such as 'Inner Sanctum' and 'Vestry', decked out with four posters and red velvet and hidden at the top of a stone staircase.

**Tigerlily** (125 George Street, 0131 225 5005, www.tiger lilyedinburgh.co.uk) has an impressive cocktail bar and basement nightclub, and is more modern in its design, right down to the iPod docks in the rooms. **Hotel Missoni** (1 George IV Bridge, 0131 220 6666, www.hotelmissoni.com) brings glamour to the Old Town; guests are greeted by men wearing kilts in the designer's trademark zig-zag weave. More effacing is **Millers64** (64 Pilgrig Street, 0131 454 3666, www.millers64.com), a smart three-room B&B in a Victorian New Town house.

For a budget option, one of the best hostels is **Art Roch** (2 West Port, 0131 228 9981, www.artrochhostel.com).

## GETTING THERE & AROUND

By train, East Coast operates a direct route from King's Cross to Waverley station in Edinburgh.

Despite a few hills, central Edinburgh is easy to walk around, especially if you find the short-cut alleyways in the Old Town, which link different levels. There are lots of buses for longer journeys – to Leith and the Shore, for example – and the long-awaited tramway is due to start operating in 2012, connecting the airport with the centre and the Shore.

---

### Cultural baggage

**Book** *Trainspotting* (Irvine Welsh, 1993)
**Film** *Shallow Grave* (Danny Boyle, 1994)
**Album** *Sunshine on Leith* (The Proclaimers, 1988)

# The Highlands

It's a long way to go for a weekend break, but if you catch the night train and/or add on an extra day, you can get stuck into some serious walking and wildlife watching. Here we concentrate on Aviemore and the vast wilderness of the Cairngorms, with a few options around the Highlands' capital and transport hub, Inverness. The first snows in Britain often fall on the Cairngorm plateau around early October, and from then on conditions for outdoor activities are unpredictable; the best time to go – unless you want to ski – is between March and September.

The Highlands are known for their scenery, with Caledonian pinewoods dominating the lower reaches, and mountain tundra at greater heights, plus expanses of dark icy water in the form of lochs and waterfalls, making the views spectacularly varied. There is always a decent range of activities to suit most pockets and tastes: mountain biking, clay-pigeon shooting, rafting, hiking for all levels of ability, mountain climbing and, in season, skiing and snowboarding, are all on offer in the areas close to Aviemore – and there are great pubs in which to taste the famous malts of Speyside.

Having the flexibility of a car is useful – you can't reach the most beautiful, remote spots without one. Note, because you're so near the sea, the weather is incredibly changeable – while it might be lovely and bright one day up in Ullapool, it could be sleeting in Kingussie.

## Fast facts

**Journey time** Train (sleeper) overnight; flight – 1 hour 25 minutes

**Festivals & events** Rock Ness (June, www.rockness. co.uk) – bands and a chance to scout Scotland's famous monster – this annual festival has been called the most beautiful in the world due to its loch-side location, but it also attracts big names such as the Chemical Brothers and Fatboy Slim; Speyfest (July, www.speyfest.com) – a six-day festival of traditional and contemporary Celtic music held in the village of Fochabers on the banks of the River Spey; Pitlochry Highland Games (September, www.pitlochryhighland games.co.uk) – hosting competitions since 1852, the Pitlochry outpost of the Highland Games still has events such as tossing the caber and stone putting

**Good for** Countryside, food, walking, wildlife

## SEE & DO

Nearby to **Aviemore** is Scotland's national outdoor training centre, **Glenmore Lodge** (01479 61256, www.glenmorelodge.co.uk), which runs courses on useful skills such as orienteering and first aid. There's also **Cairngorm** mountain itself, where there's skiing and snowboarding in the winter and a plethora of lakes and lochs. The **Rothiemurchus Centre** (01479 812345, www.rothiemurchus.net) in Aviemore offers everything from archery to canoeing, including the high-rise rope playground TreeZone, which kids love. The **RSPB Centre Loch Garten** (01479 831476, www.rspb.org) is worth a visit, and is known for its ospreys. Of course, there's plenty of walking and hiking to be done that doesn't have to be organised through a particular

Loch Garten

Cairngorm Hotel

Macdonald Aviemore Resort

Glenmore Lodge

Macdonald Aviemore Resort

company – www.walkhighlands.co.uk, for example, is very useful for planning trips.

Visit the **Dalwhinnie Distillery** (01540 672219, www.discovering-distilleries.com) south-west of Aviemore to try some of the 15-year-old single malt and see how it's made. The **Highland Folk Museum** (01540 673551, www.highlandfolk.com) is split between the nearby towns of Newtonmore and Kingussie: there are displays of old buildings, as well as artefacts from domestic life.

Take in some classic views on the drive from Inverness south-west to **Glen Affric**. Often described as the most beautiful glen in Scotland, it boasts ancient pinewoods, lochs and moorland. This journey goes via **Beauly**, a little town with a few opportunities for shopping and diversions such as the **Kilmorack Gallery** (01463 783230, www. kilmorackgallery.co.uk). Housed in a converted church, it holds decent exhibitions of contemporary art. Get in a couple of rounds at the nine-hole golf course in **Aigas** (01463 782942, www.aigas-holidays.co.uk), also home to

**Aigas Field Centre** (01463 782443, www.aigas.co.uk) which specialises in Highlands wildlife breaks and courses. North-east from Inverness, venture through the Black Isle to the port of Cromarty, where you can take the two-car ferry to **Nigg** and gaze at the dramatic oil platforms out to sea.

For history buffs, not far from Inverness, **Fort George** (01667 460232, www.historic-scotland.gov.uk) is worth a visit – the huge fortification was built to defend and pacify the Scottish Highlands after the Jacobite uprising of 1745. Further afield, east of the city, **Cawdor Castle** (01667 404401, www. cawdorcastle.com) in Nairn is a romantic, fairytale castle.

## EAT & DRINK

If you're in need of a heavy dollop of Scottishness, the **Cairngorm Hotel** (Grampian Road, Aviemore, 01479 810233, www.cairngorm.com) is the answer. Food – hearty meals such as venison casserole – is served between noon and 9pm, and there's an accordionist some nights too. For a more bistro-style place, try **Ord Bán** (Rothiemurchus, 01479 810005, www.ordban.com). Both the **Cross** and **Muckrach Lodge** guesthouses (*see right*) have notable restaurants, with more adventurous cooking than you'll find elsewhere in the region.

In Inverness, fine dining can be found at **Abstract** at the Glenmoriston Town House (20 Ness Bank, 01463 223777, www.abstractrestaurant.com), which has a Modern French influence, or **Chez Roux** at the Rocpool Reserve (Culduthel Road, 01463 240089, www.rocpool.com), where there's also a cool cocktail bar. The **Mustard Seed** (16 Fraser Street, 01463 220220, www.mustardseedrestaurant.co.uk) is a home-style restaurant in a converted church on the river. **Hootananny** (67 Church Street, 01463 233651, www.hootananny.co.uk) is the best pub for traditional live music.

If you head to Loch Ness, the **Loch Ness Country House Hotel** (01463 230512, www.lochnesscountry househotel.co.uk) offers a fine-dining experience, while the **Dores Inn** (01463 751203, www.thedoresinn.co.uk) is a family-run restaurant and pub on the shores of the loch.

## SHOP

The official **Harris Tweed Shop** (Main Street, Newtonmore, 01540 670188, www.harristweedshop.com) sells everything from plus-fours to kilts. If you make the journey up to Nigg, continue to Fearn and visit the **Anta Factory Shop** (01862 832477, www.anta.co.uk) where everything from posh tartan homeware to textiles are found – you can pick up end-of-line fabrics and there is also a tearoom. In Beauly, the **House of Beauly** (Station Road, 01463 782821, www.houseofbeauly.com) stocks Scottish goods of all sorts (some better quality than others) from scarves to oatcakes. The place for traditional Highland wear here is **Campbell's of Beauly** (Highland Tweed House, 01463 782239, www.campbellsofbeauly.co.uk), where you'll get expert fitting advice but no modern styling. Stop at the **Corner on the Square** (1 High Street, 01463 783000, www.corneronthesquare.co.uk) for superb picnic ingredients.

## STAY

The **Cross** (Tweed Mill Brae, Ardbroilach Road, Kingussie, 01540 661166, www.thecross.co.uk) is a tweed mill converted into a simple but comfortable hotel and restaurant. At the other end of the scale, the **Macdonald Aviemore Resort** complex (0844 799152, www.macdonaldhotels.com) is made up of four hotels and 18 self-catering lodges. The resort also boasts the Spey Valley championship golf course and the pools and flumes of Spey Valley Leisure. **Muckrach Lodge** (Dulnain Bridge, by Grantown-on-Spey, 01479 851257, www.muckrach.co.uk) merges a Victorian Highland lodge with a contemporary chic feel. There is also a **Hilton** (01479 810661, www.hilton.co.uk) nearby in Coylumbridge. For real peace and quiet, there's the **Boat Hotel** (Boat of Garten, 01479 831258, www.boathotel.co.uk), which has spectacular mountain views.

## GETTING THERE & AROUND

A sleeper service leaves Euston at 11pm on Monday to Friday and on 10.45pm on Sunday, and stops at a variety of places in the Highlands including Fort William, Inverness and Aviemore. This is a long journey and it's worth booking a first class ticket to get a bed and breakfast as well as a bit of privacy. The flight to Inverness takes just over an hour and a half from London. Once in the Highlands, public transport does link many of the towns and villages but obviously a car offers most choice.

Rothiemurchus

# Belfast

Before the 1994 IRA ceasefire, Belfast was pretty much off the travel radar, and the few weekenders who went there were intrepid sorts interested in the sectarian murals and the 'dark tourism' delights of a home-grown warzone. These days there is a small influx of European and American travellers most weekends, their numbers boosted by 'Titanoraks' inspired by the cheesy blockbuster film or deep-sea dive melodrama-documentaries on the telly. Shipbuilding, tobacco factories, rope-making works and engineering made the city Ireland's richest during the boom years of the Industrial Revolution, and the grandiose Victorian buildings you see all around are a reminder of this era. Billions of pounds of investment have gone some way to restoring some parts of civic Belfast and have helped turn the city into a lively, culturally rich and safe place to visit.

The city centre around Donegall Square is compact and easy to explore on foot. To the north is the main shopping district and some of Belfast's best restaurants and bars, while the area stretching east towards the River Lagan, once dominated by shipyards, now houses two of the city's largest entertainment venues – the Odyssey Arena and Pavilion and the soon-to-open Titanic Belfast. A 20-minute walk south takes you to the University Quarter, home to some of Belfast's most popular attractions: Queen's University, the Botanic Gardens and the Ulster Museum. Fun, cheap bars and restaurants cater to the student hordes, and there's always a buzz in the area.

## Fast facts

**Journey time** Flight 40 minutes; train and ferry 14 hours
**Festivals & events** St Patrick's Day Parade and Concert (March, www.belfastcity.gov.uk/events) – celebrate St Patrick's Day with a carnival and concert of pop and traditional music; Belfast Titanic Maritime Festival (June, www.belfastcity.gov.uk/events) – spectacular ships from around the world sail into Belfast harbour for this popular celebration of Belfast's maritime heritage; Ulster Bank Belfast Festival at Queen's (October, www.belfastfestival.com) – international and Northern Ireland's art and culture
**Good for** Culture, food, history, nightlife

Titanic Belfast

## SEE & DO

Before you do anything, take an organised tour with **Black Cab Tours** (07990 955227, www.belfastblackcabtours.co.uk) or a similar firm. As well as helping you get oriented for the rest of the weekend, it will give you a chance to see the murals of the Falls and Shankill roads and other reminders of the Troubles in an otherwise much-glossied Belfast.

Once you've found your feet, use them. Start your walking tour at the **Botanic Gardens** (College Park, Botanic Avenue, 9031 4762, www.belfastcity.gov.uk) near Queen's University: an important part of Belfast's Victorian heritage. Established in 1828, it's a joy to wander around the rose gardens and tropical ravine. See rare trees such as the hornbeam-leafed oak tree, planted in the 1880s, and the well-kept array of exotic flowers in the Palm House – an 1839 masterpiece by Charles Lanyon and one of the earliest examples of a curvilinear cast-iron glasshouse.

Nearby is the **Ulster Museum** (Botanic Gardens, 0845 608 0000, www.nmni.com/um), a bright, spacious medley of history, art and science. Well-laid-out displays are spread across four floors, each with a 'discovery section' that invites visitors to handle artefacts. Highlights include the display on Ireland's recent history, exquisite ceramics and Indonesian shadow puppets – and Peter, the stuffed polar bear. Admission is free.

For contemporary art, go to **Ormeau Baths Gallery** (18A Ormeau Avenue, 9032 1402, www.ormeaubaths.co.uk) housed inside a redbrick Victorian building that used to be a swimming baths. Now the modern, white-walled spaces show a roster of work by local and international artists, making it one of Northern Ireland's leading art galleries. A few streets away is **St George's Market** (*see p136*). Belfast's last covered market is housed in a handsome redbrick and ironwork Victorian building.

Belfast Cathedral

Linen Hall Library

Cross over the Lagan Bridge to **Titanic Quarter**, an area of reclaimed land on Belfast's harbour (aka Queen's Island) that's been the focus of Belfast's recent regeneration. Due to open in 2012 for the centenary celebrations of the RMS *Titanic*, **Titanic Belfast** (Queen's Road, 9076 6399, www.titanicbelfast.com) is located on the slipways where the ship was built, and its fully interactive 'Titanic Experience' exhibition will extend over nine galleries, comprising high-spec special effects, rides and full-scale replicas of the interiors of the most famous ship in the world. A Titanic Walking Tour (2A Queen's Road, 0790 4350 339, www.titanicwalk.com) guides Titanoraks (the local nicknames for the new wave of tourist) along the slipways to an enormous pumphouse and the dry dock where the *Titanic* and *Olympia* ships were built. Tours are enthusiastic and detailed, and depart twice daily from outside the Premier Inn, Titanic Quarter.

Heading back towards the city centre, the Cathedral Church of St Anne – better known as **Belfast Cathedral** (Donegall Street, 9032 8332, www.belfastcatherdral.org) – has a beautiful mosaic roof above the baptistery. Close by, and equally reverential, is **Linen Hall Library** (17 Donegall Square, 09032 1707, www.linenhall.com). Founded in 1788, it's the oldest library in Belfast and, with its stairwell and high ceilings, has retained an air of grandeur and seriousness lacking from modern libraries. It holds free talks and lectures, hosts exhibitions and has a wonderful café overlooking Donegall Square, where old-fashioned tables are spread over two rooms. It has an unparalleled Irish studies collection.

## EAT & DRINK

Fine diners should make a reservation at **Deanes** (36-40 Howard Street, 9033 1134, www.michaeldeane.co.uk), bearer of the city centre's only Michelin Star and flagship of a fleet of Deane eateries around the city. Modern, classic and locally inspired dishes include loin of Fermanagh beef with braised daube, bordelaise jelly and creamed potato, and the three-course lunch menu is excellent value at £21.50. More informal – but equally celebrated – is **Mourne Seafood Bar** (34-36 Bank Street, 9024 8544, www.mourneseafood.com), where bowls of mussels, cockles

Mourne Seafood Bar

Made in Belfast

and oysters – sourced from Mourne's own shellfish beds in Carlingford Lough – are served with Mourne Oyster stout on wooden tables. A similar warehouse-type affair with fantastic food is **Nick's Warehouse** (35 Hill Street, 9043 9690, www.nickswarehouse.co.uk). It's long-established in the Cathedral Quarter and always busy, thanks to the vibrant, light-hearted food: a sweet-fleshed salmon fillet paired with a giant potato croquette and mussels, with a verdant pea dressing. Come to **Made in Belfast** (Wellington Street, 9024 6712, www.madeinbelfast.com) for quality food and decorative intrigue, with mismatched tables, chairs, lightshades and sofas. Walls are covered in newspapers, graffiti and mirrors, making for a relaxed atmosphere, in keeping with the homely menu of fishfinger sandwiches, beef pie and scallops with black pudding.

For drinking, you'll be spoilt for choice. Belfast's most beautiful pub is without question **Crown Bar** (46 Great Victoria Street, 9024 3187, www.crownbar.com) – of such historic importance that it's owned by the National Trust. Its interior is carved, coloured and mosaic-ed to perfection; much of the work was by Italian craftsmen who came to Ireland in the 1880s to build new Catholic churches. Ten carved wooden snugs are perfect for hours of cosy drinking, but nabbing one is a rare feat, as this popular pub has become something of a tourist destination. For a similarly glittering interior but without the throng of non-locals, the **Duke of York** (7-11 Commercial Court, 9024 1062) should satisfy any cravings for an authentic Belfast drinking experience. The interior is decorated with framed football programmes, mirrors advertising old whiskey brands and artefacts from Belfast's newspaper history, as well as a museum-worthy collection of rare whiskeys. The crowd is young and friendly. A few steps away, the **Spaniard** (3 Skipper Street, 9023 2448,

www.thespaniardbar.com) heaves with happy and hip drinkers: behind the paraphernalia hides an impressive array of interesting and characterful liqueurs, spirits and beers. It has a good rota of DJs spinning northern soul and rockabilly at the weekend; great tapas is served upstairs. (The Spaniard likes its crowd trendy, though, so make an effort or be prepared to be turned away.)

## SHOP

For gifts, head to Irish institution **Avoca** (41 Arthur Street, 9027 9050, www.avoca.ie), which stocks an extensive range of homeware, clothing, cutesy children's gifts and beauty products. Upstairs is a tempting food hall, deli and café. **St George's Market** (12-20 East Bridge Street, 9043 5704, www.belfastcity.gov.uk/markets) is one of Belfast's oldest and best attractions. On Fridays the Variety Market has hundreds of stalls selling everything from fresh fish to antiques to cupcakes. On Saturday, food's the main theme, with more fish on sale as well as cheeses, pickles, fruit and vegetables, while on Sunday there is an emphasis on arts and crafts.

The area around Botanic Gardens has some impressively bohemian small shops, such as clandestine and impossibly scruffy **Bookfinders** (47 University Road, 9032 82969), a delightful second-hand and antiquarian bookshop selling an interesting selection of modern first editions, poetry, history, and literature and art books. At the back there is a café heated by a Hotpoint gas oven and serving coffee, cakes and hot meals at low prices. In the evenings it turns into a restaurant with a BYO policy with ad hoc Bluegrass performances and poetry readings. One-off vintage bargains are to be had at the **Rusty Zip** (28 Botanic Avenue, 9024 9700, www.therustyzip.com), Belfast's oldest – and grooviest – vintage clothing emporium. Two floors of vintage wonders, fancy dress and retro accessories for both men and women have kept this store filled with hipster students since 1998.

**Merchant Hotel**

**Ten Square**

## STAY

The city centre has several upmarket hotels. Perhaps the most glamorous is the **Merchant Hotel** (14 Shipper Street, 9023 4888, www.themerchanthotel.com), a handsome Italianate sandstone building only a few steps away from the cathedral. It has 62 lavish bedrooms with bespoke furniture in either art deco or Victorian styles. There are three bars, a nightclub, and the top-notch Great Room restaurant serving Modern Irish cuisine. Recent additions include a rooftop terrace, gymnasium and spa. Similarly snazzy is **Fitzwilliam Hotel** (Great Victoria Street, 9044 2080, www.fitzwilliamhotelbelfast.com) with 130 smart rooms in muted colours; king-size beds come with crisp Egyptian linen. For a more boutique experience but with the same central location, **Ten Square** hotel (10 Donegall Square South, 9024 1001, www.tensquare.co.uk) makes a good alternative. Situated at the edge of Donegall Square overlooking City Hall, the Grade I-listed building has 23 slickly appointed bedrooms with leather furniture, contemporary wallpaper and large beds, and has recently been named the coolest hotel in Belfast.

## GETTING THERE & AROUND

Flights to Belfast International Airport from London are quick (around 40 minutes) and Aer Lingus, British Airways, BMI and EasyJet all run regular services, starting from £70 return. From the airport you can get a bus (Airport Express 300) to Belfast from directly outside the terminal. The buses depart every 15 minutes and journey time is approximately 40 minutes, depending on traffic. A taxi costs about £20 to the city centre. If you don't want to fly, SailRail tickets from London to Belfast via Glasgow cost as little as £49 return and take a day and a half – departing late at night from London, arriving at Glasgow early the next morning for a transfer to Ayr, then on to Cairnryan where a ferry runs to Belfast, arriving just in time for lunch. You certainly don't need a car to explore Belfast, in fact the twisted and narrow alleyways (many of them still cobbled) are difficult to navigate for even the most intrepid driver. The city is both compact and a pleasure to walk around, and cabs are relatively inexpensive.

BELFAST

HELSINKI
p190

STOCKHOLM
p193

COPENHAGEN
p177

HAMBURG
p158

BERLIN
p164

LONDON

AMSTERDAM
p151

COLOGNE
p207

BRUSSELS
p155

LUXEMBOURG
p147

NORMANDY
p197

PARIS
p140

VIENNA
p218

LIECHTENSTEIN
p168

BERGERAC
p162

MILAN
p145

AVIGNON
p174

NICE
p215

FLORENCE
p204

PORTO
p186

BARCELONA
p200

LISBON
p231

MADRID
p210

VALENCIA
p183

PALMA
p171

GRANADA
p221

PALERMO
p228

European Hops

# Paris

Chances are, if you live in Great Britain, and especially in London, you've been to Paris at least once before. So – how do you make a trip new, fresh and exciting? Follow us, is how. At the end of 2011, Time Out launched an online listings magazine in Paris (www.timeout.fr/paris), edited by local writers and published in both French and English. So we're better placed than ever to point Londoners to what's happening right now at the other end of the Eurostar line, while of course keeping tabs on those classic cafés, restaurants, galleries and boutiques. You could easily fill a weekend with safe bets, such as the Eiffel Tower, the Pompidou and the Louvre, and these are rewarding in obvious ways – but you might find 'your' Paris if you stray from the biggies for at least part of the weekend, wandering wherever your fancy takes you and exploring the distinctive *arrondissements* and *quartiers*. Below is a rich mix of inspirational arts and culture stops, historical landmarks and secret corners, and some very Parisian indulgences to enjoy when you need a sit-down after traipsing – sorry, flaneuring – down all those endless museum corridors and longer-than-they-looked boulevards.

## Fast facts

**Country dialling code** +33
**Journey time** Train 2 hours 15 minutes
**Festivals & events** Printemps du Cinéma (March, www.printempsducinema.com) – cut-price tickets at cinemas across the city for a three-day film bonanza; La Nuit des Musées (May, www.nuitdesmusees. culture.fr) – when museums open their doors late for one night, with special events; Festival d'Automne (September-December, www.festival-automne.com) – this major annual arts festival brings contemporary, challenging theatre, dance and modern opera to the city – with an emphasis on non-Western performance.
**Good for** Culture, food, history, shopping

## SEE & DO

No matter how hard we try, we've never quite nailed croissants in London, have we? So, since you've got at least two mornings to play with, go to **Arnaud Delmontel** (39 rue des Martyrs, 9th, 01 48 78 29 33, www.arnaud-delmontel.com) and to **Poîlane** (8 rue du Cherche-Midi, 6th, 01 45 48 42 59, www.poilane.com) to start each one with delicious, freshly baked bready things.

The city is highly walkable, so long as you choose your neighbourhood and stick to it. The Marais district is especially pleasant early in the mornings. It's also awash with cultural institutions: the **Musée Carnavalet** (23 rue de Sévigné, 3rd, 01 44 59 58 58, www.carnavalet.paris.fr) tells the history of Paris in chronological order through furniture, paintings, decor and prints, and the **Maison Européenne de la Photographie** (5-7 rue de Fourcy,

Louvre

Eiffel Tower

Jardin & Palais du Luxembourg

Le Meurice

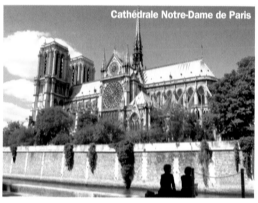
Cathédrale Notre-Dame de Paris

Printemps

4th, 01 44 78 75 00, www.mep-fr.org) is one of the city's best photography showcases (current exhibitions focus on Albania, Brazil and the work of William Klein). Neither get the queues you'll find at the mega-museums.

If you're planning on visiting the **Louvre** (rue de Rivoli, 1st, 01 40 20 50 50, www.louvre.fr), go early, right when it opens at 9am, and pre-book your ticket. For a front row view of the *Mona Lisa*, head straight to the Salle de la Joconde. It's best to see the Gothic posterchild **Cathédrale Notre-Dame de Paris** (place du Parvis-Notre-Dame, 4th, 01 42 34 56 10, www.cathedraledeparis.com) in the morning too. Make sure you climb up the towers and don't miss **La Conciergerie** (2 boulevard du Palais, 1st, 01 53 40 60 80), the medieval fortress where Robespierre, Danton and Marie-Antoinette were imprisoned. For the quintessential Paris park, wander airily through the **Jardin & Palais du Luxembourg** (place André Honnorat, 6th, 01 44 54 19 49, www.senat.fr/visite), which is full of sculptures, terraces, small sailing boats in the pond and old men playing chess.

For a panoramic view of Paris that doesn't involve climbing the Tour Eiffel, head to the **Parc des Buttes-Chaumont** (Rue Botzaris, 19th), a gorgeous 19th-century park with a lake, a belvedere and a waterfall. Alternatively, try the

**Institut du Monde Arabe** (1 rue Fossés-St-Bernard, 5th, 01 40 51 38 38, www.imarabe.org), which has an Oriental rooftop café affording fine views over the Seine – walk back into town from here if you want to do the classic riverbank thing.

Paris reigns supreme on decay and death and general romantic gloom, and in its trio of cemeteries you can do some thinking person's people-watching: the **Cimetière de Montmartre** (20 avenue Rachel, 18th, 01 53 42 36 30) houses the remains of Degas, Heine, Nijinsky and Truffaut, as well as La Goulue, the cancan star and model for Toulouse-Lautrec; the **Cimetière du Père-Lachaise** (boulevard de Ménilmontant, 20th, 01 55 25 82 10) 'has' Jim Morrison, Oscar Wilde and Marcel Proust; Sartre, Man Ray and Beckett are laid to rest at the **Cimetière du Montparnasse** (3 boulevard Edgar-Quinet, 14th, 01 44 10 86 50).

Stick with the Thanatos theme at the **Catacombes** (1 av du Colonel Henri Rol-Tanguy/place Denfert-Rochereau, 01 43 22 47 63, www.catacombes.paris.fr) – former quarry tunnels lined with the bones of more than six million Parisians. The remains were moved here in the 18th century, when the city's graveyards became insalubrious.

After all that underground exploring, you might well want to give the Métro a miss for a while. There are more than 400 kilometres of bike lanes, so a fun way to explore is via the 'Vélib' (www.velib.paris.fr), the inspiration for London's bike-hire scheme. More than 20,000 bikes are available 24 hours a day at some 1,500 Vélib stations. Finally, if you're planning on a museum-heavy trip, get yourself a **Paris Museum Pass** (www.paris museum

# Time Out

# We'll always have Paris...
# In our pockets

**Compiled by resident experts**
**Apps and maps work offline with no roaming charges**

Now FREE to download: London, New York, Paris, Manchester,
Barcelona, Berlin, Buenos Aires and Zagreb

**timeout.com/iphonecityguides**

Built by

pass.fr) for €32 for two days. It offers you access to more than 60 museums and attractions, including the Louvre and Musée d'Orsay.

Lastly, another spectacular view is to be seen after dark. The very best Paris panorama is found on the 56th floor of the **Tour Montparnasse** (avenue de Maine, 15th, 01 45 38 52 56, www.tourmontparnasse56.com), Paris's only inner-city skyscraper. From here, the whole capital (including the Eiffel Tower) unfurls before your feet in steely splendour. At night the world twinkles beneath you and the 'City of Lights' is no longer a cliché but an epiphany.

## EAT & DRINK

Lunch at Left Bank classic **La Palette** (34 rue de Seine, 6th, 01 43 26 68 15, www.cafelapaletteparis.com), an old zinc bar with a desperately romantic fresco-filled back room. It's a bar, café and bistro, serving croques monsieur and madame, beef tartare and caviar.

Have cocktails at **Le Forum** near Madeleine (4 boulevard Malesherbe, 8th, 01 42 65 37 86, www.bar-le-forum.com); indulge in a fruity, vanilla-laced Pornstar martini before you make your mind up about food. To sink a few trendy beers (after 7pm), try **L'Alimentation Générale** in Oberkampf (64 rue Jean-Pierre Timbaud, 11th, 01 43 55 42 50, www.alimentation-generale.net), where DJs spin tunes well into the night.

Come dinnertime, the aptly named **Frenchie** (5 rue du Nil, 2nd, 01 40 39 96 19, www.frenchie-restaurant.com) is run by Grégory Lemarchand, who trained with Jamie Oliver before opening this bistro. Try the gazpacho with calamari, and make sure you book in advance. **Le Meurice** (Hôtel Meurice, 228 rue de Rivoli, 1st, 01 44 58 10 55, www.meuricehotel.fr/hotel-paris) is a haze of chandeliers and gold, serving fancy and delicious dishes, such as clay-sealed turbot with celery cream or truffled sardalais potatoes.

The non-kitsch **Thai Thaïm** (46 rue de Richelieu, 1st, 01 42 96 54 67) is great for lunch – for a prix fixe of €16 you get three courses, with a choice of fish, poultry or meat each day. **Bistrot Victoires** (6 rue de la Vrillière, 1st, 01 42 61 43 78) is one for deal-lovers and is always filled with locals tucking into no-nonsense grub such as steak-frites or veal in cream sauce.

For a late-night meal, **La Tour de Montlhéry** (5 rue des Prouvaires, 1st, 01 42 36 21 82, open Mon-Fri), is perfect. Packed at midnight and open until 5am for even the hardest of partiers: try the stewed venison or rib steaks with chips. **L'Ambassade d'Auvergne** (22 rue du Grenier-St-Lazare, 3rd, 01 42 72 31 22, www.ambassade-auvergne.com) is good for a rustic meal, with cured hams, chunks of lamb in a meaty sauce and lentils cooked in goose fat.

## SHOP

First, the one-stop emporia and a couple of classics: **Le Bon Marché** (24 rue de Sèvres, 7th, 01 44 39 80 00, www.bonmarche.fr) is the city's oldest department store, housing most designers your fashion heart could desire (and the adjoining Grand Épicerie food hall is great for a lunchtime break). **Printemps** (64 boulevard Haussmann, 9th, 01 42 82 50 00, www.printemps.com) is great for fashion, too, both men's and women's, plus the assistants won't answer you with a blank stare if you ask them a question in English. Even if you're not planning on spending any money,

**Chanel** (31 rue Cambon, 1st, 01 42 86 28 00, www.chanel.com), **Louis Vuitton** (101 avenue des Champs-Elysées, 8th, 01 53 57 52 00, www.vuitton.com) and **Sonia Rykiel** (175 boulevard St-Germain, 6th, 01 49 54 60 60, www.soniarykiel.com) are worth visiting for the spectacle alone.

When it comes to boutiques, **AB33 & N°60** (33 & 60 rue Charlot, 3rd, 01 42 71 02 82) is great for unstructured garments, one-stop concept and lifestyle shop **Colette** (213 rue St-Honoré, 1st, 01 55 35 33 90, www.colette.fr) stocks everything from books to beauty products, and **L'Eclaireur** (40 rue Sévigné, 4th, 01 48 87 10 22, www.leclaireur.com) stocks some exclusive designer finds. **La Hune** (170 boulevard St-Germain, 6th, 01 45 48 35 85) is fab for specialist art and design books, plus it sells a large collection of French literature and theory.

Over in the second *arrondissement*, **Episode** (12-16 rue Tiquetonne, 2nd, 01 42 61 14 65) is an Aladdin's cave of vintage, offering a diverse selection of iconic brands and looks, from Levi 501s and Converse All Stars to 1950s

## An American in Paris: Disneyland

With two parks to explore – **Parc Disneyland** and the special-effects-focused **Parc Walt Disney Studios** – as well as the Village (restaurants, bars, nightclubs) and numerous hotels, this slice of Americana is an option for the kids if they're not overly impressed with seeing the *Mona Lisa* or sampling snails in garlic. The main Parc Disneyland is great for young kids, with the Cheshire Cat and wicked Queen of Hearts hiding away in Alice's Curious Labyrinth and cute automated toy soldiers and animals in the Small World attraction. Older kids and thrill-seeking adults will be happier on the Twilight Zone Tower of Terror, a high-altitude adrenalin ride in the Production Courtyard of the Studios park or on the megafast Rock 'n' Roller Coaster in the Back Lot. Afterwards – and definitely not before – tuck into the very un-French grub on offer: Tex Mex dishes come accompanied by a Wild West extravaganza at Buffalo Bill's Wild West Show in the Village.

Outside the hottest seasons, Disneyland Paris is always fun, but it's especially magical at Christmas and Halloween. Some Eurostar and many RER A suburban trains stop at Disneyland Paris, which is in Marne-la-Vallée, 32 kilometres east of Paris. For prices and information, call UK number 0870 503 0303 or visit www.disneylandparis.com.

dresses and biker jackets. **Andrea Crews** (25 rue de Vaucouleurs, 11th, 01 42 21 36 36) is a young art collective led by the designer Maroussia Rebecq, which creates playful, fun one-off pieces, all at affordable prices.

For the full Parisian market experience, head to the **Marché des Enfants Rouges** (39 rue de Bretagne, 3rd, 01 40 11 20 40), which runs from Tuesday to Sunday and whose lanes are lined with gourmet cheesemongers, florists and wine merchants. Finally, if you're still in need of a high fashion fix, head to **Merci** (111 boulevard Beaumarchais, 3rd, 01 42 77 00 33). It sells clothes from the likes of Isabel Marant and Stella McCartney, with an ethical stance – all its profits go to charity.

For English-language books – or just because you have read *Ulysses* and know the name – head to **Shakespeare & Company** (37 rue de la Bûcherie, 5th, 01 43 25 40 93, www.shakespeareandcompany.com). For pretty much anything your literary heart could desire, from second-hand to antiquarian, its stock is quite remarkable.

Mama Shelter

## Cultural baggage

**Book** *Parisians: An Adventure History of Paris* (Graham Robb, 2010)
**Film** *Un Témoin dans la Ville* (Edouard Molinaro, 1959)
**Album** *Fréhel 1930-1930* (2000)

## NIGHTLIFE

Some say that Paris la nuit has lost its mojo but there's actually plenty to keep you bopping till sunrise, beginning with **Silencio** (142 rue Montmartre, 2nd, www.silencio-club.com), opened in October 2011 by none other than David Lynch. It's a semi-private club, located beneath the Social Club (where music-savvy night-owls have been flocking for years), open to the public after midnight, with a line-up of DJs, film projections and artistic happenings.

For an absinthe cocktail in a former 19th-century bordello, try **Le Carmen** (34 rue Duperré, 9th, 01 45 26 50 00, www.le-carmen.fr), where live music and DJ nights also add to the entertainment. A stream of top-notch electro acts perform at **La Machine du Moulin Rouge** (right next door to the famous Cabaret, 90 boulevard de Clichy, 18th, 01 53 41 88 89, www.lamachinedumoulinrouge.com), or for Paris-style clubbing, live it up with everything from disco and house, to punk, hip hop and electro-pop at **Rex Club** (5 boulevard Poissonnière, 2nd, 01 42 36 01 96, www.rexclub.com).

## STAY

If you'd rather spend your money on baguettes than beds, there are several budget hotels to choose from (though it's unlikely you'll pay much less than €100 per night unless you're staying in a youth hostel). **Mama Shelter** (109 rue de Bagnolet, 20th, 01 43 48 48 48, www.mamashelter.com) was designed by Philippe Starck, with Marvel comic light fittings. **Hôtel les Degrés de Notre-Dame** (10 rue des Grand-Degrés, 5th, 01 55 42 88 88, www.lesdegreshotel.com) is in a lovely location – ask for rooms 47 or 501 for a view of the cathedral. Boutique hotel **Five Hôtel** (3 rue Flatters, 5th, 01 43 31 74 21, www.thefivehotel.com) is slightly more expensive but also snazzier, with fibre optics in the walls to make you feel like you're sleeping under a starry sky and a choice of four fragrances to perfume the rooms. Also slightly more expensive but still moderately priced is the charming **Hôtel de la Sorbonne** (6 rue Victor-Cousin, 5th, 01 43 54 58 08, www.hotelsorbonne.com), with bold design, carpets with quotes from French literature and an iMac in every room.

If money ain't a problem, however, there are two particularly good bets. **Le Meurice** (228 rue de Rivoli, 1st, 01 44 58 10 10, www.lemeurice.com) is the ultimate in luxury, with Louis XVI decor, jazz performances in the Winter Garden, a restaurant with three Michelin Stars and the Swiss Valmont spa. While **Le Metropolitan** (10 place de Mexico, 16th, 01 56 90 40 04, www.radissonblu.com) holds the trump of all Paris hotel cards – views of the Eiffel Tower. You also get oak floors, a cocktail bar, marble baths, a hammam and a great breakfast buffet.

## GETTING THERE & AROUND

The Eurostar (www.eurostar.com) is the most hassle-free way of getting to Paris from London. The journey takes 2 hours 15 minutes on the non-stop trains and, if you book in time, could be as cheap as £69 return.

Once in Paris, the Métro (www.ratp.fr/en) is your best bet for navigating the city swiftly. The city also has over 400 kilometres of bike lanes snaking through it, with the Vélib scheme (www.velib.paris.fr) – Paris's equivalent to London's Boris bikes – providing the vehicles.

# Milan

Milan means three things to most people: finance, fashion and football. As the business capital, it's often overlooked in favour of Florence, Venice or Rome. But for many Italians, especially northerners, this city is Italy's true heart. Home to da Vinci's *Last Supper*, Caravaggio's *Basket of Fruit*, La Scala opera house, the Duomo and lots of impressive Baroque and 19th-century neoclassical architecture – not to mention some of the world's best cafés and many of Italy's finest restaurants – Milan really is a cultural powerhouse. That said, you won't ever have to search too long for a D&G, Armani or Versace store, and you'll have to plan far in advance if you want a ticket for a derby at the San Siro Stadium. Don't go if you're looking for a fresh breath of mountain air, as the city is notorious for its smog. But that really is the only downside to visiting Milan, which is in many ways unlike any other Italian destination.

## Fast facts

**Country dialling code** +39
**Journey time** Flight 1 hour 55 minutes; train 11 hours 25 minutes
**Festivals & events** Salone Internazionale del Mobile – Milan's huge, high-profile furniture fair (April, www.cosmit.it); La Notte Bianca – when, for one night, bars, restaurants, shops, cinemas et al whoop it up from early evening to 6am (June, www.comune.milano.it); Settimana dei Beni Culturali – cultural heritage week (early spring, www.beniculturali.it)
**Good for** Food, culture, shopping

Galleria Vittorio Emanuele II

## SEE & DO

It's easy to fill a day in Milan without a guided tour or even the use of public transport. Start off your morning in the **Parco Sempione** (at the metro Cadorna, Cairoli or Lanza), one of the city's rare parks, where even the most sweaty local jogger still manages to look stylish. Head to **Pinacoteca di Brera** (via Brera 28, 02 722 631, www.brera.beniculturali.it) to take in works by Caravaggio and Modigliani, followed by a visit to Milan's cultural icon, **il Duomo** (Piazza del Duomo, 02 7202 2656), the third largest cathedral in the world. Head to the top in the lift for the best views of the city. Also check out nearby church **Santa Maria presso San Satiro** (Via Torino 19, 02 874 683) with all its trompe l'oeil apse glory. It would be a waste of a journey to leave Milan without seeing *Il Cenacolo* – da Vinci's *The Last Supper* – which you'll find in the western part of the city at **Santa Maria delle Grazie** (piazza Santa Maria delle Grazie, 02 4676 1123, www.grazieop.it), and for which you'll need to reserve a timed, 15-minute slot in advance. Even if you're not the world's biggest football fan, the 85,000-seater **San Siro Stadium** (Stadio Giuseppe Meazza, piazzale dello Sport 1, 02 404 2432, www.sansirotour.com) is definitely worth a visit. The museum and tours are both interesting, but the real spectacle is an AC Milan or Inter Milan match; if you're lucky enough to nab tickets, don't sit in either of the team's end zones, Curva Nord or Curva Sud – you won't know what 'hardcore fans' truly

means until you've experienced them here; we're talking non-stop standing, non-stop chants and the occasional missile.

## EAT & DRINK

Don't expect to return from Milan a few pounds lighter from all the sightseeing you'll be doing – the Milanese know and love their food. For at least one of your meals, do like the Italians and order an *antipasto* (starter), a *primo* (mainly pasta, fish or risotto), a *secondo* (meat or fish), a *contorno* (veggie side dish), and a dessert, fruit or cheese platter, followed by a grappa. Steer clear from fixed-price meals or places advertising a *menu turistico*, as you won't find any locals eating there. Instead, head to **13 Giugno** (via Goldoni 44, 02 719 654, www.ristorante13giugno.it) for

13 Giugno

Il Duomo

Vietnamonamour

## SHOP

Milan is fashionable – at times painfully so. If you stayed longer than a weekend, you'd soon become blasé about the many model-level lookers roaming about.

Many shops still close on Sundays and some also close between 12.30pm and 3.30pm during the week. Sales take place in January and July. For savvy outlet shopping, go to **Il Salvagente** (via Fratelli Bronzetti 16, 02 7611 0328, www.salvagentemilano.it), three floors of men's and women's fashion, arranged by both size and colour, or the more central **Dmagazine Outlet** (via Montenapoleone 26, 02 7600 6027, www.dmagazine.it), with some designer items priced at 80% off their original price. **10 Corso Como Outlet** (via Tazzoli 3, 02 2901 5130) is good for (mainly black) designer gear by the likes of Chloé and Helmut Lang. **Galleria Vittorio Emanuelle II** (between piazza del Duomo and piazza del Scala) is open 24 hours a day and known as Milan's living room. Sure, you might pay €10 for a cappuccino, but it houses all of the fashion retail bigwigs, and the intricate designs and grand architecture alone are worth visiting.

## STAY

**Petit Palais** (via Molino delle Armi 1, 02 584 891, www.petit palais.it) is exquisite, with Murano chandeliers and crystal wine glasses, located a 15-minute walk from the city centre. **Ariston** (largo Carrobbio 2, 02 7200 0556, www.ariston hotel.com) is for eco-fiends, decked out with energy-efficient lightbulbs, water-saving showers and organic food, plus free use of the hotel's bicycles. If you're travelling on a budget, **Hotel Aspromonte** (piazza Aspromonte, 02 236 1119, www.hotelaspromonte.it) is friendly, tidy and has its own garden. Another less expensive option is **Vietnamonamour** (via Pestalozzo 7, 02 7063 4614, www.vietnamonamour.com), an Italian-Vietnamese concept B&B with hardwood floors and South-east Asian decor, with breakfast (in the private garden) including fresh orange juice, bananas and mangos.

## GETTING THERE & AROUND

If booked far enough in advance, the no-frills airlines will take you to Milan Bergamo, Somma Lombarda or Milan Linate airports for under £50 return. In Milan, public transport (www.atm-mi.it) is fairly safe, but watch out for pickpockets on busy buses subways. The three metro lines run until 12.30am and there is no public transport whatsoever between 2.30am and 6am, so be prepared to pay for a cab if you're out late. Italians are famed for their crazed driving, so cycling isn't for the weak, though the recent introduction of cycle paths and expansion of pedestrianisation have made travelling by bike much easier than it was ten years ago. See www.ciclolobby.it and www.arciquartiere.org for bike tours.

Sicilian seafood in a gentleman's-club atmosphere, or **La Picolla Ischia** (viale Umbria 60, 02 5410 7410, www.piccolaischia.it) for one of the town's best pizza joints – the *pizza all'ischitana* is fantastic, laden with provolone, rocket, fresh tomatoes and grana shavings. **Antica Trattoria della Pesa** (viale Pasubio 10, 02 655 5741) is best for (very) traditional Milanese food, while **Fioraio Bianchi** (via Montobello 7, 02 2901 4390) is so romantic and delicious it makes up for the higher pricing.

### Cultural baggage

**Book** *Duca and the Milan Murders* (Giorgio Scerbanenco, 1970)
**Film** *Miracolo a Milano* (*Miracle in Milan*, Vittorio de Sica, 1951)
**Album** *Il tuo bacio è come un rock* (Adriano Celentano, 1959)

# Luxembourg

Luxembourg is primarily known for three things: castles, banks and booze. It's so small that the country's full name doesn't fully fit on most maps of Europe, and a weekend is plenty of time to get to know the capital (take Monday off and you can conquer the whole country). For such a small place, it still manages to be topographically diverse, and while it's certainly fairytale-esque, it's really the juxtaposition of farmland and medieval castles that makes it such a lovely place. Most tourists come in the summer; it's hot between May and August. If you're coming for the wine, visit in the autumn, when the Moselle Valley harvest celebrations take place. Spring is less tourist-laden, plus you'll also get to see some great flora and fauna. The national motto sums up the proud atmosphere of the area: *Mir wëlle bleiwe wat mir sin* ('We want to remain what we are'). Luxembourg's residents are said to go to bed earlier than most of their European neighbours, but below is plenty to fill two or three not-too-sleepy days.

As you're reading this chapter, chances are you don't speak Letzeburgesch, but you should be fine if you speak either French or German (both the languages of administration in the country).

## Fast facts

**Country dialling code** +352
**Journey time** Flight 1 hour 20 minutes from Heathrow; train 4 hours 45 minutes (via Brussels); car 7 hours
**Festivals & events** Printemps Musical (March-May, www.printempsmusical.lu); Blues'n Jazzrallye (July, www.bluesjazzrallye.lu); Summer in the City (June-September, www.summerinthecity.lu)
**Good for** Food

## SEE & DO

Luxembourg City was built on a promontory, so the views of the surrounding valleys and forests are spectacular; walk along **Chemin de la Corniche** to take it in. Luxembourg City's fortress, built in 1744, has since been (mostly) dismantled, but the citadel within, dating right back to 936, can still partly be seen. The foundations underneath the castle were excavated and a 23-kilometre network of tunnels, the **Bock Casemates** (Montée de Clausen Clausen, 22 28 09, open Mar-Oct) were built. Over the years they've been used to shelter soldiers, as an

Vianden

Grand-Duc Jean Musée d'Art Moderne

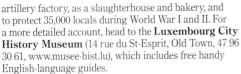

Hotel Albert Premier

Apoteca

artillery factory, as a slaughterhouse and bakery, and to protect 35,000 locals during World War I and II. For a more detailed account, head to the **Luxembourg City History Museum** (14 rue du St-Esprit, Old Town, 47 96 30 61, www.musee-hist.lu), which includes free handy English-language guides.

The **Palais Grand-Ducal** (17 rue du Marché-aux-Herbes, Old Town, 22 28 09, open July-Sept) should be pretty high up on your things-to-do list. Built during the Spanish rule in 1570, it was once a royal residence but has since been downgraded to an office for the Grand Duke and location for formal receptions. Visit the **Grand-Duc Jean Musée d'Art Moderne** (3 Parc Dräi Eechelen, Clausen, 45 37 85 22,

www.mudam.lu), Luxembourg's Modern Art Museum, created by the same architect who designed the Louvre pyramid, Ieoh Ming Pei. You'll find everything from fashion to photos and multimedia. Close to the museum is the **Philharmonie** (1 place de l'Europe, Clausen, 26 32 26 32, www.philharmonie.lu), which could absolutely hold its own against other great concert halls of the world, though the design is highly modern, looking like a gigantic white UFO.

If you're looking to venture out a little further, the town of **Vianden**, to the north of Luxembourg City, is probably the country's most romantic spot. To the south of the capital lies the vineyard-laden **Moselle Valley**. The 1,000-year-old **Château de Bourscheid** (1 Schlasswee, 99 05 70), between Esch and Ettelbrück, makes you feel like you've walked straight into an old Germanic fairytale, overlooking the Sûre River and surrounding farmland.

## EAT & DRINK

Since Luxembourg is only about 80 kilometres long and 60 kilometres wide, an adventurous weekend traveller could set out to have breakfast in Deutschland, lunch in France and dinner in Belgium. Fortunately, the capital, Luxembourg, has fabulous cuisine of its own, so you don't need to.

According to Luxembourg's tourism office, the country has more Michelin-starred restaurants per capita than anywhere else in the world. The local cuisine mixes hearty German with richly flavoured French, as exemplified by the national dish: *judd mat gaardebounen* – smoked pork with a thick cream-based sauce with potatoes and broad beans. Other popular dishes are prepared with liver, spare ribs and sauerkraut. Drink the great, fruity white and sparkling local wines (quality-labelled 'Marque Nationale du Vin Luxembourgeois'), of course, but don't ignore the beer – Diekirch, Bofferding, Simon Pils and Mousel are all worth an exploratory pint.

**Apoteca** (12 rue de la Boucherie, 26 73 77, www. apoteca.lu) serves traditional food; try the smoked pork neck in beans. Right behind the Cathédrale Notre Dame sits the Michelin-starred **Clairefontaine** (place de Clairefontaine 9, 46 22 11), serving rich dishes made with venison, truffle sauces and lobster. **Maison des Brasseurs** (Grande Rue, 41 371) serves the classics, from *coq au Riesling* to *choucroute garnie* (sauerkraut with sausages). Three kilometres from the city centre, **L'Agath** (route de Thionville 274, Howald, Hesperange, 48 86 87) is pricey, but the wine list and seven-course menu are arguably worth the splurge.

**Cantine Mousel** (montée de Clausen 46, 47 01 98) does great Luxembourgeois dishes using cuts of pork, veal and wild boar, often served with dumplings.

## STAY

The antique-filled, 14-room boutique **Hotel Albert Premier** (2A rue Albert 1er, 44 244 21, www.albet1er.lu), is just five minutes from the centre and close to a nice park. **Hôtel Casanova** (10 place Guillaume II, Old Town, 22 04 93, www.hotelcasanova.lu) is also in a good spot, near to the cathedral and in the middle of the pedestrian district, though the hotel itself is less exciting. The lavish **Grand Hotel Cravat** (29 boulevard Roosevelt, Old Town, www. hotelcravat.lu) is again in a fantastic location and known for its good customer service.

## GETTING THERE & AROUND

Take the Eurostar to either Brussels or Paris. Trains from Brussels to Luxembourg take 2 hours 45 minutes. Trains from Paris take a bit longer and cost a bit more.

Luxembourg Airport (www.lux-airport.lu) lies six kilometres east of the capital.

If you're travelling by car, wait to fill up your tank until you've arrived – petrol prices are comparatively low here.

Public transport in Luxembourg is fairly comprehensive, though it doesn't cover everything. If you're planning on sightseeing extensively outside of the capital, you'll probably need to mix trains and buses. Check the **Nationale des Chemins de Fer Luxembourgeois** (www.cfl.lu) for timetables and fares. The **Luxembourg Card** (www.ont.lu/card-en) gives you unlimited access to public transport plus discounts on admission to museums and other attractions.

LUXEMBOURG

# THE CURRENCY EXCHANGE EXPERTS

## BUY YOUR EUROS WITH GWK TRAVELEX AND GET THE BEST DEAL.

**BRANCHES IN AMSTERDAM CITY CENTER**

- CENTRAL STATION • VICTORIA HOTEL • DAMRAK 86
- LEIDSESTRAAT 103 • LEIDSEPLEIN 31A
- KALVERSTRAAT 150

**BRANCHES AT THE AIRPORT**
- SCHIPHOL PLAZA (ARRIVAL HALL 3)
- SCHIPHOL (LOUNGE 1 - GATES B/C)

# Amsterdam

Amsterdam is one of those cities that can be adapted to your desires. If you're looking for a weekend of drugs and sex, you've got it – though the coffeeshops no longer serve booze, and smoking – cigarettes or joints – is only allowed alfresco these days. If you want art and culture, not a problem. And if you're a foodie or a retail addict, you can satisfy those urges too. It's easy, however, to forget how charmingly green this city really is, so, once you've breezed through the Red Light District, snapped some tulips and munched on some cheese, leave some time to walk slowly through this beautiful, easygoing and history-rich world city. Amsterdam's cobbled streets and meandering canals – granted UNESCO World Heritage status in 2010 – can be as confusing as Venice is for a first-timer, so to get your bearings, you may want to join a bike tour. If you do get lost, most Amsterdammers speak English and are usually happy to help. Mix and match this city and give it time to grow on you: it doesn't have to be hedonism versus history – you can go for a little of both.

## Fast facts

**Country dialling code** +31
**Journey time** Flight 1 hour 10 minutes;
train 4 hours 40 minutes; car 6 hours
**Festivals & events** Realisme Art Fair (January,
www.realismeamsterdam.com); Queensday (30 April,
www.queensdayamsterdam.eu); 5 Days Off Amsterdam
(March, www.5daysoff.nl); Vondelpark Open Air Theatre
(June-August, www.openluchttheater.nl)
**Good for** Culture
For more information see www.iamsterdam.com/en
and www.timeout.com/amsterdam

## SEE & DO

The canalside **Anne Frank House** (Prinsengracht 263-367, (0)20 556 7100, www.annefrank.org) looks unassuming from the outside, but once inside you'll soon see the famous bookcase marking the entrance to the former hideaway on the top floor. Many tourists come to Amsterdam just to see the house (a million every year, apparently), so make sure you get there for 9am if you want to avoid long queues – and buy your tickets online in advance.

Within the **Museum Quarter** (Museumplein), the **Rijksmuseum** (Hobbemastraat 21, (0)20 674 7000, www.rijksmuseum.nl), opened in 1885, owns an impressive 40 Rembrandts and four beautiful Vermeers. Don't miss Rembrandt's *Night Watch* and Vermeer's *Kitchen Maid*

# COME AND JOIN US TO EAT OR DRINK IN THE RESTAURANT OR BY OUR WATERSIDE BAR.

Visit the Rock Shop and purchase one of our limited edition city tees. We are situated in the heart of the city centre.

For reservations and group bookings please contact: amsterdam_sales@hardrock.com

**MAX EUWEPLEIN 57-61, 1017 MA AMSTERDAM**
**+31 20 5237625 • HARDROCK.COM**

and *Woman Reading a Letter*. Also in the quarter, the **Van Gogh Museum** (Paulus Potterstraat 7, (0)20 570 5200, www.vangoghmuseum.nl) has no fewer than 200 paintings and 500 drawings on show, including various self-portraits and the famous sunflowers. If you're travelling with children, both museums offer treasure hunts and audio tours. For something less highbrow, head to the **Heineken Experience** (Stadhouderskade 78, (0)20 523 9666, www.heineken experience.com); a flashy tour of the former brewery includes a free beer and a virtual reality ride in which you are the Heineken bottle.

It's not necessarily a good thing to shy away from clichés in Amsterdam. Shoe fetishists and fans of carpentry might be charmed by the clog-making museum, **Klompenmakerij De Zaanse Schans** (Schansend 7, (0)20 075 681 0000, www.zaanseschans.nl). Other clichéd but enjoyable experiences are buying tulips at the **Bloemenmarkt** (Singel 610-616, (0)20 625 8282, www.keesbevaart.nl) along the Singel, and stocking up on cheese at **Wegewijs** (Rozengracht 32, (0)20 62 44 093, www.wegewijs.nl), which has over 150 different kinds on offer. Check out the most famous of Amsterdam's eight windmills, **De Gooyer** (Funenkade 5), which is right next to the oldest operational brewery in town, **Brouwerij 't IJ** (Funenkade 7, (0)20 622 8325, www.brouwerijhetij.nl).

After dark, classical fans might want to try to catch a performance at the gigantic **RAI Theater** (Europaplein 8-22, (0)20 549 1212, www.raitheater.nl), which moonlights as an exhibition and convention centre during the day and shows ballets, musicals and operas at night. **Trouw** (Wibautstraat 131, (0)20 463 7788, www.trouwamsterdam. nl) is the place for electronica, house and underground dance fans. The club also has a restaurant catering for late-night diners. Alternatively, head to **OT301** (Overtoom 301, (0)20 779 4913, www.ot301.nl), the former squat turned film school that now hosts nights such as 'Matjesdisco' (mullet disco!) and electronic new-wave night 'Pop Wave 301', and serves a range of cheap bottled beers.

## EAT & DRINK

Go for a local *biertje* (beer) at 1930s café **'t Blauwe Theehuis** (Vondelpark 5, (0)20 662 0254, www.blauwe theehuis.nl), with its big terrace in the middle of Vondelpark

**Eden Hotel**

**Anne Frank House**

– perfect for people-watching. The park itself is great for a blanket and book, but if you're in the rose garden you might want to set your phone alarm to wake you up before dusk – after dark, public sex is tolerated. You don't have to worry about seeing any bare behinds during the daytime, however.

Cheap and cheerful **Nam Kee** (Zeedijk 111-113, (0)20 639 2848, www.namkee.net), in Amsterdam's Chinatown,

Trouw

Van Gogh Museum

Bazar

has a devoted following, and rightly so; try the oysters in black bean sauce. Former church **Bazar** (Albert Cuypstraat 182, (0)20 639 2848, www.bazaramsterdam.nl), a bit kitsch but fun, serves good and attractively priced North African food. The residential De Pijp district in the south-east is perfect for a wind-down beer, while Nieuwmarkt, on the Old Side, is great for outdoors drinking when it's warm. For a dairy fix, visit **De Kaaskelder** (Singel 518, www.cheesefarms.com), a cheese cellar that stocks goudas galore.

## SHOP

Amsterdam isn't one of those cities that you might visit purely to go shopping – which doesn't mean that you'll have a hard time finding places where you can be relieved of a good amount of cash. The area known as the **Nine Streets** (www.theninestreets.com) is ideal for vintage shopping, mainly showcasing 1970s and '80s clobber, but also featuring some high-end boutiques. **Kalverstraat** (www.kalverstraat.nl) is a one-kilometre pedestrian area of shops, the busiest (and most expensive) shopping street in town. **De Bijenkorf** (Dam 1, Old Centre: New Side, 0900 0919, www.debijenkorf.nl) is Amsterdam's best-known department store, with a great household goods area and a good mix of clothing, plus a top-floor 'Chill Out' area, which caters to the coolest of young folk.

## STAY

Amsterdam suits most budgets, offering accommodation in the form of good, clean hostels, upmarket boutique hotels and apartment rentals suited to longer stays. The **Flying Pig** (Vossiusstraat 46, (0)20 428 4934, www.flyingpig.nl) hostel, opposite Vondelpark, is well located and ideal if you just want a place to crash after a long day out. If you're planning on spending more – and a bit more time in the room – **Eden Hotel** (Amstel 144, (0)20 530 7878, www.edenhotelamsterdam.com) is smarter, and has a fantastic view of the Amstel. If you're with a larger group, you could try one of the many apartment rental agencies, such as **Stay Amsterdam** ((0)20 808 0790, www.stayamsterdam.com).

## GETTING THERE & AROUND

It's just over an hour's flight from London Stansted and Luton to Schiphol (add on an extra ten minutes for Gatwick and Heathrow), so getting to Amsterdam may well cost you less time (and less money if you book in advance) than a UK break. There is a boat-train service from Liverpool Street Station via Harwich, as well as the Eurostar service via Brussels, which takes between 4-6 hours.

There are 600,000 bicycles on the streets of Amsterdam. If you're not a regular cyclist but still want to do as the 'dammers do, try an organised cycle tour, such as **MacBike's City Bike Tour** (Nieuwe Uilenburgerstraat 114, (0)20 428 7005, www.macbike.nl), which lasts between two and four hours. Pedalos are an equally enjoyable, albeit slightly slower way of getting around town. **Canal Bike** (0900 333 4442, www.canal.nl) rents out its snazzy pedalos from various locations. The **OV-chipkaart** (www.gvb.nl), similar to London's Oyster Card, gives you unlimited access to trams, buses and metro.

# Brussels

The journey from St Pancras International to Bruxelles-Midi takes less than two hours – that's faster than a trip to Paris and, some would argue, far better value and more original as a choice for a weekend escape. After flitting through the Kentish countryside and Pas de Calais, the train turns north-east to speed through *le plat pays*, the legendary flat land, with church steeples and tree crowns popping up aplenty. Once in Brussels, it can be hard to focus on anything but food, as the Belgians love their cuisine (and rightly so), but after a waffle with chocolate sauce or a few truffles, put on a comfortable pair of shoes and get walking. Although sometimes painted as dull and boring – the presence of the European Commission in various parts of the city doesn't help – the Belgian capital in fact has many quirky corners and some interestingly bohemian areas worth exploring. If you're going for a long weekend, you can also include half-day trips to either artsy, nightlife-loving Antwerp or posh, pretty Bruges.

## Fast facts

**Country dialling code** +32
**Journey time** Flight 1 hour 10 minutes; train 2 hours; car 4 hours 30 minutes
**Festivals & events** ArtisanArt (November, www.artisanart.be); Public Brewing sessions (November, www.cantillon.be); Brussels Antiques & Fine Arts fairs (January, www.brafa.be); Culinaria (May, www.culinariasquare.com); Brussels Gay Pride (May, www.blgp.be); Fête de la Musique (June, www.conseildelamusique.be)
**Good for** Culture, food

Grand Place

## SEE & DO

The city centre, the **Lower Town** area, is pleasingly walkable. The **Grand Place**, now a UNESCO World Heritage Site, was once described by French writer Victor Hugo as 'the most beautiful square in the world', and is where first-timers should start their weekend journey. The architecture around the square is impressively grandiose, in particular the **Town Hall** (Grand Place, 2 279 2343) and the **guildhalls**. Built after 4,000 properties were destroyed during the French bombardment in 1695 during the Nine Years' Wars, the guildhalls are each adorned with gold-coloured statues relating to the relevant trades – so, a gable for the boats men, hops plants for the brewer. Be sure to take a look at those on nos.1-2, Le Roi d'Espagne, a pub with Spanish King Charles II's bust on its façade. No.5, La Louve (the she-wolf), is also particularly noteworthy, with a phoenix on its top; while no.26, Le Pigeon, is the artists' guild where Victor Hugo stayed in his exile in 1852. Get the anti-climactic bronze statue of the **Manneken-Pis** (Stoofstraat 46, 2 502 7145, www.mannekenpis.be) ticked off if you must and then head to the **Belgian Comic Strip Centre** (rue des Sables 20, 2 219 1980, www.comicscenter.net) to meet Belgium's other famous fictitious son: **Tintin**. There's a Lucky Luke area, complete with Western swing doors, Smurf statues, a large collection of original sketches and drawings by Belgian artists, plus an extensive comic book shop.

On a Sunday morning, head south-west to the **Midi Market**, around Gare du Midi, one of Europe's biggest markets (450 stalls), where you'll find everything from clothes to food to flowers.

The **Upper Town** area, sandwiched between the Lower Town and EU Quarter, is the neoclassical, stately and museum-heavy area of town. Certainly have a look at the **Magritte Museum** (place Royale 1, 2 508 32 11, www.musee-magritte-museum.be), ordered chronologically from the third floor down to the ground, with each floor representing a different period in René Magritte's life. Anyone remotely interested in classical music will enjoy the **Musée des Instruments de Musique** (rue Montagne de la Cour 2, 2 545 0130, www.mim.be), housing the world's largest collection of instruments with over 6,000 varieties; plus, there are regular free music events, and the top-floor restaurants offers great views of the city below.

## EAT & DRINK

Foodie fact fans will be glad to hear that Belgian restaurants won 114 Michelin Stars in 2010, more per capita than France, and that the city has more than 2,000 restaurants and counting. Of course it needn't all be posh – don't leave this city without having at least one portion of *moules-frites*, mussels and chips, a national favourite. Just as important as eating is drinking – beer, in particular.

Over 600 varieties of beer are brewed in Belgium; most bars serve 20 different kinds, others stock over 200.

As far as value for money goes, try **Le Cirio** (rue de la Bourse 18, 2 512 1395), a café named after an Italian grocer (complete with pre-war toilets); it's also great for people-watching while sipping a *half-en-half*, part sparkling and part still wine. **Divino** (rue des Chartreux 56, 2 503 3909, www.restodivino.be) is a retro-minimalist Italian restaurant that serves oversized and tasty goat's cheese and parma ham pizzas, while **Thiên-Long** (Arteveldestraat 12, 2 511 3480) is an outlandishly decorated Vietnamese restaurant where meals are generously proportioned and delicious. Also included on your culinary to-do list should be **Le Cap Sablon** (Lebeaustraat 75, 2 512 0170), a simple, art deco brasserie serving homely Modern European cuisine, such as roasts and grills and large wicked desserts.

If you want to go native, **Belga Queen** (Wolvengracht 32, 2 217 2187, www.belgaqueen.be) will cater to your Belgian blowout needs. Occupying a one-time bank building adorned with a stained-glass skylight and original pillars, it's best known for its seafood platters and oyster bar – don't let the transparent doors of the unisex toilets put you off.

And, for classic *moules-frites*, either head to the no-nonsense **Bij den Boer** (quai aux Briques 60, 2 512 6122, www.bijdenboer.com) or **La Roue d'Or** (rue des Chapeliers 26, 2 514 2554, www2.resto.be/rouedor) for slightly chunkier chips.

Beer fans should grab a pint or five at **Chez Moeder Lambic Fontainas** (place Fontainas 8, 2 503 6068, www.moederlambic.eu/sitebar), which serves 40 draughts (and a good selection of wines) in an old townhouse. The aptly named **Délirium Café** (impasse de la Fidélité Carmes 4A, 2 514 4434, www.deliriumcafe.be) serves 2,000 Belgian and international beer varieties; ask the friendly staff if you have any queries, but do keep an eye on the alcohol content of the beers if you don't want to be carried home.

## SHOP

You may be tempted to spend all of your shopping dosh on beers and chocolates, but the boutiques aren't to be overlooked. While Grand Place is tourist trap-heavy, you don't have to walk too far for the proper goodies. The **Galleries Royales St-Hubert** (1000 City of Brussels, 2 513 8940, www.galeries-saint-hubert.com), Europe's first arcade, built in 1847, is worth a visit. **Place du Jeu de Balle** (open daily from 7am to 2pm), in the bohemian Marolles district, is the place for flea market fiends. Vendors spread out their stock – of varying value and quality – on sheets on the floor. Get there around 6am, which is when the vendors unpack and the pros lurk about – Tuesday is considered the best day but it's packed with goodies on weekends too.

The **Musée du Cacao et du Chocolat** (Guldenhoofdstraat 9, 2 514 2048, www.mucc.be) at the Grand Place should give you a hint as to how big a part of the culture chocolate is for the Belgians. Try the **Leonidas** chain (rue au Beurre 34, 2 223 1745, www.leonidas.com), originally named after a Greek man in 1913, for various kinds of pralines sold by weight, meaning you can mix and match as you please. Alternatively, walk over to the Sablon area and visit **Pierre Marcolini** (rue des Minimes 1, 2 514 12 06, www.marcolini.be), which opened 12 years ago and is expanding fast (with stores in London, Paris, Tokyo and New York). It's famous for its Earl Grey and chocolate and cream ganache fillings with spices.

## STAY

Considering its size, Brussels has a large number of hotels. Around the Grand Place, **Hotel Amigo** (rue de l'Amigo 1-3, 2 547 4747, www.hotelamigo.com) has elegant and comfortable-sized rooms, with wood-heavy decor and traditional tapestries – you'd never guess it used to be a prison. The stylish **Hotel Orts** (Auguste Ortsstraat 38-40,

# Trips out of town: Bruges and Antwerp

Only 40 minutes by train from Brussels, **Antwerp** is known for its Rubens, diamonds, architecture, food, fashion and clubbing.

During the day, the **Grote Markt** (Market Square) with its 16th-century Stadhuis and guildhouses is a good starting point. The Brabo statue, built in the 19th century, is the symbol of the city. As Da Vinci is to Florence, so Rubens is to Antwerp, with his art scattered all around the city. There are 21 of his oils and sketches in the **Royal Museum of Fine Arts** (Leopold de Waelplaats 2, 238 7809, www.kmska.be), and the **Rubenshuis** (Wapper 9-11, 3 201 1555) is a memorial dedicated to the artist, housed within a Flemish Baroque mansion built by Rubens himself in 1611. Go to the diamond district, west of Centraal station, to see three floors of gem-themed displays at the **Diamantmuseum** (Koningin Astridplein 19, 3 202 4890, www.docdiamond.com).

With some of the best clubs in northern Europe, it's worth checking out www.noctis.com and www.fishandchips.be before planning your night(s) out in Antwerp. The famous **Café d'Anvers** (Verversrui 15, 3 226 3870,

www.cafe-d-anvers.com) is worth a visit – a former church and cinema before it was revamped into a club in the early 1990s, its local DJs mostly play progressive house. For a more laid-back night, head to **Petrol** (D'Herbouvillekaai 25, 3 226 4963, www.petrolclub.be), where doormen don't mind trainers and the music varies from funky house to drum 'n' bass to reggae.

**Bruges**, meanwhile, has a population of 116,000, but attracts over three million tourists each year. The city has a historical and romantic feel, and is sometimes dubbed the Venice of the North. It's 50 minutes from Brussels by train, and is compact and pretty traffic-free, so can easily be navigated on foot. Your starting point should be the main square, the **Markt**, with its impressive Halle, or cloth hall, and Belfort, the belfry – both symbols of the city's mercantile power and civic pride. From here, it's a short walk to another square, the **Burg**, which is surrounded by Gothic architecture – don't miss the Stadhuis (Dijver 12), built in 1376, and Heilig Bloed Basiliek (Burg 15), the Romanesque Basilica of the Holy Blood, built in the 12th century.

Galleries Royales
St-Hubert

Belga Queen

Chez Moeder Lambic Fontainas

Place du Jeu de Balle

Pierre Marcolini

322 450 2200, www.hotelorts.com) is in a great location for both sightseeing and nightlife, with colour-themed rooms, while nautically themed **Noga** (rue du Béguinage 38, 322 218 6763, www.nogahotel.com) provides the kitsch factor, with knick-knacks, pictures of royals and assorted bric-a-brac all about (bath-lovers will find no lathery joy here as the rooms only have showers). If you're after peace and quiet, don't book a hotel near the Grand Place or a busy street, as many Belgians are honk-happy. Many of the hotels are expense account-funded (yep, that's your tax upping the weekday rates), which is beneficial to anyone travelling at weekends or during the summer, so make sure to check for deals before booking.

## Cultural baggage

**Book** *Dreadful Lies* (Michele Bailey, 1994)
**Film** *Brussels by Night* (Marc Didden, 1984)
**Album** *Boîte à bonbons* (Box-set compilation of Jacques Brel, 2003)

## GETTING THERE & AROUND

Only Eurocrats and fat cats fly to Brussels – from Heathrow, if you must. The Eurostar is the most obvious and straightforward mode of transport, with services from St Pancras leaving almost every couple of hours. All tickets to Bruxelles-Midi will also get you to or from any other Belgian station, included in the price.

Whether in the Lower Town or Upper Town, walking is the ideal way to get around. **Villo!** (http://en.villo.be) is the local cycling scheme, allowing you to pick up and drop off bikes from one of 180 stations around town. Public transport in the city is very efficient, and tickets can be used for up to an hour once validated, on any type of transport. The **Brussels Card** (www.brusselscard.be) is worth buying for anyone who wants to use public transport frequently and visit a few museums; available for one-, two- or three-day periods, it gets you free entry to 30 museums and free transport around town, plus a few other discounts.

# Hamburg

Think of Germany's urban powerhouses, and your mind may immediately switch to Berlin, Frankfurt or even Munich. Yet Hamburg is Germany's newspaper, insurance and internet hub and, some – especially proud Hamburgers – would say, the German capital of relaxed cool. Where in the past tourists might be drawn to the Reeperbahn (the city's most famous street, known for its nightlife) or to Beatles-themed circuits, 21st-century Hamburg offers more cosmopolitan attractions, with museums, beaches, lots of greenery and a wealth of culture. It's a surprisingly beautiful city, and was named European Green Capital in 2011, in recognition of its eco-consciousness.

Hamburg is on the water – or in the water, if you see it from above – which gives it its maritime feel. That it is Germany's biggest port (in action since the Middle Ages) has contributed to its current multiculturalism. And that's not the only thing that will make a Londoner feel at home – the famous *Schmuddelwetter* (literally, 'mucky weather') can certainly hold its own with the best of London showers.

Hamburg harbour

## Fast facts

**Country dialling code** +49
**Journey time** Flight 1 hour 35 minutes; train 15 hours; car 9 hours 30 minutes
**Festivals & events** Alstervergnügen (August, www.hamburg.de/alstervergnuegen), an annual street fair held around the lake; Hafengeburstag (May, www.hamburg.de/hafengeburtstag-english), Hamburg's huge port festival; Reeperbahn (September, www.reeperbahnfestival.com), a music and culture festival held in various venues around the city
**Good for** Culture

## SEE & DO

You'll get the best view of the city if you enter the **Alte Elbtunnel** (Bei den Sankt Pauli-Landungsbrücken 6, www.hamburg-port-authority.de) – a 100-year-old tunnel under the Elb river – and walk through to the southern exit to look back at the city. Alternatively, go to the **Tower Bar** in the **Hotel Hafen Hamburg** (Seewartenstrasse 9, (0)40 31 11 30, www.hotelhafen.hamburg.de), which is 62 metres high and even attracts locals, thanks to the view. Hamburg's skyline is busy with churches, dark-brick Hanseatic buildings, Gothic architecture, large warehouses and cranes. At first glance, the city may seem more industrial and grey than it actually is – between all these layers of architecture are vast amounts of water and plenty of green areas. That

Planten un Blomen

East hotel

Schanzenviertel

said, the port is incorporated within the city, not apart from it, as it has always been Hamburg's main source of money and power.

Unless you actively hunt them out, neither the Beatles nor the Reeperbahn are rammed in your face. But if it's your first visit and you want to tick off a couple of classics – or clichés – a walk down the **Reeperbahn**, still a *Vergnügungsmeile* ('pleasure mile') to this day, will soon lead you to the newly opened **Beatlemania** (Nobistor 10, (0)40 85 38 88 88, www.beatlemania-hamburg.com). Smack in the middle of the former stomping ground of the Beatles' formative years (1960-62), the museum is devoted solely to the band, housing 11 themed rooms. For finer culture, head to the **Hamburger Kunsthalle** (Glockengiesserwall, (0)40 428 131 308, www.freunde-der-kunsthalle.de), which

showcases a bountiful collection of expressionist painting. The three connected buildings house pictures by Picasso, Klee, Caspar David Friedrich, Dürer, Cézanne and Gauguin. It really is a fine museum.

A large part of the harbour area is known as **HafenCity** and is a confusing maze of waterways and wharfs for anyone who doesn't work there, as well as a poster child for Hamburg's ongoing redevelopment. Take a look at the new home of the **Elbe Philharmonic** (Am Kaiserkai, (0)40 3 80 88 00, www.elbphilharmonie.de), being built here at the dockside; it has generated a big debate for the fact that the project is becoming more and more expensive, with the completion date being pushed further and further back.

The area around the concert hall is known as the **Speicherstadt**, meaning 'warehouse district', with its rows of late 19th-century warehouses, each one linked to its neighbour by walkways built over the canals. It's all very photogenic, as is the gold bull at **Argentinienbrücke** the 'Argentinian Bridge'.

**Planten un Blomen** (Klosterwall 8, (0)40 42 8 54 47 23, www.plantenunblomen.hamburg.de), in the heart of the city, is the botanical garden. It has the largest Japanese garden in Europe, as well as mini-golf, and concerts in the music pavilion. Oddly enough, the name isn't German but low Saxon or Plattdeutsch, a west Germanic language spoken in parts of northern Germany and the eastern parts of the Netherlands.

Heading away from the water and through the park, you find yourself in the former meatpacking district and neighbouring **Schanzenviertel**; here, you're likely to find

# Hamburg – all included

**Hamburg's  MUST SEE**
Alster Lake, Elbe River, Elbphilharmonic Hall, St. Pauli,
BEATLEMANIA

**Hamburg's Culture**
Hamburg State Opera, Hamburg Art Gallery, Bucerius Art Forum

**Hamburg's Shopping**
Mönckebergstrasse, Neuer Wall, Karolinenviertel, Schanze

**Hamburg's Port**
Historic Warehouses, Harbour City, Miniature Wonderland,
International Maritime Museum

**Hamburg's Events  2012**
DOM Beer Festival, Port's Birthday,
ELBJAZZ, Reeperbahn Festival

**Discover the city with
the Hamburg CARD!**

yourself surrounded by hipsters. The area used to be genuinely hip during the dot com boom in the late 1990s when it was a centre for the new economy, but has now become largely gentrified, with high rents and people who head there to see and be seen. Still, the many bars, restaurants, boutiques, vinyl- and skate shops make for a pleasant stroll, and it still houses Hamburg's lefty scene.

Don't let the skull-and-crossbones flags of this area fool you – they represent the district and the football team, St Pauli, a symbol adopted by the fans of the team, previously used as the symbol of squatters. If you go a little further east, you'll arrive at the interesting **Karolinenviertel**, a 1970s former working class area that has managed to fight off being gentrified (at times even with violence) and is now a multicultural centre, with some great shops.

Hamburg is almost completely surrounded by water. It sits at the confluence of rivers – the Elbe being the largest – and lakes, and the many narrow canals spread the aquatic theme to every corner of the city. For a maritime feel, seek out the **Alster** river, surrounded by trees, parks, banks, waterside cafés and yachts. You can explore the river (and city) by many means, whether you buy tickets for a ferry, boat or steamer ride or rent a boat yourself (www.alstertouristik.de).

If you're planning on visiting the famous **Fischmarkt** (Grosse Elbstrasse 1, (0)40 30 05 13 00, www.hamburg-tourism.de), don't stay out too long the night before – open Sundays from 5am to 9.30am, it is loud, traditional and, most of all, charming. A Hamburger staple since 1703, anything and everything gets sold here – not just fish.

## EAT & DRINK

Meat-lovers should head to former slaughterhouse **Bullerei** (Lagerstrasse 34B, (0)40 33 44 21 10, www.bullerei.com) in the Schanzenviertel area. It's run by TV chef Tim Mälzer, as famous in Germany as Jamie Oliver is in Britain, and his kitchen turns out beef tartare, *pata negra* ham, salmon with apple and fennel and fresh burrata cheese with own-made bread.

**Das Feuerschiff** (Vorsetzen, (0)40 36 25 53, www.das-feuerschiff.de), close to St Pauli, is a bar and restaurant set within a converted lightship, now moored close to the free port. Watch the river traffic while enjoying some seafood and fine German beers.

**Fischereihafen** (Grosse Elbstrasse 143, (0)40 38 18 16, www.fischereihafenrestaurant.de), in Altona-Altstadt, is great to visit on a sunny day, as you can sit outside looking at the Elbe. In a former warehouse in a former fishing port – yes, Hamburg is all about regeneration – fish fiends will have plenty to choose from. Try the oysters from the popular oyster bar as well as the freshly caught flounder and herring.

## STAY

You don't have to spend a lot of money on accommodation in Hamburg – there are cheap choices aplenty. The **KiezBude Hostel** (Lincolnstrasse 2, (0)40 74 21 42 69, www.kiezbude.com) is within the district of St Pauli, right by the Reeperbahn. Rooms (decked out in pure kitsch) are two- or four-beds, with bedlinen costing an extra €3 and towels €1.50. The **Hotel Motel One** chain (one is at Kieler Strasse 171, (0)40 89 72 06 90, www.motel-one.com)

has four hotels in Hamburg. The rooms are cheap and clean, like an upmarket hostel.

The **Hotel Atlantic** (An der Alster 72-79, (0)40 2 88 80, www.kempinski.com) is on the fancy side, with grand architecture and a great rooftop view of the city; many rooms also have views of the Aussenalster river. And if none of that sways you, Cary Grant and Gustav Klimt were once guests here. **East** (Simon-von-Utrecht-Strasse 31, (0)40 30 99 30, www.east-hamburg.de) is more urban. Occupying a former steel foundry close to the Reeperbahn, it belongs to an Asian-fusion restaurant-bar group. The rooms (ranked S to XXL and spread over five floors) are all colour- and scent-coded, after oriental flowers and spices. Check out the spa on the top floor and the roof terrace, which houses saunas and masseuses.

## GETTING THERE & AROUND

Lufthansa, British Airways, Ryanair and EasyJet all fly between London airports and Hamburg Airport and Hamburg Lübeck (a bit further out). You can also take the sleeper trains of the Eurostar and Deutsche Bahn (www.db.de), changing in Paris, though this will take much longer and is likely to cost more.

Hamburg's public transport, the **HVV** (www.hvv.de), is simple to use; the S- and U-Bahns are reliable, the buses drive around the clock, and tickets are valid on the ferries within the city too (a nice trip, for instance, is from Landungsbrücken to Finkenwerder and back). Buy a three-day **HamburgCard** for unlimited travel and reduced entry prices to some of the local cultural attractions.

Bullerei

# Bergerac & Around

Although this town shares its name with France's famous large-nosed swordsman, Cyrano de Bergerac never actually came here. Nevertheless, the hero of Edmond Rostand's famous play has been adopted as a local icon, and two statues of him act as (rather nonchalant, low-key) tourist attractions. The town is about as unspoilt as you get in Western Europe, having retained its peaceful squares, original fountains, 16th-century archways and timber-framed buildings. Foodies will recognise this area of the south-west for some of France's best-known specialities, such as foie gras, confit duck, prunes and truffles. It's hard to get far without seeing rows of vines dividing the landscape – the town is at the centre of a region with 12 appellations, which produce some of the finest wine in the country. As well as being the epitome of a picturesque French town, Bergerac acts as a gateway to the Dordogne. A weekend isn't enough for a deep exploration of *la France profonde*, but if you do all of the following you'll get a proper taste of the place – and will probably be tempted to come back to the region again.

## Fast facts

**Country dialling code** +33
**Journey time** Flight 1 hour 40 minutes
**Festivals & events** Jazz Pourpre Festival (May) – now in its ninth year, this is a unique festival for jazz-lovers, with performances in different venues around town and a successful competition for amateur bands; Sarlat Theatre Festival (July-August) – Sarlat is an hour and a half's drive away from Bergerac but hosts this important cultural occasion founded in 1952. More than 20 classical plays are performed in the beautiful medieval town centre for three weeks of the summer
**Good for** Countryside, food, wine

## SEE & DO

Start with a walk through Bergerac's old town, the centre of which is now pedestrianised. It features many medieval houses, such as the **Maison dite La Vieille Auberge** (27 rue des Fontaines) and the Romanesque **Church of St Jacques** (rue St-Jacques, 0553 736749), which lies on what in French is referred to as the 'Saint-Jacques-de-Compostelle' pilgrimage route towards Spain's Santiago de Compostela.

Bergerac was once a major centre for tobacco production (which is still grown in the area today). The intriguing **Musée du Tabac** displays smoking paraphernalia such as intricate pipes, snuff boxes and cigarette holders. It's housed in the early 17th-century **Maison Peyrarade** (place du Feu, 0553 630413), which Louis XIII once stayed in.

The other temple to pleasure is the **Maison des Vins**, in the 16th-century cloisters of the **Cloîtres des Récollets** (1 rue des Récollets). Here you can explore the winemaking process through interactive displays and tastings.

The best way to get to know the area's wines, though, is by visiting the individual châteaux, which are all within driving-distance of Bergerac (a 'spitoon' is always available). Cycling to the vineyards is also a nice way to take in the beautiful (but fairly hilly) landscape.

The **Monbazillac** area, a 15-minute drive south of the river, produces a syrupy, golden sweet wine that ranks second only to Sauternes – the grapes have to be affected by 'noble rot' to classify. Taste the nectar at the **Château de Monbazillac** (route de Mont-de-Marsan, 0553 636500, www.chateau-monbazillac.com), an imposing building with pepperpot towers, a moat, and fantastic views. The privately owned **Tirecul La Gravière** (0553 574475, www.vini bilancini.com) nearby has also produced top-class wines, and owners Bruno and Claudie will be happy to arrange a tasting. For reds, **Pecharmant** (literally 'charming hill') is the oldest collection of vineyards in the region, producing full-bodied fruity wine that matches the local cuisine.

If you want to go further afield, the old market town of **Eymet** (a 30-minute drive from Bergerac) specialises in fruit preserves, and has the signature grid layout and central square of a typical *bastide* (fortified French town). A haven for expats, its shops also sell Farrow & Ball paint and jars of Marmite. **Issigeac**, 25 minutes away, is another pretty town packed with small streets and alleyways. There is a famous antiques market several times a year, where you can pick up great crockery and trinkets (check with the local Office du Tourisme for dates: 0553 587962). The town is also famous for glassblowing, and you can visit **L'Atelier des Verriers** (route d'Eymet, 0553 732256) for exhibitions and sales.

If you're feeling active, the Dordogne is a great river for kayaking. Some 20 minutes' drive away in Gardonne is **Canoe Attitude** (0680 880672), where you can arrange to paddle anywhere from three to 34 kilometres along the river.

## EAT & DRINK

Apart from the sights listed above, the real pleasure of Bergerac is just to stroll around the town – especially early in the morning and as dusk falls – and find little bars and cafés in which to recharge. If you're a foodie, you'll want to get out of town to try the rural cuisine, but **L'Imparfait** (6-10 rue des Fontaines, 0553 574792, www.imparfait.com) is a jolly restaurant in the old town that gives traditional dishes a bit of a contemporary makeover. It has a neighbouring sister bar, **Le Plus-Que-Parfait**, that often has live music.

Tirecul La Gravière

Begerac

Château de Monbazillac

Château des Vigiers

**La Grappe d'Or** (Le Peyrat, 0553 611758), near Monbazillac, is a great place to go for a long lunch after visiting the château. It serves specialities such as *civet de canard* (duck casserole) and *ris de veau* (sweetbreads of veal).

If you're serious about bread, you won't regret the 30-minute car journey into Lot-et-Garonne to seek out **Lo Pan del Puech** (St-Quentin-du-Dropt, 0553 360455, www.lo pandelpuech.blogspot.com), the bakery of two-man team Laurent (French) and Jim (American), who have reinstated the art of sourdough in an area where the quality of the average boulangerie has dropped.

During the summer months, most towns have night markets where local producers prepare food such as steaks, duck kebabs and snails, and you can take it back to long tables shared with the rest of the village. In Bergerac, this happens on Fridays, and in Monbazillac on Mondays.

## SHOP

The city's name is said to stem from the Gallic word *braca*, which refers to a manufacturer of the Gauls' traditional baggy breeches. Unfortunately, the town seems to have lost its flair for haberdashery, and fashion shops are few and far between. However, Bergerac does have some interesting home decoration shops, and on the first Sunday morning of each month there's a flea market in the old town.

What's definitely worth bringing home is the food. On Wednesday and Saturday mornings, a **farmers' market** encircles the church of Notre-Dame, where you can pick up the obligatory tin of *confit*. If you miss the market, **Valette** (24 rue St-James, 0553 571715, www.valette.fr) specialises in foie gras. From December to February it's truffle season, and Bergerac hosts a special market (ask for **Marché aux Truffes**) on the usual market days.

## STAY

In the centre of town, the **Hôtel de Bordeaux** (38 place Gambetta, 0553 571283, www.hotel-bordeaux-bergerac.com) and **Hôtel de France** (18 place Gambetta, 0553 571161, www.hoteldefrance-bergerac.com) are both in old properties and offer simply furnished rooms and swimming pools. **Le Logis Plantagenet** (5 rue de Grand Moulin, 0553 571599) is a gem of a bed & breakfast in a restored 12th-century house, with three bedrooms and its own peaceful courtyard. For a more isolated weekend, the **Château des Vigiers** (0553 615000, www.vigiers.eu), 25 minutes outside Bergerac, is set within beautiful grounds and has a spa.

## GETTING THERE & AROUND

Flights to Bergerac from London operate from Gatwick with Flybe, or from Stansted with Ryanair. Once there, you'll need a car, and there are various car rental offices at the airport. Bergerac town centre is about ten minutes' drive from the airport. If you're planning on sticking within Bergerac itself, you can take a taxi from the airport, as from there it's easy to walk around. If you're planning to go on wine tastings but not to spit, or just want to indulge over lunch/dinner, use local taxis for trips out of town. For bicycle hire, **Apolo Cycles** (31 boulevard Victor Hugo, 0620 645925, www. apolo-cycles.com) offers everything from mountain bikes to carbon road bikes to children's bikes.

# Berlin

Berlin, like London, is vast and sprawling and scruffy round the edges. Many of the tourist hubs, such as Potsdamer Platz, the area around the Brandenburg Gate, and Alexanderplatz, are walkable, but it pays to get accustomed to using public transport if you want to explore the inner city properly. Unlike some other European cities – Berlin's transport system (known as the BVG) doesn't wind up with the chime of midnight, and it stretches way out into the suburbs.

You could happily travel to Berlin for a nocturnally themed weekend of dining, drinking and clubbing. Or wear yourself out taking in all the Cold War history, art galleries, museums and shops. But our favourite weekend in Berlin is one that combines a little bit of all of these things – so it pays not to make sleep a priority here.

Reichstag

## Fast facts

**Country dialling code** +49 for Germany, plus 30 for Berlin if calling from abroad
**Journey time** Flight 1 hour 50 minutes; train 10 hours 20 minutes; car 11 hours
**Festivals & events** Lange Nacht der Museen (Late Night at the Museums) (February & August, www.lange-nacht-der-museen.de), when around 100 of Berlin's museums stay open into the early hours; Berlinale International Film Festival (February, 259 200, www.berlinale.de/en); Karneval der Kulturen (May/June, 6097 7022, www.karneval-berlin.de), a celebration of Berlin's ethnic and cultural diversity; Christopher Street Day Parade (June, 2862 8632, www.csd-berlin.de), one of the summer's most enjoyable and inclusive street parties; Christmas markets from late November
**Good for** Culture, history, nightlife

## SEE & DO

Berlin is very walkable. Start off with a stroll past an icon, for a taste of the city's history: the **East Side Gallery** (Mühlenstrasse 1, 251 7159, www.eastsidegallery.com) is a 1.3-kilometre stretch of the **Berlin Wall** left standing in Friedrichshain, which was handed over to 118 artists to beautify in 1990. Here you'll see many famous murals; sadly, the most well-known one of Honecker and Brezhnev kissing, by artist Dmitri Vrubel, was painted over in 2009, though a new version has since been created. You can also still see the famous big-lipped cartoon heads by Thierry Noir. Some Berliners turn their noses up at the 'gallery', however, and savvier guides or locals may point you to the random chunks of untouched wall that remain around the city, in all their grey glory. See www.berlin.de/mauer/verlauf for a full list of locations.

The Potsdamer Platz and the ugly Sony Center (Kemperplatz 1) are best seen in a hurry, but slow down for the **Brandenburg Gate** (Strasse des 17 Juni). Walk north for two minutes and you'll find the **Reichstag** (Platz der Republik 1), with its famous glass dome by Norman Foster (and huge queues – visit early in the day if you want to go

inside). Heading west from here – along Strasse des 17 Juni and then through the **Tiergarten**, Berlin's large chunk of green – you come to the **Siegessäule** (Grosser Stern 1), or Victory Column, a monument built in 1871 to celebrate the last wars won by the Prussians against Denmark, Austria and France in the late 1800s. The column is victoriously adorned by captured (and now gilded) French cannons and cannonballs, and topped with a gold Goddess of Victory.

South of here – and all of a few minutes' walk – is the **Memorial to the Murdered Jews of Europe** (Denkmal für die ermordeten Juden Europas, Cora-Berliner-Strasse 1, 2639 4336, www.holocaust-denkmal.de), a city-block-size field of 2,711 sloped concrete blocks representing the Jewish victims of World War II.

Head east from the Brandenburg Gate, and you'll pass many of the sights people associate with Berlin, particularly along Unter den Linden, which then turns into Karl-Liebknecht-Strasse. Here you'll pass the history-laden **Hotel Adlon Kempinski Berlin** (Unter den Linden 77, 261 2222, www.hotel-adlon.de), featured in numerous films and books; the original building was ruined in 1945, but was completely revamped in 1997. The **Guggenheim** (Unter den Linden 13-15, 202 0930,

**Brandenburg Gate**

**Ostel Hostel Berlin**

Weekend

Alexanderplatz

www.deutsche-guggenheim.de) features ever-changing
exhibitions, so check the website for details. Other landmarks
along your walk include the chilling **Nazi Book Burning
Memorial** (Bebelplatz 1), the **German State Opera**
(Unter den Linden 7, 2035 4555, www.staatsoper-berlin.
org), the **Berliner Dome** (Am Lustgarten), and, finally,
**Alexanderplatz**, with its golfball-on-a-knitting-needle
television tower – or the 'Alex', as Berliners fondly call it.

Monsieur Vuong

Flohmarkt am Mauerpark

KaDeWe

# EAT & DRINK

Few people would travel to Berlin purely for its cuisine, but that isn't to say that you can't dine well in this city. It's strong on sausages and snack food and boasts a variety of ethnic cuisines, and there are plenty of hearty Middle Eastern delis, fantastic Indian restaurants, and cake-laden coffee houses – ideal if you're there on a winter visit.

You can't leave Berlin without having tried a currywurst: a big sausage in the kind of curry sauce English chippies use (you'll probably be asked whether you want it '*mit oder ohne Darm*', which means with or without intestines). Sample one at Konnopke's family-run **Imbiss** (under the U-Bahn tracks at the corner of Danziger Strasse and Schönhauser Allee), in business since 1930, for the real deal. Some snack joints serve it with champagne, in keeping with Berliners' ironic angle on life in general. Kaffee und Kuchen – coffee and cake – is a German staple more prominent in the Western cities, but popular in Berlin too. Head to **Café Einstein am Stammhaus** (Kurfürstenstrasse 58, 261 5096, www.cafeeinstein.com) or **Café im Literaturhaus** (Fasanenstrasse 23, 882 5414, www.literaturhaus-berlin.de) for a spread of cakes and decent coffee.

Berlin is home to the world's largest Turkish expat community, and the first proper foreign-friendly doner kebab was reputedly sliced and served here in 1971. You can rely on the city's many Turkish eateries for cheap and cheerful shish and doner dishes, and falafel with houmous. You'll never have to walk far to find a good doner place in the city, but the areas around Prenzlauer Allee and Eberswalder Strasse are good bets – check out **Miro** (Raumer Strasse 28-29, 4473 3013, www.miro-restaurant.de) and **Bistro Yilmaz Kardesler** (Kottbusser Damm 6). There are also a good number of relatively cheap sushi bars – the **Ishin** (Schlossstrasse 101, 797 1049, www.isihin.de) chain serves maki rolls that easily rival much more expensive sushi joints in London.

If you find yourself around Hackescher Markt, Vietnamese restaurant **Monsieur Vuong** (Alte Schönhauser Strasse 46, 9929 6924, www.monsieurvuong.de) – famous for its glass noodle salad – and Modern Asian **Pan Asia** (Rosenthaler

East Side Gallery

## Cultural baggage

**Book** *Russian Disco* (Wladimir Kaminer, 2002)
**Film** *Good bye, Lenin!* (Wolfgang Becker, 2003)
**Album** *Berlin Trilogy* (David Bowie and Brian Eno, 1970s)

Strasse 38, 2790 8811, www.panasia.de) are worth a visit. For a hangover cure, head to the **Schwarzes Café** (Kantstrasse 148, 313 8038, www.schwarzescafe-berlin.de), something of a Berliner institution that serves breakfast – including typical German seeded bread rolls, sliced cheeses and meats, and huge milky coffees – 24 hours a day.

## SHOP

Berlin has two one-stop shopping strips: **Hackescher Markt** in the east, and **Kurfürstendamm** (often referred to as 'Ku'damm') in the west. **Hackescher Markt** (formerly a marsh before the market square was laid out in the late 1700s), and the area surrounding it, is now filled with a variety of shops. There are trendy restaurants and cafés amid the retail offerings, so you can refuel in between browsing.

The Ku'Damm offers straight-to-the-point shopping: start at the Wittenbergplatz U-Bahn station – where you'll see the famous department store Kaufhaus des Westens, referred to as **KaDeWe** (Tauentzienstrasse 21-24, 302 1210, www.kadewe.de), then walk along Tauenzienstrasse and the Ku'Damm. The shops are a mix of quality high street and high-end labels.

Berliners love a good bargain, and many visit the city's flea markets religiously every week, both to sell and buy. The **Flohmarkt am Boxhagener Platz** (Boxhagener Platz 1, 0174 946 7557, www.boxhagenerplatz.de), open on Sundays from 10am to 6pm, is very arty, while the **Flohmarkt am Mauerpark** (Bernauerstrasse 45, 0176 2925 0021, www.mauerparkmarkt.de), held on Sundays from 8am to 6pm, is the largest and busiest in Berlin.

## NIGHTLIFE

Many people come to Berlin purely for the bars and clubs. The choice can be bewildering. Our favourite picks include **Clärchens Ballhaus** (Auguststrasse 24, 282 9295, www.ballhaus.de) for old-school nostalgic charm; the infamous **Berghain/Panorama Bar** (Rüdersdorfer Strasse 70, 2936 0210, www.berghain.de), one of Europe's best techno clubs; **2BE** (Klosterstrasse 44, 8904 873 10, www.2be-club.de) for hip hop fiends; **Weekend** (Alexanderstrasse 7, 2463 1676, www.week-end-berlin.de) for great DJ sets (2ManyDJs, DFA) and fantastic cityscape views; and **Kleine Nachtrevue** (Kurfürstenstrasse 116, 218 8950, www.kleine-nachtrevue.de), in the spirit of Sally Bowles and Marlene Dietrich.

## GAY & LESBIAN

Berlin has one of the world's best gay and lesbian scenes. Check out the city's longest-running dance institution, **SchwuZ** (Mehringdamm 61, 693 7025, www.schwuz.de) on a Saturday night; hardcore sex den **Lab.oratory** (Am Wriezener Bahnhof, www.lab-oratory.de) has the regular Naked Sex Party on Thursdays (with all sorts of props at your disposal); or the psychedelic **Hafen bar** (Motzstrasse 19, 211 4118, www.hafen-berlin.de) for a quieter night, which hosts a pub quiz in English on the first Monday of the month.

**Prinz Eisenherz** (Lietzenburgerstrasse 9A, 313 9936, www.prinzeisenherz.com) is one of Europe's finest gay bookshops, while the flashy **Boyz'R'Us** (Maasesnstrasse 8, 2363 0640, www.boyz-r-us.de) and theatrical 1950s-'70s second-hand shop **Waahnsinn** (Rosenthalerstrasse 17, 282 0029, www.waahnsinn-berlin.de) are both worth visiting if you're after some original fashion.

## STAY

Berlin is still one of the cheaper large European capitals as far as hotel prices go – which doesn't mean that it doesn't have luxe and designer options, if that's what you're after. For 'Ossi' (the nickname for 'East German') nostalgia, stay at the **Ostel Hostel Berlin** (Wriezener Karree 5, 2576 8660, www.ostel.eu), a 1970s DDR replica hostel close to Ostbahnhof station, with original wallpaper, box radios and food ration coupons that you exchange for breakfast in the mornings. The **Hotel Q!** (Knesebeckstrasse 67, 810 0660, www.loock-hotels.com), winner of various design and interior awards, is at the pricier end of things, but well worth it, if you can afford it – the spa is fantastic, rooms have their own temperature control and are creatively designed – bed and bath are part of the same wooden unit (with separate showers and toilets) – and the location is very central. The family-friendly **Hotel Pension Columbus** (Meinekestrasse 5, 881 5061, www.columbus-berlin.de) is a cheap and cheerful option just off the Ku'damm, as is the **CityStay Hostel** (Rosenstrasse 16, 2362 4031, www.citystay.de), which is right by Hackescher Markt, yet still quiet and friendly. If you're a luxury fiend and have the money to spend on 'destination hotels', the **Hotel de Rome** (Behrenstrasse 37, 460 6090, www.roccofortecollection.com) is the one you want to pick. Originally the headquarters of a bank, the 19th-century building is grand but informal. Rooms are decked out in wood, marble and velvet, with a spa in a former jewel vault and great views from the rooftop champagne terrace.

## GETTING THERE & AROUND

Both EasyJet and Ryanair fly to Berlin Schoenefeld two or three times a day, while BA and Lufthansa fly to Berlin Tegel (until it closes in June 2012, when flights will land at the newly opened Berlin Brandenburg Airport).

Eurostar is scheduled to open a direct connection between London and Cologne in summer 2012, after which travelling to Berlin by train will be relatively quick and simple. (The journey from Cologne to Berlin is around five hours on the Deutsche Bahn. Currently, London to Cologne takes five hours 20 minutes and includes a change in Paris. Alternatively, you can travel via both Brussels (Eurostar) and Cologne (ICE), which takes just under ten hours.)

Once in Berlin, take the S-Bahn from Schoenefeld Airport or a TXL bus from Tegel Airport (which is part of the BVG). Berlin's buses, U-Bahn (underground train network), S-Bahn (overground train network) and trams (mainly in the east) are easy to use; see www.bvg.de for English-language info. On weekends, most lines run through the night. The 100 bus, a regular line, moonlights as a very cheap sightseeing tour bus, as it passes many important spots, from Zoologischer Garten to Prenzlauer Berg. And while you shouldn't always presume a Berliner will be fluent in English, most Berliners speak some and will happily point you in the right direction.

Many Berliners cycle, and there are cycle paths along most pavements in the city. Make sure you rent a helmet as police will stop you and pedestrians will shout at you if you don't. Check out www.fattirebiketours.com/berlin for guided tours and www.pedalpower.de, if you want to rent a bike.

For more useful information, visit www.visitberlin.de/en, www.berlin.de and www.timeout.com/berlin.

# Liechtenstein

Liechtenstein, just 25 kilometres long and six wide, is a little larger than Manhattan island and you could feasibly walk the whole country in a long weekend – which, in fact, wouldn't be a bad idea, as the country is deep in the Alps, landlocked between Switzerland and Austria, and ideally suited to hiking and cycling (there are 90 kilometres of bike trails) as well as picnicking, landscape painting, or simply gawping. It's the last remnant of the Holy Roman Empire and became a sovereign state in 1806, with the monarch residing in a Gothic castle on a hill, straight out of a fairytale. His subjects are proud and prefer not to be compared to their neighbours. December to April is skiing time, May to October is the trekking season. If you want quirky, Liechtenstein does the trick: its national anthem has the same music as England's, it has wines made by an international footballer and it's the world's largest producer of dentures. And most of your mates probably haven't been there…

## Fast facts

**Country dialling code** +423
**Journey time** Flight 1 hour 50 minutes to Zurich, then 1 hour by train or car
**Festivals & events** Christmas markets (December, www.eventfactory.li); Liechtenstein State Celebration (15 August, www.tourismus.li); Vaduz Film Festival (July, www.filmfest.li)
**Good for** Food, walking, wine

Schloss Vaduz

St Florin Cathedral

## SEE & DO

The capital, **Vaduz**, is a good place to start sightseeing. Walkable and spread over just 17 square kilometres, it houses around 5,350 of Liechtenstein's 34,000-strong population. There aren't many 'attractions' per se, but the big grey block that is the **Kunstmuseum** (Städtle 32, 9490 Vaduz, 235 03 00, www.kunstmuseum.li), the city's main art gallery, and the **Postage Stamp Museum** (Postmuseum, Städtle 37, 9490 Vaduz, 239 68 46, www.postmuseum.li) are right in the centre. The gallery has a collection of international modern art, including artists such as André Thomkins, Rolf Ricke and Joseph Beuys. Don't turn your nose up at the stamp museum – a Liechtenstein postage stamp is very sought after by collectors. If you walk south of here, you'll soon come to the 1873 neo-Gothic **St Florin Cathedral** (Sankt Florinsgasse 15, 9490 Vaduz, 232 36 16) and the 1905 government building **Regierungsgebäude** (Städtle 49, 9490 Vaduz, 239 63 00).

Prince Hans-Adam, the country's monarch, lives in the Gothic Vaduz castle, **Schloss Vaduz**, which is visible from almost everywhere in the town. Occupied by the royal family since 1712, but built in the 12th century, it's a private

Parkhotel Sonnenhof

residence and closed to the public (but still pretty from the outside). Liechtenstein's royals are very unlike most – it's quite possible that you'll see them during your weekend here, even if it's just in a car marked with their birth year on the licence plate. The national anthem, 'Oben am jungen Rhein', uses the tune of England's 'God Save the King', which was the first song ever to be used as a national anthem, so many other countries nicked it, including Hawaii and Sweden, though the latter two no longer use it.

For a café pitstop, try the **Confiserie-Konditorei-Café Wanger** (Landstrasse 27, 9494 Schaan, 232 40 04, www.wangerag.li) just north of Vaduz, or the **Vanini Café-Bar** (Herrengasse 2, 9490 Vaduz, www.adler.li), which serve freshly baked breads, pastries and cakes. There's not an awful lot of shopping to be done in Vaduz (this is a place where the sole McDonald's is signposted on numerous traffic signals), but if you're looking for a nice gift to bring home, head to the aforementioned stamp museum or buy a local wine – most of the 15 hectares of vineyards are close to Vaduz. The **Hofkellerei** (Feldstrasse 4, 9490 Vaduz, 232 10 18, www.hofkellerei.li) is the prince's winery.

If you have a hire car or catch the local 'Post Bus', you can make the journey up to **Triesenberg**, a village overlooking Vaduz, where you can see down the Rhine Valley and beyond to the peaks of the Swiss and Austrian Alps. Liechtenstein looks after its hikers – because of the high demand, the tourist board has a page where you can choose a pre-planned route or create your own bespoke tour, factoring in duration, distance and elevation (see www.tourismus.li). Another fantastic option, if you're feeling energetic, is to hire a bicycle; Liechtenstein has more than 90 kilometres of cycling trails, through the valleys, around the mountains and along the river. Check out www.lie-cycling.li, www.sigis-veloshop.li or www.bikegarge.li.

Finally, if you're not content with seeing just one country on your weekend, it's easy to just pop over to Austria for some coffee and cake or to Switzerland to stock up on emmental.

## EAT & DRINK

Almost all of the bakeries around Liechtenstein are fantastic (including the ones mentioned above), so you won't have any difficulty sourcing a good breakfast or hiking supplies. There are a few Michelin-starred restaurants and

**Kunstmuseum**

many other outstanding eateries. The local food is hearty, and very influenced by its neighbours; *Käsknöfle* is a typical dish, similar to *Spätzle* but with cheese and onions. As in Germany and Austria, the main meal of the day is typically eaten at lunchtime, and dinner is often an open meat or cheese sandwich. Restaurants, of course, offer main meals in the evening too.

Pleasant and reasonably priced, the **Old Castle Inn** (Aeulenstrasse 22, Vaduz, 232 10 65) is in the heart of the capital and serves authentic dishes. The menu changes daily, but there's always a good selection of steak dishes, Schnitzel and pasta dishes.

The **Parkhotel Sonnenhof** (Mareestrasse 29, 9490 Vaduz, 239 02 02, www.sonnenhof.li) has a rather romantic restaurant (the view from the outdoor area is fantastic), serving dishes such as smoked salmon tartar and home-made veal ravioli, but it can be pricey. The **Engel Ratskeller** (Städtle 13, 9490 Vaduz, 3236 17 17, www.restaurant-engel.li) is less expensive but no less yummy, serving Swiss, German and Austrian dishes such as Schnitzel, Spätzle and hefty glasses of beer.

There are quite a few vineyards in Liechtenstein – with 178 wine growers, you can buy good wine at all the supermarkets and tourist shops. There are quite a few wine-tasting options, for instance at the Hofkellerei (www.hofkellerei.li) mentioned earlier, or at the **Harry Zech Winery Cantina** (Vorarlbergerstrasse, Schaanwald, 370 11 00), run by a former defender from the national football team.

## STAY

The aforementioned **Parkhotel Sonnenhof** is certainly worth staying at if you're not after a budget hotel; rooms with views of the Rhine Valley are especially nice. **Landgasthof Au** (Austrasse 2, 9490 Vaduz, 232 11 17, www.gasthof-au.li) is more traditional, ten minutes away from the city centre and with an adjoining beer garden. Breakfast is included and the hotel hosts lively BBQ parties in the warmer months.

The **Hotel Residence** (Städtle 23, 9490 Vaduz, 239 20 20, www.residence.li) is business-like and minimalist, with large king-sized beds, flatscreen TVs and steam showers (or whirlpool baths, in some cases). **Hotel Gasthof Löwen** (Herrengasse 35, 9490 Vaduz, 238 11 44, www.hotel-loewen.li) is in a 600-year-old house, with appropriately kitschy rooms (most notably the ornamental, high-backed dark wooden headboards) and decent prices.

## GETTING THERE & AROUND

You'll have a harder time getting to Liechtenstein than you'll ever have getting around it. Due to its size, there isn't an airport in the country – the closest are in Friedrichshafen in Germany and Zurich in Switzerland. Liechtenstein is only about an hour away from Zurich by train or car (115km), and Innsbruck is two hours away (and a lovely drive). Check the Swiss railway schedule at www.sbb.ch, Austria's on www.oebb.at/en and the Liechtenstein bus schedule on www.lba.li. If you're getting there by car, the Swiss Autobahn A13/E34 will get you to Liechtenstein, along the Rhine.

The official language of Liechtenstein is German, though you should be fine with English in most places. The temperature is mostly mild, ranging from 15°C in winter and 28°C in summer, thanks to the south-west wind, the Föhn.

# Palma

Although many visitors to Mallorca still never set foot in its cosmopolitan capital – heading straight from airport to resort – the growing number that do are normally pleasantly surprised by its assured character and sophistication. As well as varied and characterful eating opportunities, and an impressive number of boutique hotels for such a small city, you'll also find frenetic shopping streets, fine *modernista* architecture, cool seafront bars and an expanding contemporary art scene; think of it as a sort of mini-Barcelona, but without the suffocating tourist droves and related street crime. For, despite the exponential development of the wide bay that it dominates, this city of a third of a million people remains resolutely Spanish (or, as the locals would insist, *Mallorquí*) and in most of the city's cafés, restaurants and bars you'll find as many locals as visitors. Add in the ease of getting out into Mallorca's spectacular mountains or to the sea, and it's easy to see why Palma has become so popular as a weekend break destination for those in the know.

Catedral de Palma

## Fast facts

**Country dialling code** +34
**Journey time** Flight 2 hours 20 minutes
**Festivals & events** Jazz Voyeur Festival (April-December, www.jazzvoyeurfestival.com) – a series of hugely popular jazz concerts; Copa del Rey (July-August, www.copadelreyaudimapre.com) – arguably the most important regatta in the Mediterranean; Nit de l'Art (September, www.jamartmallorca.com) – the annual 'art night', when galleries stay open till late, and there's a genuine buzz around town
**Good for** Beaches, culture, food

## SEE & DO

Palma's most interesting area is its pristine historic core, within which lies a clutch of compelling sights secreted among its twisting medieval streets. The modern city, fanning out behind it, is fairly bland in contrast, with few real attractions for the average visitor. A bigger draw is the café-specked waterside, stretching from the modern **Parc del la**

Castell de Bellver

Plaça Major

Palau March

Hotel Tres

La Bóveda

Mar, in front of the cathedral (*see below*), east to the old fishing harbour of now-trendy **Portitxol**, and west to below the impressive **Castell de Bellver**, which contains the city-history museum (Calle Camilo José Cela s/n, 971 73 06 57).

On the old town's shoreline, cruise ships and yachts are dwarfed by Palma's landmark and top attraction: the mighty **Catedral de Palma**, known locally as **La Seu** (Plaça de l'Almoina s/n, 971 72 31 30, www.catedral demallorca.info). In addition to some daring renovations by Antoni Gaudí, the cathedral's newest addition – completed in 2007 – is a stunning 300-square-metre ceramic mural by Mallorcan artist Miquel Barceló, representing the miracle of the loaves and fishes. The cathedral was built in the 13th century on the site of a mosque – the Moors ruled Mallorca for 400 years, and the Islamic seat of power, the **Palau de l'Almudaina** (C/Palau Reial s/n, 971 21 41 34) still stands next door. Just to the west, **Sa Llotja** (Plaça Llotja, 971 71 17 05) is a 15th-century merchants' exchange. It gave its name to Palma's historic quarter, where narrow streets team with shops, bars and restaurants opening out on to leafy squares.

The narrow streets that meander eastwards from the cathedral are some of the city's most characterful. This district is known as **Sa Calatrava** and contains a number of diverting museums and mansions, including the **Museu de Mallorca** (Portella 5, 971 71 75 40, www.museude mallorca.es); if you have any interest in the island's prehistory, an hour here is time well spent.

Head north of the cathedral and you'll come to **Plaça Cort**, a key hub of the city since the 13th century. It's easily identified by the twisted 1,000-year-old olive tree that sits in its centre. The square is dominated by the 16th- to 17th-century **Ajuntament** (Town Hall). Walk further north, up Calle Carnisseria, and you'll come to the lovely **Plaça Salvador Coll**, home to some nice lunch spots. To the left along Calle Bosseria is a conjunction of narrow streets at Plaça Marquès de Palmer, where two of the city's finest *modernista* buildings sit side by side: private residence **Can Rei** and former department store **L'Aguila**. Just beyond them is the large, arcaded **Plaça Major**, Palma's central square, and the haunt of mime artists, buskers and touristy cafés.

Contemporary art-lovers are well catered for by two grand public exhibition spaces, the **Palau March** (Calle Palau Reial 18, 971 71 11 22, www.fundacionbmarch.es), featuring the work of such international sculptors as Rodin and Henry Moore, and the **Es Baluard** museum of modern Spanish art (Plaça Porta de Santa Catalina 10, 971 90 82 00, www.esbaluard.org). The latter, housed in a 16th-century Renaissance fortress, contains pieces by Picasso and Miró, and has some excellent temporary exhibitions. Its restaurant has a huge terrace with amazing views of Palma's port.

The former home of Joan Miró – who lived and worked in Mallorca for 40 years – lies a few miles south-west of the centre, and forms part of the **Fundació Pilar I Joan Miró** (Calle Joan de Saridakis 29, 971 70 14 20, http://miro.palmademallorca.es), which is filled with the celebrated artist's works.

There is no shortage of nearby attractions on this compact island, but one of the most accessible and charming day trips is a ride on the old-fashioned brass and mahogany narrow-gauge train **Ferrocarril de Sóller** (971 75 20 51, www.trendesoller.com) north through the mountains and orange groves to the little town of **Sóller**. From there, it's a short ride to the picture-perfect mountain village of **Deià** – once a denizen of expat artists and writers centred around Robert Graves, now a second home for a host of celebs, including Bob Geldof and Michael Douglas. With stone houses, winding streets and a backdrop featuring the Tramuntana mountain range, it's a romantic setting.

## EAT & DRINK

Traditional, rustic Mallorcan cuisine includes *pa amb oli* – bread smeared with tomatoes and olive oil, served with local cheese and/or ham; *sobrassada*, a chorizo-type sausage; and tasty *ensaïmadas* – spiral-shaped breakfast pastries. All of these are available in cafés all over the city. Pork is the most common meat on restaurant menus, while seafood also features heavily.

Palma has an impressive number of high-quality restaurants. The majority of noteworthy places are located around the Passeig des Born in the centre, and in Sa Llotja and Santa Catalina, with old-school spots, such as tapas joint **La Bóveda** (Paseo Sagrera 3, 971 72 00 26, www.tabernadelaboveda.com) – serving classic *tortilla*, local cheeses and hams, seafood, and good-value wines and sherries – competing for custom with a new wave of places that includes *pintxos* bar **La 5a Puñeta** (Calle de les Caputxines 3, 971 71 15 71), popular with Palma's arty set, and the modern, clean-lined **Tast** (Calle Unió 2, 971 72 98 78), for top-notch tapas.

For cheap, local cuisine served in a high-ceilinged dining room plastered with bullfighting posters, head north of the centre to Plaça Bisbe Berenguer de Palou, where you'll find **Celler Sa Premsa** (no.8, 971 72 35 29, www.cellersa premsa.com). For the opposite experience, dine at one of Palma's many high-end restaurants; **Simply Fosh** (Calle de la Missió 7A, 971 72 01 14, www.simplyfosh.com), Marc Fosh's seasonally focused fine-dining establishment, is one of the best and also least stuffy.

Palma has a thriving café society, with its residents' keenness on 'doing coffee' exemplified by the success of the home-grown **Cappuccino** chain (www.grupocappuccino.com), whose best-known and most atmospheric branch is the Grand Café on Calle Sant Miguel.

For evening drinks, there's **Ábaco** (Calle Sant Joan 1, 971 71 49 39, www.bar-abaco.com), Palma's most talked-about establishment, full of kitsch flowers, fountains, theatrical decor and colourful cocktails. For a trendier vibe, head to the districts of Ciutat Jardi and Portitxol.

## SHOP

Palma's shopping is concentrated in two main areas that run into each other: along **Passeig des Born** and the mainly pedestrianised streets running east towards Plaça Major and bounded by Calle Unio; and the streets running east and north of **Plaça Major**, including Calle Sindicat, Calle San Miquel and Calle Oms. One of Mallorca's best-known brands is shoe chain **Camper**, which has a branch on Calle Sant Miquel (no.17, 971 22 85 88, www.camper.com). For traditional Mallorcan foodstuffs, head to **Sobrasada** (Calle Santo Domingo 1, 971 71 48 87). For traditional coloured glassware, try the Palma outlets of the famed **Gordiola** factory (Calle Victoria 2, 971 71 15 41, and Calle Jaime II 14, 971 71 55 18) – but be prepared for high prices.

## STAY

Palma has a limited number of budget options, but plenty of boutique-style hotels. Most of the latter are found in the old town, with bigger chains strung along the Passeig Maritim.

One of the best bets in the mid-range hotel bracket is the charmingly old-world **Hotel Born** (Calle Sant Jaume 3, 971 71 29 42, www.hotelborn.com), set in a 16th-century palace.

Our favourites from the many boutique hotels are **Hotel Tres** (Calle Apuntadors 3, 971 71 73 33, www.hoteltres.com), with its white, minimalist rooms; **Hotel Santa Clara** (Calle San Alonso 16, 971 72 92 31, www.hotelsantaclarahotel.es) – renowned for its sunbathing roof terrace and cathedral views; and, over in Portixtol, the Swedish-owned **Hotel Portixol** (Calle Sirena 27, 971 27 18 00, www.portixol.com), with ultra-suave decor and cool details such as binoculars in each room. Back in the old town, **Hotel Can Cera** (Calle San Francisco, 971 71 50 12, www.hotelcancera.com) has been gaining column inches for its beautifully converted 13th-century building and amazing spa.

## GETTING THERE & AROUND

There are daily EasyJet flights from Gatwick and Stansted, and daily Ryanair flights from Stansted. From Palma's Son Sant Joan Airport, eight kilometres outside the city, take bus no.1, which runs between the airport and the bay-side Passeig Maritim via Plaça Espanya every 15 minutes (from 6am to 2.15am daily) and costs around €2. A taxi between the airport and the city centre will set you back around €22.

Palma's old town is compact enough to be easily explored by foot. To get to the further reaches of the city, it's worth hiring a bike, which will also allow you to take advantage of the waterside cycle path that runs most of the way around the Bay of Palma. A range of bus routes also circumnavigate the old town (almost all passing through Plaça Espanya) and run along the coastal roads either side of the bay.

# Avignon

The legacy of Avignon's brief spell under papal rule is everywhere you look. You can see it in the many churches dotted around the historic centre, in the dramatic Gothic architecture of the Palais des Papes and in the artistic gems hanging on the walls of Avignon's galleries and museums. Little wonder UNESCO has granted the city World Heritage Site status. The Place de l'Horlogue, the main square, is the perfect spot for people-watching while enjoying Provençal cuisine washed down with the local Rhône wine. In July, the pace of Avignon life is ramped up considerably as it hosts a performing arts festival to rival that of Edinburgh. But throughout the rest of the year, the mood is pleasantly relaxed.

St Bénezét Bridge

## Fast facts

**Country dialling code** +33
**Journey time** Flight 1 hour 45 minutes to Marseille then 53-minute train journey; train 5 hours 49 minutes
**Festivals & events** Festival d'Avignon (July, www.festival-avignon.com/en) – for three weeks each summer, Avignon becomes the backdrop for hundreds of performances, from premières by big-name directors to impromptu street theatre. Don't be perturbed by the oddly dressed characters accosting you on all sides. They're actors peddling tickets to their shows; Tremplin Jazz (August, www.trempjazz.fr) – Avignon's other summer festival, which takes place in Avignon's Cloître des Carmes, is a celebration of all things jazz. Set up in 1992, Tremplin Jazz offers a platform to the best young talent and established jazz musicians; Fête des Côtes du Rhône Primeurs (November, www.millevin.fr) – get a taste of the Rhône Valley at this annual wine festival, which takes place at Les Halles covered market and various participating restaurants across town; Festival Les Hivernales (February, www.hivernales-avignon.com) – from hip hoppers to tango teachers, choreographers and dancers of all sorts descend on Avignon each winter for this week-long contemporary dance festival
**Good for** Culture, food, wine

## SEE & DO

Avignon's cobbled streets were made for meandering. Pick up a map from the tourist office (41 cours Jean Jaurès, (0)4 32 74 32 74) and go for a saunter around the *centre-ville* (town centre), ending up at **Le Palais des Papes** (6 rue Pente Rapide, www.palais-des-papes.com). This imposing Gothic palace was the official residence of Clement V and the subsequent generations of popes who made this city their home in the 14th century. With 25 rooms, including the fabulously ornate pope's bedroom, there's plenty to explore on the inside too.

Just around the corner is the site without which no visit to Avignon would be complete. **Le Pont d'Avignon**, or to give it its official name, St Bénezét Bridge (rue Ferruce, www.palais-des-papes.com), was made famous by French school kids (and French language learners) singing the catchy ditty 'Sur le Pont d'Avignon'. We wouldn't recommend dancing on the medieval bridge, which has suffered flood damage over the years and now ends halfway across the Rhône.

If you plan to do anything remotely cultural – as well you should here – grab an **Avignon Passion** pass, free when you pay full price at the first attraction you visit. This gives you discounted entry to Avignon's many museums. The **Musée du Petit Palais** (place du Palais des Papes, (0)4 90 86 44 58, www.petit-palais.org), once a residence for archbishops, now holds a permanent collection of art from

Le Palais des Papes

Hôtel de la Mirande

the Middle Ages to the Renaissance, while the Collection Lambert caters for contemporary art-lovers with exhibitions of work dating from the 1960s to the present day by Cy Twombly, Jean-Michel Basquiat and others.

If you're prepared to set aside a day, a jaunt to nearby **Nîmes** is highly recommended. The train ride takes about an hour; there you will find some of the best-preserved Roman architecture in the world. Head straight to the main square to ogle the **Maison Carée**, a magnificent temple, complete with dramatic Roman columns. Another must-see is **Les Arènes**, a first-century amphitheatre. In the past a bloodthirsty audience of 23,000 would flock here to watch gladiators slaughter each other, but today, save for the occasional bullfight, it's the serene setting for concerts and theatrical performances.

## FOOD & DRINK

Being the so-called 'gateway to Provence', Avignon isn't short of decent eateries. Be sure to make a reservation for **La Fourchette** (17 rue Racine, (0)4 90 85 20 93), a traditional bistro deservedly popular with tourists and locals. **Le Brigadier du Théâtre** (17 rue Racine, (0)4 90 82 21 19, www.lebrigadier.com) is worth visiting as much for the delightfully kitsch interior as the tasty Provençal dishes.

Guests of the **Hôtel de la Mirande** (4 place de l'Amirande, (0)4 90 14 20 20, www.lamirande.fr) should

nip to the excellent restaurant downstairs for some of the best fine dining in Avignon. Head chef Frédéric Duca also gives cookery classes and on Tuesdays and Fridays invites diners to eat with him around the kitchen table. Restaurant **Christian Etienne** (10 rue de Mons, (0)4 90 86 16 50, www.christian-etienne.fr) offers set menus, themed around tomatoes or truffles, depending on the season, and stunningly good à la carte options, including the chef's signature dish: roasted lobster claws with asparagus and ginger.

With gleaming piles of fresh fruit and veg and mountains of cheese at every turn, **Les Halles** (place Pie, www.avignon-leshalles.com) is a proper French market and ideal for stocking up for a picnic. Every Saturday at 11am, leading local chefs drop into *la petite cuisine* (the little kitchen) to share their expertise and good humour via cookery demonstrations and tastings.

The local wine is lip-smackingly good and can be sampled by the glass at **AOC Cave et Bar à Vins** (5 rue Tremoulet, (0)4 90 25 21 04), a tiny wine bar down an unassuming side road. Don't be put off by the shabby exterior, the wine here is excellent. AOC also serves tasty, reasonably priced platters of charcuterie and other food to line the stomach. Buy a bottle (or several) to take home from the well-stocked cellar.

## STAY

A word of warning: Avignon is positively heaving with visitors during the theatre festival, so if you plan a weekend break here during this time, sort out your accommodation well in advance. Avignon has ample choice of places for weary Londoners to lay their heads. If you're on a tight budget, the **Pont d'Avignon Campsite** (10 chemin de la Barthelasse, (0)4 90 80 63 50, www.camping-avignon.com), just across the river on Île de la Barthelasse, is open from March to November. Similarly good value, but a tad cosier, **Hotel Mignon** (12 rue Joseph Vernet, (0)4 90 82 17 30, www.hotel-mignon.com) offers dinky rooms and a warm welcome. In the mid-range, **Hotel Bristôl** (44 cours Jean Jaurès, (0)4 90 16 48 48, www.bristol-avignon.com/uk) is well located for sightseeing in the historic centre. If you're after something swankier, try **Hôtel de la Mirande** (4 place de l'Amirande, (0)4 90 14 20 20, www.lamirande.fr), a former cardinal's palace, which boasts sumptuous decor and Michelin-starred dining.

## GETTING THERE & AROUND

There are no direct flights from London to Avignon. British Airways and EasyJet both fly from Gatwick to Marseille in an hour and three-quarters and a connecting train from the airport to Avignon city centre takes just 53 minutes. Between July and September you're best off taking the Eurostar from London St Pancras to Avignon town centre station, arriving right outside the city walls in just under six hours. If you're keen to travel by rail outside the summer months, you can change at Lille. The journey takes up to 6 hours 25 minutes. You'll arrive a few miles from the town centre, at Avignon TGV Station, but hop on a *navette* (shuttle bus) and you'll be there in ten minutes. Within Avignon there is a bus service but, given the town's relatively dinky size, you're best off exploring by foot or on a *vélopop*, Avignon's answer to the Boris Bike.

# Copenhagen

Copenhagen always does well in those surveys of the world's most liveable cities, and arriving in the city provides ample evidence as to why. The fast metro link to the city will take you direct to the centre in just 15 minutes, meaning that you can be shopping in fabulous design and fashion boutiques, eating superb New Nordic cuisine, cycling around the famous blue bike lanes, or taking the kids on one of the rollercoasters in the supremely *hygge* (a Danish concept meaning 'cosy' or 'comforting') Tivoli pleasure park in no time at all. As well as the unbeatable cycling culture, Danes also embrace healthy, outdoor city living through the city's harbour baths, which are now clean enough to swim in, or by strolling along the spruced-up waterfront, with its impressive new architecture and cultural centres. And linking everything up is the local obsession with good, functional design applied to everyday life. Copenhagen may not be the world's cheapest city, but it's certainly one of the most stylish – yet it remains friendly and unintimidating in that classic Scandinavian way.

## Fast facts

**Country dialling code** +45
**Journey time** Flight 1.5 hours; train 20 hours
**Festivals & events** Queen Megrethe's Birthday Parade (16 April, 33 92 64 51) – join thousands of Danes at the foot of the public balcony of the Amelienborg Palace, where the Queen appears at noon; Copenhagen Cooking (August, www.copenhagencooking.dk) – when the city's top chefs get together to cook up a New Nordic feast; Tivoli Christmas Season (November-December) – for a truly *hygge* (cosy) Scandinavian atmosphere. Christmas markets sell *Gløgg* and *æbleskiver* – Danish versions of mulled wine – along with decorations, gifts and delicious seasonal foodstuffs
**Good for** Culture, food, shopping

Christianshavn

## SEE & DO

It's easy to get your bearings in Copenhagen. Most of the sights are in a compact area to the east of the city, with much new development along the waterfront. The city's medieval centre has a plethora of museums and royal palaces, along with ample shopping and fine dining, making it the perfect place to begin your Copenhagen exploration. Start at the lakes of the Østre Anlæg park, which follow the lines of the city's old defensive moat. Here you'll find the **Statens Museum For Kunst** (Sølvgade 48-50, 33 74 84 94, www.smk.dk), a world-class collection of Danish and European art. The main focus is, of course, Danish artists (Vilhelm Hammershøi, JT Lundbye and CW Eckersburg, to name a few), but there is a cleverly curated new wing with a fine selection of works by Matisse, Braque, Munch and Picasso, as well as sculptures by Kai Nielsen and Astrid Noack. The old wing has Titians, Rubens, Rembrandts, Poussins and Fragonards; you'll need several hours to explore.

Diagonally across from the Statens Museum, the fairytale, Dutch Renaissance **Rosenborg Slot** (Øster Volgade 4A, 33 15 32 86, www.rosenborgslot.dk) started life as a small

Islands Brygge

# SHOPPING... DINING...
# MUSIC... ART...
# METRO...

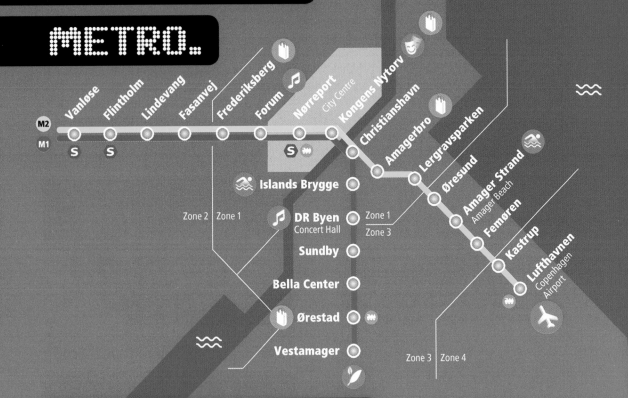

Vanløse · Flintholm · Lindevang · Fasanvej · Frederiksberg · Forum · Nørreport (City Centre) · Kongens Nytorv · Christianshavn · Amagerbro · Lergravsparken · Øresund · Amager Strand (Amager Beach) · Femøren · Kastrup · Lufthavnen (Copenhagen Airport)

M2 · M1

Islands Brygge

DR Byen (Concert Hall) · Sundby · Bella Center · Ørestad · Vestamager

Zone 2 | Zone 1

Zone 1 | Zone 3

Zone 3 | Zone 4

## Timetable
The Metro operates 24 hours a day, all week. Trains leave every 2-6 minutes during the day and every 8-20 minutes at night.

## Airport
The Metro runs to and from Copenhagen Airport. The trip from the city centre takes 14 minutes.

## Tickets
You can purchase tickets from the Metro ticket machines located at all Metro stations. Ticket prices

vary depending on the number of zones you travel. Valid for one or two hours.

**10-clip card** – Same as tickets, but with up to a 40% discount. Remember to stamp the card at the start of your journey.

**City Pass** – Unlimited travel throughout central Copenhagen (all Metro stations) for a 24- or 72-hour period.

Find more travel info at **intl.m.dk**

**M**
Let's go

summer house, extended by Christian IV between 1606 and 1634 and still jam-packed with the king's fancies: toys, architectural tricks, inventions, art objects and jewellery. The 24 rooms on show offer an unparalleled insight into the lives of Renaissance kings, and the treasures it houses – such as Christian IV's gold, pearl and jewel-encrusted saddle and crown – are jaw-dropping. A special late-night, torch-lit tour takes place once a year on **Kulturnatten** (*see p177* **Fast facts**).

Head east of the Rosenborg Slot, down Gothersgade, and you'll come to **Kongens Nytorv** (literally, 'King's New Square'), which has had a recent facelift. Home to the Royal Theatre, **Det Kongelige Teater**, **Gamle Scene** (Old Stage), it's also a popular spot for a stroll, and leads to Copenhagen's most famous strip: **Nyhavn** – the canalside stretch famous for its colourful 17th-century houses, three of which (nos.18, 20 and 67) were former residences of Hans Christian Andersen. The street is often swamped with tourists, but it's still an essential sight. Head to the end of Nyhavn and you'll see the impressive new Royal Danish Playhouse – **Skuespilhuset** – in a prime spot overlooking the water. On the other side is Henning Larsen's **Opera House** – something of a new architectural icon for the city – while walking further north along the waterfront brings you to another of the city's older icons – Edward Eriksen's (somewhat overrated) statue depicting Andersen's **Little Mermaid** (Den Lille Hayfrue).

The characterful neighbourhoods of **Vesterbro**, **Frederiksberg** and **Nørrebro** are to the west, and this is where the locals live, drink, eat and shop.

To reach Nørrebro, cross the lake via Nørrebrogade, or another of the bridges, and head to the graceful cemetery to see the resting place of Copenhagen's elite. **Assistens Kirkegårde** (Jagvej and Nørrebrogade, 35 37 19 17, www.assistens.dk) 'has' many a great Dane, including Hans Christian Andersen and philosopher Søren Kierkgaard. Hundreds of varieties of trees make this a shady (in every sense) spot for a picnic, and it is used by many as a local park. Nørrebro is now one of the city's trendiest districts, and a match for Vesterbro, to its south, when it comes to attracting creatives. Both house excellent fashion and design boutiques – along with several of the city's many bike shops – and are interesting neighbourhoods to wander around. Slightly further out is the more refined neighbourhood of Frederiksberg, home to, among other green spaces, **Copenhagen Zoo** (Zoologisk Have, Roskildevej 32, 72 20 02 00, www.zoo.dk).

Another spot that makes a similarly pleasant day out when skies are blue is the former industrial area of **Islands Brygge**, a key part of the city's strategy for revitalising 42 kilometres of former docklands. The construction of the **Copenhagen Harbour Baths** (Islands Brygge 7, 23 71 31 89, www.kubik.kk.dk/islandsbryggebad) here in 2003 has created a popular summer bathing destination. Open from the end of May to the end of August, the harbour water is clean (and constantly monitored), and many parts have been given a Blue Flag.

Finally, no visit to Copenhagen is complete without a wander into the commune of **Christiania** – a self-declared independent state. A mess of historic military buildings (it used to be an army barracks until 1971), individually built, sometimes eccentric houses, and adhoc-style businesses, Christiania has to be seen to be believed (especially as photography is banned – you'll see signs

Café Wilder

Christiania

Radisson Blu (SAS) Royal Hotel

Vesterbro

warning against snapping away). Home to around 1,000 people, it is one of Copenhagen's biggest tourist attractions, and until recently it was a community that existed outside of Copenhagen's laws and regulations, complete with soft drug stalls alongside groceries in the local market. Now a 'legalisation' process has demolished much of the obvious illegal activities, although most residents remain committed to their alternative lifestyle.

If you have time for a day trip out of Copenhagen, make sure it's to the **Louisiana Museum For Modern Kunst** (Gammel Strandvej 13, Humlebaek, 49 19 07 19, www.louisiana.dk), 40 minutes' by train. There may be larger modern art collections in the world, but surely none is located in more blissful surroundings.

## EAT & DRINK

Rene Redzepi's **Noma** restaurant (Strandgade 93, 32 96 32 97, www.noma.dk), in Christianshavn, has been at the top of many a 'world's best restaurant' list for the past few years, becoming the city's most prominent symbol for New Nordic cuisine, which emphasises local ingredients, such as berries, foraged wild produce, root vegetables, pickled fish, and organic dairy and meat. But while the restaurant does live up to the hype, getting a reservation there is another matter. You may have more luck at Nørrebro's well-regarded **Relae** (Jaegersborggade 41, 36 96 66 09, www.restaurant-relae.dk), established by ex-Noma chefs.

Make sure you fit in a meal at the Meatpacking District – **Kødbyen** – in Vesterbro during your stay. **Fiskbaren** (Flæsketorvet 100, Vesterbro, 32 15 56 56, www.fiskebaren.dk) is the mini-district's trendy seafood restaurant, which serves the freshest of fish in an industrial space. Oysters from the icy depths of Limfjorden, Øresund mussels with raspberry and walnut dressing, or fish and chips are some of the tasty offerings – along with an excellent northern European wine list. Other good Kødbyen restaurants include **Mother** pizza parlour (Høkerboderne 9-15, 22 27 59 98, www.mother.dk) – whose pizza bases are made with sourdough – and **PatéPaté** (Slagterboderne 1, 39 69 55 57, http://patepate.dk), which is part of a five-strong portfolio of excellent bars and eateries spread around the city. The

Frederiksberg

Hotel Fox

## Cultural baggage

**Book** *The Complete Fairy Tales* (Hans Christian Andersen)
**Film** *Festen* (Thomas Vinterberg, 1998)

Meatpacking District is now Copenhagen's number one drinking spot too, so follow your meal with a few Carlsbergs at one of the numerous bars (**Bakken i Kødbyen** is a current favourite).

For wallet-conscious dinners, try modern Danish cuisine at the centrally located **Madklubben** (Store Kongensgade 66, 33 32 32 34, www.madklubben.info). Furnished in typically Danish wood panelling with long, canteen-style tables, this is a fun place to eat with a group of friends, with the menu featuring classics such as steak with Jerusalem artichokes and catch of the day with roasted fennel. Another spot that's great for Danish classics is Vesterbro's **Dyrehaven** (Sdr. Boulevard 72, 33 21 60 24, www.dyrehavenkbh.dk) – one of the best spots in town to try *smørrebrod* (traditional open sandwiches).

Brunch is a strong Copenhagen tradition, with **Meyers Deli** (Gammel Kongevej 107, 33 25 45 95, www.meyers deli.dk) providing some of the tastiest (and most expensive) offerings, such as rye bread with smoked salmon, incredible cinnamon-flavoured pastries, and top-notch coffees, teas and hot chocolate – to eat in or take away. Another popular brunch spot is Christianshavn's **Café Wilder** (Wildersgade 56, 32 54 71 83, www.cafewilder.dk), a lovely café-bar with fresh, cheap and simple fodder (pasta, salads, sandwiches) and charming service.

Finally, don't miss Copenhagen's new covered gourmet food market, **Torvehallen** (Frederiksborggade 21, 70 10 60 70, www.torvehallernekbh.dk), which opened in autumn 2011 right by Nørreport station, in the centre. Open daily, it's the best place to get an introduction to modern Nordic cuisine.

## STAY

Hotel rates in Copenhagen are famously high, although in the past decade or so a growing number of low- and mid-range hotels have sprung up. Most budget hotels are situated in Vesterbro, just west of Central Station. **Hotel Fox** (Jarmers Plads 3, Vesterbro, 33 95 77 55, www.hotelfox.dk) is a good bet; the rooms are designed by some of Europe's top graphic designers, illustrators and graffiti artists, and downstairs houses a sushi bar. You can rent bikes from reception.

Lower rates can be had at nearby **Hotel Sct Thomas** (Frederiksberg Allé 7, Fredericksberg, 33 21 64 64, www. hotelsctthomas.dk), a small and intimate hotel with a welcoming atmosphere, in one of the most sought-after residential areas of town. Breakfast is included, but only 26 of the 44 rooms are ensuite.

Another central and low-cost place to stay is at **DanHostel Copenhagen City** (HC Andersens Boulevard 50, Vestebro, 33 18 83 32, www.dghi-byen.dk/hostel), a huge 'five-star hostel', kitted out with trendy Scandinavian furniture with fantastic views over the Langebro Bridge. You can rent a whole room by paying for the extra beds, which will still work out cheaper than any of the two- or three-star hotels nearby.

Those on a larger budget should consider staying at **Radisson Blu (SAS) Royal Hotel** (Hammerischsgade 1, 33 42 60 00, www.radissonblu.com), designed – both the building itself and the original interior, down to the cutlery – by Arne Jacobsen, Denmark's most famous architect-designer, in 1960. While the interior has been modernised, one room (no.606) has retained the original

*Mad Men*-esque mid-century modern decor, while other rooms have fabulous views over Tivoli.

But to really splash out, it has to be the five-star **Nimb Hotel** (Bernstorffsgade 5, 88 70 00 00, www.nimb.dk), a converted 1909 Moorish-inspired building right next to Tivoli Gardens.

## SHOP

The majority of retail therapy can be had on and around the seemingly endless **Strøget** in the city centre, with edgier, more fashion-forward items sold at the boutiques of Nørrebro, Frederiksberg and Vesterbro.

Not far from Kongens Nytorv is **Antique Toys** (Store Strandstræde 20, 33 12 66 32, www.antique-toys.dk), one of Copenhagen's cutest stores, selling antique toys in all shapes and sizes – some dating as far back as the 17th century. For more contemporary Danish design, head to **Stilleben** (Niels Hemmingsensgade 3, 33 91 11 31, www.stilleben.dk), just off Strøget, selling a range of candle holders, woollen rugs and other supremely stylish Scandinavian homewares, as well as modern jewellery. On Strøget itself, don't miss **Royal Copenhagen** (Amagertorv 6, Strøget, 33 13 71 81, www.royalcopenhagen.com), which is famous for its porcelain, and which also encompasses upmarket homewares store **Illums Bolighus** (Amagertorv 10, Strøget, 33 14 19 41). Further along, with entrances on Østergade, is Copenhagen's best department store, **Illum** (Østergade 52, Strøget, 33 14 40 02, www.illum.dk), which should delight fans of Scandiavian fashion labels, and which also houses a great food hall.

Copenhagen is particularly strong on cool menswear labels, with **Norse Store** (Pilestræde 4, 33 93 26 26, www.norsestore.com) one of the best of the bunch, selling workwear-inspired own-label garments as well as a selection of items from Folk, Acne, Levis and the like. Women can find similarly cutting-edge style at **Parterre** (Gammel Kongevej 103, 31 54 43 13, www.parterre.dk), in Frederiksberg, while home-grown brand **Wood Wood** (Grønnegade 1, 35 35 62 64, www.woodwood.dk) caters for both sexes.

For gourmet foodstuffs, meanwhile, head to the excellent new covered market, **Torvehallen** (*see left*).

## GETTING THERE & AROUND

Flight time from London to Copenhagen's Kastrup Airport is roughly one hour and 30 minutes, and the Copenhagen Metro link has recently been extended as far as the airport, taking just 15 minutes to reach Central Station (København H). If you'd rather go by train, you'll need to go via Amsterdam, from where you can catch a DSB train (De Danske Statsbaner – Danish State Railways).

Although Copenhagen has excellent public transport (the Metro was named the world's best in 2010, and local buses are efficient and clean), the city has the most bike-friendly infrastructure in the world, with blue bike lanes safely separating cyclists from other road traffic. Hire a bike to experience the city from a local perspective; City Bike is the official summer bike hire scheme (equivalent to Boris Bikes). Otherwise, the best bike-hire rates can be had at Baiskeli (Turensensgade 10, 26 70 02 29, www.baisikeli.dk).

In summer, boat tours are a great way to see the city. DFDS Canal Tours (33 96 30 00, www.canaltours.com) depart from Nyhavn and Gammel Strand half-hourly.

# Valencia

'The melon of Castile is for self-abuse; the melon of Valencia for eating,' wrote Hemingway, hinting at the laid-back attitude to pleasure in Valencia – not to mention a gastronomical heritage borne of being located in one of Spain's most blessed agricultural regions. With Mediterranean breezes to keep it cool, and a smallish size to keep it relatively calm – there is none of the try-hard tension of Barcelona or Madrid here – Valencia is very visitor-friendly. It's also a city that's fascinatingly (and occasionally infuriatingly) in flux; a tragic flood in 1957 resulted in the Turia's old riverbed being turned into an 18-kilometre-long park ending at the sea, where, in the preamble to hosting the 2007 America's Cup, a slew of futuristic buildings has given the city a deserved reputation for architectural ambition. New bars and restaurants, both in the old town and around the sleek new marina district, have added to an already varied nightlife. And then there are those paellas…

Ciudad de las Artes y las Ciencias

## Fast facts

**Country dialling code** +34
**Journey time** Flight 2.5 hours; train 20 hours
**Festivals & events** Las Fallas (March, www.fallasfromvalencia.com), a festival of fireworks, bonfires and all-night drinking; Benicassim annual music festival takes place in a coastal town near Valencia (July, www.fiberfib.com); the infamous Tomatina tomato-throwing festival (August, www.latomatina.org) takes place in Buñol, a 35-minute drive from Valencia
**Good for** Beaches, culture, food

## SEE & DO

You don't need to be an architecture buff to appreciate Valencia's beautiful historical district. The perfectly preserved 19th-century bullring, **Plaza de Toros** (10 Pje del Doctor Serra, 963 883 738, www.museotaurino valencia.es), is a good place to orientate yourself. Walk west to find the **Torres de Quart** (89 Guillem de Castro)

– towers that were part of the medieval wall, and which are still pockmarked by a French invasion in 1808. The **Cathedral** (Plaza de la Reina, 963 918 127, www.catedral devalencia.es) also claims to house the mother of all religious relics: the Holy Grail. Its 'El Miguelete' bell tower rival's any Gothic interior and boasts two Goyas.

The **Plaza Redonda** (circular 'square') gives a glimpse of old Valencia and is a must-see. It houses a market on Sundays that sells keepsakes, clothing and religious paraphernalia. If you're after modern art, head to **IVAM** (118 C/Guillem de Castro, 963 863 000, www.ivam.es), a futuristically designed gallery holding the city's best contemporary work. Alternatively, there are classic works from Velázquez, Murillo and El Greco at the belle époque **Museo de Bellas Artes** (San Pio V 9, 963 870 300, www.museobellasartesvalencia.gva.es).

Ricardo Bofil's transformation of the Turia riverbed into a lush park, complete with winding clusters of orange trees, fountains and bridges, makes the **Jardines de Turia** a good point from which to explore further. Inland, at its western end, the newly constructed **Bioparc** zoo (Avenida Pio Baroja 3, 902 250 340, www.bioparcvalencia.es) is home to elephants, lions and panthers inhabiting impressively natural-looking enclosures. It's a great draw for families,

IVAM

but so too is the park's eastern end, where the much-celebrated science and arts complex, the **Ciudad de las Artes y las Ciencias** (Prolongacion Paseo Alameda 48, 902 100 031, www.cac.es), can be found. Looking like some mad scientist's version of a space station, the marvellous skeletal structure, set around vast fountains, houses an opera house, IMAX cinema, science museum and world-class aquarium. From here, it's a short walk – or better yet, cycle – to the elegant design of the **Juan Carlos 1 Royal Marina** (963 812 009, www.marinarealjuancarlosi.com), built in the lead-up to hosting the 2007 America's Cup race. Adjoining Malvarossa beach is great for cafés, restaurants, people-watching and, of course, paella.

## EAT & DRINK

Valencians take their paella seriously. **La Pepica** (Paseo Neptuno 6, 963 710 366, www.lapepica.com) does a lobster variation that attracts celebrity clients, including Antonio Banderas. **El Rall** (Calle Tundidores 2, 963 922 090, www.elrall.es) does a more affordable but still authentic take on the dish. Closer to the cathedral, **La Lola** (Subida del Toledano 8, 963 918 045, www.lalolarestaurante.com) serves Modern European cuisine as flamenco dancers slink through the waiters. For award-winning Spanish-fusion, **Seu-Xerea** (Conde de Almodovar 4, 963 924 000, www.seuxerea.com) is unbeatable, while, down at the port, **Casa Montana** (Calle José Benlliure 69, 963 672 314, www.emilianobodega.com) has some of the best tapas in Spain. For something different, **Casa Guillermo** (Marina Real Juan Carlos I 9, 689 909 277, www.elreyde laanchoa.com) specialises in marinated anchovies. And for something *really* different, dine in the bowels of the **Oceanogràfic** aquarium (www.cac.es/oceanografic) at the ultra chi-chi **Submarino** (booking essential on 961 975 565).

## SHOP

The **Mercado Central** (Avenida Barón de Cárcer, 963 829 100, www.mercadocentralvalencia.es) is a foodie's dream, with around a thousand stalls hawking everything from eels to precious saffron. For high-street fashion, head to Calle Colón. Luxury brands such as Roberto Cavalli and

Bioparc

Catedral de Valencia

Juan Carlos 1 Royal Marina

Mercado Central

Hermès can be found at Calle Poeta Querol. The shops in El Carmen are a mixed bag of hip clothing, antique booksellers and taxidermists. One charming oddball is the 150-year-old fan shop **Abanicos Carbonell** (Calle Castellón 21, 963 415 395, www.abanicoscarbonell.com), which has been owned by the same family for four generations. If it's bargains you're after, head to **Plaza Luís Casanova** on a Sunday; vendors lay out blankets with pre-loved clothes and knick-knacks for one of the city's biggest flea markets.

## STAY

Close to the cathedral, the **AdHoc Monumental** (Calle Boix 4, 963 919 140, www.adhochoteles.com) is a B&B in a handsome late 19th-century townhouse in the historic Xerea quarter. **Hostal Antigua Morellana** (Calle En Bou 2, 963 915 773, www.hostalam.com) is very reasonable and has a homely atmosphere. **Hilux Valencia** (Calle Cadirers 11, 963 914 691, www.feetuphostels.com) is a cosy youth hostel close to the train station with free internet and no curfew. For those wanting to stay near the beach, **Hotel Sol Playa** (Paseo Neptuno 56 , 963 561 920, www.hotelsolplaya.com) is a basic but clean option with seaside views. With views over the marina, **Hotel Neptuno** (Paseo de Neptuno 2, 963 813 717, www.hotelneptunovalencia.com) is a cut above, offering a rooftop jacuzzi and a fully equipped gym.

## GETTING THERE & AROUND

EasyJet flies to Valencia from Gatwick; Ryanair from Stansted. The airport is five miles from the centre and there's a metro link. A **Valencia Tourist Card** (www.valenciatouristcard.com) allows visitors to use public transport for 48 hours, as well as access to some museums. Valencia is pretty flat and easy to navigate, so well suited to hiring a bike; there are hire shops dotted around town and in the Turia gardens, or many will deliver to your hotel.

Casa Montana

# Porto

Dramatically climbing up from the River Douro, Portugal's second city, with its vertiginous bridges and narrow streets of picturesque semi-ruins, has a flair for the dramatic. It's also a city in transition: the long-neglected and depopulated downtown area has seen an influx of new businesses, bars and restaurants in the last few years, and looks set to regain some of the urbane elegance and edge of its heyday. Away from the tourist magnet of the riverside area (and the inevitable visit to a port wine warehouse), Porto's brooding quality and mercantile reserve become apparent, and its parks and squares and stunning diversity of architecture make for an eccentric and intriguing urban experience that really repays intensive on-the-ground exploration.

## Fast facts

**Country dialling code** +351
**Journey time** Flight 2 hours 15 minutes
**Festivals & events** São João (23-24 June) – a huge street festival dedicated to St John the Baptist, featuring fireworks and street food stalls, that takes over the centre of the city starting in the early evening and going through the night; Serralves em Festa (late May, www.serralvesemfesta.com) – a free, high-profile contemporary arts fair; Fantasporto (February-March, www.fantasporto.com) – the local film festival
**Good for** Beaches, culture, wine

## SEE & DO

One of the great pleasures in Porto is wandering: streets are densely packed and steep. For a committed cityphile, the fabric of the place peels away to reveal successive eras of development, style and taste, from high Baroque to chilly modernism. A particular joy is the city's shopfronts, which visit every idea of retail from severe 19th-century book dealers to 1970s outfitters for the funky man-about-Porto. As an introduction to the heart of the city, a good alternative to hoofing it is the historic tram system. Line 22 starts at **Praça de Parada Leitao** and heads down past the elaborate 18th-century church **Igreja e Torre dos Clérigos** (Rua São Filipe de Nery 10), across the bottom of the **Praça da Liberdade** and up towards the superb modernist (though only sporadically open) **Cinema Batalha** (Praça de Batalha), before finishing perched above the river near the funicular railway, a stretch of medieval city wall and the Romanesque **Cathedral**.

From here, those with a good head for heights can cross the upper walkway of the **Ponte Luis I.** Often misattributed to Gustav Eiffel (who was responsible for the Ponte Maria Pia, just upstream), this steel bridge is not for the faint-hearted, but the brave are rewarded with amazing views up and down the Douro, and of the facing **Ribeira** and **Gaia** areas. The latter is where you'll find the city's port wine lodges. Almost all offer tours and tastings: try **Graham's** (Rua Rei Ramiro 514, 22 377 6484,

Cathedral

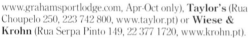
Pensão Favorita

Pedro Lemos

www.grahamsportlodge.com, Apr-Oct only), **Taylor's** (Rua Choupelo 250, 223 742 800, www.taylor.pt) or **Wiese & Krohn** (Rua Serpa Pinto 149, 22 377 1720, www.krohn.pt).

Other notable landmarks are the deco **Coliseu** (Rua Passos Manuel 137) and the **Pavilhão Rosa Mota** (Rua Dom Manuell II) in the **Jardins do Palacio de Cristal**, a splendidly eccentric copper-domed sports hall from 1953, with a handy workers' canteen-style restaurant in the basement.

The striking **Serralves** museum of contemporary art (Rua Dom João de Castro 210, 226 156 500, www.serralves.pt) is a tasteful white monolith in a landscaped park outside town, from Portugal's biggest-name architect, Siza Viera. It hosts meaty temporary shows and runs a wide range of talks and cultural events. In the centre of the city, the **Centro Português de Fotografia** (Campo Mártires da Pátria, 222 076 310, www.cpf.pt) is housed in a remarkable former prison, many of whose fittings remain intact.

If culture and toiling up hills loses its lustre, the beaches at **Foz** and **Matosinhos** are within easy striking distance on public transport, with a commanding sweep of the Atlantic to soothe and revivify.

Suitably refreshed, you can hit some nightlife; the best bets are around the **Clérigos** area, downtown. Ruas de Galeria Paris and Cândido dos Reis are full of bars and bar-clubs. Try **Plano B** (Cândido dos Reis 30, www.planob porto.com) for hipster-interest art, DJs and hanging out, and **Casa do Livro** (Rua Galeria de Paris 85), evoking Porto's literary image.

## EAT & DRINK

Tripe is big in Porto, though not as ubiquitous on menus as it once was. **Tripeiro** (Rua Passos Manuel 195, 222 005 886, www.restaurantetripeiro.com) near the Coliseu has some authentic dishes, though it's on the pricey side. Downtown, **Canelas de Coelho** (Rua Elisio de Melo 29-33, 222 015 824) has great tapas and a generally deserved sense of its own worth, while **Santiago** (Rua Passos Manuel 226, 222 055 797) is good for *francesinhas* (literally, 'little Frenchies') — Porto's contribution to world cuisine — a multi-meat-packed sandwich smothered in sauce.

Foz is a good area for eating out. Grab lunch at **Homem do Leme** (Avenida de Montevideu, 226 182 963), or push the boat out at **Pedro Lemos** (Rua Padre Luis Cabra 974,

# EXPLORE FROM THE INSIDE OUT

Time Out Guides written by local experts

Walk with a llama in Britain, discover a secret garden in London, get a rockabilly haircut in New York.

With original and inspirational ideas for both tourists and seen-it-all-before locals, there's always more to be uncovered.

## visit timeout.com/shop

POCKET SIZED GUIDE

220 115 986, www.pedrolemos.net), in the old part of the area, a bit removed from the sea. It's expensive, but among Porto's finest restaurants. Finally, if you want to dine out in the eccentric Porto style to which you have now become accustomed, we recommend **Café Vitória** (Rua José Falcao 156, 220 135 538, www.cafevitoria.com), a slightly too-cool-for-school bar with a remarkably elegantly appointed restaurant upstairs with plenty of modish tat and variable well-intentioned food, or **Café de Galeria de Paris** (Rua Galeria de Paris 56): the food's passable, the wine's cheap and plentiful and if you're lucky a mime will appear with nine trained cats and perform for your startled enjoyment.

## SHOP

While you would hardly describe Porto as a shopping destination, browsing here is a real pleasure, since there are still so many small independent shops, particularly around the Baixa and downtown areas. In a city well supplied with bookshops, **Lello** (Rua de Carmelitas 144) stands out. Its fantastical Gothic nouveau interior supposedly inspired JK Rowling, while civil engineering fans will marvel at its unconventional use of concrete. To the east, Rua Santa Catarina is a fairly straightforward shopping drag, while chi-chi boutiques are popping up around Rua Miguel Bombarda in the north-west. Nearby, the picturesque Praça de Carlos Alberto hosts a craft and flea market on Saturdays. No one should visit the city, however, without a trip to the **Mercado de Bolhão** (Rua Sá da Bandeira), a manic two-storey souk crammed with stalls selling fish, fruit, flowers, bits and bobs and pretty much anything else you might require.

## STAY

If you want to splash out, the five-star **Yeatman** (Rua do Choupelo, 22 013 3100, www.theyeatman.com), which styles itself as a 'luxury wine hotel', is in the port lodge area of Gaia and has a cellar stocked with 25,000 bottles. Its restaurant is headed by Michelin-starred chef Ricardo Costa, the spa offers 'vinotherapy' and the rooms are decorated with themes representing the 11 wine regions of Portugal.

The venerable **Grande Hotel do Porto** (Rua Santa Catarina 197, 22 207 6696, www.grandehotelporto.com) is in a usefully central location and, after a renovation a few years ago, has recovered some of its 19th-century charm, with a splendid colonnaded salon and the modish Windsor Bar for a drop of pre-dinner port.

Boutique hotel fans could opt for **Pensão Favorita** (Rua Miguel Bombarda 267, 22 013 4157, www.pensao favorita.pt), a chic minimalist take on a traditional townhouse with designer touches. Also central is the **Hotel Aliados** (Rua Elisio de Melo 27, 22 200 4853, www. hotelaliados.com), just off Avenue Aliados – a modest pension with loads of 1950s charm, above one of the city's best-preserved café-restaurants, where there is live music most nights.

## GETTING THERE & AROUND

Fly TAP from Heathrow or Gatwick, EasyJet from Gatwick, or Ryanair from Stansted. Apart from Porto's old-school tram system mentioned above, the city has an extensive bus network serving the outer suburbs and up and down

Grande Hotel do Porto

Yeatman

the coast. Journeys can take a while, since the routes are dense with bus stops and oversubscribed, and the streets are rather winding. The city is proud of its new rapid-transit system, the Metro. More a tram than a tube, it's a reliable if dull way of getting across town, though its ace in the hole is line D, which links Porto and Gaia and runs across the upper level of the Ponte Luis I: 20 seconds of sheer horror/exhilaration.

# Helsinki

In Helsinki, people don't cross the road when the little man's on red, even when there's not a car, tram or bike in sight. There's no public disorder, litter, rudeness or dirt. You bump into people you've seen elsewhere, and they acknowledge you. A sense of old-fashioned gentility, juxtaposed with a cool, quirky, contemporary scene, extends to the physical city. Neoclassical good looks jostle with compact granite blocks and art nouveau structures and buildings inspired by the idea of independence from Russia, which finally came about in 1917. The climate's surprisingly warm – no, really – and in summer there's almost round-the-clock sunlight, with locals lining the boulevards enjoying prolific street entertainment and the outdoor cafés heaving. Hemmed in by water on three sides and with numerous parks, it's a stylish, modernist-inspired timewarp that offers a wealth of attractions and activities.

## Fast facts

**Journey time** Flight 3 hours
**Country dialling code** +358
**Festivals & events** The Helsinki Festival (August, www.helsinkifestival.fi) hosts Finland's top musicians and vocalists, as well as featuring poetry, circus acts, theatre and more. In the Huvila alternative and world music tent it can lay claim to one of the city's stand-out venues; Helsinki International Film Festival (September, www.hiff.fi) – when as many as 15,000 people flock to see what's hot in Finnish and international cinema; Big Band Jazz Festival (April, www.apriljazz.fi) – concert halls, restaurants and other venues host Finnish and international jazz performers throughout the month
**Good for** Culture, shopping

Kauppatori

## SEE & DO

Experience up close the Finnish design phenomenon in the district around Diana Park. The area is home to the **Design Museum** (Korkeavuorenkatu 23, 09 622 0540, www.designmuseum.fi), charting the evolution of Finnish design over the last 100 years. Just down the road there's the **Museum of Finnish Architecture** (Kasarmikatu 24, 09 8567 5100, www.mfa.fi), showcasing the work of Finland's best architects past and present, as well as the **Design Forum** (Erottajankatu 7, 09 6220 8130, www.designforum.fi), where you can pick up the latest in kitchen appliances and become the well-travelled envy of your friends.

A 15-minute ferry ride out in the harbour from Market Square takes you to **Suomenlinna Fortress** (09 684 1850, www.suomenlinnatours.fi), a massive sea fortress and UNESCO World Heritage Site, built by Sweden in 1747 to unsuccessfully fend off Russia, and used post-independence by the Finns as a prison. A slice of Finnish everyday life can be found at the **Kauppatori** (Market Square), located at the harbour's edge, where merchants sell straight from the boats and temporary cafés serve up succulent sausages and fish. The market over on the Esplandi side sells many a local delicacy, including honey, smoked fish and Finnish cheeses.

If it's cold, take a dip at the magnificent **art deco pool** built by Väinö Vähäkallio in 1928 (Yrjonkatu 21, 0 9 3108 7401). Locals will advise you to get waxed prior to jumping in naked (men and women swim at different times), and you can say hello to your new friends outside afterwards: look out for the knowing nod and wink.

One of the city's most famous sons is Alvar Aalto, and evidence of the spare, elegant style he inspired is everywhere; it's perhaps best seen at Yrjö Lindegren and Toivo Jäntti's functionalist yet elegant 50,000-seat **Olympic Stadium** built for the cancelled 1940 games (climb the 72-metre tower for views across the Baltic). Aalto's own **Finlandia Hall** (Mannerheimvägen 13, 09 40 241, www.finlandiatalo.fi) hosts regular classical concerts and recitals. If nothing's on it's still worth going on a tour of the building – these last about an hour and are held twice-weekly.

The white, curving spaces of **Kiasma** (Mannerheiminaukio 2, 09 1733 6501, www.kiasma.fi) will remind art-lovers of New York's Guggenheim, but its original contemporary art programme is very much its own, with four floors dedicated to permanent collections, an annually changing thematic collections exhibition, smaller quarterly shows and studio spaces with individually curated programmes.

Slightly further afield, the **Kaapeli** cultural centre (Tallberginkatu 1, C15, 09 4763 8330,

Design Museum

Kiasma

Finlandia Hall

Hotel Fabian

Suomenlinna Fortress

www.kaapelitehdas.fi) is home to hundreds of artists, designers and craftsmen, many of whom display their work in the three museums and 13 galleries of this former factory. It's a great place to catch new graphic art and illustration, and meet up-and-coming artists in their studios. The location, in the waterside Ruoholahti district, is excellent too. For more conventional Nordic art, the **Ateneum Art Museum** (Kaivokatu 2, 09 173 361, www.ateneum.fi) is home to the country's national art collection.

Take the water bus from the South Harbour or no.24 bus to **Seurasaari Island open-air museum** (09 4050 660, www.nba.fi), which offers an insight into traditional Finnish architecture and craft, with building styles stretching back over four centuries. It's a delight in summer, when the restaurant opens and it's warm enough to swim and sunbathe on the large beach.

In winter, the city glows with the **Season of Light** installation (held each January) and there's outdoor skating everywhere – try the Ice Park in Railway Square.

## EAT & DRINK

The influence of Russia and Sweden looms large in Finnish cuisine, and you don't have to look hard to find Thai, Chinese or Italian restaurants. Finnish food shuns complicated preparations, concentrating on natural flavours and ingredients sourced from the surrounding land and sea – mushrooms and berries from the forests, fish caught from the Baltic. Herring is the fish of choice, either pickled as a snack or baked with layers of potato and cream. Sausages sizzle on street grills, and are a fast-food favourite. If you get the chance try *Mustamakhara*, a black sausage usually served with lingonberry jam. Finnish vodkas, schnapps and liqueurs are made with local berries, and Salmari, a fiery vodka cocktail, is also a popular choice. During winter you'll be offered *Glogi*, a type of mulled wine with almonds and blackcurrant juice, while for beer drinkers, Lapin Kulta is a good local brew.

Breakfast on warm doughnuts in tiny plywood booths lit by red wall-lamps at the **Hakaniemi Market Hall** (www.hakaniemenkauppahalli.fi), an indoor marketplace with around 70 shops over two floors specialising in Finnish delicacies.

**Elviira** (Punavuorenkatu 3, 050 554 4050, www. ravintolaelviira.fi) serves succulent hors d'oeuvres and a good range of fish dishes. A three-course meal is encouraged, though with modest portion sizes don't expect to leave feeling full.

**Bali-Hai** (Iso Roobertinkatu 35-37, 09 179 904, www. balihai.fi) is a hip café-cum-restaurant with chequered panel flooring and minimalist decor. A range of salads and light bites are served, as well as hearty burgers, fish and the house delicacy, sautéd reindeer.

The interiors and wall paintings are reasons alone to drop by **Seahorse** (Kapteeninkatu 11, 09 628 169, www.seahorse.fi). It's the go-to place for classic Finnish fare – meatballs, or perch with horseradish butter and mushroom sauce. The portions tend to be generous and the staff are friendly.

If you'd like a tipple on public transport while seeing the sights, then take a ride on a pub tram – the bright red trams converted into pubs that do circular trips of Helsinki during the summer months. They set off from the Central Railway Station and are recognisable by the no-nonsense destination board reading 'Pub'.

## SHOP

Helsinki's retro vibe isn't just in the fabric of the buildings and their interiors. There's a positively post-war 'make-do and mend' trend sweeping the city's creative citizens too.

The **Design District**, a small area centred on Uudemenkatu, Iso Roobertinkatu, Fredrikinkatu and Punavuorenkatu, is filling up with shops such as **Edel City** (Fredrikinkatu 33, 044 270 9329, www.edelcity.com),

where Finnish designers such as Mifuko sell jewellery made in Kenya from recycled safety pins and beads, or denim jeans turned into pretty dresses, or old beach towels run up into colourful patch-pocket skirts.

At **Globe Hope** (Lasipalatsi, Mannerheimintie 22-24, 50 530 2103, www.globehope.com), aptly housed in Lasipalatsi – a streamlined 1930s concrete prefab that's now a cultural centre and arthouse cinema – gorgeous dresses are made from parachutes, bright pink coats from Swedish Army snow coats, and all manner of clothing, accessories and homewares from old hospital materials, boat sails and army tents. And vintage is everywhere – Albertinkatu and Roobertinkatu are great streets for finding all manner of old stuff. **Lumi on 14** (Pursimiehenkatu 14, 04 4271 2622, www.lumion14.com) is a sprawling fashion concept store with a focus on young Finnish designers. Their mantra is to make something every day. If you've always fancied a white felt hat, or would like a chic bag to take with you down the supermarket, then look no further. **Marimekko** is the Finns' most beloved design brand, a textile and clothing firm renowned for its original prints and colourful designs. The **Marimekko Factory Shop** (Kirvesmiehenkatu 7, 09 758 7244, www.marimekko.com) is packed with new-season stock, samples and off-cuts. **Pop Antik** (Iso Roobertinkatu 14, 04 581 5395, www. popantik.fi) is a tiny outpost of oddness, featuring cute antique collectibles, old toys made of tin, teddy bears and other curios.

## STAY

The 1928 **Hotel Helka** (Pohjoinen Rautatiekatu 23, 09 613 589, www.helka.fi) offers authentic Helsinki heritage combined with funky decor, rooms with private bathrooms and facilities that include saunas and whirlpools. The brand-new **Hotel Fabian** (Fabianinkatu 7, 09 6128 2000, www.hotelfabian.fi) has a great central location and the rooms are comfortable and spacious, with good beds, large bathrooms and built-in entertainment systems. **Finn** (Kalevankatu 3, 09 684 4360, www.hotel lifinn.fi) is a modestly sized, reasonably priced hotel, about a third of a mile from the main railway station. Rooms have basic facilities, with a pool and sauna next door. **Arthur** (Vuorikatu 19, 09 173 441, www.hotel arthur.fi) is a smart, recently refurbished hotel located in the heart of the shopping district boasting a top-notch restaurant on-site. **Hotel Kamp** (Pohjoiesplanadi 29, 09 5840 9520, www.hotelkamp.fi) combines luxury and tradition, with restored good looks that date originally from 1887. The service is excellent, and its location, by the Esplanadi, is ideal. The breakfast buffet will set you up for the day.

## GETTING THERE & AROUND

Flights operate from all over Heathrow and Gatwick. Finnair operates a shuttle bus from the airport to the central train station, departing every 20 minutes (€5.90), or a taxi costs around €40. Flying to Tallinn and catching a cheap 35-minute Finnair flight to Helsinki is another option. There's no significant cost difference and you'll at least get a glimpse of another city. Better still, glide into Helsinki on board a hovercraft from Tallinn. The trip lasts 90 minutes and costs just €30 one way.

---

### Cultural baggage

**Book** *The Kalevala* (Elias Lönnrot, 1849)
**Film** *Sauna* (Antti-Jussi Annila, 2008)
**Album** *Miero* (Värttinä, 2006)

# Stockholm

Stockholm offers that rarest of urban commodities: space to think. The city is made up of one third water and one third green space, which means just one third urbanity. It's a Venice of the north, spread across 14 islands, where the air and the streets are seemingly always clean. For a city of 1.9 million people, Stockholm has made a significant impact on the world: its history is full of home-grown success stories, from Strindberg and Bergman to Acne, Ericsson, Skype and Spotify. Perhaps the thinking space has something to do with it, but creativity is first and foremost born of functional simplicity – a mantra at the very root of Sweden's soul. There's no getting away from the fact, however, that Stockholm makes a pretty expensive weekend getaway, from finding a place to stay to eating out, but in return you get both substance and style, and enough northern chic to fill your baggage allowance on the way home.

## Fast facts

**Country dialling code** +46
**Journey time** Flight 2.5 hours
**Festivals & events** Stockholm Design Week (February, www.stockholmdesignweek.com) – Sweden's top creatives are in town for this world-class design event; Stockholm Jazz Festival (June, www.stockholmjazz.com) – one of the biggest annual events in Stockholm, the festival takes place at Skansen and attracts big names; Popaganda (August, www.popaganda.se) – this music festival has been growing in size and reputation since it started in 2006, attracting acts such as Arcade Fire and Lykke Lee in recent years; Crayfish parties (August) – a late summer phenomenon to mark the closing of the season; crayfish are eaten outdoors in a setting decorated with colourful paper lanterns
**Good for** Culture, food, shopping

Gamla Stan

Vaxholm

## SEE & DO

The narrow, winding streets of the old town, **Gamla Stan**, are tourist-central, yet make a good starting point. The **Royal Palace** (Slottsbacken 1, 08 402 61 30, www.royalcourt.se) is the main sight on this, the most central island, though there's also the high-tech **Nobelmuseet** (Borshuset, Stortorget, 53 48 18 00, www.nobelmuseum.se) – which tells the history of the Nobel Prizes – and Stockholm's de facto cathedral, **Storkyrkan** (Trangsund 1, 08 723 30 16, www.stockholms domkyrkoforsamling.se). The best approach is to wander at will, soaking up the atmosphere and taking in the colourful 18th-century buildings before stopping for coffee in Gamla Stan's main square, Stortorget.

Cross over the locks at nearby **Slussen** and you'll enter **Södermalm**, the former working-class district, now Stockholm's unofficial capital of cool. At the **Stockholm Stadsmuseum** (Ryssgården, 08 50 83 16 20, www.stadsmuseum.stockholm.se) you can learn all about the city's history before getting the lift opposite to the **Katarinahissen** (Stadsgarden 6, 08 642 47 86), a 38-metre viewing platform that provides stunning views of the city.

Fotografiska

Filippa K

Just past Katarinahissen, next to the water, is the new **Fotografiska** gallery (Stora Tullhuset, Stadsgårdshamnen 22, 50 900 500, www.fotografiska.eu), a huge exhibition space for world-class photography. Afterwards, wander down nearby **Götgatan**, and into the area of Södermalm known as **SoFo** (an acronym for 'South of Folkungagatan'), which is full of cool shops, galleries and cafés.

A great way of getting a feel for Stockholm is to take a boat trip – either as a form of transport, or as a more expensive tourist excursion. There are several Djurgårdsfärjen boats (www.waxholmsbolaget.se) an hour connecting Slussen with the nearby city islands of Djurgården and Skeppsholmen. Get off at lovely **Skeppsholmen** for the **Moderna Museet** (08 51 95 52 00, www.modernamuseet.se), Stockholm's premier contemporary art venue, housed in a former naval exercise building. The acres of undeveloped land on **Djurgården**, meanwhile, are great for picnics, walking and cycling. The island is home to many of Stockholm's best museums, including the **Nordiska Museet** (Djugardsvagen 6-16, 51 95 46 00, www.nordiskamuseet.se), which holds historical and cultural artefacts from all over Scandinavia; **Skansen** (Djurgårdsslatten 49-51, 442 80 00, www.skansen.se), an open-air museum organised like a miniature Sweden, with Scandinavian animals and traditional buildings; and the jaw-dropping 17th-century *Vasa* ship at the **Vasamuseet** (Galärvarvsvägen 14, 08 51 95 48 00, www.vasamuseet.se). The largest and best-preserved ship of its kind in the world, the *Vasa* made waves at the time of her discovery in 1956. Also on Djurgården, perched on the edge of the island, next to where you board the Djurgårdsfärjen ferry, is amusement park **Gröna Lund**

(Lilla Allmanna Grand 9, 58 75 01 00, www.gronalund.com), combining old-school charm with fairground thrills.

A boat trip to Stockholm's archipelago – consisting of some 24,000 islands and islets – is an essential feature of any visit to Stockholm. Ferries leave from Slussen and from outside the Grand Hôtel (*see p196*). Two of the most popular islands to visit are **Vaxholm** and **Grinda**, but note that both get busy during the summer, when locals head out to their summer houses for a dip in the crystal-clear water.

## EAT & DRINK

One of the best openings in Stockholm from the last few years is Gamla Stan's **Frantzén & Lindeberg** (Lilla Nygatan 21, 08 20 85 80, www.frantzen-lindeberg.com), which has two Michelin Stars. The owners grow their own vegetables and herbs in the restaurant garden, while other raw ingredients come from local farmers, fishermen and wine-makers. The amuse-bouches are very imaginative (macaroon with foie gras and pear, for instance), with the set menu providing an avant-garde taste extravaganza.

A vegetarian Chinese restaurant is a rare breed, but **Lao Wai** (Luntmakargatan 74, 08 673 78 00, www.laowai.se) proves it can be done. The decor is plain, but there's plenty of sparkle in the food – a mix of dishes from Taiwan and the Sichuan province of China. Everything is delicious, from the smoked tofu to the bean noodles with water chestnuts, so be bold and choose what you like the sound of.

A Stockholm classic, **Tranan** (Karlbregvagen 14, 08 52 72 81 00, www.tranan.se) ticks more than one box: in the basement there's a bar popular with hipsters and the after-work crowd, while upstairs there's a restaurant serving contemporary Swedish cuisine. It's one of the best places to try *köttbullar* – Swedish meatballs – served with the traditional accompaniments of mash and lingonberry sauce.

Situated in Södermalm (southern island), **Pelikan** (Blekingegatan 40, 08 55 60 90 90) is an old-school restaurant in a former beer hall, serving Swedish classics, such as meatballs, smoked salmon, *smör, ost och sill* (butter, cheese and herring), and fried pork with onion sauce. For extra authenticity points, try a glass of *brännvin* (schnapps) with your food – elderflower is one of the most popular flavours.

A favourite local spot for lunch is **Blå Porten** (Djugårdsvägen 64, 08 663 87 59, www.blaporten.se), next to the Liljevalchs Konstahall art gallery on Djurgården, serving local lunch classics as well as delicious cakes and pastries. Its piazza-like garden is packed in summer.

The café is to the Swedes what the pub is to the Brits. Swedes love coffee – they drink more of it per capita than every other nation apart from Finland – and *fika*, the mid-afternoon ritual of coffee and a snack, is a widely observed tradition. The *kanelbulle* (cinnamon bun) is a typical *fika* treat year-round, while seasonal favourites include the *lussekatt* (saffron-flavoured bun) at Christmas, and the *semla* – an epic creation of pastry, almond paste and whipped cream – at Easter. Stockholm is heaving with places for *fika*, with the **Cinnamon Bakery & Coffeeshop** (Verkstadsgatan 9, 08 669 22 24) in Södermalm among the best.

Hotel Rival

Frantzén & Lindeberg

## SHOPS

Stockholmers are a stylish bunch, and local brands such as **Acne** (Hamngatan 10-14, Östermalm, 08 20 34 55), **Filippa K** (Götgatan 23, Norrmalm, 08 55 69 85 85, www.filippak.com) and **Whyred** (Mäster Samuelsgatan 3, Norrmalm, 08 660 01 70, www.whyred.se) have made a name for themselves globally, with subtly innovative designs and new takes on urban classics like the parka jacket. These and other stores can be found on and around **Biblioteksgatan**, one of the city's best shopping streets, which sits on the edge of the district of **Östermalm** – an area synonymous with designer shops. Other popular labels include the tennis star's eponymous **Björn Borg** underwear line, and **Fjällräven** – which makes the ubiquitous Kånken backpacks that are now popular worldwide.

For department stores, there's the ultra-smart **NK** (Hamngatan 18-20, 08 676 00 00, www.ahlens.se) in Norrmalm; a sort of Swedish Selfridges, with an iconic revolving sign on its roof, it's good for fashion, homewares, beauty products and gourmet food.

Vintage clothing is extremely popular in Stockholm right now, with many vintage shops located on trendy Södermalm. **Beyond Retro** (Åsögatan 144) is Swedish, and has several branches in town, while **Judit** (Hornsgatan 75, 08 84 45 10, www.judits.se) and **Herr Judit** (Hornsgatan 65, 08 658 30 37, www.herrjudit.se), 100 metres from each other in Hornstall, stock a well-edited range of designer vintagewear, from 1950s jewellery and accessories to Balenciaga shirts.

SoFo

Herr Judit

Hotel Hellstens Malmgård

Stockholm is also heaven for design fiends. **Design Torget**, with a branch underneath Kulturhuset in Norrmalm (Sergels Torg, 08 21 91 50, www.designtorget.se), and one on Götgatan in Södermalm, is great for gifts, while **Svenkt Tenn** (Strandvägen 5, Östermalm, 08 670 16 00, www.svenskttenn.se) is a Stockholm classic, selling exquisite textiles and furniture based on the designs of Josef Frank, since 1924.

Lastly, the grand **Östermalms Saluhall** (Östermalmstorg, Östermalm, www.ostermalmshallen.se), housed in a beautiful 19th-century building, serves gourmet (read: expensive) treats for the well-heeled.

## STAY

For budget accommodation with a difference, the **STF Hostel af Chapman & Skepppsholmen** (Flaggmansvägen 8, 08 463 22 66) provides cabin accommodation on an iconic white yacht, complete with masts and rigging, on the island of Skeppsholmen. The rooms are small but cosy and the facilities basic, but it remains a popular choice (book well in advance). Otherwise, **Hostel Bed & Breakfast** (Rehnsgatan 21, 08 15 28 38) is a centrally located youth hostel with shared bathroom facilities, laundry room and kitchen. There are 36 beds in two-, four-, eight- and ten-bed rooms.

**Hotel Hellstens Malmgård** (Brännkyrkagatan 110, 08 4650 5800, www.hellstensmalmgard.se) offers mid-range accommodation in a mansion in Södermalm. The rooms are stylish and unpretentious, with clean wooden surfaces, sturdy furniture and subtle colour schemes. Some of the doubles include four-poster beds, and 12 of the hotel's 52 rooms contain handmade porcelain stoves from the 1770s.

Owned by Benny from Abba, **Hotel Rival** (Mariatorget 3, 08 54 57 89 00, www.rival.se) combines the best of parts of the 1930s hotel that once stood here with plush modern comforts. Guest rooms are comfortable and stylish, all with widescreen TVs and iPod stereo connectors. The hotel's cocktail bar and red-velvet cinema are art deco treasures, while the next-door Cafe Rival is popular for meetings and *fika*.

For a taste of deluxe Stockholm, check yourself into the **Grand Hôtel** (Södra Blasieholmshamnen 8, 086 79 35 00), which overlooks the water in Norrmalm. The hotel's Cadier Bar is one of the hottest places in town on a Friday evening, particularly around the time of the Nobel Banquet, when visiting royals and rock stars rub shoulders with newly crowned Laureates, who traditionally stay here after the awards ceremony.

## GETTING THERE & AROUND

Fly direct to Stockholm Arlanda with British Airways, Norwegian or Scandinavian Airlines, or to Stockholm Skavsta – much further away from the city – with Ryanair. From Stockholm Arlanda, take the bright yellow Arlanda Express train, which gets you to the centre of the city in 20 minutes. From Stockholm Skavsta, it's a 1.5-hour bus journey.

Unless you're up to your ankles in snow during winter, central Stockholm can be covered on foot, though it's sensible to invest in a travelcard for the metro, bus and passenger ferry services, as not everything worth seeing is in the centre. They can be purchased at metro stations and some newsagents and last for 1, 3 or 7 days.

## Cultural baggage

**Book** Stieg Larsson's *Millennium* crime trilogy (2005, 2006, 2007)
**Film** *Wild Strawberries* (Ingmar Bergman, 1957)
**Album** *Robyn* (Robyn, 2005)

# Normandy

Normandy, less than 100 miles from the Sussex and Hampshire coasts, is a great choice for a weekend break from London, involving a shortish journey but allowing visitors to really feel they've been abroad. The beaches are synonymous with the D-Day beach landings, but there are 375 miles of coastline in total and a huge swathe of pure French countryside inland. The whole region is rich in historical sites from the Roman era – Emperor Diocletian established Normandy's boundaries in the third century – and from the period of Viking rule in the eighth century. In 1066, William II of Normandy defeated King Harold II at the Battle of Hastings, the story of which can be followed in the Bayeux Tapestry.

To get the most out of the region, you'll need a car – especially if you want to see both the coastal loveliness and the rural hinterland.

Le Mont St Michel

## Fast facts

**Country dialling code** +34
**Journey time** Flight 2 hours; ferry 4 hours; car 6 hours
**Festivals & events** Bayeux Medieval Festival (July) – the town comes alive with a medieval market and street performances; Automne en Normandie festival (October-November, www.automne-en-normandie.com) – music, theatre and dance events held across the region, and shuttle buses between the venues to allow easy access; American Film Festival (September, www.festival-deauville.com) – held in Deauville, Calvados, this showcases new films by rising American directors
**Good for** Beaches, culture, food, walking

## SEE & DO

**Caen**, the capital of Lower Normandy, is a good base for exploring the region. Looming over the city is the splendid **Château Guillaume-le-Conquérant** (www.chateau-guillaume-leconquerant.fr, 02 31 41 61 44, place Guillaume le Conquérant), founded in 1060 by William the Conqueror. A five-minute walk along rue Guillaume le Conquérant, and you can even see William's thigh bone at the **Abbaye-aux-Hommes** (Esplanade Jean-Marie Louvel, 02 31 86 37 21, www.abbaye-aux-hommes.cef.fr).

The **Mémorial – Un Musée pour la Paix** (Esplanade Général Eisenhower, 02 31 06 06 45, www.memorial-caen.fr, closed Mon and from Nov-Feb) is only a ten-minute drive from the city centre (or you can catch the number 2 bus from place Courtonne if you fancy a rest from the wheel).

Abbaye-aux-Hommes

Ivan Vautier

Bayeux

La Rapiere

Providing a vivid account of the background and drama of the Battle of Normandy, it's an impressive affair, with animation, sound and audio testimonies alongside the usual artefacts. There's even an underground bunker used by the Germans in 1944 and now dedicated to winners of the Nobel Peace Prize.

The Normandy beaches are 30 minutes away by car (and there are also regular trains from Caen to Bayeux). The golden sands and glorious coastline belie the horrors of D-Day, but on **Omaha Beach** – perhaps the best known of the battlegrounds, and the one where the fighting was arguably most intense – you can still observe remnants of the struggle. Shell holes are still visible in the cliffs, German bunkers line the coast, and overlooking the beach is the 172-acre St-Laurent Military Cemetery, where more than 9,000 American World War II heroes have been laid to rest.

The 11th-century **Bayeux Tapestry**, celebrating the Duke of Normandy's victory over England, hangs in the **Musée de la Tapisserie de Bayeux** (www.tapisserie-bayeux.fr, 02 31 51 25 50 ), a 15-minute drive from Omaha.

Take the one-and-a-half hour drive to the other side of the coast to visit **Le Mont St-Michel** (www.ot-mont saintmichel.com, 02 33 60 14 30). This volcanic island, a UNESCO World Heritage Site, is France's third most popular tourist attraction, and the 1,000-year-old monastic citadel has been a place of pilgrimage for centuries (save a brief spell in the late 18th century, when it was used as a prison). It's strategically placed for confinement, with one kilometre of sand separating the island from the shore, and the sea washing over the causeway at high tide. Nowadays, it's full of tourist shops, but it has charm in abundance and the cobbled streets are quaint enough. The drive back to Caen passes by **Champrepus Zoo** (02 33 61 30 74, www.zoo-champrepus.com), which has a Sumatran tiger and penguins.

## EAT & DRINK

Normandy is famous for fish, camembert cheese and apples, as well as *moules à la crème Normande*: mussels cooked with white wine and Normandy cider. The faint-hearted might want to avoid fowl in Rouen, where the birds are strangled to ensure as much blood as possible gets into the sauce. Normandy's extensive coastline means there's plenty of seafood on the menus, and the shores are lined with restaurants. Among the best is **La Rapière** (rue St-Jean 52, 02 31 21 05 45, www.larapiere.net) in Bayeux. Expect to pay around £25 for a three-course meal: the 'fisherman's pot' contains monkfish, cod and salmon combined with local vegetables and potatoes. Also worth a visit is **La Fleur de Sell** (Les Marais 73730, 04 79 37 49 98, www.restaurant-fleurdesel.fr), in Port-en-Bessin-Huppain, and **Boeuf & Cow** (6 boulevard Allies, 02 31 86 37 75, www.boeufandcow.fr), in Caen, which serves excellent steak.

Food markets show off farm and other local produce all over Normandy. On Sundays, there's a bustling market at place Courtonne in Caen, and at the Port en Bessin in Bayeux. Boats unload right behind the stalls, so the fish are flappingly fresh.

Come dessert, a tipple of calvados is an essential. It's a brandy brimming with the scent of zesty apples, perfect with a bowl of *teurgoule*, a rice pudding flavoured with cinnamon. The latter is serious business in Lower Normandy, with its own brotherhood in the resort of Houlgate charged with safeguarding the official recipe.

## STAY

Normandy has all manner of accommodation, from campsites to boutique hotels. If you're travelling around using public transport, stick to the cities. In Caen, the **Ivan Vautier** (avenue Henry Chéron 3, 02 31 73 32 71, www.ivan vautier.com) has 19 boldly decorated rooms – all leather, walnut and plain colours – and a great restaurant. A 30-minute drive away, the **Hotel Churchill** (rue St-Jean 14-16, 02 31 21 41 66, www.hotel-churchill.fr) is situated in the heart of Old Bayeux, and has charm in abundance, including framed photos hanging throughout the building depicting Liberation in 1945. The hotel offers a daily shuttle to Mont St-Michel. From April to September you can camp by Omaha Beach in a mobile home (rue de la Hérode, 02 31 22 41 73, www.camping-omaha-beach.fr). The **Château de Bouceel** (Cahuzac, 50240 Vergoncey, 02 33 48 43 61, www.chateaudebouceel.com) is a family-run hotel in a beautiful park between Mont St-Michel and Fougères. Built in 1763, it has wood-panelled bedrooms; there are cottages if you prefer something cosier.

## GETTING THERE & AROUND

The easiest route is to take the Eurostar to Paris (2hrs 15 mins) and switch to Saint-Lazare station to catch the train to Caen (2hrs); it's bookable through Rail Europe, 0844 848 4064, www.raileurope.co.uk). CityJet offers four direct flights a week to Deauville Normandy Airport (0871 663 3777, www.cityjet.com). The flight takes just 2 hours and the airport is an hour's drive from Caen. There are plenty of car-hire firms in Caen. If you want to take your own car, it's best to take the ferry from Dover over to Calais (www.poferries.com, 0871 664 2121). From there, it's a four-hour drive to Caen hugging the coast. Finally, Brittany Ferries (0871 244 0744, www.brittany-ferries.co.uk) links Portsmouth to Caen (5hrs 45mins) and Cherbourg (3hrs) and Poole with Cherbourg (2hrs 30mins).

Omaha Beach

# Barcelona

Catalonia's distinctiveness has its roots in centuries of cultural and linguistic separation and in decades of Spanish nationalism during the Franco era. Catalonians have put their stamp where they might have been stamped out, and regional pride is strong – don't be alarmed if you are dismissed for attempting Spanish rather than the local lingo. Barcelona is no longer riding the rebranding wave that started with the 1992 Olympics, but it is established as a 'classic' European holiday destination on a par with London or Paris. The city has a cosmopolitan vibe you don't get anywhere else in Spain, and the number of long-term expats from across Europe suggests that it remains a great place to live as well as have fun. The recession has stalled progress to some extent, but gentrification schemes in previously no-go areas, such as the Raval, the Bicing public bicycle scheme (www.bicing.com), started in 2007, and the ongoing fame of the Catalan capital's culinary scene keep 'Barna' (Barca is the footy team) moving forward.

## Fast facts

**Country dialling code** +34
**Journey time** Flight 2 hours
**Festivals & events** Sónar – the night-time music festival favouring electronic, techno, house and experimental artists (June, www.sonar.es); Festival del Grec – the city's major cultural festival of the year for theatre, music and dance, held in the Greek amphitheatre built on Montjuïc for the 1929 Universal Exhibition (June-August, www.bcn.cat/grec); Festes de la Mercè, a week-long celebration of the city's patron saint, Our Lady of Mercy, with more than 600 events including *sardanas* (circle dances) (September, www.bcn.cat/merce); Festival Internacional de Jazz de Barcelona – one of Europe's most respected jazz festivals (October to November, www.theproject.cat)
**Good for** Culture, food, nightlife

## SEE & DO

The best way to see the city is on foot. Get lost and it won't be long before an iconic sight comes into view. The **Gothic Quarter** is a good place to start, with its narrow streets and quiet squares. Walk along **La Rambla**, the city's famous boulevard. The medieval **Cathedral** (Pla de la Seu, 93 342 82 60, www.catedralbcn.org) is spectacular, but indefinitely covered in scaffolding, but **Santa Maria del Mar** (Plaça de Santa Maria, 93 310 23 90) offers an alternative in Catalan Gothic.

The **Raval**, while still a red-light district, has shed its seedy image (but it's wise to be on your guard at night) and is now home to the **MACBA** (Museum of Contemporary Art of Barcelona, Plaça del Àngels 1, 93 412 08 10, www.macba.cat), a giant minimalist space with an excellent permanent collection. The area also hosts monthly 'Living Moon' parties on Calle Lluna, celebrating local artistic talent.

A walk around the **Eixample** district at the centre of the city might follow a trail of 'Modernisme' buildings, particularly on the block known as **Manzana de Discordia**, with Gaudí's **Casa Batlló** (Passeig de

Sagrada Família

La Rambla

Park Güell

Platja de Barceloneta

Hotel Murmuri

Gràcia 43, 93 216 03 06, www.casabatllo.es) being the most photographed. Gaudí's **Sagrada Família** (Calle Mallorca 401, 93 207 30 31, www.sagradafamilia.cat) has been controversial in its status as a city emblem, but the five million visitors each year are funding its ongoing construction. Equally jaw-dropping is the **Palau de la Música Catalana** (Calle Sant Francesc de Paula 2, 93 295 72 00, www.palaumusica.org), worth a visit just for the stained-glass ceiling. Combine architecture with a picnic in the charming surroundings of **Park Güell**, and if the Modernisme on the streets is not sufficient, head to the **Museu del Modernisme Català** (Calle de Balmes 48, 93 272 28 96, www.mmcat.cat) to find out more about the movement.

Rent a bicycle and ride along the waterfront towards the city's beach, **Platja de Barceloneta**, then finish with a walk through the leafy Montjuïc hill, which is home to the **Fundació Joan Miró** (93 443 94 70, www.fundaciomiro-bcn.org) and has the **Pavelló Mies van der Rohe** (93 423 40 16, www.miesbcn.com) at its base – the 1986 replica of

Blow by Le Swing

Plaça Reial, Barri Gòtic

La Boqueria

H1898

the pavilion built by Mies van der Rohe for the 1929 World Exhibition. The outdoor cinema **Sala Montjuïc** (www.salamontjuic.org) is also a deservedly popular attraction during July and August.

## EAT & DRINK

One of the foodiest regions in Spain, the influence on Catalonia from neighbouring France and the Basque Country has led to a cuisine that is constantly evolving. Tapas are largely skipped over in favour of hearty dishes, though the Basque trend that has caught on is for *pintxos* (bite-size open sandwiches speared with toothpicks) – the best example of which is at **Euskal Etxea** (Placeta Montcada 1-3, 93 310 21 85, www.euskaletxeak.org).

**La Boqueria** market (La Rambla 89, 93 318 25 84, www.boqueria.info) is an essential stop, and if you go as it's opening – between 8am and 9am, before the crowds hit – it's a great place to pick up picnic ingredients. The grand **Café de l'Opera** (La Rambla 74, 93 317 75 85) is an atmospheric spot for coffee, while **La Granja** (Calle Banys Nous 4, 93 302 69 75) offers thick shots of hot chocolate to keep energy levels up.

If it's tapas you're after, compare the fine, fresh seafood on offer at old-fashioned **Cal Pep** (Plaça de les Olles 8, 93 310 79 61, www.calpep.com) with Ferran Adrià disciple Carles Abellan's quirky modern take on small dishes at **Tapaç24** (Calle Diputació 269, 93 488 09 77, www.tapac24.com). The master of molecular gastronomy himself has opened a tapas bar called **Tickets** (Avinguda del Paral·lel 164, 93 292 42 50 www.ticketsbar.es).

For Catalan staples, such as boar stew and partridge *escabeche* (where the bird is poached in vegetables, herbs and wine), try **Can Culleretes** (Calle d'en Quintana 5, 93 317 30 22, www.culleretes.com), the second-oldest restaurant in Spain, or **Cinc Sentits** (Calle Aribau 58, 93 323 94 90, www.cincsentits.com), for more experimental versions.

Up in Montjuïc, **La Font del Gat** (Passeig Santa Madrona 28, 93 289 04 04) has an excellent set lunch menu.

MACBA

La Vinya del Senyor

For a taste of a different region, **Las Fernández** (Calle Carretas 11, 93 443 20 43, www.lasfernandez.com), run by sisters from Leon, is homely and inviting. **Vinateria del Call** (Calle Sant Domènec del Call 9, www.lavinateria delcall.com) and **La Vinya del Senyor** (Plaça Santa Maria 5, 93 310 33 79) are both cosy wine bars with home-made food to match.

## Cultural baggage

**Book** *The Shadow of the Wind* (Carlos Ruiz Zafón, 2001)
**Film** *Biutiful* (Alejandro González Iñárritu, 2010)
**Album** *Corrientes Vital: 10 Años* (Ojos de Brujo, 2010)

## SHOP

The centre of Barcelona is crammed with retail outlets, with major chains occupying the high streets. There's still an abundance of old, specialist shops and local independent shop owners selling everything from votive candles to Catalan sausages. The Raval is the area for vintage clothing, with **Blow by Le Swing** (Calle Doctor Dou 11, 93 302 36 98) and **Produit National Brut** (Calle Ramalleres 16-20, 93 268 27 55) leading the pack. **On Land** (Calle Princesa 25, 93 310 02 11, www.on-land.com) is where local hipsters buy contemporary streetwear.

Stock up on the traditional *espardenyes* (local style of espadrilles) at **La Manual Alpargatera** (Calle Avinyó 7, 93 301 01 71, www.lamanual.net), where the colour range is fantastic. You can get a sense of the old town at **Casa Gispert** (Calle Sombrerers 23, 93 319 75 35, www.casagispert.com), whose shelves groan with nuts, nuts and more nuts, all freshly roasted on the premises. Nearby, **El Rei de la Màgia** (Calle Princesa 11, 93 319 39 20, www.elreidelamagia.com) is a magic shop from a bygone era.

## STAY

Thanks to the credit crunch, Barcelona's hotel scene has improved, both in terms of the price and the range of accommodation on offer. At the budget end, many hostels are in grand old buildings with elaborate doorways and beautiful staircases; the **Alberg Mare de Déu de Montserrat** (Passeig de la Mare de Déu del Coll 41-51, 93 210 51 51, www.tujuca.com) and **Hostal L'Antic Espai** (Gran Via de les Corts Catalanes 660, 93 304 19 45, www.anticespai.com) are two great examples.

**Barcelona Urbany** (Abda Meridiana 97, 93 245 84 14) is one of the best newer style hostels, with all mod cons and a swimming pool. Mid-range options include the antique-filled **Hostal Girona** (Calle Girona 24, 93 265 02 59, www.hostalgirona.com) and the minimalist **Market Hotel** (Passatge Sant Antoni Abat 10, 93 325 12 05, www.markethotel.com.es).

**Casa Fuster** (Passeig de Gràcia 132, 93 255 30 00), in a historic Modernista building, is the luxury option for old-world class. **H1898** (La Rambla 109, 93 552 95 52, www.hotel1898.com) can't be beaten for its central location, and newcomer **Hotel Murmuri** (Rambla Catalunya 104, 93 550 06 00, www.murmuri. com) is glitzy and chic.

## GETTING THERE & AROUND

British Airways flies from London City to Barcelona Airport (El Prat), and EasyJet flies from Gatwick, Luton and Stansted. Ryanair flies to both Reus and Girona (both a 1-hour bus or train journey to/from Barcelona).

Once in the city, the public transport system is highly integrated, with tickets valid for up to three changes of transport on bus, tram, local train and metro lines. The metro is the quickest and easiest option for getting around, with all lines operating from 5am to midnight Monday to Thursday, Sunday and holidays, and until 2am on Friday and 24 hours on Saturdays. Journeys are a flat fare of €1.40. Black and yellow taxis are also readily available and have a base charge of €2.

# Florence

Florence may now have a state-of-the-art tram system (Tramvia) and a few examples of cutting-edge architecture, but that's not fooling the millions of visitors who come here for one thing – the Renaissance art. UNESCO estimates that Italy is home to around 60 per cent of the world's most important works of art, over half of which are located here. And, indeed, if Michelangelo himself were to return to Florence to see how the slab of marble he turned into *David* was holding up after 500 years, he would find this city of tiny cobbled streets, medieval bridges, elegant palazzi and churches in many ways unchanged – on the surface, at least.

Its diminutive size also makes Florence a dream weekend break, with most major sights within walking distance of any other central point. And with the often-visible dome of the Duomo and the River Arno's four central bridges acting as reference points, it's practically impossible to get lost. The majority of the main sights and museums are clustered north of the two central bridges (ponte Vecchio and ponte Santa Trinità), in the area around the Duomo. But make time to explore the other areas around this rectangle too: Santa Maria Novella, San Lorenzo, San Marco, Santa Croce and, across the Arno, Oltrarno – a great area in which to hang out.

## Fast facts

**Country dialling code** +39
**Journey time** Flight 2 hours 20 minutes
**Festivals & events** Maggio Musicale Fiorentino (late April-early July, www.maggiofiorentino.com) – Florence's 'Musical May' is one of the best festivals in Italy for opera, concerts and dance performances; Estate Fiorentina (July-August, www.firenzestate.it) – a feast of arts and cultural events; Calcio Storico (June, 055 290832), Florence's rugby-football-boxing hybrid, with teams representing the ancient quarters; Calici di stelle (10 August, www.movimentoturismo.vino.it) – about 50 Tuscan 'Città del vino' participate in this 'wine under the stars' event
**Good for** Culture, food

**Michelangelo's David**

## SEE & DO

If you're not into art, you're in the wrong town. Florence's unrivalled artistic wealth – it has more works of art per square metre than anywhere else on the planet – makes it an art-lovers' paradise, but unless you're organised you could end up spending most of your weekend queuing to see it – a terrible waste when you could be inside the Accademia ogling *David*'s spectacular torso. You can pre-book a number of galleries via **Firenze Musei** on 055 294883 (www. firenzemusei.it), or better still buy a €50 **Firenze Card** (www.firenzecard.it), which gives you instant access to 33 museums, including all the key ones, and free travel on public transport for 72 hours from activation.

So, which to see? The **Uffizi** (piazzale degli Uffizi 6, 055 2388651, www.uffizi.firenze.it) is the grand daddy, housing some of the world's greatest Renaissance art – notably works by Da Vinci, Michelangelo, Lippi, Uccello and, in room 10, Botticelli's *Birth of Venus*. The **Accademia** (via Ricasoli 58-60, 055 2388609, www.uffizi.firenze.it/musei/

accademia) runs it a close second, with Michelangelo's *David* lording it over all. If you can't be bothered queuing to see him, a copy dominates the 13th-century piazza della Signoria near the Duomo, which is where you'll also find Giambologna's sexy nymphs and satyrs surrounding Ammannati's *Neptune* fountain (nicknamed 'il Biancone' or 'big whitey'), and the wonderfully Gothic crenallated Palazzo Vecchio – film fans might recognise its balcony as the location of Hannibal Lecter's grisly disembowelling of police inspector Rinaldo Pazzi, in *Hannibal*. Other galleries and museums worth visiting are the **Museo di San Marco** (piazza San Marco 1, 055 2388608, www.firenze musei.it/sanmarco), a former monastery largely dedicated to the ethereal paintings of Fra Angelico, who lived here with his fellow monks in the 15th century; **Palazzo Pitti** (piazza Pitti 1, via Romana, 055 2654321, www.palazzopitti.it), home to the vast collection of art amassed by the Medici family; and the **Bargello** (via del Proconsolo 4, 055 2388606, www.sbas.firenze.it/bargello), housing Florence's most eclectic and prestigious collection of sculpture.

Duomo

Société Anonyme

JK Place

'Ino

Once you've done with the museums, it's time to check out a church or two. Brunelleschi's glorious **Duomo** (piazza del Duomo, 055 2302885, www.duomofirenze.it) never fails to astound: the cathedral and its dome are so enormous that there's no spot nearby from where you can see the whole thing, though a walk through the surrounding streets will be punctuated by glimpses of its red-tiled dome, completed in 1436, 140 years after construction had first started on the cathedral. The façade is utterly beguiling, its white Carrara, green Prato and red Maremma marbles reflecting the variety of time periods that work on the building covered.

Given such scale and exterior decoration, the interior's a little disappointing, but worth visiting for a series of stunning frescoes and, of course, the precarious climb up 463 steps to the lantern perched on the double-shelled cuppola of the 37,000-tonne dome (constructed with more than four million bricks, fact fiends). The piazza's also home to the elegant three-floor, 414-step **Campanile**, designed by Giotto in 1334, and leads on to piazza San Giovanni, where the octagonal **Baptistery**, with its famous Ghiberti doors, faces the main doors of the Duomo. If you're pressed for

time, you can get a lot of pleasure from just seeing the exteriors of the Duomo complex and exploring the interiors of one of three equally compelling churches; the **Santa Maria Novella** (piazza Santa Maria Novella, 055 219257, www.chiesasantamarianovella.it), the illustrious-tomb-filled **Santa Croce** (piazza Santa Croce 16), and **San Marco** (piazza San Marco, 055 287628) – check out Giambologna's 16th-century Cappella di Sant'Antonino inside, where you can now, creepily, see the whole dried body of the saint.

Had enough of being cooped up? Cross the Arno via tat-filled **ponte Vecchio** into Oltrarno for the **Boboli Gardens** (055 2651816, 2651838) or – heading south-east from the river through this vibrant, arty area – costa San Giorgio and the **Giardino Bardini** (via de' Bardi 1r, costa San Giorgio 2, 055 290112). Nearby, the **Porta di San Niccolò** offers a lovely Tuscan village feel until the evening, when the wine bars and *osterie* along via de' Renai open up, but by the evening you should be up at Florence's most famous viewpoint, **piazzale Michelangelo**, on the hill directly above piazza Poggi. Laid out in 1869 by Giuseppe Poggi, it's dominated by another *David*, this one a bronze replica of Michelangelo's original. Buses 12 and 13 take the scenic route in opposite directions round Poggi's *viali*, but it's also a pleasant walk along via San Niccolò to Porta San Miniato, then up via del Monte alle Croci, and left up the long flight of stone steps winding between handsome villas and gardens. Alternatively, take the rococo staircase that Poggi designed to link piazzale Michelangelo with the piazza in his name below. Above here, the exquisite **San Miniato al Monte** (via delle Porte Sante 34, 055 2342731) is one of the city's loveliest churches – time your trip to coincide with the Gregorian chant sung daily by the monks (4.30pm winter, 5.30pm summer) if you can, then clamber back down to the piazzale to watch the sun set.

## EAT & DRINK

In the last few years Florence has embraced new ways of eating and drinking. A host of laid-back *enoteche* and foodie bars have sprung up, particularly in the lively Oltrarno and Santa Croce areas. The best of these are **Ganzo** (via de' Macci 85r, 055 241067, www.ganzoflorence. it), **Brac** (via dei' Vagellai 18r, 055 0944877, www.libreria-brac.net) and **Baldobar** (via San Giuseppe 20r, 055 02260107, www.cafebaldobar.com) in Santa Croce, and Oltrarno's vegetarian option **5 e Cinque** (piazza della Passera 1, 055 2741583), serving organic food and wine. The piazza it sits on has three other great *trattorie*, including **Caffè degli Artigiani** (via dello Sprone, 055 287141, www.firenze-oltrarno.net/caffeartigiani), which also runs a separate artisanal ice-cream parlour opposite. Round the corner, **Vivanda** (via Santa Monica 7, 055 2381208, www. vivandafirenze.it) boasts a wine list of over 120 organic and biodynamic labels, as well as fantastic modern Tuscan dishes. Equally appealing is **Bevo Vino** (San Niccolo 59r, 055 2001709), in the bustling San Niccolò neighbourhood, also home to likeable, relaxed **Enoteca Fuori Porta** (via Monte alle Croci 10r, 2342483, www.fuoriporta.it).

The tradition of serving *aperitivo* with drinks in the early evening continues to draw young crowds to bars in and around Oltrano's piazza Santo Spirito – check out **Pop** (piazza Santo Spirito 18a/r, 055 213852, www.popcafe.it), **Volume** (piazza Santo Spirito 5r, 055 2381460, www. volume.fi.it) and **La Cité** (borgo San Frediano 20r, 055 210387, www.lacitelibreria.info), which all stay open until the wee small hours. Also here is **Olio e Convivium** (via Santo Spirito 4, 055 2658198, www.conviviumfirenze.com), a gourmet grocer with two cosy dining rooms as well as delicious food to go.

In the historic centre, things get trickier, but **Caffetteria della Biblioteca delle Oblate** (via dell'Oriuolo 26, 055 2639685, www.caffetteriadelleoblate.it), with great views of the Duomo and a lovely terrace, is a real gem, and **'Ino** (via de' Georgofili 3r-7r, 055 219208, www.ino-firenze.com), a stone's throw from the Uffizi, makes a great lunchtime stop.

For a real blowout, meanwhile, it has to be **Enoteca Pinchiorri** (via Ghibellina 87, 055 242757, www.enoteca pinchiorri.com) in Santa Croce, or the spectacular **Moba** (costa San Giorgio 4/a, 055 2008444, www.moba.fi.it), overlooking the city from the elegant Bardini gardens.

## SHOP

Away from the tourist tat and gaudy jewellery on the ponte Vecchio, and the leather 'workshops' around San Lorenzo market, a vibrant artisan scene in Santa Croce and Oltrarno ensures lots of independent shops and ateliers selling original designs. **Ethic** (borgo degli Albizi 37r, 055 2344413) and **Société Anonyme** (via Niccolini 3/f, 055 3860084, www.societeanonyme.it) are two great Italian boutiques in Santa Croce, selling hip men's and women's fashion and unusual homewares. In Oltrarno, head for **Laudato** (via Santa Monaca 17r, 055 292229) for sandals and **Alessandro Dari** (via di San Niccolo 115r, 055 244747, www.alessandrodari.com) for jewellery. **Giorgia Atelier** (via de' Ginori 58r, 055 280374), in San Lorenzo, focuses on clothing and fashion accessories by local designers.

Fans of big designer brands will love the stores on and around via de' Tornabuoni. And for gifts, it has to be the beautifully packaged soaps and toiletries sold at **Officina Profumo-Farmaceutica di Santa Maria Novella** (via della Scala 16, 055 216276), an ancient herbal pharmacy located in a 13th-century frescoed chapel.

Foodies should head to San Lorenzo's **Ortolano** (via degli Alfani 9r, 055 2396466, www.osteriafirenze.com) or **Sant Ambrogio** market in Santa Croce, for a wide range of local produce and deli goodies. The chocoholic's fix is best dealt with at **La Bottega del Cioccolato** in Santa Croce (via del Macci 50, 055 2001609, www.andreabianchini.net).

## STAY

Florence has a terrific range of accommodation, from high-ceilinged, frescoed rooms in centuries-old *palazzi* for £50 a night, to designer boutique spaces near the Duomo for hundreds. Two great examples of the former sit spendidly in Santa Maria Novella: the **Hotel Burchianti** (via del Giglio 8, 055 277300, www.hotelrosso23.com) and **Scoti** (via de' Tornabuoni 7, 055 292128, www.hotelscoti.com), housed in a 15th-century townhouse. In nearby San Lorenzo, the **Hotel Bellettini** (via De' Conti 7, 055 213561, www.hotel bellettini.com) is similarly decorative, while the boutique **Hotel dei Macchiaioli** (via Cavour 21, 055 213154, www. hoteldeimacchiaioli.com) is stuffed with work by the little-known Tuscan group of avant-garde artists 'I Macchiaioli'.

The **Black 5 Townhouse** (via Giuseppe Verdi 5, 055 0505147, www.black5florencesuite.it) and the pricier **Torre Guelfa** (borgo SS Apostoli 8, 055 2396338, www.hoteltorre guelfa.com) both give guests access to private roof terraces, but if you're after more grandeur, the **Golden Tower Hotel** (piazza Strozzi, 055 287860, www.goldentowerhotel.it), the penthouse suites at **JK Place** (piazza Santa Maria Novella 7, 055 2645181, www.jkplace.com), and opulent recent newcomers **Il Salviatino** (via del Salviatino 21, 055 9041111, www.salviatino.com) and **Hotel L'Orologio** (piazza Santa Maria Novella 24, 055 277380, www.hotelorologio florence.com) will appeal.

## GETTING THERE & AROUND

Amerigo Vespucci Airport at Peretola is by far the easiest way to reach Florence, but only CityJet from London City Airport and Meridiana from London Gatwick fly here. Pisa's Galileo Galilei Airport has frequent flights from London, but is a train or coach journey away. A third choice is Bologna's Guglielmo Marconi Airport.

Walking is the quickest way to get around central Florence, with the electric bus service a good backup if you're feeling weary.

# Cologne

In Germany's highly competitive cultural stakes, Cologne has long been overshadowed by Berlin. But, as well as arguably being the gay capital of Germany, the city's Belgian Quarter is drawing a cool, young-ish crowd, with independent fashion boutiques, new galleries in the bohemian Agniesviertel district, and a thriving café culture giving the city a laid-back, cosmopolitan feel.

Cologne also knows how to party, with a busy calendar of social and cultural events throughout the year celebrating everything from food, film and comedy to literature, music and art. The climax is the annual Cologne Carnival, which officially kicks off at 11 minutes past 11 on 11 November and goes on for over three months, peaking in mid February. The other biggie, Cologne Pride, takes place each year in July and attracts over a million visitors, culminating in the politically charged Christopher Street Day parade. But no matter when you visit, with well over 100 galleries, 42 museums and countless shops, pubs, restaurants and cafés, Cologne guarantees a weekend crammed with culture.

## Fast facts

**Country dialling code** +49
**Journey time** Flight 1 hour 20 minutes;
train 4 hours 30 minutes
**Festivals & events** Art Cologne (April,
www.artcologne.de); Cologne Carnival (November-
February, www.koelnerkarneval1.de); Cologne
Pride/CSD Parade (July, www.csd-cologne.de);
Christmas markets (late November-December)
**Good for** Culture, nightlife, shopping

## SEE & DO

Heavy bombing in World War II destroyed most of Cologne but, despite being hit 70 times, the **Kölner Dom** (*see right*) – Cologne Cathedral – survived. As well as being a magnificent structure inside and out, it's also a useful landmark in a city with no fewer than 86 distinct quarters, and the place to get your bearings before setting off on a walking tour of the city.

Pick up a map at the **Tourist Information** office (Kardinal-Höffner-Platz 1), opposite the cathedral, and join the locals for morning coffee at the traditional German **Café Reichard** (Unter Fettenhennen 11, 0221 2578 542, www.cafe-reichard.de). It has the best cake selection in town, and an enormous geranium-fringed terrace with uninterrupted views of the **Dom** (Dompfarramt, Domkloster 3, 0221 17940 200, www.koelner-dom.de) – and the cathedral bells for a soundtrack. After a sugar hit you'll be better placed to climb the 509 stairs to the top of the cathedral for a view of the city. The Gothic building took over 600 years to complete, is a UNESCO World Heritage Site, and remains the city's best-known symbol. It also contains an exquisite stained-glass window by artist, and honorary citizen of Cologne, Gerhard Richter, which replaced one damaged in World War II. It features a staggering 11,500 pieces of hand-blown glass in 72 colours.

Next door is **Museum Ludwig** (Heinrich-Böll-Platz, 0221 22126 165, www.museum-ludwig.de), a fantastic modern art gallery with a relaxed vibe. On display are works by Picasso, Mondrian and Matisse and the biggest pop art collection outside America. One of the city's oldest museums, it was recently relocated, and its shiny new premises now house 2,000 years of Western culture under one roof.

On exiting Museum Ludwig, stroll down towards the Rhine and you'll stumble upon the **Hohenzollern Bridge**, otherwise known as the 'kissing bridge' due to the 40,000 'love-locks' that adorn it: for years now it's been a local custom for lovers to attach a personalised padlock to the iron bridge before kissing and throwing the key into the Rhine.

Continue upstream along the Rhine's tree-lined banks and you'll find a string of restaurants and pubs perfect for an alfresco lunch. Afterwards, go across to the jetties where boat companies tout river cruises. **KD Rhine** (Frankenwerft 35, 0221 2088 318, www.kdrhine.com) operates boats between Cologne and the Romanesque town of Mainz, a stretch of river lined with steep-sloped Riesling vineyards and watched over by countless war ruins and medieval castles. Buy a **KD Rhine Pass** and hop on and off all day as you please (note: most cruises only operate April to November).

Once back in Cologne, carry on towards Rheinau harbour to the **Chocolate Museum** (Am Schokoladenmuseum 1A, 0221 9318 880, www.chocolatemuseum-cologne.com), where you can taste raw cocoa as well as drink from a fresh chocolate fountain. Wrap the day up with a whiff of 'eau de Cologne': head back towards the main cathedral square via the **Farina Fragrance Museum** (Obenmarspforten 21, 0221 3998 994, www.farina.eu), and, if you fancy a giggle, book the 'special tour', on which an actor (melo)dramatises the company's history and secrets.

The city has some beautifully maintained gardens and parks. On a sunny day, head to the **Aachener Weiher** (Richard-Wagner-Strasse, 0221 5000 614, www.biergarten-aachenerweiher.de) beer garden and join the university crowd enjoying barbecued meats and local Kölsch beers while looking out on to the lake. If you're lucky there may be a free gig on too.

For more information, visit www.koeln.de and www.cologne-tourism.com.

## EAT & DRINK

Cologne's culinary credentials have soared in recent years, with an explosion of fine dining and international restaurants, as well as a café culture to rival some French cities. There are more than 3,000 restaurants and pubs, and dining out is a sociable, convivial experience. Those after sophisticated fine dining should head to stylish **Taku** (Trankgasse 1-5, 0221 2703 910, www.excelsiorhotel ernst.com), at the Excelsior Hotel Ernst. It has a glass-covered stream flowing underfoot and serves elegant

Modern Asian food – the tasting menu is superb. After dinner, pop to the hotel's Riesling Lounge to sample the region's most famous wines.

For a local experience, head to family-run **Malzmeulhe** (Heumarkt 6, 0221 210 117 www.muehlenkoelsch.de), the oldest brewery in the Old Town. Packed with Germans quaffing *stangens* (small, thin glasses) of Kölsch beer, it serves hearty traditional dishes, with lots of pork, potatoes and sauerkraut on the menu.

To experience Cologne's café culture, avoid the tourist-packed places by the cathedral and head into the Belgian Quarter, where the caffeine-addicts hang out. Down an unassuming sidestreet, **Kleines** (Auf dem Berlich 7, 0221 16935 271, www.kleines-koeln.de) has a tranquil secret garden and serves delicious salads and snacks. A quirky option is **Die Wohngemeinschaft** (Richard-Wagner-Strasse 39, 0221 39760 904, www.die-wohngemeinschaft.net), a bar and hostel designed to feel like a family home; you can sprawl on a couch with a book, chat in the VW campervan or mingle in the kitchen. In the daytime, enjoy coffee on the buzzy sun terrace, and in the evenings, sink a drink or two in the bar. **Madame Miam Miam**'s wacky, colourful cakes (Antwerpener Strasse 39, 0221 94998 519, www.madamemiammiam.de) are another don't-miss.

If you're after a lively night out then head to the **Friesen Quarter**, or, for a younger vibe, the **Latin Quarter** has a mix of bars to choose from.

Hohenzollern Bridge

B&B Cologne Filzengraben

Museum Ludwig

**Excelsior Hotel Ernst**

**Madame Miam Miam**

**Die Wohngemeinschaft**

**Agnesviertel Quarter** has a bohemian buzz about it. Independent designers, bars and galleries sit alongside beautiful historical monuments – such as Fort X, built to protect the city from French attacks.

## STAY

There are some 26,000 guest beds in Cologne, covering all budgets, from bargain youth hostels and well-equipped campsites to stylish B&Bs and bland conference hotels. The three-star **Hotel Domstern** (Domstrasse 26, 0221 1680 080, www.domstern.com) offers great value for money. Hidden down a sidestreet close to the city centre, it's peaceful and has 16 basic but modern rooms.

Those after luxury for less should try **B&B Cologne Filzengraben** (Filzengraben 1-3, 0221 8011 812, www. bedandbreakfastcologne.com), an intimate apartment just minutes from the city centre, with two gorgeous guest rooms. With great views of the cathedral and a very big breakfast, it suits those seeking affordable but stylish accommodation and a homely welcome.

Blow the budget at five-star **Excelsior Hotel Ernst** (Trankgasse 1-5, 0221 2701, www.excelsiorhotelernst.com), which has 142 beautifully decorated rooms and suites, many with views of the Dom. With a sauna, steam room and gym and an award-winning restaurant, it's one of the most luxurious places to stay in the city and – seconds from the station and the cathedral square – one of the most convenient.

## GETTING THERE & AROUND

Fly to Cologne Bonn Airport from Gatwick with EasyJet; German Wings operates regular flights from Cologne Bonn to Stansted. It's possible to reach Cologne by Eurostar, with a change at Brussels – the shortest journey time is just over four hours. In 2013, Germany's state rail company, Deutsche Bahn (DB), is due to operate a direct train service from London to Cologne.

Once in Cologne, the best way to explore the city is on foot. Maps can be found at the tourist centre opposite the cathedral (Kardinal-Höffner-Platz 1). If you're planning on using public transport, buy a **Köln WelcomeCard**, which allows you free travel plus up to 50 per cent off at more than 100 attractions in the city.

## SHOP

Many tourists who visit Cologne do not leave the city centre – Schildergasse rivals Oxford Street as Europe's busiest shopping street and sucks in the mugs – but the city's best stores are spread around the 86 *Veedel* (districts). The **Belgian Quarter**, which radiates out from Brüsseler Platz, is the new hub for young creatives and designers, and is full of independent studios selling one-off clothing items, jewellery and accessories. This area also has a great selection of vintage stores, as well as cool little cafés.

Adjacent is the **Latin Quarter**, popular with students and home to a few good-value independent shops, as is the **Nippes** district: Neusser Strasse has become one of the liveliest shopping streets and is the pitch for Cologne's oldest and biggest market every weekday morning.

### Cultural baggage

**Book** *Group Portrait with Lady* (Heinrich Böll, 1971)
**Film** *A Dangerous Method* (David Cronenberg, 2011)

COLOGNE

# Madrid

In Madrid the old and new bubble together, its history a mosaic of peoples and cultures that its present reflects. The grandeur of Madrid is still there for the taking, whether in the Habsburg-created area around Plaza Mayor or the lavishly decorated buildings lining Gran Vía, but the city's true soul lies in the backstreets and distinctive *barrios* (neighbourhoods): the hipster hangouts in Malasaña, bohemian Lavapiés, and Chueca, home of the country's best gay scene. By night, Madrileños live up to their nickname of *gatos* ('cats'), with bars and clubs open until dawn.

Reminders of the city's illustrious past are everywhere: ignore at your peril the Prado, Thyssen or Reina Sofía, which house some of the finest art collections in Europe. Among the relics of its chequered history, new buildings clamour for attention, with the Jean Nouvel-designed Reina Sofía extension as incongruous as it is successful. In the unlikely event that you're lost for ideas, looking up can provide inspiration; for while there's no beach or great river running through it, Madrid's blue skies are unrivalled.

Puerta del Sol

## Fast facts

**Country dialling code** +34
**Journey time** Flight 2.5 hours
**Festivals** Veranos de la Villa (July/August, www.veranosdelavilla.esmadrid.com) – an open-air summer festival that takes place at venues throughout the city, with performances by national and international artists, ranging from classical ensembles to rock, pop and flamenco acts; Rock in Rio (August, www.rockinriomadrid.es) – the Madrid edition of the international pop and rock music festival, held in the outskirts of Madrid; PhotoEspaña (June/July, www.phedigital.com) – international festival of photography and visual arts in Madrid; Ojo Cojo International Film Festival (October, www.elojocojo.org) – an annual film festival aiming to promote cultural and social integration, with international shorts and features of every conceivable genre
**Good for** Culture, food, nightlife, shopping

## SEE & DO

A good starting point is the **Puerta del Sol**, the official centre of Spain. It's where big public events happen, from protests, to bringing in the New Year. A short walk and you're in Huertas, Madrid's historic literary district, now a tourist hotspot, with sherry bars, and tapas joints scattered around its centrepiece, **Plaza de Santa Ana**. For regal pomp, the closeby **Royal Palace** (Viaducto, Calle de Bailén 6, 915 59 74 04, www.patrimonionacional.es) is open to the public, though royal watchers beware – no Spanish monarch has lived in it for over half a century.

Plazas and parks are an essential part of any trip to Madrid. On Sundays, bring in the new week with ad hoc drumming celebrations in the **Retiro** park (Calle de Alfonso XII 14). Relax with a *caña* (small beer) by day or join the party by night in **Plaza 2 Mayo**. For performance art, impromptu public gatherings and

Museo del Prado

Estado Puro

Room Mate Oscar

street music, head to **Plaza de Lavapiés**, the
unofficial heart of Madrid's immigrant community.

Madrid's great art triumvirate – the state-owned **Prado**
(Calle de Ruiz De Alarcón 23, 913 30 28 00, www.museo
delprado.es) and **Reina Sofía** (Calle de Santa Isabel 52,
917 74 10 00, www.museoreinasofia.es), and the privately-
owned **Thyssen-Bornemisza** (Paseo del Prado 8,
902 76 05 11, www.museothyssen.org) – are looking
better than ever after substantial renovations. The Prado
has the most extensive collection of Goya and Velázquez
paintings in the world, and a visit to Picasso's *Guernica*
in the Reina Sofía should definitely feature on your
itinerary. Less established but worth a visit is the free to
enter **La CaixaForum** (Paseo del Prado 36, 913 30 73 00,
www.lacaixa.es), and the house and museum of Spanish
painter **Joaquim Sorolla** (Paseo General Martínez
Campos 37, 913 10 15 84, www.museosorolla.mcu.es).

La Musa de Espronceda

A trip to Madrid's **Filmoteca Española** (Calle Magdalena 10, 914 67 26 00, www.mcu.es/cine) will reward both cinephiles and non-filmgoers, housed in a 1920s building with a façade of jaw-dropping beauty. Films shown range from established classics to obscure world cinema, taking in all manner of curios in between.

Sunday isn't Sunday in Madrid without a trip to **La Latina**, the former Islamic citadel and Madrid's oldest *barrio*. Arrive early to pick up a bargain at the **Rastro** (Calle de la Ribera de Curtidores 21, 605 54 19 99) – the renowned flea market – before escaping to one of the many tapas bars on **Cava Baja** and **Cava Alta**.

## FOOD & DRINK

Easily accessible from Lavapiés metro, the small, brightly lit **Café Melo** (Calle de Ave Maria 44, 915 27 50 54) is no looker, but is famous among locals thanks to its *zapatillas* – massive open sandwiches served with a variety of toppings (the word means 'slipper'). Cheap, filling grub – and perfect for late-night munchies. The *barrio* is also the location for the excellent new-wave tapas bar **La Musa de Espronceda** (Calle Santa Isabel 17, 915 39 12 84). For other great tapas bars, head to La Latina, where you'll find a whole host of well-known tapas joints, including **Juanalaloca** (Plaza Puerta de Moros 4, 91 364 05 25), renowned for serving one of the best *tortillas* in town.

The recently refurbished **Mercado de San Miguel** (Plaza de San Miguel 1, 915 42 49 36, www.mercadode sanmiguel.es) is the oldest covered market in Madrid. The choice and quality of fruit, cheese, fish and delicatessen products are about as good as it gets in Madrid (though the prices are steep). Grab a beer or a glass of wine and go from stall to stall, sampling the different offerings.

Plaza Mayor

El Retiro

Peseta

Sol is home to **El Sobrino de Botín** (Calle de los Cuchilleros 17, 913 66 42 17, www.botin.es), which claims to be 'the oldest restaurant in the world'; though this is hard to verify, it's still going strong after 300 years. Always popular with tourists, it serves a mean roast, as well as the traditional Spanish favourite: *cochinillo* (suckling pig). Its nooks and crannies add up to an atmospheric – if a little cramped – dining spot. As if it didn't need another selling point, it's where Hemingway himself used to dine.

There are increasing numbers of vegetarians, and places that cater for them, in traditionally carnivorous Madrid. **Artemisa** (Calle Ventura de la Vega 4, 914 29 50 92, www.restaurantevegetarianohuertascortes.com) was the first, and probably still the best, its decor nondescript, but its salads bigger and more creative, and soy burgers more flavoursome.

To star spot while you eat, try **Casa Lucio** (Calle de Cava Baja 35, 913 65 32 52, www.casalucio.es); its famous patrons including King Juan Carlos, Bill Clinton and Penelope Cruz. The secret to its success is rumoured to be the coal-fired oven and the use of the best olive oil. Star dishes include *solomillo* (beef steak) and a starter of lightly fried eggs on a bed of thinly cut chips. Be sure to ask for a table on the first floor.

## Cultural baggage

**Book** *As I Walked Out One Midsummer Morning* (Laurie Lee, 1969)
**Film** *Women on the Verge of A Nervous Breakdown* (Pedro Almodóvar, 1987)
**Album** *Mecano* (Siglo XXI)

La Cava Baja

Caixa Forum

Taller Puntera

Mercado de San Miguel

## SHOP

The ubiquitous department store **El Cortes Ingles** (translation: the polite English) is along the lines of Marks & Spencer, stocking clothes, jewellery, food and more (tip: the café atop the Callao branch has some of the best views of the city). **Calle Fuencarral**, leading into the trendy Malasaña district, answers all your high-street fashion needs, featuring Spanish chains such as **Custo** (Calle Fuencarral 29) and **Desigual** (Calle Fuencarral 36). For vintage, you can often find a gem trawling the streets around Tribunal metro, or visit established vintage outfitters **Pepita is Dead** (Calle Doctor Fourquet 10, 91 528 87 88, www.pepitaisdead.es), which stocks clothes and accessories to buy or rent dating from the 1950s up until the present day. For lovely bags and accessories, don't miss **Taller Puntera** (Plaza Conde de Barajas 4, 913 64 29 26, www.puntera.com), set in a lovely square in Los Austrias, and Malasaña's **Peseta** (Calle Noviciado 9, 915 21 14 04, www.peseta.org); both are great for gifts. If you're looking for foodie gifts, **Patrimonio Comunal Olivarero** (Calle Mejia Lequerica 1, 913 08 05 05) is the one stop shop for olive oil, while Spanish ham, other cured meats and manchego cheese can be bought at any one of the many branches of the **Museo del Jamón** (Gran Vía 72, 915 41 20 23, www.museodejamon.es), dotted about town.

## STAY

From swanky hotels to backpacker hostels, Madrid isn't short of places to stay, and some of the best properties are in the mid-market price range. At the cheaper end of the spectrum, **Hostal Delvi** (Plaza Santa Ana 15, 915 22 59 98, www.hostaldelvi.com) is within walking distance of all the major sights and housed inside the eccentric Casa de Guadalajara building, the entrance hall decorated with ceramics of winged cherubs. The hostel, run by an elderly couple, provides basic facilities. For a more contemporary edge, **Room Mate Oscar** (Plaza Vázquez de Mella 12, 917 01 11 73, www.room-matehotels.com), in gay district Chueca, is a showcase of modern Spanish hotel design. One of four Room Mate hotels in Madrid, its rooms are all designer curves and funky colour schemes and, booked in advance, represent good value for money. The **Hotel Ritz** (Plaza de la Lealtad 5, 917 01 67 67, www.ritzmadrid.com), situated centrally near the major museums, provides a taste of belle époque grandeur, though the large and glitzy **Hotel Meliá a Gaigos** (Calle de Claudio Coello 139, 915 62 66 00, www. es.solmelia.com) gives it a run for its money. Located in the heart of the business district, Hotel Meliá's 11 conference rooms suit business travellers, though the free bar and gym make it popular with the leisure set too.

## GETTING THERE & AROUND

Flights to Madrid Barajas take two and a half hours and are offered by British Airways and Iberia airlines from London Heathrow. Ryanair offers a budget service from Gatwick and Stansted, while EasyJet runs flights out of Gatwick and Luton. Once there, Madrid's city centre is easily accessible by foot, though if you do want to use public transport, there are travel passes for tourists lasting for 1, 2, 3, 5 and 7 days, valid for both the metro and buses. Prices range from €6 for a one-day pass to €25 for a week.

# Nice

Less glitzy than neighbouring Cannes and St Tropez, Nice has the calmer, kinder air of a city that has had its moment in the limelight and quietly moved on. What present-day visitors find is beautiful Italianate architecture, wonderful views of the Mediterranean and a wealth of artistic treasures. There is also a thriving (and indelibly French) local community that has remained remarkably unfazed by the super-yacht brigade that descends every summer. Lively Vieux Nice's labyrinthine alleys are filled with pastel-coloured buildings and shops selling local produce, such as lavender-scented castile soaps and hot slices of *socca*, the latter a Niçois delicacy made from olive oil and chickpea flour. The new city, meanwhile, has its fair share of disenchanted youths on skateboards, and the police keep themselves busy arresting *sans-papiers*. But Nice's appeal lies in that simple fact of being a decidedly modern city that has grown from the grandiose remains of the 19th century.

## Fast facts

**Country dialling code** +33
**Journey time** Flight 1 hour 50 minutes
**Festivals & Events** Carnaval de Nice (February/March, www.nicecarnaval.com) – a famous Mardi Gras festival that sees flower-strewn boats competing for a prize, ending with the burial of the Carnival King on the promenade des Anglais; La Nuit des Musées (May, www.nuitdesmusees.culture.fr) – participating museums and galleries open their doors free of charge from 9pm to 1am; Fête de la Mer (June) – a traditional fishermen's procession from the church (L'Eglise du Jesus) to the seafront, culminating in the ceremonial burial of a boat
**Good for** Beaches, food, shops

Promenade des Anglais

## SEE & DO

Nice's pebbly beach can get incredibly crowded in high season, but you'll always find a spot in which to sunbathe. Head to the bathing area across the road from the war memorial at **quai Rauba Capeu**, between the Old Town and the port, which is normally happily devoid of tourists, even in the busy months. The blocks of sun-baked rock are perfect for a picnic.

A leisurely stroll along Nice's seaside promenade, the **promenade des Anglais** – carefully avoiding the hundreds of joggers, lapdogs and inline skaters – takes in the art deco palaces that line the strip, including the **Musée Masséna** (65 rue de France/35 promenade des Anglais, 04 93 91 19 10); built as a winter residence for the aristocratic Victor Masséna, the carefully restored rooms in this Italianate villa are impressively decorated in elaborate mosaics and friezes, ornate carvings and marble pillars.

Discover some of the city's artistic treasures, starting at the **MAMAC** (Musée d'Art Moderne et d'Art Contemporain, promenade des Arts, 04 97 13 42 01, www.mamac-nice.org). There's plenty of work from the Nice School, as well as New Realism and pop art pieces, and the roof terrace is dotted with minimalist sculptures by Yves

Hi Hôtel

Les Distilleries Idéales

Nice harbour

Musée des Artes Asiatiques

**NICE**

and recent releases (in original language) caters to the film tourists – classic flicks filmed in the area (remember Cary Grant's tussle in Cours Saleya flower market in *How to Catch a Thief?*) are often screened.

It is easy to venture further afield from Nice, with buses travelling up and down the coast. Neighbouring former fishing village, now trendy hotspot, **Villefrance-sur-Mer** is filled with lovely chapels and quaint views. Jean Cocteau's Chapelle de St-Pierre-des-Pêcheurs (western end of the Port) is a gem of lively frescoes depicting the life of St Peter.

## SHOP

The flower market at the **Cours Saleya** is an explosion of colour six days a week, and also has food stalls selling such delights as plump swollen olives, perfectly ripe apricots, and local goat's cheese. On Mondays, it is replaced by an excellent flea and antiques market, as brocanteurs take over, selling bric-a-brac, second-hand clothes and books; it's a great spot for finding costume jewellery to give your weekend trip a 1950s Riviera flavour. In the evenings, the market has more arty stalls.

The main shopping district in Nice is **avenue Jean-Médicin**, which runs the north-south length of the modern city centre. It has the usual high-street mix of shops and chains: Galeries Lafayette, Fnac, Zara, Sephora et al, as well as a few surprises: **Nice Etoile** is a smallish indoor shopping mall with four floors of shops and cafés. The craft and hobby shop Loisirs et Creation on the top floor is often full of delightful homeware ideas at very cheap prices.

It is the independent boutiques in Vieux Nice that are the main shopping attractions, however. Gleaming vats of local olive oil line the walls of shop-cum-kitchen **Oliviera** (8bis rue du Collet (04 93 13 06 45, www.oliviera.com); buy a few bottles to take home or sample one of the liberally doused dishes served at mealtimes. Another top spot for beautifully packaged olive oil – and related products – is Nice stalwart **Nicolas Alziari** (14 rue St-François de Paule, 04 93 62 94 03, www.alziari.com.fr), near the opera house. All kinds of hats – from handmade panamas to wool-lined leather deerstalkers – are sold at **La Chapellerie** (36 Cours Saleya, 04 93 62 52 54, www.chapellerie.com), while Italian-run **gLOVE Me** (7 rue du Marché, 04 93 82 50 23) has a rainbow-like collection of handmade Italian leather gloves and purses.

Klein, who was born in Nice. At 3pm on Sundays, participate in a traditional tea ceremony under the gingko trees at the **Musée des Artes Asiatiques** for €10 (405 promenade des Anglais (04 92 29 37 00, www.arts-asiatiques.com). Entrance to the white marble-and-glass museum (designed by Japanese architect Kenzo Tange) is free and the collection spans a 12th-century Japanese Buddha to the latest in Asian high-tech design. The museum also holds masterclasses in calligraphy and ceramic painting.

Entry is also free to Matisse's 17th-century villa, **Musée Matisse** (164 avenue des Arènes, 04 93 81 08 08, www.musee-matisse-nice.org), which displays sketches, paintings and sculptures by the artist, as well as personal belongings. Highlights include the spectacular paper cut-outs and sketches for his Vence chapel, Chapelle du Rosaire.

Rodin's *The Kiss* is housed at the **Musée des Beaux Arts** (33 avenue des Baumettes, 04 92 15 28 28, www.musee-beaux-arts-nice.org) – a beautiful Genoese-style villa built for a Ukrainian princess in 1878 – alongside works by Pierre Bonnard, Raoul Dufy and Jules Cheret.

To escape the heat, an air-conditioned cinema, such as **Cinémathèque de Nice** (3 esplanade Kennedy, 04 92 04 06 66, www.cinematheque-nice.com) can be a godsend in mid-summer. Its international selection of classic films

## EAT & DRINK

An intimate affair, **Chez Palmyre** (5 rue Droite, 04 93 85 72 31) serves Niçois specialities in style. The menu changes daily but includes items such as ratatouille, fresh fish, calamari and deep-fried courgette flowers. Book in advance to ensure a place.

Get a table on the terrace at **Les Pêcheurs** (18 Quai des Docks, 04 93 89 59 61) for a view of the port. Making the most of the Mediterranean's fresh fish and seafood, the menu has a distinct Asian/Creole accent, featuring prawns with ginger and lemongrass, served with spicy courgette purée, or *bourride* (fish soup) made with rockfish and plenty of saffron. The main courses are expensive but the set menus offer a good deal.

For a budget bite, try local delicacy *socca* – an unleavened pancake made with chickpea flour and olive oil, served in thick slices sprinkled with black pepper – at **Chez René Socca** (2 rue Miralheti, 04 93 92 05 73). There is no table service here – collect your piping-hot food, take it to one of the wooden tables, and eat like the locals with your fingers.

For an after-dinner drink, head to casual, cool and convivial **Les Distilleries Idéales** (24 rue de la Prefecture, 04 93 62 10 66), a welcome antidote to the swanky Riviera cocktail bars of terracotta-tanned holidaymakers that pepper the port. Local atmosphere abounds at **Le Bar des Oiseaux** (5 rue St-Vincent, 04 93 80 27 33), a popular theatre, bar and restaurant, with main courses starting at €12 for a generously sized Niçoise salad.

'Bar-Electro-lounge' **Le Smarties** (10 rue Defly, 04 93 62 30 75) has 1970s-style decor and a mainly gay crowd.

## STAY

Occupying an 18th-century convent in Vieux Nice, **Villa de la Tour** (4 rue de la Tour, 04 93 80 08 15, www.villa-la-tour.com) has 14 small but stylish bedrooms, several with a small balcony overlooking the rabbit-warren streets of the Old Town. The hotel also has a rooftop garden.

The funky decor at **Hi Hôtel** (3 avenue des Fleurs, 04 97 07 26 26, www.hi-hotel.net) makes it the hippest place in Nice, with a rooftop pool and nine 'concept' rooms decorated in sweetie colours. Each has something special to recommend it: 'White & White' has a transformable four-poster bed-to-bathtub, while 'Indoor Terrasse' channels a Balinese beach hut vibe. At the weekends, guest DJs hold garden soirées, and yoga classes are offered on Saturday mornings.

On a similar vein, the 25 'artists' rooms' at **Hôtel Windsor** (11 rue Dalpozzo, 04 93 88 59 35, www.hotelwindsornice.com) are individually decorated by artists, making it a mecca for bohos. The Wi Jungle garden has a palm-fringed pool and breakfast is served on the small mosaic-topped tables.

Breakfasting outside on the terrace is de rigueur at **Hôtel Suisse** in Vieux Nice (15 quai Rauba Capeu, 04 92 17 39 00, www.hotels-ocre-azur.com), perfectly positioned for easy access to the Old Town and the beach; its simply kitted-out rooms have magnificent panoramas across the bay. For budget travellers, youth hostel **Hôtel Belle Meunière** (21 avenue Durante, 04 93 88 66 15) has doubles from €45, or stay in the dorms for €15. Hostel dinners are held in the small garden, and the sea is only a few moments' walk away.

## GETTING THERE & AROUND

Flights from London take about two hours. Nice Côte d'Azur Airport is 8 kilometres west of the city centre, along the promenade des Anglais, and bus no.98 runs past Vieux Nice to the *gare routière* (bus station), while no.99 stops in the New Town and the main SNCF station (every 20 mins Mon-Sat, every 30 mins Sun). Tickets can be bought when boarding the bus. A taxi to the city centre will cost around €35. Buses from the *gare routière* will also take you to the neighbouring towns along the coast and into the hills: check at the information desk.

# A Day in Marseille

In France's oldest city, medieval churches, Roman remains, 19th-century palaces and tiny cottages on hilly streets jostle with huge housing estates, louche cafés and avant-garde architecture. There may be glorious sea views at every turn, but Marseille – a lovely two-hour drive from Nice (particularly if you take the Corniche road) that passes Cannes and Cassis en route – is proudly, defiantly urban: not a seaside resort out to fleece tourists, but a year-round working city with a lively cultural scene, where you might just happen to join the locals for a swim on the beach.

If the *French Connection* movies and, more recently, Robert Guédiguian's *La Ville est Tranquille* haven't exactly painted a pretty bouillabaisse-suffused picture of the city, other images capture its upbeat energy: the omnipresent blue and white of football team Olympique de Marseille (OM); Luc Besson's *Taxi* films, packed with local humour and colour; and the nationwide success of France's most popular soap opera, *Plus Belle la Vie*. Of late, Marseille has been undergoing an ambitious programme of urban renewal, which has brought a sleek new tramway; what's more, it has been chosen as the European City of Culture for 2013.

This is a city of fascinating contradictions. The sun almost always shines, but the ferocious winds of the Mistral chill the bones in winter. The architecture can be stunning but, despite much restoration in hand, many buildings are crumbling and Marseille has its share of modern eyesores. Yuppies dine in the Vieux Port's smart restaurants, while boy racers charge around in souped-up cars late at night. Some of the neighbourhoods behind the Vieux Port remain relatively poor, while the Corniche coastal road to the south is peppered with grand stucco villas. A dangerous reputation lingers, but the crime rate is no higher than in other major French cities and continues to drop.

Bouillabaisse, *méchoui* (roasted lamb), *pizza* and *nems* (spring rolls) illustrate the ethnic mix, but France's second city offers so much more. Loud-mouthed and welcoming to those who appreciate their city, its citizens first and foremost consider themselves Marseillais.

# Vienna

Vienna is a city you can enjoy as much travelling solo as in a couple. Yes, it's romantic, but not in the same in-your-face manner as Paris or Venice. If you're a lover of the arts, history, hedonism or just good old people-watching, the city will treat you kindly, and not leave you feeling like a loner. After all, this is the city that played classical music in subways to (successfully) win over local drug dealers – charm is in its very make-up. Vienna's circular structure of 23 districts has served it as a sort of architectural bulwark against its enemies, and the central streets still look very much the same as they did during the Turkish sieges in the 16th and 17th centuries. You could spend an entire week wandering through the Innere Stadt alone, with its palaces, churches and world-class museums and art galleries, not to mention relaxing in the city's many green spaces and parks, and enjoying the Kaffeehaus culture.

## Fast facts

**Country dialling code** +43 1
**Journey time** Flight 2 hours 30 minutes; train approximately 17 hours, with interchanges in Brussels and Cologne
**Festivals & events** OsterKlang (Easter, www.osterklang.at); Donaufestival (late April-May, www.donaufestival.at); Viennale (October, www.viennale.at)
**Good for** Culture, food, history

Stephansdom

**Priceless Tip**

New five-star hotel Sofitel Stephansdom is an 18-storey glass-and-steel tower designed by French architect Jean Nouvel. MasterCard is accepted at 32 million locations worldwide. www.mastercard.co.uk

## SEE & DO

The heart of Vienna – called variously the Erster Bezirk (first district), Innere Stadt (inner city) or simply 'die Innenstadt' – is supremely walkable. (A note about addresses – the first number is that of the district, the second the street number.) The **Stephansplatz** and its cathedral, **Stephansdom** (1, Stephansplatz, 51552 3526, www.stephanskirche.at), are useful landmarks when wandering about town; the one-and-a-half towers of the cathedral dominate the city's skyline. Open from as early as 6am (and until 10pm) from Monday to Saturday, and from 7am on Sundays, the cathedral is free to enter. Lovingly nicknamed the 'Steffl' by the Viennese, this Gothic building has seen and survived two Ottoman sieges, the Napoleonic French and World War II.

You won't get through the weekend without a little bit of Mozart, even if it's just a symphony playing in the background in a swanky bar, or his face emblazoned on the dark chocolate and marzipan sweets known as *Mozartkugeln*. The **Mozarthaus Wien** (1, Domgasse 5, Schulerstrasse 8, 512 1791, www.mozarthausvienna.at), where he lived between 1784 and 1787, is the wunderkind's only extant ex-residence in Vienna. Also known as the Figarohaus, because he wrote *The Marriage of Figaro* here, it displays original sheet music, letters and instruments.

Vienna would not be the place it is today without the Habsburg monarchy, which ruled Austria until the collapse of Austria-Hungary in 1918. Even the modern-looking **MuseumsQuartier** (www.mqw.at) – a must-visit cultural complex that includes the stunning Leopold Museum with its collection of works by Egon Schiele – is converted from the former Imperial stables. Walk through **Maria-Theresien-Platz** (with the huge statue of the Empress surrounded by allegories of the four virtues – important military figures of her time as well as a young Mozart) to the **Naturhistorisches Museum** (1, Burgring, 7, 52177, www.nhm-wien.ac.at), which contains Franz I's huge collection of (often extinct) animals and plants, including a dinosaur skeleton. On the opposite side you'll find the **Kunsthistorisches Museum** (1, Burgring 5, 52524 0, www.khm.at), which houses some of Vienna's most important paintings, including *Tower of Babel* by Pieter Brueghel, Giuseppe Arcimboldo's *Summer* and many

MuseumsQuartier

Prater

Café Aida

other Dutch and Italian masterpieces. If you cross over the Ringstrasse – which surrounds the inner district – you come to the **Hofburg Imperial Palace**, with its parks, gardens, chapels and squares. Take a look at the **Kaiserappartements/Sisi Museum** (1, Innerer Burghof Kaistertor, 533 7570, www.hofburg-wien.at) to get a fascinating glimpse of Habsburg life. Walk east to the **Kaisergruft & Kapuzinerkirche** (1, Tegetthoffstrasse 2, 512 6853 16, www.kaisergruft.at), where crowned heads lay encrypted in stone. Further afield, the Hapsburgs yellow-painted palace, **Schloss Schönbrunn** (13, Schönbrunner Schlossstrasse, 811 13 239), is easily accessible from central Vienna on the U-Bahn.

For a taste of more recent history, don't leave Vienna without seeing the iconic **Secession** (1, Friedrichstrasse 12, 587 5307, www.secession.at); you can combine this with a trip to the scenic **Naschmarkt** (4, Linke und Rechte Wienzeile) next door: food Monday to Friday, plus a great

Hotel Residenz Palais Coburg

flea market on Saturdays. More modern still is Rachel Whiteread's austere monument to the Austrian victims of the Holocaust (in Judenplatz), unveiled in 2000.

For some slightly cheesy fun, visit the **Prater** (2, Prater 90, 7295430, www.wienerriesenrad.com), containing one of the world's first Ferris wheels, the Riesenrad, which dates back to 1897, takes 20 minutes to ride and is 65 metres high. The 60-square-kilometre former aristocratic hunting ground, opened to the public in 1766, is perfect for a Sunday stroll or a spot of jogging, with gigantic oak and chestnut trees, rowing boats on the old Danube, cafés, beer gardens and a fun fair that is open between mid March and the end of October.

## EAT & DRINK

Vienna is the coffee-and-cake metropolis of Europe – you could easily spend a long weekend just café-hopping. Kitschy **Café Aida** (1, Stock-im-Eisen-Platz 2, 512 2977, www.aida.at) delivers a typical (and typically indulgent) Kaffeehaus experience – the pink neon logo makes branches of the chain easy to spot. More upmarket, **Café Sacher Wien** (1, Philharmonikerstrasse 4, 512 1487, www.sacher.com) is famous for its Sachertorte, as is **Demel** (1, Kohlmarkt 14, 535 1717, www.demel.at), a bakery and café with gloriously pretty window displays and a nice line in chocolates. For a less expensive coffeehouse experience, drink a *Melange* (a milky coffee that's the city's preferred drink), in an atmospheric spot such as **Café Hawelka** (1, Dorotheergasse 6, 512 8230, www.hawelka.com) or **Café Prückel** (1, Stubenring 24, 512 6115, www.prueckel.at).

Leave room for the savoury stuff too. If you're hankering for an authentic *Wiener Schnitzel*, head to **Figlmüller** (1, Wollzeile 5, 512 6177, www.figlmueller.at) or **Zu den Zwei Lieseln** (7, Burggasse 63, 523 3282); for other Viennese classics such as *Tafelspitz* (beef boiled in broth) served with apple sauce and horseradish, spinach-filled *Palatschinken* (thin pancakes) or any fruit-filled *Knödeldessert*, go to **Gasthaus Poeschl** (1, Weihburggasse 17, 513 5288).

**Kaiserappartements/Sisi Museum**

---

### Cultural baggage

**Book** *The Piano Teacher* (Elfriede Jelinek, 1988)
**Film** *The Third Man* (1949, Carol Reed)
**Album** *The K&D Sessions* (Kruder & Dorfmeister, 2007)

If you're looking for a smart but affordable lunch or dinner, check out **Österreicher im MAK** (1, Stubenring 5, 714 0121, www.oesterreicherimmak.at). Specialities include soup with liver dumplings, goulash with *Knödel* (potato dumpling) or the typical *Krautfleckerl* (pasta with cabbage); the wine-bottle chandelier, winter garden and alfresco bar give the venue and its guests an artsy feel. If you're visiting the Naschmarkt, pop into friendly **Amacord** (4, Rechle Wienzeile 15, 587 4709) for brunch.

*Heuriger*, or wine taverns, are a popular option, especially in the warmer months; **10er Marie** (16, Ottakringer Strasse 222-224, 489 4647, www.fuhrgassl-huber.at) and **Zawodsky** (19, Reinischgasse 3, 320 7978, www.zawodsky.at) are authentic and entertaining, and not just for tourists.

## STAY

Like the majority of Vienna's sights, most of the accommodation is in the Innere Stadt, but if you want to save a bit of money, venture just outside (still close enough to walk) to somewhere like **Pension Wild** (8, Lange Gasse 10, 406 5174, www.pension-wild.com).

If you've got cash to spend and fancy staying in a neo-classical palace, book yourself a room in the **Hotel Residenz Palais Coburg** (1, Coburgbastei 4, 51818-0, www.palais-coburg.com). Built in 1857, it boasts a spectacular entrance, a spa, a rooftop pool and views of the Stadtpark.

**Do&Co Hotel** (1, Stephansplatz 12, 24188, www.doco.com), smack in the middle of the city, has a great view of the Stephansdom. It's a modern hotel with exceptionally friendly staff, and a popular bar on the sixth floor. **Das Triest** (4, Wiedner Hauptstrasse 12, 589 180, www.dastriest.at) is Vienna's original boutique hotel, designed by Sir Terence Conran in 1995. A new addition is the ultra-modern **Sofitel Stephansdom** (2, Praterstrasse 1, 906 160, www.sofitel.com).

**Pension Christina** (1, Hafnersteig 7, 533 2961-0, www.pertschy.com) and the slightly pricier **Pension Pertschy** (1, Habsburgergasse 5, 534 49-0, www.pertschy.com) belong to the same group and are both fantastic value for money, in quiet but central locations; some of the rooms in Pension Pertschy include kitchenettes.

## GETTING THERE & AROUND

British Airways, Lufthansa, Austrian Airlines and EasyJet all fly to Vienna. Once there, you won't necessarily need to use public transport, as much of the city is very compact and walkable; but if you do, you'll find that it's pleasingly user-friendly and barrier-free. The trams, buses and underground trains are safe and reliable, and most U-Bahn stations have multilingual vending machines. For a weekend visit, a Vienna Card is a good choice – providing 72 hours worth of travelling on all routes, plus over 200 discounts on museums, restaurants and even *Heuriger*, for €18.50. You can find out more fares and general information on www.wien.info/en. If in doubt, the tourist office Tourist-Info Wien (1, Albertinaplatz, 211 14-22, www.vienna.info) is open every day between 9am and 7pm and is stacked with brochures, tickets, maps, tours, money exchange and hotel booking services.

# Granada

Granada is widely regarded as the epitome of *España profunda*: deepest Spain, where traditions hold firm, flamenco echoes around the whitewashed streets and the people speak the most impenetrable form of Castilian. As far as visitors are concerned, that has long been the charm of this Andalucían city, along with its scenic location at the foot of the Sierra Nevada and Alpujarras mountains.

However, spurred on by a lively international student scene and the need to remain competitive in the tourist market, the past five years have seen a more modern outlook adopted around Granada. So, what will you find now if you arrive for a flying weekend visit to the city known as *Graná* in the locals' lazy tongue?

The ultimate icon of Granada – and many people's main reason for visiting the city – is the Alhambra, the palace-fortress that looks down on the city from its dominant hilltop setting. Facing the Alhambra are the beautifully preserved narrow cobbled streets of the Albaicín district, the city's other important marker of Moorish influence, and which has undergone something of a rebirth over the past few years.

Alhambra

## SEE & DO

Since Washington Irving's 'rediscovery' of the **Alhambra** (information 958 22 95 75, tickets 902 441 221, www.alhambra-patronato.es) in the early 19th century, and the subsequent flood of panegyrics celebrating its wonders that issued from the pens of Romantic travellers, this remarkable palace has been one of the major tourist destinations not just in Andalucia, or Spain, but in the whole of Europe. The complex of buildings and gardens started life in the 11th century as a basic structure of blush-coloured walls and fortified towers, which gave the site its name: qu'lat al-Hamra or the 'Red Castle'. Its strategic location on the inaccessible hill of al-Sabikah attracted Mohammed I, the founder of the Nasrid dynasty (1237-1492), who set up a hydraulic system of aqueducts and cisterns to support an independent township. The most spectacular period of Nasrid architecture came in the mid to late 14th century during the reigns of his successors, Yusuf I and Mohammed V, who built the Palacio de los Leones and the Palacio de Comares. The subsequent additions of Christian monarchs rankle with many visitors and certainly disrupt the aesthetic unity of the Alhambra, yet the Palacio de Carlos V and the Convento de San Francisco are undeniably beautiful in their own right and heighten the Alhambra's sense of history.

After Carlos V left in the mid 16th century, the whole site gradually fell into ruin and went on to suffer terrible abuse at the hands of Napoleon's troops, who were stationed here in 1812. Yet 20 years later Washington Irving's bestselling book, *Tales of the Alhambra*, put Granada firmly on the tourist map and the Spanish government finally allotted funds to the site's restoration; it remains an ongoing project.

The recommended route through the site allows a slow immersion in the historical contexts. It begins at the **Alcazaba** military fortress to the west, followed by the **Palacio de Carlos V**, the **Palacios Nazaríes** (the highlight of any visit), with a stroll through the **Generalife** gardens forming a sensual coda.

The tour of the entire complex takes at least three hours, and involves quite a lot of walking, so wear comfy shoes and bring something to drink, particularly in summer. The Alhambra's immense popularity has resulted in an admission policy that limits the daily number of visitors. This means that, effectively, tickets must be bought in advance (although it is possible to turn up on the day, it's not advised). If you buy the **Granada City Pass** (*Bono Turístico* – see http://caja.caja-granada.es), then your Alhambra entry slot and ticket are part of the package.

Aside from the Alhambra, there is plenty of other interest to be found in Granada's less celebrated district, which looks back at the Alhambra from the other side of the picturesque Darro Valley. Known as the **Albaicín**, this maze of whitewashed houses built by the Moors contains

Parador

plenty of surprises – not least because it's impossible to master the layout of narrow cobbled streets. More by accident than design you will come across tiny squares with orange trees and fountains, traditional bars and a growing number of gourmet restaurants. But the biggest draw might be the unexpected viewpoints, known as *miradores*, which offer sweeping views of the city, the Alhambra and –weather permitting – the backdrop of the snow-capped mountains. The best (but busiest) of the *miradores* is San Nicolás, which provides equally spectacular views by day and night (a night-time visit will bring more respite from the ubiquitous crusty musicians and hyperactive schoolchildren).

The streets and squares of Granada's city centre, particularly around the cathedral – specifically **Plaza Bib-Rambla** and **Fuente de la Batalla** – have a more recognisably elegant, continental feel. Here you'll find the boutiques, art nouveau flower stalls and large decorative fountains that grace many old European city centres. However, a lot of work has been carried out in recent years to give Granada's old town a more modern atmosphere, nowhere more so than along the main thoroughfares of **Gran Vía de Colón** and **Avenida de la Constitución**, where Cubist street lamps and other contemporary street furniture have changed the feel of the area. But then, just off Gran Vía, you can dive straight back into the Moorish past with a walk around the **Alcaicería**, a less hectic but still charming version of an Arabic bazaar.

Although Granada's not a great destination for a family-oriented break, there is one attraction that will keep the kids' attention. The **Parque de las Ciencias** (www.parqueciencias.com), located in the south of the city, features well-designed interactive exhibits and hands-on activities that explain a wide variety of scientific thinking – things you should probably know as a grown-up but could do with some refreshing. Fittingly, given the popularity of the city's traditional *miradores*, the park's centrepiece is a 12-storey viewing platform with fantastic views across Granada and its environs.

Spaniards from outside Granada often speak of the feeling of melancholy that hangs over the city's people due to centuries of hardship. It's little wonder, then, that it reverberates to this day with the soulful but haunted sounds of flamenco. Far from being a tourist gimmick, flamenco is a living, breathing (and wailing) lifestyle in evidence throughout Granada's more time-worn areas. To prove the point, the family many view as the founders of contemporary flamenco, the Morentes, hail from the secluded streets of the Albaicín.

For an accessible and enjoyable introduction to this musical force of nature, head to the orange terrace of flamenco club **Peña de la Platería** (7 Placeta de Toqueros, 958 21 06 50, www.laplateria.org.es). Meanwhile, the cosy bar of **La Porrona** (Plaza Larga) seems to be a venue of choice for singers and enthusiasts alike.

The most authentic flamenco is found in the legendary heartland of Spanish gypsy culture: **Sacromonte**. Even without the attraction of flamenco this district is worth a visit, mostly thanks to its scenic (but precarious) hillside pathways and whitewashed cave dwellings. But to get a true sense of Sacromonte, spend some time in the evening checking out the homespun flamenco venues dotted along the Camino de Sacromonte.

Albaicín

## EAT & DRINK

Start your busy day with an enormous sugar rush of *churros con chocolate* at one of the many cafés on **Plaza Bib-Rambla** or **Plaza Pescadería**; this sugar-sprinkled batter with a rich chocolate dip is adored all over Spain, and is popular as a post-clubbing treat.

Granada has kept up the custom of free tapas. No matter how aware of this tradition you may be, it always comes as a pleasant surprise to have a delicious free dish put in front of you along with your drink (the price of which rarely feels like it subsidises the food). The dishes range from manchego cheese and toasted bagels to small portions of paella, but the tastiest *tapa* is perhaps the tender ham from the Alpujarras mountains, a dish said to have gained in popularity as persecuted former Jews attempted to prove their conversion to Christianity in the 15th century. For a wide selection of free tapas, head to **Bodega Mas Que Vinos** (Calle Tundidores), set in a tiny street off Calle Zacatín. Or for a more alfresco experience, trek up to the top of the Albaicín to **Bar Kiki** (no phone), just beside Mirador San Nicolás. Another surprising local speciality, and a perfect accompaniment to the tapas on offer, is the sweet red wine from the surrounding mountains. Although at first it tastes like a fortified wine, it turns out to be a gluggable and warmly intoxicating variety, best experienced beside the idyllic Darro River at **Bar Minotauro** (23 Carrera del Darro, 958 22 13 99, www.minotaurotapasbar.es).

With all the free food on offer don't forget to leave some room for finer cuisine, a great choice for which would be **Restaurante San Nicolás** (3 Calle San Nicolás, 958 80 42 62, www.restaurantesannicolas.com). With its beautifully presented terrace and incredible views of the Alhambra, this venue is surprisingly quiet even at peak times. And the food's not at all bad either, with succulent pork shoulder a particular highlight.

## NIGHTLIFE

Granada starts – and finishes – having fun even later than other Spanish cities. It's perfectly reasonable to head out at 11pm and not hit a club until 2am or 3am. So don't be put off if you enter an empty club at midnight – you may have to wait for the atmosphere to get going. Kill some hours enjoying free drinks on **Calle Elvira** – look out for the 'reverse chuggers' giving out coupons to redeem beers or shots in the studenty bars. If you prefer your drinking in more upmarket surroundings, nearby **Seco** (57 Calle Reyes Católicos) is a well-liked staple of the city's bar scene.

Starting from Calle Elvira or the streets between Gran Vía and Plaza Nueva, your night can pan out in one of two ways. One, stay in the city centre, perhaps crawling the small, scruffy bars along Calle Molinos, before ending the night dancing to cheesy Spanish pop in the ever-popular **Granada 10** (Calle Cárcel Baja 10, 958 22 40 01). Converted daily from cinema to club, the venue is known for its chintzy furniture, international student crowd and less-than-proficient DJs. Still, it's welcoming and upbeat and can round off a good night out.

The artful alternative is to head along the riverside **Carrera del Darro**, taking in bars along the way. Then, at 2am, head up to Sacromonte to **El Camborio** (Camino del Sacromonte 47, 958 22 12 15, www.elcamborio.com) for an unforgettable night-time experience. Like many of the houses round here, this club occupies tunnels built into the hillside (making for some interesting acoustic effects). When you start to flag, take to the terrace above to sit back and watch the sun rise over the stunning valley, with the Alhambra in the foreground, the city and mountains in the background. Magical.

## STAY

Tucked in among the city's shopping streets, the **Room Mate Leo** (Calle de los Mesones 15, 958 53 55 79, www.room-matehotels.com) blends a traditional building with contemporary touches and has very reasonably priced rooms.

The **Zaguán del Darro** (Carrera del Darro 23, 958 21 57 30, www.hotelzaguan.com) is a more stately affair in the Albaicín but offers good-value double rooms from around €45 a night.

To really immerse yourself in the legends of the Alhambra, splash out on a night at the **Parador** (Real de la Alhambra, 958 22 14 40, www.parador.es), set at the palace's heart.

## GETTING THERE & AROUND

There are no direct flights to Granada from the UK so the quickest option is to fly to Málaga and continue by road. EasyJet flies from Gatwick, Luton and Stansted, with British Airways operating routes from Gatwick and City. Once in Málaga it's a quick bus ride to the coach station, from where 18 daily Alsa coach services (www.alsa.es) run to Granada in around 90 minutes. Check the time of the last coach before booking your flight as the latest departures can be relatively early. If you hire a car in Málaga airport it frees you up to make a few excursions into the Andalucían countryside around Granada – some of the mountain roads are quite spectacular.

In Granada itself, a tram–metro network – another sign of creeping modernity – is currently under construction but will not be complete any time soon. But with most of the city built on the flat plain between mountain ranges (the Alhambra and Albaicín apart), walking around is relatively easy. Taxis, too, are a simple option given the fairly inexpensive rates.

# Europe's Best Ski Resorts – by Train

This chapter is definitely aimed at long weekenders – those who want to get off, say, Thursday night or Friday and stay away till late Monday. Travelling by train is lovely, and more affordable than you might expect – but it's not always speedy. It's best to think of the overland journey as part of the break. Indulge in nocturnal picnics, buffet car booze-ups or the Agatha Christie romance of being rocked to sleep by the rhythms of the train, before waking up in a snowscape many miles away. The times given are for the 2011/2012 season and subject to change; check and co-ordinate timetables, and book rail travel with Eurostar (www.eurostar.com), Rail Europe (www.raileurope.co.uk), Railbookers (www.railbookers.com) and Deutsche Bahn (www.bahn.com). Visit www.snowcarbon.co.uk for more flight-free skiing ideas. Oh, and you can fly to all these places too, if you're in a hurry.

Verbier

## Clavière, Italy

Don't let this lesser-known resort fly under you skidar. You'll find Clavière's traditional village, which is at an altitude of 1,760 metres, brimming with Alpine charm. In the heart of the 400-kilometre Milky Way ski area, the snow record is excellent, and the fact that so many of the runs are tree-lined is a big visual plus. Although the resort doesn't offer a great deal for late-night party people, lively Montgènevre is just a two-kilometre walk or taxi ride over the French border.

**MasterCard Priceless Tip**

The rotating terrace of the Gipfel Restaurant in Söll, Austria, provides a 360-degree tour of the Hohe Salve mountain range as you eat. MasterCard is accepted at 32 million locations worldwide. www.mastercard.co.uk

**Stay** All three classes of bedroom at the Hotel Bes & Spa, Clavière (via Nazionale 18, +39 0122-878637, www. hotelbes.com) are brightly decorated and the hotel is close to the ski-lifts.
**Depart** St Pancras on the 10:25 Eurostar, change in Paris and take the 15:24 TGV, arriving Oulx 20:05; then it's a 15-minute taxi ride.

## Les Arcs, France

It's hard to fault the skiing in Les Arcs. For beginners, there's a *ski tranquille* area above each village, while for intermediates, the huge network of runs means care-free carving all day. And there are challenging slopes for experts, the legendary Aiguille Rouge-Villaroger being just one example.

Of the several traffic-free villages that make up the resort, the newest is Arcs 1950. It's a superb ski-in, ski-out set-up – you can literally ski through the village. The traditional buildings look great, but the almost too neatly arranged

Crans Montana

layout can make it feel like a ski version of the *Truman Show*. Another option is to stay in Bourg St-Maurice – a working town that offers great value for money – and take the funicular each day.

**Stay** At the three-star Grand Hotel Paradiso (Village de Charmettoger, +33 4 79 07 65 00, www.grandhotelparadiso. com), at the foot of the slopes; with large terraces and balconies off almost every room, the views are fab.

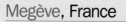

**Depart** St Pancras on the 10:00 Eurostar Direct Ski Train, arriving Bourg St-Maurice at 18:51, then a seven-minute ride by funicular train to Arcs 1600.

## Megève, France

The crazy thing about Megève is how long the powder snow lasts. You can get back up the slopes day after day and it's still sitting there, untouched. This isn't due to some magical meteorological quality in the region; it's simply because Megève's clientele mostly likes to stay on piste.

The resort was founded in the 1920s by bon viveurs and the restaurants are legendary, particularly on the slopes; try to have at least one meal at the rustic Ravière hut, in the woods at Mont d'Arbois. At the end of the day, Megève's medieval village has a grand, cobbled main square, which is a blissful setting for a glass of steaming hot wine.

**Stay** The family-run Au Coeur de Megève (44 rue Charles Feige, +33 4 50 21 25 30, www.hotel-megeve.com) is in the centre, and the tartan-esque decor gives it a cosy country lodge feel.

**Depart** St Pancras on the 18:02 Eurostar, change in Paris and take the 23:02 Corail Lunea sleeper train, arriving St Gervais at 08:43.

## Söll, Austria

No one does après-ski like the Austrians, and few resorts do it better than Söll. By the end of a weekend here you'll have made new friends, danced on tables and been gently marinated in beer and *gluhwein* in bustlingly warm bars such as Moonlight. Be warned, however. Local legend DJ Oetzi has carved a living from creating cheesy remixes and you will hear these again and again and again.

The ski area is the real draw. Part of the 279-kilometre Ski Welt, it has loads of intermediate runs and the north-facing runs above Söll hold their snow well. The views over the Wilder Kaiser are fabulous from every angle.

**Stay** The Tyrolean-style Hotel Mödlinger (Dorfbichl 30, +43 5333 5339, www.moedlinger.at) is family-friendly and has a ski bus stop outside the door.

**Depart** St Pancras on the 16:02 Eurostar, change in Paris and take the 20:20 City Night Line sleeper train, arriving Woergl at 09:41, then it's a 15-minute taxi ride.

## Crans Montana, Switzerland

If you like sunny, varied pistes and long lunches, Crans-Montana – actually two villages linked by a free shuttle bus – is a solid choice. The panoramic views over the Rhône

Valley are stunning, and the varied skiing is from 1,500 metres up to 3,000 metres at Plaine Morte. It's mostly rolling reds and easy blue runs, and you can see the appeal for families, while on slope you are spoilt for mountain restaurants – the rustic Cabane des Taules, which used to be a cowshed, is excellent. **Stay** Ultra-modern Helvetia Intergolf (Route de la Moubra 8, +41 27 485 88 88, www. helvetia-intergolf.ch), recently renovated, is perched on a high plateau overlooking the Rhône Valley. **Depart** St Pancras on the 08:02 Eurostar, change in Paris and take the 12:58 TGV, changing in Martigny to arrive Sierre 18:03, then a 15-minute ride by funicular train.

## St Anton, Austria

St Anton's status as a mecca for powder snow-lovers and partygoers is well earned. There are reams of off-piste to be explored, and lots of challenging slopes for advanced skiers. Any day's exploring should end at the legendary daily on-slope après-ski parties at the Moosewirt bar.

The village has character and bustle, and the railway station was recently moved to a location metres away from the centre. The journey, via Zurich through the Arlberg valleys, is a constant vista of lakes and mountains, and the final leg is on the very comfortable new RailJet train. **Stay** In downtown St Anton, Hotel Post (Walter-Schuler-Weg 2, +43 5446 22130, www.hotel-post.co.at) is intimate and elegant and sits right beside the ski lifts. **Depart** St Pancras on the 06:22 Eurostar, change in Paris and take the 10:24 TGV, changing in Zurich, to arrive St Anton am Arlberg 18:57.

## Train tips

### Get low fares
Book early to get the lowest prices. If your journey involves more than one train, try booking each train separately to get a lower overall fare. Indeed, don't always trust the prices you see online – phone a rail company or booking expert and ask them to help.

### Find a package
Look for rail-inclusive ski packages from tour operators such as Inghams and Crystal, which include rail travel at preferential rates and transfers from station to resort too.

### RER, not Métro
If changing station between Gare du Nord and Gare de Lyon, use the RER, not the Métro. It's far quicker and there are escalators and lifts between platforms.

### Pre-booked Paris taxi transfers
You can cross Paris by taxi using Paris City Line, a pre-booked taxi service that meets you at the end of the Eurostar platform. Its eight-seater vehicles cost €30 and the English-speaking drivers point out scenery on the way.

## Serre Chevalier, France

The nightly sleeper train from Paris deposits you directly in Briancon, the first of several unpretentious villages that make up the resort of Serre Chevalier. Much loved by the French for its superb terrain, it's relatively undiscovered by the British. It's a really good choice for families, with good ski schools and nursery slopes such as those at Serre Ratier or Grande Alpe, plus bags of intermediate terrain to progress to.

Of the villages, Chantermerle is suited to families while Villeneuve has a few bars, although don't expect wild nightlife here – save your energy for the slopes. **Stay** The Auberge du Choucas (Briançon, +33 4 92 24 42 73, www.aubergeduchoucas.com) is a small, smart hotel with wood-clad rooms and an excellent restaurant. **Depart** St Pancras on the 17:32 Eurostar, change in Paris and take the 22:05 Corail Lunea sleeper train, arriving Briançon at 08:30, then it's a 20-minute bus or taxi ride.

La Clusaz

St Anton

Les Arcs

## La Clusaz, France

Ask most British skiers about La Clusaz and they'll reply, 'Where?' It's a resort that should really be far better known, because it ticks a lot of boxes. Located up the hill from the city of Annecy, the village shares a 222-kilometre ski area with Le Grand Bornand. It is intermediate nirvana and there are easy off-piste options near most slopes. While the skiing isn't high altitude, the snow holds well and the views of the magnificent Aravis mountain ranges make one of the most picturesque settings in the Alps. If you come for the last weekend in January, you can ski over to neighbouring Manigold for the Rhône-Alpes Husky Dog Challenge.

**Stay** The Hotel Chalet Alpage (1872 route du Col de la Croix-Fry, +33 4 50 02 63 28, www.chalet-alpage.com) is in an ex-Savoyard farmhouse, which has been transformed into a cosy place to stay.

**Depart** St Pancras on the 09:00 Eurostar, change in Paris and take the 13:50 TGV, arriving Annecy 17:30, followed by a 40-minute taxi ride.

## Verbier, Switzerland

Verbier's unparalleled off-piste options, animated nightlife and informality mean that it attracts a varied crowd from a range of countries. Some of the best off-piste options are the steep, open slopes off the Mont-Gele cable car; afterwards, for a rocking sun terrace and bands playing from the afternoon, pick the Après Ski Bar.

The resort has cult status among snowboarders because of its extreme terrain, natural kickers and cliffs jumps, and has hosted the Freeride World Tour, where extreme snowboarders compete in jaw-dropping terrain.

**Stay** Hip Central Hotel (place Centrale, +41 27 771 5007, www.verbiercentral hotel.com) is superbly situated in the heart of the picturesque village.

**Depart** St Pancras on the 08:02 Eurostar, change in Paris and take the 13:09 TGV, changing Geneva and Martigny to arrive Le Chable 18:39, then a 12-minute ride by cable car.

## Meribel, France

Meribel has long since been a mecca for those who like a proper dose of nightlife with their skiing, and hosting the week-long Little World Festival for two years running has put it on the live gig circuit too. Don't stay out too late, though: the resort sits in the heart of the 600-kilometre Three Valleys area, which has enough pistes to fill a long, long weekend.

**Stay** The Club Med Meribel Aspen Park (Rond-Point des Pistes – BP 62 – Les Allues, www.clubmed.co.uk) is a wellness hotel with the usual Club Med comforts.

**Depart** St Pancras on the 10:00 Eurostar Direct Ski Train, arriving Moûtiers at 18:13, then a 20-minute transfer taxi.

# Palermo

Unlike some other Italian cities, Sicily's capital is as much at ease with modern traditions as it is with time-honoured ones. You can sip fancy cocktails in high-ceilinged bars that host literary events, eat smoked tuna in artsy cafés, drink beer in punk-rock bars or watch open-air ballet. Being smack bang in the middle of the Mediterranean, Sicily has been fought over by invading empires since Palermo was founded in the eighth century BC. Romans, Byzantines, Normans, Germans, French and Spanish have all had their stay on the island, and the 19th-century unification of Italy finally allowed the island to be its distinct, diverse self, complete with recent influences from Tunisia and China. The local cuisine is also a big draw here – it's not for nothing that the place has been nicknamed 'God's Kitchen'. From *cannoli* to *cassata*, Sicilian cuisine is world famous, while the wines and olive oils from the slopes of Etna can be picked up from the city's celebrated food markets. The beautiful island is firmly on the tourism map, and yet the city never quite feels as tourist-mobbed as other parts of Italy – perhaps due to decades of news about the local mafia.

Teatro Massimo

## Fast facts

**Country dialling code** +39
**Journey time** Flight 2 hours 50 minutes
**Festivals & events** Festino di Santa Rosalia (14 July, www.festedisicilia.it) – the holy day dedicated to the patron saint of Palermo, with processions, fireworks and street parties throughout the week; Festival di Morgana (November, www.museomarionette palermo.it) – the city's principal puppetry festival; Semana Santa (Easter, www.sicilytourism.com) – the Holy Week's parades are spectacular
**Good for** Culture, food, history

## SEE & DO

The **Quattro Canti** is a crossroads dating from the 17th century that separates the four quarters at the centre of the oldest part of town: Albergheria, Il Capo, Vucciria and La Kalsa. The baroque, octagonal piazza is a good starting point for a tour of the town, or to use as a meeting point.

Just south-east of the Quattro Canti, down via Maqueda, **Santa Maria dell'Ammiraglio** (piazza Bellini, 091 616 1692), or **La Martorana**, is the mother of all Palermo's churches. Originally planned as an Eastern Orthodox church and then donated to Benedictine nuns in 1433, the design is a slightly odd mixture of Baroque and Byzantine. The glittering mosaics that survived the nuns' refurbishment include portraits of Roger II and

Mercato della Vucciria

Alla Kala

Santa Maria dell'Ammiraglio

Antica Focacceria di San Francesco

George of Antioch, and the cupola's Christ and four angels are magnificent. A more humble church is just a few strides away on the same piazza. The **Chiesa di San Cataldo** (piazza Bellini, 091 616 1692) is a 12th-century Norman chapel and not at all flashy, though it still houses the original mosaic floor and main altar. The architecture is Arabian-Norman, a style unique to Sicily. The church was briefly used as a post office in the 18th century.

If you walk east down via Vittorio Emanuele (straight towards the ocean), you'll find the district of **La Kalsa**, one of Europe's oldest Arab localities. You might want to make use of the numerous eateries and drinking dens, but if you fancy a walk or an alfresco picnic, head to the botanical garden, **Orto Botanico** (via Lincoln, 091 623 8241, www.ortobotanico.unipa.it). It dates from the 19th century and comprises 25 acres of exotic plants, including fig trees, huge hibiscus bushes, a Mediterranean herb garden and coffee trees – just don't visit at dusk when mosquitos are out aplenty. Afterwards, stroll north along the water down Foro Umberto to catch a show or visit an exhibition at the nearby **Museo Internazionale delle Marionette – Opera dei Pupi** (via Butera 1, 091 132 8060, www.museomarionette palermo.it), a combined puppet museum and theatre. The place is home to more than 3,500 handmade antique puppets from all over the world; if you're into puppets at all, this is the best museum of its kind.

Just west of the botanical garden (and south of the Quattro Canti) is the **Expa Galleria di Architettura** (Scuderie Palazzo Cafalà, via Alloro 97, 091 617 0319, www.expa.org), occupying former stables. It's not a tourist staple, but the gallery hosts everything from exhibitions to festivals, debates and workshops, with a great roof terrace. The **Kursaal Kalhesa** (Foro Umberto, 091 616 0050, www.kursaalkalhesa.it) is also a stone's throw away from the botanical garden, right on the water; here, you can visit art exhibitions, browse the bookstore with its many foreign newspapers, watch a live music or literary event, or just sip a cocktail and people-watch.

*Godfather* fans should head north from the Quattro Canti to the **Teatro Massimo** (piazza Giuseppe Verdi, 06 4807 8400, www.teatromassimo.it) – just under ten minutes' walk from the Expa, in relatively sedate and leafy Il Capo. It's a 19th-century opera house, where scenes from the third instalment of the trilogy were filmed.

The **Civica Galleria d'Arte Moderna** (via Sant'Anna 21, 091 843 1605, www.galleriadartemodernapalermo.it), just east off via Roma, is housed within a 15th-century *palazzo* but displays 19th- and 20th-century Sicilian art, as well as regular exhibitions. Make sure to check out the gift and bookshop too, as well as the arty café in the courtyard.

After a day's sightseeing, the **Hammam** (via Torrearsa 17, 091 32 0783, www.hammam.pa.it) is a welcome leftover of the Moorish influences of the city. Here you can get the day's joint-pains (or previous night's excesses) scrubbed and steamed out of you and pretend you're in Turkey for a few hours.

The town of **Mondello**, 12 kilometres north along the ocean, is great for a day trip, especially if you're travelling during the hotter months. The beach on the **Mondello Lido** stretches for two kilometres and is peppered with multicoloured fishing boats – remnants of the city's fishing village past. The town boasts a great variety of restaurants serving traditional Sicilian grub, such as **Bye Bye Blues** (via del Garofalo 23, 091 684 1415, www.bye byeblues.it) and **Charleston Le Terrazze** (Stabilimento Balneare, viale Regina Elena). If you're visiting in July or August, be sure to get there early (via the no.806 bus from piazza Sturzo) to get a good spot at the water.

The local tourist information centre is Libertà (piazza Castelnuovo 35, 091 605 8111, www.palermotourism.com).

# EAT & DRINK

Sicily is famous for its produce. You'll turn your nose up at any tomato you can buy in the UK once you've seen and tasted the juicy, gigantic ones sold in Sicily. Sweet-toothed visitors also won't know where to begin here, what with the *cassata* cakes, fruit-shaped marzipan and, especially, the *cannoli siciliani* – tube-shaped fried pastries stuffed with a sweet ricotta filling. Of course, pasta is found in nigh every restaurant. As is fresh fish and seafood. And the mix of cultures also means an extremely diverse culinary scene.

The informal **Antica Focacceria San Francesco** (via Alessandro Paternostro 58, 091 320 264, www.afsf.it) serves fast/street food, Sicilian style, and is very popular with the locals (and was once popular with famous Mafia boss 'Lucky' Luciano). Try the traditional stuffed rice balls, *arancini di riso*. Or, if you're brave enough, the *maritata*, a Palermitan snack made of veal innards and ricotta cheese.

**I Grilli** (largo Cavalieri di Malta 2, 091 334 130, www. igrillirestaurant.it), open only between 8pm and 10.30pm, is hidden away behind a plain door but serves delicious traditional food; the fish (swordfish and squid) and pasta dishes steal the show. **Osteri dei Vespri** (piazza Croce dei Vespri 6, 091 617 1631, www.osteriadeivespri.it) is more expensive, but worth the extra: the wine list is the best in Palermo, and dishes include cuttlefish ravioli, chestnut and purple potato dumplings filled with porcini mushrooms, and quail and prunes cooked in a marsala wine reduction.

If you've got a bit of a sweet tooth, don't miss **Bar Alba** (piazza Don Bosco 7, 091 130 9016, www.baralba.it); the savoury selection is fine, but the sweet dishes are fantastic,

---

## Cultural baggage

**Book** Andrea Camilleri's 'Motalbano' series
**Film** *The Godfather Part II* (Francis Ford Coppola, 1974)
**Album** Anything by Etta Scollo

---

especially the *cassata* (sponge cake made with candied fruit and chocolate) and *frutta martorana* (marzipan shaped like fruits and vegetables). One of the best *gelaterie* in town is **Massaro 2** (via Brasa 6-8), sandwiched between the large Corseo Re Ruggero and via Ernesto Basile. The decor is futuristic – some might say odd – but the ice-creams are delicious, as is the coffee.

For more of an alternative scene, check out **Rocket Bar** (piazza San Francesco di Paola 42) after 10.30pm, where you'll be surrounded by pictures of the Ramones, Blondie and other punk and rock singers, or **Exit Drinks** (piazza San Francesco di Paola 40, www.exitdrinks.com) right next door, a popular gay bar with plush decor and fabulous cocktails.

Note that many restaurants, shops and bars close in August, when most locals leave the island to escape the heat.

# SHOP

Some people visit Palermo purely for the markets, and once you've seen them, you'll understand why. The **Mercato della Vucciria** (piazza Caracciolo, just off via Vittorio Emanuele or via Roma) sells super-fresh vegetables, pungently ripe fruits and lots of fish (if you go early morning you'll see whole swordfishes being filleted outside). The street is narrow and busy, but the colours are fantastic. **Mercato di Ballarò** (via Ballarò Centro, just west off via Maqueda down via del Bosco) is popular with tourists, yes, but is still big with the locals for its fruit and veg and its animated stallholders. If you're looking to bring some local produce home, buy some Etna olive oil, a local wine such as the Nero d'Avola, or cheeses made out of both cow's and sheep's milk, such as caciocavallo.

# STAY

Whether bolthole, B&B, boutique or five-star, Palermo's got it. **Panormous** (via Roma 72, 091 617 5826, www.bb panormous) is five minutes' walk from Stazione Centrale, and really good value for money, with great views of the city, high ceilings and art nouveau decor (although no en suites).

**Hotel Tonic** (via Mariano Stabile 126, 091 581 754, www. hoteltonic.it) is very well priced, especially considering its central location, close to theatres and shops.

**Alla Kala** (via Vittorio Emanuele 71, 091 743 4763, www. allakala.it) is a very boutiquey B&B, with large windows that give you a great view of the port, and pretty rooms.

The **Grand Hotel et Des Palmes** (via Roma 398, 091 602 8111, www.grandhoteldespalmes.com) is top-of-the-range but not overpriced. Founded in 1874, it has a marbled atrium, reading rooms and stately furnishings, as well as a great new spa, a bar and a top-notch restaurant, Palmetta. Two B&B websites worth checking out are www.bandbilmezzanino delgattopardo.it and www.aibottai.com.

# GETTING THERE & AROUND

Falcone-Borsellino Airport is 30 kilometres from the centre. EasyJet flies direct from Gatwick, Ryanair from Stansted. Alitalia and Air France also fly there, but include a stopover. You can catch a bus outside the airport to take you to Palermo, which will set you back €5 for the 30-50-minute journey, depending on traffic, but only runs between 5am and noon. A train station nearby gets you there until 10.40pm, also for €5 in 45 minutes.

# Lisbon

Most people arrive in Lisbon by air these days, and the view from the plane takes in the great curve of the River Tagus and its estuary, and the tangle of streets below. Traditionally, though, visitors arrived by water on one of the ferries. However you arrive, there are few more spectacular entrances to a major European city: across the vast estuary of the Iberian peninsula's longest river is the 'peaceful harbour' – 'Alis-Ubbo' in Phoenician – from which Lisbon took its name. It dictated the city's position and later defined its 'maritime vocation', weaving a complex web of trade and colonial relationships across the world.

Clinging on to the western edge of Europe, Portugal is an Atlantic country, its southern warmth tempered by ocean winds. The culture is neither Latin American nor completely Mediterranean. To visitors from more northerly climes, however, similarities with other southern European countries are more evident. Seniors gather in leafy squares to play cards, and youngsters mill outside bars at night. And while the esplanades now dotted around town are a relative novelty, local festivals have always been open-air parties that anyone can join.

## Fast facts

**Country dialling code** +351
**Journey time** Flight 2 hours 45 minutes
**Festivals & events** Peixe em Lisboa (April, www. peixemlisboa.com) – Lisbon's big gastronomic event focuses on the local speciality: fish; Festas dos Santos Populares (June) – a whole month of parties, during which the 'people's saints' – António, João and Pedro – have their days; Delta Tejo (July, www.delta tejo.com) – this event in Monsanto Forest is a good way to get to know local bands
**Good for** Culture, history, nightlife, shopping

## SEE & DO

A good place to start off a day of sightseeing is at the centrally located **Castelo de São Jorge** (Rua de Santa Cruz do Costelo, 21 880 0620, www.castelosaojorge.egeac.pt), the hilltop castle from where you can get an overview of the city. Hop on a no.28 tram up the hill to reach it. From here, you can walk down to the **Museu-Escola de Artes Decorativas** (Largo das Portas do Sol 2, 21 888 1991, www.fress.pt), if you have a taste for the applied arts, or detour to the **Museu do Teatro Romano** (Pátio du Aljube 5, Rua Augusto Rosa, 21 882 0320, www.museuyeatroromano.pt), the Roman Theatre Museum, underlining Lisbon's importance as a Roman outpost. A bit further down still, **Igreja e Mosteiro de São Vicente de Fora** (Largo de São Vicente, 21 882 440), also on the no.28 tram route, is a church and beautiful cloisters, decorated with 18th-century tiles, its foundation stone laid down in 1147 by Portugal's first king, Alfonso Henriques.

A tram ride over to Chiado will take you to the **Igreja de São Roque** (Largo de Trinidade Coelho, 21 323 5000), a lavish Baroque church, built in 1573, with a gold, ivory and lapis lazuli side chapel dedicated to St John the Baptist, originally built in Rome to be blessed by the pope.

Art-lovers, meanwhile, may want to schedule a visit to the very Portuguese **Museu Nacional de Arte Antiga** (Rua

Padrão dos Descobrimentos

das Janelas Verdes, 21 391 2800, www.mnarteantiga-ipmuseus.pt) or the wide-ranging **Museu Calouste Gulbenkian** (Avenida de Berna 45, 21 782 3461/50, www.museu.gulbenkian.pt). The latter has a lovely garden, but keen botanists will find more to marvel over close to hand in the **Jardim Botânico da Faculdade de Ciências** (Rua da Escola Politécnica, 21 392 1893) in Príncipe Real.

At least half a day of a weekend trip to Lisbon should be set aside to explore **Belém**, west of the centre, a district that will be forever linked with 'the Discoveries', the golden age of Portuguese maritime exploration. The stone **Padrão dos Descobrimentos** monument, built in 1940, glorifies the age. As well as key examples of the late-Gothic Manueline style of architecture – in particular at the **Mosteiro dos Jerónimos** and **Torre de Belém** (Mosteiro Praça do império, 21 362 0034, www.mosteirojeronios.pt) – the area has museums galore and a fine modern art collection. Take a break from culture to indulge in some of the famous custard tarts of the **Antiga Confeitaria de Belém** (*see right*): it's considered a sin by *lisboetas* to walk past here without stepping inside to munch a few of its specialist *pastéis de Belém*.

Over on the eastern side of town is the **Parque das Nações**, the former site of Expo 98, whose theme was the oceans and the Discoveries. It has attractions for visitors of all ages, with the **Oceanário** (Esplanada Dom Carlos 1, Doca dos Olivais, Parque das Nações, 21 891 7002/6, www.oceanario.pt) the prime exhibit.

You can't come to Lisbon without becoming acquainted with fado music, providing the city's soundtrack with songs of jealousy, failed relationships, betrayal and impossible longings. It's not hyper cheerful, no, but it is beautiful, fascinating and gripping. Two of the best *casas de fados* are **Mesa de Frades** (Rua dos Remédios 139, 91 702 9436), a former chapel that serves dinner but which is really all about the singers, especially as the night progresses; and **A Parreirinha de Alfama** (Beco do Espírito Santo 1, 21 886 8209), a low-ceilinged restaurant owned by fado legend Argentina Santos.

## EAT & DRINK

The Portuguese take their time when it comes to eating: you won't see too many fast-food joints, unless you're in the big shopping malls.

Lisbon is a fantastic city for seafood fiends. **Sr Peixe** (Rua da Pimenta, Parque das Nações, 21 895 5892, www.cidarte.pt/senhorpeixe) offers fish fresh from the port 50 kilometres away, with a catch coming in six mornings a week, while **Casa do Peixe** (Rue Engenheiro Vieira da Silva, Mercado 31 de Janeiro, 21 354 4233), known as 'the market canteen', is cheap and cheerful, though open for weekday lunches (noon-3pm) only. **Tavares** (Rua da Misericórdia 35, Chiado, 21 342 1112, www.restaurante tavares.pt) is the oldest restaurant in the city, with old-school decor to prove the point. Using mainly seasonal and organic ingredients (try the roasted red mullet with cuttlefish), it recently got its first Michelin Star. Another well-respected restaurant is **Vin Rouge** (Rua Fernandes Tomás 1, Cascais, 21 468 4439, www.restaurantevinrouge.com), which offers an excellent French-infused *menu de degustação* (tasting menu) for around €40.

If you're a vegetarian and get sick of ordering only side dishes for dinner, check out **Os Tibetanos** (Rua do Salitre 117, Avenida, 21 314 2038, www.tibetanos.com), where you can get Tibetan dishes, seitan and tofu on the patio. Carnivores, on the other hand, should head to **Casa Liège** (Rua da Bica de Duarte Belo 72, Bica, 21 342 2794), a charming, inexpensive *tasca* (family-run canteen) with grilled meats galore.

And for a stylish gourmet feast, be sure to visit **Bocca** (Rua Rodrigo da Fonseca 87D, Rato 1250-190, 21 380 8383, www.bocca.pt), which serves Portuguese cuisine in novel guise: local favourite *buchechas de porco* (pork cheeks) is here cooked in wine and served with caramelised apple and blood sausage.

Finally, no trip to Lisbon is complete without sampling one (make that several) traditional, creamy custard tarts, *pastéis de nata*. The best place in town to try them is the **Antiga Confeitaria de Belém** (Rua de Belém 84-92, 21 363 7423), where, on an average weekday, 10,000 *pastéis* are sold – with the figure rising to over 20,000 on weekends.

## SHOP

Shopping in Lison is a tale of two cities: a range of restrictive lease laws has long allowed charming (or fusty) small businesses to survive, paying tiny rents, despite fierce competition from the other city of chain stores and giant shopping malls. Many neighbourhood markets are still operating too. A stroll around **Chiado** and **Baixa**, still Lisbon's focal retail areas, as they have been since the late 18th century, does not suggest decline to the casual observer. But the truth is that even here family shops are

York House

Tavares

**AIRPORT**
**Arrivals**
7 am to 12 pm
Tel: 218 450 660

**Lisbon Shop**
Rua do Arsenal, 15
9.30 am to 7.30pm
Tel: 210 312 820

**BAIXA**
**Rua Augusta**
10 am to 6 pm
(Closed 1 pm to 2 pm)
Tel: 213 259 131

Tourist Information

808 781 212

**BELÉM**
**Jerónimos Monastery**
Tuesday to Saturday
10 am to 6 pm
(Closed 1 pm to 2 pm)
Tel: 213 658 435

**LISBOA WELCOME CENTER**
Praça do Comércio , 25
Pátio da Galé
9 am to 8 pm
Tel: 210 312 810

**PALÁCIO FOZ**
**Praça dos Restauradores**
9 am to 8 pm
Tel: 213 463 314

**Y LISBOA**
Rua Jardim do Regedor, 50
10 am to 7 pm
Tel: 213 472 134

**STA. APOLÓNIA TRAIN STATION**
Estação CP - Stª Apolónia
Terminal Internacional
International Terminal
7am to 1pm
Tuesday to Saturday
Tel: 218 821 606

**CASCAIS**
Rua Visconde da Luz, 14
10 am to 1am/2 pm to 6 pm
Tel: 214 822 327

**ESTORIL**
**Arcadas do Parque**
10 am to 1 pm/2 pm to 6 pm
Tel: 214 687 630

**ERICEIRA**
Rua Dr. Eduardo Burnay, 46
10 am to 1 pm/2 pm to 6 pm
Tel: 261 861 095

**SINTRA**
Praça da República, 23
9.30 am to 18 pm
Tel: 219 231 157

**SINTRA TRAIN STATION**
10 am to 12.30 pm/2.30 pm to 6 pm
Tel: 211 932 545

## www.askmelisboa.com

· online information and sales

# LISBOA CARD

## OUR VISITING CARD FOR LISBOA!

Free access to public transports, museums monuments and discounts at other sites of interest.

## Prices

|  | 24 hours | 48 hours | 72 hours |
|---|---|---|---|
| ADULTS | 18,50 euros | 31,50 euros | 39 euros |
| CHILDREN (5-11) | 11,50 euros | 17,50 euros | 20,50 euros |

Prices valid until March 31st 2013
Available at "Ask Me" counters

Torre de Belém

gradually disappearing. In Baixa, Lisbon's traditional downtown, there are still streets, however, where trades have clustered for centuries: jewellers linger on Rua do Ouro (Rua Aurea), Rua dos Sapateiros is still a 'street of shoemakers' and Rua dos Fanqueiros is home to a number of textile merchants and fabric shops.

If you'd like to buy some of the famous Portuguese *azulejos* (tiles), one of your best bets is to head to the **Museu Nacional do Azulejo** (Rua da Madre de Deus 4, Madre de Deus, 21 810 0340, http://mnazulejo.imc-ip.pt). After touring the musuem, which charts the history of *azulejos*, you can head to the museum shop for a beautiful selection for sale, as well as a collection of books on the decorative arts.

## NIGHTLIFE

For some eclectic tunes, head to **MusicBox** (Rua Nova do Carvalho 24, Cais do Sodré, 21 343 0107, www.musicbox lisboa.com). The managers of this club have music industry connections and exploit them creditably. It is one of the city's most interesting venues, with a regular programme of rock and world music bands, electronic live acts, singer-songwriters and DJ sets (all night on Fridays). The space has an underground feel and look and is located on one of Lisbon's seediest streets.

Lisbon's trendiest club, though, is **Lux** (Avda Infante Dom Henrique, Amazém A, Cais da Pedra a Santa Apolónia, 21 882 0890, www.luxfragil.com), with two dancefloors (one loungey, one sweaty) and a roof terrace overlooking the river. As the hip furniture indicates, it is a see-and-be-seen place rather than one of pure hedonism, but the crowd is friendly and the measures Lisbon-large. House and guest DJs offer everything from electro and hip hop to bursts of '80s music.

For something a little less energetic, check out **Pavilhão Chinês** (Rua Dom Pedro V 89, Príncipe Real, 21 343 4729) in the centre, which is known for having Lisbon's most interesting bar decor, courtesy of Luís Pinto Coelho. The warren of rooms is lined with floor-to-ceiling glass cases stuffed with toy battleships, eastern European army officers' hats and other grim ornaments. This museum of kitsch is not cheap, but is definitely worth a look. The 'Chinese Pavilion's' back room is also an atmospheric setting for a frame of pool.

## STAY

If you're travelling on a budget, **Residência Mar do Açores** (Rua Bernadim 14, Estefânia, 21 357 7085, www. residencial-mar-dosacores.h-rez.com) is great – quiet, clean, and with free Wi-Fi and a generous breakfast; ensuites are extra. You also get excellent value for money at the moderately priced **York House** (Rua das Janelas Verdes 32, 21 396 2435, www.yorkhouselisboa.com), which has a lovely green courtyard and a gourmet Mediterranean fusion restaurant.

If you're going to splash your cash, do it on the **Bairro Alto Hotel** (Praça Luis de Camões 2, Bairro Alto, 21 340 8288, www.bairroaltohotel.com), a boutique hotel with fabulous river views, a rooftop bar and terrace and 'Igloo' lounge. Slightly more grand is **Pestana Palace** (Rua Jau 54, Ajuda, 21 361 5600, www.pestana.com), an 18th-century hilltop palace full of 19th-century Portuguese art, and with a lovely spa and a cute little chapel.

Castelo de São Jorge

Pestana Palace

Mosteiro dos Jerónimos

Igreja e Mosteiro de São Vicente de Fora

Bairro Alto Hotel

## GETTING THERE & AROUND

EasyJet has direct flights between London and Lisbon, which take about 2 hours 45 minutes. British Airways and TAP Portugal (www.flytap.com) also fly there.

Lisbon is famously hilly, so take a pair of good walking shoes. The **Lisboa Welcome Centre** (Praça do Comércio, 21 031 2810, www.visitlisboa.com) can provide transport and sightseeing advice, and also sells the Lisboa Card, which comes in 24hr, 48hr or 72hr units, and gets you unlimited public transport and free or reduced entry to various key attractions. To get a feel of the city, make sure to hop on a tram at least once, but don't expect it to be a swift way of travelling. The Metro is absolutely fine but won't get you everywhere, while buses should be avoided during rush hour if you don't like being packed in like a sardine.

# Europe's Winter Wonderlands

Every Christmas, London is treated to visiting European markets, but for a real festive indulgence why not venture abroad and immerse yourself in the real thing? Whether in the historic squares of Prague or at Copenhagen's famous retro theme park, Tivoli, the following markets give you plenty of opportunities to pick up unique presents and decorations, to sample local seasonal food and drink, and experience European traditions.

Another way to get that winter wonderland feel is to venture into the Scandinavian wilderness, or head up into one of Europe's snow-covered mountain ranges. The juxtaposition of outdoor pursuits in snug winter gear with warming hot chocolates by the fire is the ideal way to embrace winter.

Plaisirs d'Hiver, Brussels

Berlin

## CHRISTMAS MARKETS

### Barcelona

Dating from 1786, the Fira de Santa Llúcia is a traditional Christmas fair that has expanded to more than 300 stalls selling all manner of handcrafted Christmas decorations and gifts, along with mistletoe, poinsettias and Christmas trees. The most popular figure on sale for Nativity scenes is the curious Catalan figure of the *caganer* ('crapper'), a small figure crouching over a steaming turd with his trousers around his ankles. Kids line up for a go on the giant *caga tió*, a huge, smiley-faced 'shitting log' that poops out pressies upon being beaten by a stick; smaller versions are on sale in the stalls. There's also a Nativity scene contest, parades and a life-size Nativity scene in Plaça Sant Jaume.
**Where** Pla de la Seu & Avda de la Catedral, Barcelona, Spain.
**Stay** Casa Camper (Calle Elisabets 11, +34 933 426 280, www.casacamper.com/barcelona), a boutique hotel located in Barcelona's old town.

### Berlin

Germany has some of the best Christmas markets in Europe, and seemingly one in every city – the ones in Cologne, Nuremberg and Frankfurt are particularly good, but Berlin could easily be described as the capital of the Traditional Christmas Market if judged on quantity alone – it has over 50 across the city every year. The market at the city's Kaiser Wilhelm Gedächtniskirche is the biggest and most popular, receiving around four million visitors each year who come to peruse the jewellery, decorations and artwork on sale as well as to indulge in the more clichéd seasonal pleasures such as chestnuts and mulled wine.
**Where** Kaiser Wilhelm Gedächtniskirche, Berlin, Germany.
**Stay** Circus Hotel (Rosenthalerstrasse 1, +49 30 2000 39 39) offers individually designed rooms in a location ideal for the Christmas markets.

### Brussels

Christmas in Brussels seems to get bigger every year. The Plaisirs d'Hiver (Winter Wonders) Christmas market now extends along the streets from Grand Place to place Ste-Catherine, covering almost two kilometres. Each of

Dog sledding, Finland

Nobis Hotel, Stockholm

## Budapest

Traditional food, folk dances and live music can be found daily in among the cottage-esque market 'stalls' of Vörösmarty tér from mid November. Based at the centre of the Pest district near the start of 'Fashion Street', this market regularly has up to 150 stalls, and plenty of local art and culture, including puppet theatres. To add to the authenticity of celebrations, all products sold in the market are guaranteed as traditionally handmade by a professional jury from a variety of organisations. Look out for the daily Advent calendar window displays at the 19th-century Gerbeaud Café.
**Where** Vörösmarty tér (Vörösmarty Square), Budapest, Hungary
**Stay** Lánchíd 19 (I.Lánchíd utca 19, +36 1 419 1900, www.lanchid19hotel.hu). The most splendid boutique hotel in town, bedecked completely in Hungarian design.

## Copenhagen

Like many European cities, Copenhagen is decked out in decorations and illuminations at this time of year. But, unlike most, the atmosphere is less commercial and more authentically 'Christmassy' (maybe the sub-zero temperatures have something to do with it). From mid November Tivoli turns into a vast Christmas grotto with a special Christmas market, Yuletide grub and an infestation of *nisser* (Danish Christmas pixies).

For this season, Tivoli will introduce a Russian theme; a mini-city has been built, complete with St Basil's Cathedral and a version of the Trans-Siberian railway where visitors can journey through landscape featuring choirs and Fabergé eggs. The traditional Western Father Christmas will be replaced by the Russian Father Frost, dressed in icy blues. Look out too

the 240 market stalls is a little wooden-roofed hut selling mainly arts and crafts or food and drink, all of them having a pan-European flavour. By the time you reach place Ste-Catherine and the quays beyond, not only are you decently warmed up, but you're at the heart of the festivities. The quaint stalls continue, punctuated every now and again by a 35-metre toboggan slope, a big-wheel illuminated with 18,000 lights and, of course, the 61-metre-long skating rink.

Other great Belgian Christmas markets are held in Antwerp (Grote Markt) and Bruges.
**Where** Grand Place to place Ste-Catherine, Brussels, Belgium.
**Stay** Sofitel Brussels (place Jourdan 1, +32 2 355 100, www.sofitel.com), for comfort without breaking the bank.

for the Hotel d'Angleterre's spectacular Christmas decorations. The gardens also offer an ice rink, rollercoaster and theme park rides for those up for more than just a leisurely amble round the handicraft stalls. Based in the centre of the capital, it attracts up to a million visitors, so expect crowds.
**Where** Tivoli (Vesterbrogade 3, +45 33 15 10 01, www.tivoli.dk), Copenhagen, Denmark.
**Stay** Kong Arthur (Nørre Søgade 11, +45 33 11 12 12, www.kongarthur.dk), a family-run hotel in the centre, offering quality accommodation at a competitive price.

## Prague

Prague's Christmas market takes place in Old Town Square and Wenceslas Square (as in Old King Wenceslas). Here visitors seek unusual food and drink rather than gifts and decoration – in the week leading up to the Vánoce (Christmas) holiday, the streets sport huge tubs of water filled with carp, the traditional Czech Christmas dish – and you should definitely make time to try the grog and honey liquor – a traditional Czech beverage. Czech carols can be heard round the market and visitors are also treated to the views of the beautiful surrounding architecture and dazzling lighting at night.
**Where** Wenceslas Square, Prague, Czech Republic
**Stay** Alchymist Grand Hotel & Spa (Trziste 19, +420 257 286 011, www.alchymisthotel.com) – where Prague's most decadent Habsburg days are still on tap.

## Stockholm

Skansen is Stockholm's outdoor mini 'village', oriented at families and featuring Scandinavian wildlife and original traditional houses and stores (most of which where moved here piece by piece from all over Sweden). Its ultra-traditional Christmas market has been held annually since 1903. Look out for Swedish craft products, traditional Christmas ornaments made of straw, a wonderfully range of hand-dipped candles and Christmas food and drink such as smoked sausage, eel, salmon, delicious *pepparkakor* (gingersnaps), warming *glögg* (mulled wine) and saffron buns.
**Where** Skansen (Djurgårdsslätten 49-51 (+46 8 442 80 00, www.skansen.se), Stockholm, Sweden.
**Stay** Nobis Hotel (Norrmalmstorg 2-4, +46 8 614 10 00, www.nobishotel.se) is one of Stockholm's most stylish design hotels, and very centrally located.

## Vienna

Winter is the most quintessentially Austrian time of year: snow (sometimes) blankets the city and the Christmas markets appear. Christkindlmärkte are Advent markets that appear in mid November. Christmas for the Viennese is a social affair, where people meet up at the markets for *Punsch* or *Glühwein* (the local mulled wine), chestnuts and spicy Christmas cookies. The principal hotspots are Rathausplatz market; the more upmarket Schönbrunn

Palace market; the cosy and arty Altwiener Christkindlmarkt at the Freyung; and Spittelberg market. Rathausplatz market's stalls are rather tacky, but still worth a visit for a glimpse of the Advent windows on the Town Hall, decorated by local artists, and the enchanting tree illuminations in the park. Spittelberg market, meanwhile, is one of the loveliest, set in the cobbled streets between Burggasse and Siebensterngasse in the 7th district, and offering goods not found elsewhere.
**Stay** Altstadt (7 Kirchengasse 41, +43 1 522 6666, www.altstadt.at), close to Spittelberg, one of the most atmospheric markets.

# SKI-FREE WINTER FUN

## Ice fishing

Fly fishing is technical and coarse fishing can be a real test of patience. But ice fishing is great fun. Using a saw or chisel, a small hole is cut into lake ice and then you sit on a stool or, on some trips, in your very own mobile cabin – known as an ice shanty – and wait for a bite. There's ice fishing throughout the sub-Arctic region, and typical catches include perch, white fish, grayling, brown trout, Arctic char and rainbow trout. By late winter, the ice may turn 'rotten', i.e. soft, so only super-keen local anglers will chance it then.
**Contact** Explore (0845 013 1537, www.explore.co.uk), to do a spot of ice fishing in Swedish Lapland, combined with reindeer rides and sledding.
**Stay** Ice Hotel (Marknadsvägen 63, Jukkasjärvi, +46 980 66 800, www.icehotel.com) offers both warm and cold accommodation, depending on your bravery.

## Glacier walking

If you're feeling brave – or cool and hard – hike across the glaciers of southern Norway. The largest mainland ice-sheet lies in Jostedalsbreen National Park, its arms stretching into smaller glaciers hanging above the rivers that wind through the valleys beneath. Don't try this alone – gorges, dozens of metres wide, and deep enough to look very dark indeed, open up into the moving glaciers and may be thinly disguised by fallen snow.
**Contact** Visit Norway (+47 22 00 25 00, www.visitnorway.com); Exodus offers glacier hikes in Norway and elsewhere (0845 805 7267, www.exodus. co.uk).
**Stay** Jostedal Hotel (Gjerde, +47 57 68 31 19, www.jostedalhotel.no) is a family-run hotel near the glacier.

## Dog sledding

In Finland's remote wilderness, along its border with Russia, lies an expanse of ancient, silent forest and frozen lakes. From your base at the Border Inn (+358 400 202 270, www.theborderinn.com), a team of dogs and a wooden sled will lead you to the heart of the landscape, covering up to 100 kilometres in a day and racing after wild reindeer and elk.

Glacier walking, Norway

Tivoli, Copenhagen

Kong Arthur, Copenhagen

Back at the lodge, saunas and Lappish stone fireplaces will keep you warm and cosy.
**Contact** Visit Finland (www.visitfinland.com); the Adventure Company offers packages in Finland that combine husky dog sledding, snowmobile safari, shoehorning and cross-country skiing (0845 450 5316, www.adventurecompany.co.uk).
**Stay** Border Inn (+358 400 202 270, www.theborderinn.com) provides comfort to contrast with the wilderness.

## Horse riding on ice

No, it's not a Christmas TV special starring Clare Balding. Icelandic horses were brought to the country by Vikings in the ninth century and have remained pure-bred ever since. Icelanders have a special affection for horses – they say the ratio of horses to people here is the highest in the world – and there are strict rules relating to the animals. One is that no horse leaving the island can ever return. One recommended ride is up to the Mrdalsjökull glacier. You probably won't have the skills to do hoof-skating but Icelanders love performing tricks on horseback on the ice. Catch a show if the opportunity arises.
**Contact** Icelandic Mountain Guides (+354 587 9999, www.mountainguides.is).

## Snowmobiling

Between the old Swedish villages of Jukkasjärvi and Kaupinnen, the Arctic Circle becomes a playground for adventurous travellers. Day excursions on snowmobiles pierce deep into the wilderness, but you can also learn to build an igloo and drive your own dog sled. A night at the Ice Hotel, made from 40,000 tonnes of snow and ice that melts into the river every year, can be included.
**Contact** Why Don't You… (0845 838 6262, www.whydontyou.com).
**Stay** Camp Ripan (Campingvagen 5, Kiruna 98135, +46 980 630 00, www.ripan.se) is situated on the edge of the Arctic Circle, and offers everything from personal chalets to luxury accommodation.

## Ice climbing

If you're feeling slightly suicidal, scale the icy peaks in the Alps on a rock climbing tour that will lead you up the daunting ascents of Mont Blanc, the Matterhorn and the Eiger. Seasoned climbers take on the vertical drops and hair-raising views of the North Face. Entry-level courses designed for complete beginners are available for first-time alpinists.
**Contact** Alpine Guides (07940 407533, www.alpine-guides.com); Activity Breaks (028 9094 1671) offers ice-climbing trips that aren't quite so hardcore, combined with snow-rafting and sledging.
**Stay** Mercure Chamonix Les Bossons (59 Route de Vers le Nant Les Bossons, +33 4 50 53 26 22, www.mercure.com) is situated at the foot of the mountains, and has phenomenal views of Mont Blanc, as well as a range of creature comforts, including a spa and indoor pool.

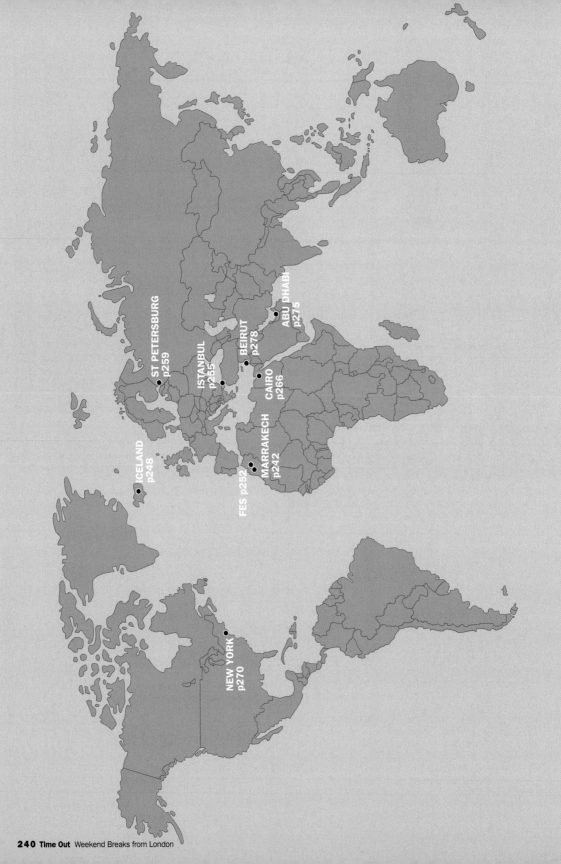

ST PETERSBURG
p259

ISTANBUL
p255

BEIRUT
p278

ABU DHABI
p275

CAIRO
p266

ICELAND
p248

MARRAKECH
p242

FES p252

NEW YORK
p270

# Big Weekends

# Marrakech

Marrakech isn't a city full of 'sights', like Paris or Rome. If need be, you could view all the principal places in under a day, and with time for breakfast, lunch and dinner in between. The city is, however, full of many other attractions – colours, storytellers, musicians, fragrances and, most importantly, spirit. It may be geographically close to Europe, but it's worlds apart in terms of atmosphere. If you're a first-time visitor, Marrakech can seem bewildering and overwhelming at times, but it needn't – the lack of things that you have to tick off your mental to-do list turns out to be rather relaxing, meaning you can enjoy getting lost in the alleyways without worrying about missing the opening hours of an overbooked exhibition. People-watchers love the city; it's easy to spend half a day here sitting in a café, looking out on the goings-on of the locals. Curious consumers and general rummagers, meanwhile, will love the Medina, where there's a magic scene to behold – and a carpet seller to shrug off – around every corner.

## Fast facts

**Country dialling code** +212
**Journey time** Flight 3 hours 30 minutes
**Festivals & events** Marrakech Biennale (February, even years only, www.marrakechbiennale.org) – showcases the best of Moroccan and international contemporary art, with a series of lectures, discussions and talks at Vanessa Branson's luxury Riad El Fenn, at the edge of the Medina; Marrakech Popular Arts Festival (July) – this five-day event is one of the biggest on the calendar and features fireworks, Berber musicians and spectacular belly-dancing performances at El Badi palace; Eid al-Fitr (October) – a three-day feast marking the end of Ramadan is a foodie celebration, complete with goat and sheep slaughtering rituals.
**Good for** Culture, food, shopping

Koutoubia Mosque

## SEE & DO

The Red City is divided into two parts: the Medina, or the old city, within the city walls, and the new city, outside them. The **Medina** is the perfect area to idle in. Its religious centrepiece, **Koutoubia Mosque**, originally built in 1147, is probably the city's most recognisable icon. Mosques are off-limits for tourists, so the architecture can only be admired from outside. This one is only 77 metres high, yet still manages to rise above the flat buildings and palm trees. A few strides away is Marrakech's real soul, **Jemaa El Fna**, the largest open space in the city. It's full of life during the day but at night is an assault on the senses and a place for gathering, entertaining and eating. Even if you don't understand Arabic, and especially if you're lucky enough to have a translator, coming across one of the local storytellers is truly a treat – they usually begin their storytelling around 5pm.

The **Musée de Marrakech** (place Ben Youssef, 024 39 09 11, www.museedemarrakech.ma) is open daily, displaying rotating exhibitions and old photographs of the city. The building itself, however, is the main attraction, with a tiled central court and huge chandeliers. If you're interested in what Moroccan artists are producing now, head to contemporary gallery **Musée de la Palmeraie** (Dar Tounsi, route de Fès, www.museepalmeraie.com), which has a gallery dedicated to up-and-coming Moroccan artists, as well as one for more established artists, such as My Youssef Elkafai. There are wonderful sculpture gardens to wander through and a cacti orchard. The owner is a perfumier and can often be found in his shed at the end of the garden.

The **Saadian Tombs** (rue de Kasbah, Bab Agnaou), south-west of Jemaa El Fna, house the holy tombs of sultans in three pavilions off a courtyard, and contain a Prayer Hall and the Hall of 12 Columns. Some 400 metres to the east of the tombs is the **Badii Palace** (place des Ferblantiers), which had walls and ceilings covered in gold that came from Timbuktu until 1598, but is now so dilapidated that you enter via a gaping hole in the outer wall. The space inside is vast, and the original Koutoubia Mosque minbar within – fashioned in the 12th century – is ornate to say the least.

The **Menara Gardens** (avenue de la Menara, Hivernage, 024 43 95 80) are a national attraction. Moroccans come to gawp at the ancient – and huge – carp and use the picnic

Jemaa El Fna

Saadian Tombs

Menara Gardens

Badii Palace

MARRAKECH

pavilion. The backdrop of the Atlas Mountains makes it a good spot for a break from the noise of the city. Another city-centre green spot, the **Jardin Marjorelle** (rue Yves Saint Laurent, avenue Yacoub El Mansour, 05 24 31 30 47, www.jardinmarjorelle.com), was established by French painter Jacques Marjorelle in 1947. It's a glittering urbane paradise of banana trees, tinkling fountains and the beautiful modernist house, painted in what is now known as Marjorelle Blue. Yves Saint Laurent was a later owner of the house and gardens, and he bequeathed it to the Fondation Pierre Bergé.

An unmissable Moroccan experience is a visit to a hammam: a steam room where a vigorous scrubbing down (*gommage*) is administered, followed by the soothing application of orange blossom and Argan oils. You'll come out feeling newborn and perhaps a little mystified: in most hammams, there is a 'trainer' simultaneously barking instructions at you and dousing you with buckets of water. Seriously opulent surroundings (marble everywhere, an enormous circular library with a central fountain) at **Palais Rhoul** (route de Fès, Palmeraie, 024 32 94 94, www.palaisrhoul.com, by appointment only) make a hammam here the closest thing most of us will get to royalty. After your hammam, you are bathed and polished to perfection with whole oranges, leaving you smelling goddess-like.

Al Fassia

## EAT & DRINK

For really fine Moroccan food, head to **Al Fassia** (55 boulevard Zerktouni, Guéliz, 024 43 40 60), run by all-female staff and serving fantastically large tagines and pastillas; or to **Dar Moha** (81 rue Dar El-Bacha, 024 38 64 00, www.darmoha.ma), which serves Moroccan fusion (the chef trained in Switzerland) – book in advance to get a table outside by the pool.

The words glamorous and sophisticated apply to both the decor and the food at **Le Comptoir Darna** (avenue Echouhada, Hivernage, 05 24 43 77 02, www.comptoir marrakech.com), with its exciting and well-executed French-influenced menu of dishes such as sea bream carpaccio, lobster ravioli with foie gras, and simple steaks with clever Asian dipping sauces. Although hardly cheap, this is five-star cooking at a fraction of European prices.

If dining on a budget, **Chez Chegrouni** (Jemaa El Fna, 065 47 46 15) is a favourite, with both a ground floor and rooftop terrace, plus quick service and menus in English. Veggies will be delighted that the vegetable soup and couscous are made without meat stock.

Another great budget eaterie is **Restaurant Toubkal** (48 Jemaa El Fna, 024 44 22 62), popular with both locals and backpackers. The premises are basic but, in return, the food is really cheap, serving all the basics such as tagines, couscous, chicken and lamb.

Certainly the cheapest (and possibly the most fun) way to eat, however, is to head to **Jamaa El Fna** after dark for a cornucopia of stalls selling hot, fresh and popular street food. The stalls are numbered and organised by cuisine: a handful of snail stalls line the rear (selling ladlefuls of hot, salty snails in a cinnamon-spiced stock), while at the front, marinated meats, fresh fish, couscous and fried vegetables are the order of the day. Pick one that appeals and plonk yourself on the canteen-style tables outside. Stalls nos.22, 42 and 31 are especially good.

Dar Moha

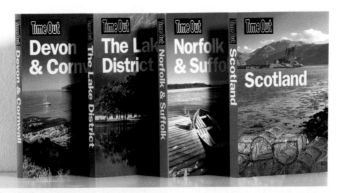

## SHOP

In a way, Marrakech revolves around shopping. You'll probably have the most diverting shopping experience if you head to the souks, where you can find everything from the beautiful to the bizarre to the bogus. Be prepared for the haggling, though, as it's been cultivated into a real art in Morocco. There are a few Moroccan treasures you should certainly keep an eye out for. Argan oil is fantastic for all kinds of things, from reducing scars and wrinkles to lowering cholesterol levels and unblocking arteries; **Scènes de Lin** (70 rue de la Liberté, Guéliz, 024 43 61 08) is a reliable stockist.

**Founoun Marrakech** (28 Souk des Teinturiers, Medina, 024 42 62 03) makes fantastic lanterns, and **Miloud El Jouli** (6-8 Souk Smat El Marga, Medina, 024 42 67 16) sells leather bags bought by buyers from fashion capitals all over the world. **Amazonite** (94 boulevard El Mansour Eddahbi, Guéliz, 024 44 99 26) and **Bazaar Ikhouan** (15 Marché Sidi Ishak, Medina, 024 44 36 16) are good places to buy antiques, from Berber jewellery to daggers and oil paintings. If you're looking to take home a carpet, check out **Bazaar les Palmiers** (145 Souk Dakkakine, Medina, 024 44 46 29), run by a fourth-generation carpet dealer who knows his stuff.

## STAY

If you're travelling on a budget, or would rather spend your money on a shopping expedition in the souks than a hotel room, stay at **Dar Fakir** (16 Derb Abou El Fadal, 024 44 11 00, darfakir@yahoo.fr), which has a slight Buddha Bar vibe, or the small riad **Jnane Mogador** (116 Riad Zitoun El Kedim, 024 42 63 24, www.jnane mogador.com), one of the best-value hotels in town.

**Caravanserai** (264 Ouled Ben Rahmoun, 024 30 03 02, www.caravanserai.com) is moderately priced, with a magnificent swimming pool and some rooms that have their own courtyards and even pools. In the same price bracket, **Riad Mabrouka** (56 Derb El Bahia, 024 37 75 79, www.riad-mabrouka.com) is a minimalist's dream, with a very cool, stylish design and a nice little terrace, in which breakfast is served in a shaded area.

If you're planning on digging deep into your pockets, however, the world-famous **Mamounia** (avenue Bab Jdid, 524 388 600, www.mamounia.com) is the place to stay. Morocco's most famous hotel was recently renovated, making it as luxurious as ever. Opened in 1923 (Winston Churchill was a regular), it was once the definition of a destination hotel, and is still the place to stay if money isn't an issue.

An alternative to a hectic weekend in the Medina is to stay outside the city. The French-owned **Beldi Country Club** (Km 6, route du Barrage, 'Cherifia', 05 24 38 39 50, www.beldicountryclub.com) must be one of the most beautiful places to stay in the whole of Morocco. Its 15 gardens (roses, figs, olives and oranges) and 29 individually decorated rooms make this a glorious countryside retreat – only 20 minutes' drive from the city centre. This former farm has been lovingly nurtured to life by its owners and has a fully functioning spa and hammam, two swimming pools and two organic restaurants (as well as a home cinema), making it a perfect place to bring the whole family.

## GETTING THERE & AROUND

Both EasyJet (www.easyjet.com) and Ryanair (www.ryanair.com) fly to Marrakech from London for around £70 return in just over three and a half hours. The airport, Aéroport Marrakech Menara, is only a ten-minute drive from the city centre, with a taxi to the Medina costing approximately 70 dirham (£5.50). If you're not planning on venturing far out of the city, you won't need anything other than a good pair of walking shoes to get around Marrakech. If you do require a cab, however, *petits taxis*, the equivalent to our minicabs, are cheap and will get you anywhere within the city limits. Anything outside the city limits, you need a *grande taxi*.

Founoun Marrakech

Jnane Mogador

# Iceland's Golden Circle

Half an hour after arriving at Keflavik Airport you can be in the Blue Lagoon, with everything but your head submerged in tropically warm water regulated by a friendly volcano. You'll have a pint of Viking lager in one hand and if it's winter you may even have the Northern Lights above you. It will have taken you three hours to fly here but you'll definitely feel you're in a foreign and faraway land: that language that kind of sounds familiar but is incomprehensible, the mind-blowingly beautiful but treeless landscape, steam rising out of the earth, crazy woollen sweaters, spurting geysers, fluffy ponies. Quite unlike any other weekend break, Iceland is surprisingly easy to get to and impossible to get out of your mind afterwards. Go in summer for festivals, late-night action and sun-filled days; go in winter for romance, surrealism and cosy suppers.

Blue Lagoon

## Fast facts

**Country dialling code** +354
**Journey time** Flight 3 hours
**Festivals & events** Thorrablot or Thursablot (January-February) – a midwinter festival with a Viking theme, honouring the god Thor; Sjomannadagur, the 'Festival of the Sea' (June) – also referred to as the 'Seaman's Day', this festival is dedicated to those Icelanders who work at sea. Activities include fishing, rowing, as well as eating fresh seafood; Menningarnótt (Culture Night) (August, www.menningarnott.is) – one of Reykjavik's most popular festivals, a carnival of live music, street food stalls and fireworks
**Good for** Walking, wildlife, shopping

## SEE & DO

For a weekend, some travellers just zoom from the airport to Reykjavik and go clubbing, café-hopping, shopping (second mortgage at the ready) and sightseeing. But for a proper introduction to Iceland, the so-called Golden Circle – a 300-kilometre road trip – is the best option. Hire a car (get a 4WD if you plan to go off road at all) and you can drive across to see the highlights of the country's south-west corner, containing the **Blue Lagoon**, **Reykjavik**, **Thingvellir**, **Geysir** and **Gullfoss**. You can even feast your eyes on **Eyjafjallajökull** – the volcano that made headlines in 2010.

There are even things to do around the airport area. Bed down near the Blue Lagoon's own 'clinic hotel' (Grindavik, 420 8800, www.bluelagoon.com) after a steamy dip in the lagoon itself, and start the following morning with a 9am quadbiking trip around **Reykhanes Peninsula** (412 4444,

Gullfoss

Strokkur

Solfar

www.icelandtotal.com). If it's winter, it might still be dark but you'll be whizzing over lava, past a lighthouse and a shipwreck that had been blown inland, and be able to take in views of the Blue Lagoon – steaming all day and with plenty of excess heat to generate electrical power for this region of Iceland.

**Rejkjavik** is the next obvious stop. Park up along the front or at your hotel if you're staying over and wander around the old town. Iceland has 300,000 inhabitants, and its capital fewer than 120,000, but it has more indie stores and good coffee shops than many far bigger European cities. Walk along **Laugavegur**, the main shopping drag, and then up the incline of **Frakkastigur**, popping into design and woollens shops along the way.

At the top of the hill, in front of the city's main church, the 74.5-metre, volcano-shaped **Hallgrimskirkja** is a statue of Leifur Eiriksson (aka Leif the Lucky), the man who discovered Vinland – probably Newfoundland – at the beginning of the 11th century. The monument is a beauty: he has a head like Thor, and calves – appropriately enough – like Captain America.

**Reykjavík Art Museum** (590 1200, www.artmuseum.is) has three venues around the city – in Hafnarhus, Kjarvalsstadir and Asmundarsaf – and hosts more than 20 exhibitions a year. Pick up a map at your hotel or at the tourist information centre (Adalstraeti 2, 590 1550, www.visitreykjavik.is) and use your walk between the venues to see the city's public parks and quiet residential streets. Have a stroll along the front too, to see the Solfar or *Sun Voyager*, a dramatic stainless-steel sculpture of a ship on granite slabs, and have a wander around the new **Harpa Concert Hall** (Austurbakki 2, box office 528 5050, www.harpa.is) – a good place to come back to in the evening if you fancy listening to some music.

Reykjavik

**Thingvellir National Park** (www.thingvellir.is), 48 kilometres east of Reykjavik on highway 36, is a legendary site for Icelanders because of its association with the first Althing – a tenth-century legal council and precursor to the modern parliament. At its heart is **Thingvallavatn Lake**, at the bottom of which lies the Mid-Atlantic Ridge, slowly opening a cleft in the earth's crust at the dizzying rate of two to three centimetres a year. There are some easy hikes here, and you can see where the Öxurá ('Axe River') flows over an escarpment in a pretty waterfall. Women sentenced to be executed were drowned in the pool formed at the bottom, while men were either beheaded – hence the name – or hanged.

Iceland gave the world the word 'geyser', and while the Great Geysir – which used to blow to a height of 70 metres – has been largely dormant since 1916, its neighbour, **Strokkur**, is very much alive. If you stay overnight at the Hotel Geysir (*see p251*), you can visit the hot pools and Strokkur when there are no tourists around.

It's half an hour's drive from Geysir to the **Gullfoss waterfall**. Around 32 metres high and about 100 metres wide, its most striking feature is the many levels it crashes on to during its journey down, creating a booming noise and sending up clouds of cool spray. If you go in winter, Gullfoss is part frozen, with the water straining through the ice-filled chasms. From the walkways above the fall, you can see far into the distance, to several mountain peaks and the creamy white top of the **Langjökull glacier**. Gullfoss has a lovely restaurant serving coffee, sandwiches and, on cold days, Icelandic lamb stew.

Loop south on highway 35 towards **Selfoss** for a drive through rural Iceland. You see volcanoes everywhere when driving around. Most are dead or dormant but even infamous **Eyjafjallajökull** is close enough to the route to visit – double-back down the island's main coast road, highway 1, for an hour to get up close. Steam pours from the ground everywhere you look, and most hotels and chalets have either a private hot pool or a geothermally heated swimming pool.

For your final day in Iceland, book a horse trek on one of the famous Icelandic horses at a reputable equestrian centre such as the **Ishestar Riding Centre** (Sorlaskeid 26, Hafnarfjördur, 555 7000, www.ishestar.is) or **Eldhestar** (*see p251*), both close to Reykjavik and the Golden Circle road. Small, strong, placid and gorgeously hairy, pure-bred

**Gullfoss waterfall**

**Leif Ericson statue, Reykjavik**

Thingvellir

Icelandic horses are the only horses allowed into the island. They are great to ride, not least because they have, as well as the usual walk, trot and canter/gallop gaits, one or sometimes two special gaits coded into their genes. The *tölt* is a fast walk with four distinct beats as hooves strike the floor in rhythm, and the less common fifth gait is called the *pace* or *flying pace*, involving the left hind and front legs moving together followed by the right together, rather like a camel or a giraffe. Both the *tölt* and *pace* are less spine-shaking than trotting so, as you glide smoothly over the lava landscape, you'll feel dignified and almost Viking-like.

## EAT & DRINK

At its worst, the cuisine of Iceland the nation can be rather like the products of Iceland the shop: frozen pizzas, Arctic-hue vegetables, non-prime beefburgers. But if you head for the right places, you'll be lavished with quality smoked salmon, *rollmops*, haddock dumplings, roast lamb, cured cold cuts and exotic dishes such as gull and shark's meat. At the end of meals, try *brennivín*, a digestif of local schnapps flavoured with caraway seeds – it's sold under the brand name Black Death.

Rejkjavik has lots of snug cafés and a few good pubs and bars, and is the best place for exploring the national diet. Decorated like a rich grandma's living room, **Við Tjörnina** (Templarasundi 3, 551 8666, www.vidtjornina.is) is considered to be one of Reykjavik's best seafood restaurants: try out the marinated cod chins with estragon sauce, a house speciality.

Cosy, romantic **Fish Company** (Vesturgötu 2a, Grófartorg, 552 5300, www.fishcompany.is) has an awesome and appetising range of fish and seafood dishes, such as slow-cooked, spruce-smoked haddock and fried langoustines, and fried monkfish and monkfish cheek with pistachio-crusted ratte potato.

**Café Loki** (Lokastígur 28, 466 2828, www.textil.is), opposite the Hallgrimskirkja, serves traditional Icelandic fare such as meat soups, trout tarte, skyr cake (skyr is a runny cheese, ubiquitous in Iceland) and, er, sheep-head jelly, turnip and bean-salad sandwich.

**Kaffi Mokka** (Skólavörðustig 3A, 552 1174, www. mokka.is) is Iceland's oldest café and serves a selection of cakes and coffee.

For eating options in Geysir and Gulfoss, see the relevant hotels below.

## STAY

Reykjavik can be used as a base for daytrips into the Golden Circle, and has the full spectrum of hotels. The **Hotel Borg** (Posthusstraeti 11, 551 1440 www.hotelborg.is) is a smart art deco-style four-star hotel right in the heart of the capital. **101 Hotel** (Hverfisgata 10, www.101hotel.is) is a boutique hotel with a stylish monochrome theme. The **Hotel Leifur Eiríksson** (Skolavordustigur 45, 562 0800, www.hotelleifur.is) is a less expensive, family-run hotel in the old centre of Reykjavik.

Despite the name, the **Blue Lagoon Clinic Hotel** (Grindavik, 420 8800, www.bluelagoon.com) is a pleasantly airy, cleanly designed property. The 15 rooms have verandas overlooking moss-covered lava fields, the LAVA restaurant serves sushi, salads and burgers and the geothermal centre is five minutes walk away.

In Geysir, the **Hotel Geysir** (Haukadalur, 480-6800, www. geysircenter.is) is just across the road from the geyser park (closed in January). The restaurant serves an à la carte menu featuring minke whale carpaccio, crispy salt cod and, randomly, naan bread with chicken salad. The hotel has a volcano-heated outdoor swimming pool.

The quiet 16-room **Hotel Gulfoss** (Brattholt, Blaskogabyggd, 486 8979, www.hotelgullfoss.is) is on the main road, midway between Geysir and Gulfoss; its restaurant is known for country-style cooking.

Ideal for the horse riding, **Eldhestar** (Völlum 810, Hveragerði, 480 4800, www.eldhestar.is) is a large, functional hostel-type complex, with stables next door. During spring, summer and autumn the hotel has a restaurant, but in winter guests have to travel to nearby **Hveragerði**, where there are a couple of basic restaurants.

## GETTING THERE & AROUND

Icelandair lies to Keflavik from Heathrow, Iceland Express from Gatwick. You'll need to hire a car at the airport or in Reykjavik to drive round the island. Discover the World (01737 218800, www.discover-the-world.co.uk) can arrange a four-night self-drive tour of the Golden Circle.

# Fès

While Marrakech has been attracting tourists for some time, Fès has only recently become a desirable destination for weekend breakers. From the smells coming from the market to the 'hee-haws' of the donkeys and the huddled housing, the city retains a medieval feel. Islamic architecture, which is everywhere you turn, is at its most impressive in the beautiful mosques and religious schools. During the ninth century, Fès became a capital for culture, learning and religion, and it's said that Pope Silvester II studied mathematics at the world's first university in the city. While these remain the city's monuments to history, the labyrinthine Medina, souks and narrow passages (even the widest streets in the old quarter are too narrow for a car) teem with activity. Fès is far from sleepy.

## Fast facts

**Country dialling code** +212 55
**Journey time** Flight 3 hours 20 minutes
**Festivals & events** Fez Sacred Music Festival (June, www.fesmusicfestival.com), featuring musicians from Morocco, Pakistan, Egypt and elsewhere; Culinary Arts Festival (October, www.moroccofestivals.co.uk), a celebration of Moroccan gastronomy; Jazz in Riad (October, www.moroccofestivals.co.uk). For more information on things to do, see www.visitmorocco.com and www.visit-fez.com
**Good for** Culture, food, shopping

Sofitel Palais Jamaï

Dar Roumana

## SEE & DO

Fès has three distinct areas. To the north is **Fès El-Bali**, or 'Old Fès', housing the core of the Medina, or town centre. In the south-west is **Fès El-Jedid**, or 'New Fès', containing both the Jewish quarter and the inaccessible Royal Palace, with its 82 hectares of palace grounds hidden behind large bronze doors. And, past the city walls, even further in the same direction, is the **Ville Nouvelle**, the French-created newest part of town.

If you were to look at Fès from above – which you should, from either the Borj Sud, a 16th-century fortress, or the Merenid tombs, which once belonged to 14th-century sultans – you'll see many predominantly plain, ∂white cubic buildings with flat roofs. This style of house is typical for Morocco, with people using their roofs to hang out washing or simply for fresh air, as most houses don't have gardens. At ground level, it's all colours and movement and overarching Islamic architecture. Fully accept that once you've entered the old town you will get lost; addresses won't mean anything (hence the lack of them in this text), though locals are always happy to be of help. Rue Talaa Kebira ('the big slope'), running downhill, takes you to the main souk area. Once you pass the **Cherabliyin Mosque** to your right, shops start popping up more frequently, from cobblers to bookbinders to slipper-makers, until you reach the **souk El-Attarine**, where a vast selection of spices is sold.

If you walk even further east down rue Talaa Kebira you reach the **henna souk** and **carpenters' souks** as well as the **Souk des Teinturiers** or Dyers' Souk. The multi-coloured dyes in the pools are made with seeds and minerals and are used on fabrics and wool. Downriver come the famous tanneries, or **Chaoura**. If you walk down rue El-Mechattine from place Seffarine, you'll soon get a whiff of the hides being dunked in water, salt, limestone and pigeon droppings (for the ammonia). Watch from the terrace of **Terrasse de Tannerie** (10 hay Labilda Chouara). The city's prized possession is the **Karaouiyine Mosque and Library** right in the middle of Old Fès, founded in 857 and doubling up as the world's first university.

On the opposite end of Talaa Kebira, towards the west, sandwiched with rue Talaa Seghira, you'll find the **Medersa Bou Inania**, the largest and most beautiful Koranic school in town, built between 1350 and 1356. The Merenid monument is classic Moroccan, with an olivewood ceiling, stucco work and mosaic tiling (called *zelije*).

Café Clock

South of Bou Inania down Talaa Seghira is the **Musée Dar Batha** (rue Zerktouni, 212 55 63 41 16, www.maroc.net/museums), a 19th-century Hispano-Moorish palace with a lovely, lush garden with many labelled trees (the most predominant being a giant green oak tree), and Moroccan arts and crafts exhibits (note: photography isn't allowed). The 19th-century **Palais Glaoui** (1 Derb El-Hamia, Ziat, 067 36 68 28), south of Talaa Seghira, belonged to the Glaouis, a family who once ruled southern Morocco. The interior decoration is extraordinary, from the stuccoed walls and high ceilings to the 100-year-old bathroom containing a green marble sink, and the harem area that once housed 100 women but is now inhabited by pigeons.

## EAT & DRINK

**Restaurant Laanibra** (Fès El-Bali, 61 Aïn Lkhail, 055 74 10 09), in the middle of the Medina, is housed in a tiny 14th-century palace. The food is served in the courtyard, and prices are low. The six set menus include chicken and lemon tagine and pastilla with pigeon. **Café Clock** (Fès El-Bali, 7 derb El-Magana, Talaa Kebira, 035 63 78 55, www.cafeclock.com) is run by a former Wolseley maître d' and occupies a lovingly restored Medina house. The views from the roof terrace are great, but the real treat is the food: order the Fès Platter (dates, nuts, samosas, aubergine purée, curried cauliflower), followed by a main meal and a lemon tart or marble cake.

**Dar Roumana** (Fès El-Bali, 30 derb El-Amer, Zkak Roumane, 035 74 16 37, www.darroumana.com) serves French food Tuesdays to Saturdays from 8pm onwards, and requires reservations as there are only four tables. It's a very atmospheric place to dine, with candles and flamenco-guitar music, and the owner – a Cordon Bleu-trained chef – cooks seasonal dishes, including goat's cheese soufflé and cinnamon-honey-chocolate mousse.

If you've never had a proper Moroccan mint tea, head to **Café Ba Bouchta** (Sagha Square, north of the souqs by Talaa Kebira), an old joint that would never pass UK health and safety standards, but where local men play cards and you can enjoy a glass of the (addictive) tea – grab a spot near the windows to watch the goings-on in the square below the café.

Tanneries

FÈS

**Fès El-Jdid**

**Orange blossom water**

## SHOP

You needn't worry about leaving Fès without some stylish souvenirs – the town is the archetypal rummager's paradise. Immerse yourself in the souks, and you can find almost anything – gold, beef jerky, faux Viagra… you name it. If you want a bargain, however, you'll have to hone your negotiating skills, as the Fassi traders are good hagglers, especially with tourists. **Art Naji** (Ville Nouvelle, 20 Quartier Industriel, Ain Nokbi, 035 66 91 66, www.artnaji.net) is a factory in the ceramic quarter, where www.moroccofestivals.co.ukyou can watch items being made and designed and buy numerous items from the showroom. **Made in M** (Fès El-Bali, 246 Talaa Kebira, 011 05 48 63) is rather chic, with unique leather bags, passport holders, perfumes and more. **Rue Sekkakine**, within the jewish quarter in **Fès El-Jdid**, is an entire street of shopping, mostly specialising in gold and silver; the trading of gold and silver was once forbidden within Islam, so the Jewish community set up the goldsmith shops in the 14th century. The **Parfumerie Medina** (7 Henna Souk) is a small stall that houses seemingly endless variations of perfumes, essential oils and cosmetics, as well as a henna artist.

## STAY

When you arrive at **Riad Al Bartal** (Fès El-Bali, 21 rue Sournas, Ziat, 035 63 70 53, www.riadbartal.com), you're greeted with mint tea and biscuits, after which you're shown your room, which will contain a huge bed and Berber carpets on the walls. **Riad Maison Bleue** (Fès El-Bali, 33 derb El-Miter, Talaa El-Kebira, Ain Azliten, 035 74 18 73, www.maisonbleue.com) has a courtyard pool surrounded by orange trees, plus a terrace with great views. Although on the pricey side, the 12 suites are individually designed, the location is fantastic, and it even has a spa. **Riad Tizwa** (Fès El-Bali, 15 derb Guebbas, Batha, 035 63 78 74, www.riadtizwa.com) has a relaxed and informal air about it, serving breakfast all day long, with coffee delivered to your room in a thermos every morning, while the **Sofitel Palais Jamaï** (Fès El-Babi, Bab Guissa, 035 63 43 31, www.sofitel.com) has fantastic views of the city, with a big Andalucian garden, three restaurants and a hammam.

## GETTING THERE & AROUND

Fès is no fun in August, as it gets very hot and humid; you'll be making every effort to escape the sun at midday, so don't travel then if you're after a milder climate. Fly to Fès with Royal Air Maroc from Heathrow via Casablanca in six hours, or fly direct with Ryanair (www.ryanair.com) from London Stansted.

There's a set price (under £10) for a cab from the newly refurbished airport into town; if you want to pay less, find other travellers and share it. There are still quite a few fake tourist guides around Fès, though less than there once were. If you're after a proper personal tour guide, hire one through your hotel and check he/she has the proper ID. Bear in mind that they receive commissions on any shops they take you to – some shops even offer up to 30% discount if you come without a guide.

# Istanbul

The only city in the world to straddle two continents, Istanbul is bursting with history and culture. In fact, the struggle that Istanbul has gone through over the centuries has defined what we know as Asia and Europe. The city carries this burden well, with East and West forged together to form a unique combination that sees a thriving modern Turkey alongside an equally energetic past. From the Harem inside the Topkapi Palace, where women fought to catch the sultan's eye, to the buzzing bars of Beyoğlu and the food markets of Kadıkoy, to the deep pleasures of a hammam experience, Istanbul has everything you'd want for a weekend of sights and sensations. The city has grown up around the Bosphorus and once you've got over the thrill of being able to simply drive over a bridge or take a ferry to another continent you can take a short cruise on the water to see how the city might have looked and felt to travellers in earlier centuries. Istanbul is one of those rare cities you arrive in knowing that now is its time – and a long weekend here could well be one of the best trips you'll ever make.

## Fast facts

**Country dialling code** +90
**Journey time** Flight 4 hours
**Festivals & events** Istanbul Fashion Week (February and September, www.ifw.com.tr) – the best of Turkey's up-and-coming fashionistas show that Turkey has become a main player on the fashion stage; Art Bosphorus (March, www.artbosphorus.com) – a showcase of the most distinguished names in Turkish and global contemporary art; Istancool (May, www.liberatum.org.uk) – a weekend of the world's most talented designers, editors, actors, writers, poets, dancers, musicians and filmmakers, with film screenings, talks and workshops.
**Good for** Culture, food, nightlife, shopping

**Tokapı Palace**

## SEE & DO

Sultanhamet is the 'proper' Istanbul. It is the cultural district, with classic Turkish sights such as minarets and domes. With the sea on three sides, it was the epicentre of the Ottoman Empire and remains a good place to start exploring.

**Tokapı Palace** (Bab-ı Hümayün Caddesi, Gülhane, 0212 512 0480, www.topkapisarayi.gov.tr) was the military command centre of the Ottoman Empire and home to the sultans and their courts for nearly four centuries. Visit the Harem inside the second court for intricate mosaics and fountain gardens. Just south-west of the palace is **Hagia Sophia** (Sultanahmet Square, 0212 522 1750), one of the most impressive sights in Istanbul. The massive dome means the museum – formerly a cathedral for both the Eastern Orthodox and Roman Catholic churches, and later a mosque – is visible from most areas of the city; however, it is the interior that has the 'wow factor'. Right next to the museum, on the south-west side, is **Yerebatan Sarnıcı** (Yerebatan Caddesi 13, 0212 522 1259, www.yerebatan.com), where you can be like James Bond in *From Russia with Love*, cooling yourself down in the most impressive of the city's subterranean reservoirs.

Hagia Sophia

Embrace Istanbul's burgeoning art scene and visit Turkey's equivalent of the Tate Modern, the **Istanbul Modern** (Meclis-i Mebusan Caddesi, Liman I letmeleri Sahası, Antrepo no.4, Karaköy, 0212 334 7300, www. istanbulmodern.org). Situated on the waterfront in Karaköy in a former customs warehouse, Turkish as well as international artists exhibit here. There are also temporary shows which often feature photography and video art.

After a long day sightseeing, haggling or cruising, keep an hour or two free to visit a traditional Turkish hammam to pummel your stress away. The **Çemberlitaş Hamamı** (Vezirhan Caddesi 88, Çemberlitaş, 0212 5227974, www.cemberlitashamami.com.tr), situated near the Grand Bazaar, is a great place for a hammam virgin.

In the main tourist sights and in the **Grand Bazaar** you'll get to see Istanbul close up. To get a calmer view, take a cruise along the **Bosphorus**, leaving from Boğaz Iskelesi terminal near the Eminönü tram stop by the Galata Bridge. On the government-run tourist ferries you can opt for either a short, two-hour cruise or a longer three-hour cruise. Get off at Anadolu Kavağı, the last harbour before the Black Sea, for lunch in one of the many fish restaurants or clamber up to Yoros Castle.

## EAT & DRINK

Scrumptious eateries can be found all over Istanbul, but it is the *meyhanes* (meze bars) that offer the definitive Turkish dining experience. A locals' favourite, **Nevizade Sokak** in Beyoğlu is an alley lined with *meyhanes* and cheap beer joints that has the vive of a street party most evenings. **Krependeki Imroz** (Nevizade Sokak 16, 0212 249 9073) is one of the oldest *meyhanes* and serves solid food (and raki) at reasonable prices.

### Cultural baggage

**Book** *Istanbul: Memories and the City* (Orhan Pamuk, 2004)
**Film** *From Russia with Love* (Terence Young, 1962)
**Album** *Dudu* (Tarkan, 2003)

Nevizade Sokak

Reina

If it's fine dining and spectacular views you're after, then head south-west from Nevizade Sokak to **Leb-I Derya Richmond** (Sixth Floor, Richmond Hotel, Istiklal Caddesi 445, 0212 243 4375, www.lebiderya.com). Dishes are simple but perfectly delivered and with probably the best restaurant view in Istanbul, it's the place to go. As Istanbul is where two seas converge, there is an abundance of fresh fish and seafood. Head to **Kumkapı**, which is famous for its seafood restaurants. **Çapari** (Çapari Sokak 22, 0212 517 7530, www.capari.net) is one of the district's oldest establishments. To relieve your weary feet after a jaunt around the Grand Bazaar, slurp some Turkish coffee at **Şark Kahvesi** (Yağlıkçılar Caddesi, 134 Grand Bazaar).

For bar-hopping and to soak up the atmosphere of new Istanbul, Beyoğlu is the place to be. Bars, restaurants, boutiques and artists' ateliers make up this area, at the heart of which is **Istiklal Caddesi**, the lively road where the entire city goes to shop, work and play. Çukurcuma is laden with antiques shops and boutique hotels, while Cihangir boasts stylish cafés. Nevizade Sokak is buzzing with life and there's a party atmosphere in the evening.

Since the early 17th century, hubbly bubbly (*hookah*, or *nargile* as the Turks call it) has come in and out of fashion in Turkey and it is definitely in right now. Hubbly bubbly cafés serve tea and coffee, but no alcohol. You'll find students, couples and families enjoying hubbly bubbly at any time of day or night. The best place to go is the nameless pedestrian strip on the south-west side of the Nusretiye Mosque by Tophane Square, which is lined with *nargile* cafés. On the southern side of the Golden Horn, the most popular place is **Me ale** (Arasta Bazaar 45, 0212 518 95662), where tourists and locals join to enjoy hubbly bubbly and nightly performances of Turkish classical music and dervish dancing shows on weekends.

**Grand Bazaar**

## NIGHTLIFE

A constantly busy venue, **11:11** (Tepebaşı, Mahallesi, Me rutiyet Caddesi 69, 0212 244 8834, www.1111.com.tr) has several different areas, and a range of music, and is popular with a mature crowd. Aptly named, **360** (Mısır Apartmani 32/309, Istiklal Caddesi, 0212 251 1042, www.360istanbul. com) has 360-degree panoramic views over the city. High-tech design, über-cool cocktails and an upbeat crowd turn this bar-restaurant into a show-stopping club after midnight.

If you just want a drink while gazing out over the Bosphorus, **5.Kat** (Fifth Floor, Soğancı Caddesi, 0212 293 3774, www.5kat.com) in Cihangir has fabulous views over the Asian shore. It also serves good food, and dance music takes over from chilled jazz later on.

The place to be seen, **Reina** (Muallim Naci Caddesi 44, Ortaköy, 0212 259 5919, www.reina.com.tr) is Istanbul's most famous nightclub. Situated on the waterfront and with an outdoor dancefloor and bar, Reina attracts playboys, celebs, rich brats and wannabes. Expect loud Euro Med music.

## SHOP

North-west of the cisterns is the **Grand Bazaar** (Kapalı Çarsi, Beyazit, 0212 522 3173, www.kapalicarsi.com.tr), said to be the world's oldest shopping centre. For Turkish rugs, go straight to Zincirli Hanı, in the north-east quarter of the bazaar, where you'll find the Grand Bazaar's most famous carpet dealer, Sisko Osman. Don't miss out on the ancient heart of the bazaar, the Old Bedesten where the atmosphere is much quieter, while Kalpakçilar Caddesi, on the south side shows that all that glitters is gold. Tip: haggle! And be ready to drink a lot of Turkish apple tea while you're doing it.

**Çukurcuma** is the place to go for art, antiques and collectibles. With dozens of dealers, the streets of Bostanba ı Caddesi and Turnacı Ba i Sokak are the best for a wander.

For a great excuse to visit the Asian shore, **Kadıkoy** has a prolific range of superb Turkish regional produce. Visit the top end of Yasa Sokak for delis and Güne libahçe Sokak for shops devoted to one produce, such as honey or olive oil.

## STAY

Istanbul has a great variety of places to stay. Sultanahmet is the area where much of the sightseeing is to be had, and there are plenty of small hotels and *pansiyons* here. At the budget end, right next to Haghia Sophia, is **Orient Hostel** (Akbıyı Caddessi 13, 0212 518 0789. www.orient hostel.com), where belly dancing, barbecues and a bar make it a backpacker hub. A mid-range option in the same area is the **Hotel Niles** (Ordu Cadessi Dibekli, Cami Sokak 19, 0212 517 3239, www.hotelniles.com), conveniently located near to the Grand Bazaar, with beautiful French-influenced Ottoman guest rooms and a leafy roof garden.

On the northern side of the Golden Horn, nearer the restaurants and bars of Nevizade, is the moderately priced **House Hotel** (Firuza a Mah, Bostanba ı Caddesi 19, Beyoğlu, 0212 252 0422, www.thehouse-hotels.com), which boasts a top-floor bar with Chesterfield sofas.

If you're looking for style, there's the **Witt Istanbul** (Defterdar Yokusu, 26, Cihangir, 0212 293 1500, www.witt istanbul.com). Designed by Autoban, with painstaking attention to detail, including Nespresso machines and iPod docks, this is a hotel that makes you want to stay inside.

**Witt Istanbul**

# St Petersburg

St Petersburg is the world's northernmost city, with a population of more than a million souls. Its latitude and relative isolation from other European cities has given it a distinct character and individualistic spirit, as well as the dreamily insomniacal 'white nights' of midsummer and bone-chilling black winters. In the last decade of the 20th century, the city shook off its Soviet straitjacket and engaged in small-scale youthful revolutions, from setting up squats in historical buildings to throwing rave parties in abandoned prisons. In 2003, St Petersburg celebrated its 300th birthday (it was the Russian capital from 1712 to 1918) and since then Vladimir Putin's hometown has become the symbol of new Russian prosperity. Siberian oil receipts, rising tax revenues and five million tourists every year have swelled the coffers and the city has been able to restore entire districts. A new seaport, located on a huge artificial island, was opened in summer 2011, and a newly completed 32-kilometre flood dam stretches across the Gulf of Finland as part of the 142-kilometre, eight-lane ring road around the city. The major sights have all been buffed up, while blingy new bars, clubs and galleries regularly pop up around the historical centre; 90 per cent of these soon disappear without trace, but their momentary buzz and hype are key to the new way of life in 'St Petes'.

## Fast facts

**Country dialling code** +7
**Journey time** Flight 3 hours 30 minutes
**Festivals & events** City Day (27 May) – St Pete's official birthday is celebrated with partying around the Palace Square, fireworks and a multitude of events around the city; International Ballet Festival Mariinsky (February, www.mariinsky.ru) – leading ballet companies perform at the theatres around the Teatral naya Ploshad for an entire week; White Nights Festival (May-July, www.balletandopera.com) – an international arts festival that takes advantage of the fact that the sun doesn't set. Ballet, opera and music events from Russian and international stars. Book well in advance as St Petes is very popular at this time with Russians as well as overseas travellers. The official White Nights are 11 June-2 July
**Good for** Culture, history, nightlife

Hermitage

## SEE & DO

Several classic and arguably unmissable sights (especially for a first-time visitor) are within easy walking distance of each other. A stroll down **Nevskiy Prospekt**, the main thoroughfare and cultural heart of the city, will turn up the early 19th-century **Cathedral of Our Lady of Kazan**, statues of **Gogol** and **Catherine the Great**, the pretty blue **Armenian church**, the **Siege Plaque** (relating to the 900-day siege of Leningrad by the Nazis in 1941-44) and the cafés and shops of the **Gostinyy Dyor arcade**. The **Literary Café** (Nevskiy Prospekt 18) is something of a landmark, as it's where Pushkin claimed to have met his double before setting off for the duel that would end his life. The food is only OK, but the setting is grand.

You're pretty close to the **Hermitage** (Dvortsovaya nab. 30-38, 812 710 9079, www.hermitagemuseum.org), so steel yourself for a hike round one of the world's most

Mariinsky

Kempinski Bellevue Brasserie

Church of the Saviour on Spilled Blood

Mikhailovksy Theatre

Astoria

## Skating rinks

If you visit St Petes during the winter, you'll probably want to get into the groove – the icy, difficult, swirling groove of the neighbourhood ice rink. The largest open-air skating rink (around four acres) can be found in the park behind the **TV tower** (Aptekarsky 16, £4 adult). The cosiest rink is in the heart of **Tavrichesky Garden** (www.tavrsad.com), one of the oldest parks in the city, and – bonus! – it's free (although pro-quality ice will cost you £5 per day or night); it stays open until 5am.

However, the best place to have fun all night long is on the rink at **Sports Palace SKA** (Zhdanovskaya Street 2, 812 230 7819). The ice (and the skates) are all but perfect, although hundreds of people crowd it every night. It's £5 for a night, or £3 for an hour and a half during the day.

superlative and largest art collections. The grand ensemble of buildings on the banks of the Neva has many miles of corridors, lined with masterpieces by Da Vinci, Rembrandt, Rubens, Titian, Picasso, Matisse, Gaugin, as well as room after room devoted to prehistoric, Classical and Oriental art. See as much as the 'art' side of your brain allows and don't feel guilty when you exit – it's been said it would take a visitor 11 years to examine every one of the museum's exhibits. Leave at least a little time to see the architectural features of the building – including the palace square, designed by Carlo Rossi, the opulent Winter Palace built for Tsarina Elizabeth in the 1750s and the impressive Pavilion Hall, with its striking granite columns and chandeliers.

If you've not overdosed, the nearby **Russian Museum** (Inzhenernaya ulitse 4, 812 595 4249, www.rusmuseum.ru) holds the largest collection of Russian art in the world, spread over six buildings, plus the historic Summer and Mikhajlovsky gardens. Behind it is the **Church of the Saviour on Spilled Blood** (Griboedova 2, 812 315 1636, www.cathedral.ru), perhaps the most eccentric architectural monument in the city. It's built on the spot where Alexander II (the tsar who emancipated the serfs in Russia) was assassinated, though nobody knows exactly why his mourning descendants decided to build a giant, multicoloured cake in this place of grief. In the 1930s, it was used for a time as a vegetable store, prompting the nickname 'Saviour on Potatoes'.

To get a feel for the city's thriving contemporary arts and culture scene, the **Loft Project Etazhi** (Ligovsky Prospekt 74, 812 458 5005, www.loftprojectetagi.ru/en) is a modern art spot that occupies a five-storey bakery in the centre of the city. The Loft went on to inspire **Erarta** (Vassiljevsky Island, line 29, 812 324 0809, www. erarta.com), a brand-new art museum on Vasiljevsky Island. Between these lies the thick red line that is **Dumskaya Street**, a bar-hopper's dream, with a small club in every door and window. Another nightlife landmark, **Konushennaya Square**, was transformed into a fashionable restaurant location just a few years ago. Obscure artists, poets, punks and freaks have since ceded it to tourists lost among museums, and CEOs lost in their spare time.

## EAT & DRINK

Almost all the good restaurants in St Petersburg belong either to the **Ginza Project** or to the **Probka Family**. The former combines very specific Russian eccentricities with a European veneer (its restaurants are equally popular in Moscow and New York). **Mari Vanna** (Lenina 18/4, 812 230 5359, www.marivanna.ru) provides a kickback to student flat-sharing days, though it may be a bit too cosy for those who haven't experienced life without a private kitchen and toilet. The firm's most distinctive restaurant is **Mansarda** (Pochtamtskaya 3, 812 946 4303, www. ginza-mansarda.ru), with a fashionably ascetic attic with great views over St Isaac's Cathedral.

The Probka Family prefers Italian cuisine and design and runs the most pleasant out-of-town restaurant – **Riba na Dache**, or 'Fish in the Cottage' (Sestrorezk, 921 574 0701, www.probka.org).

However, if you're looking for real Russian cuisine, you should try **Kalitka** (Nekrasova 34, 812 923 7761, www.nekrasova34.org), with its refreshing take on the country's traditions. No heavy cushions or dolled-up girls, just straight plywood interiors and an outstanding menu, with lots of pies, soups, game, fish, liqueurs, meads and beers. Similarly first-rate is the **Kempinski Bellevue Brasserie** (Mojka 22, 812 335 9111, www.kempinski.com/ ru/stpetersburg), with its breathtaking panoramic views over all the must-see palaces and churches, and a great spot to watch the concerts that take place in Palace Square.

If you wander down the busy Nevskiy Prospekt, there are dozens of cafés to stumble across, as well as countless ice-cream vendors. To splash out on a culinary extravaganza, go to **Palkin** (Nevskiy Prospekt 47, 812 703 5371, www.palkin.ru), where the likes of Dostoevsky and Gogol dined. Outstanding 'Imperial Russian' and French cuisine fits the grandiose interior – and the wine list is formidable.

### Cultural baggage

**Book** *The Siege* (Helen Dunmore, 2002)
**Film** *The Burglar* (Valeri Ogorodnikov, 1988)
**Album** *The Seventh Symphony* (Dmitri Shostakovich, 1941)

## MUSIC & BALLET

Ballet is big in St Petersburg, so much so that during the winter holidays you can go to a dozen versions of *Swan Lake* back-to-back (if that's what you feel like). Only the **Mariinsky** (Teatralnaya, 812 326 4141) and **Alexandrinsky** (Ostrovskogo 6, 812 380 8050, www. alexandrinsky.ru) theatres stand out for quality and both are always exploring new works and treatments at the same time as resurrecting Dyagilev plays or historical ballets last performed 100 years ago. Their only near-rival is the **Mikhailovksy Theatre** (Italjanskaya 1, 812 595 4305, www.mikhailovsky.ru), which, under new management and with new money being pumped in, has been host to stars such as Nacho Duato or Hubbard Street Dance Chicago.

## NIGHTLIFE

Dumskaya Street is the easy way to tap into St Petersburg's nocturnal naughtiness, though the clubs and bars seem to blend into one another, with people wandering between venues willy-nilly. Locals say you can speak any language you want in these watering holes safe in the knowledge that someone will understand you. **Mishka Bar** (Fontanka 40, www.mishkabar.ru), not far from the Dumskaya area, is cramped and dark, but the buzzing atmosphere, cheap drinks and good DJs mean there's always a party atmosphere. If that's not your thing, try moving on to Stirka 40 (Kazanskaya 26, www.40gradusov.ru), where you can have a drink while doing your laundry, or **Estrada** (Sadovaya 17), which is rather more glamorous.

The best spot to find yourself in at dawn is **Griboedov Hill** (Griboedova 2A, www.griboedovclub.ru), the oldest club in the city, situated in a converted bomb shelter. While it's civilised during the day, you can still find a crazy party or a good Russian band going on here in the wee hours.

## STAY

The **Astoria** (Bolshaya Morskaya 39, 812 494 5770, www.thehotelastoria.com) exudes old-school elegance. Don't be surprised if you find yourself dining alongside political royalty. Similarly, the **Silver Age** (Vosstaniya 13, 812 275 3466, www.silverhotel.ru) is homage to turn-of-the-19th-century Russian glamour.

The **Brothers Karamazov Hotel** (Sotsialisticheskaya Ulitse 11a, 812 335 1185, www.karamazovhotel.ru), which opened in 2005, is close to the Dostoevsky House Museum: each room is named after one of his female characters. A more atmospheric and good-value hotel with literary connections is **Domik V Kolonne** (Nab Kanala Griboedova 174A), where Pushkin wrote several books between 1816 and 1818, and where the decor hasn't really been refurbished since then.

## GETTING THERE & AROUND

SAS and S7 fly from Heathrow, AirBaltic and Aeroflot from Gatwick. Ryanair flies from Luton to Tallinn, which is the cheaper option, even when you factor in bus or train tickets to St Petersburg (around €20).

# In Search of Winter Sun

January through to early March can be a dark time. Once the Christmas lights have been packed away, the British winter becomes more of a slog than a season. But if you're feeling starved of sunlight and SAD is kicking in, take comfort in the fact that you could be thawing on a beach in a matter of hours. Bookend your weekend with a couple of days off work and jump on a plane – none of the destinations in our list are any more than five hours from London (average January high: 6 degrees), meaning you could be pulling on your sunhat first thing Saturday morning.

The Algarve

## Marrakech

**Average high in January** 18 degrees

January is the ideal month for visiting the Red City, when the North African heat is more forgiving. First timers are easily overwhelmed by the heady blend of Arabian and French culture, but few leave without their passions provoked – for better or worse. If you've any Christmas money left over, save it up for a raid on the souk, making sure you approach it from the bustling Jemaa El-Fna square, soaking up all the warmth and atmosphere this legendary city has to offer en route. *See also pp242-246.*

**Stay** Push the boat out and stay in the style to which Mick 'n' Keef have become accustomed: Es Saadi Palace & Villas (+212 5 2444 8811, www.essaadi.com) was the Rolling Stones' base during a well-documented visit to Marrakech in the 1960s. Jagger and Richards are known to revisit the city regularly, though probably for the culture these days, rather than the vegetation.

**Getting there** EasyJet flies from London to Marrakech.

## Madeira

**Average high in January** 19 degrees

Wine, scabbardfish and volcanic vistas rising from the ocean – it all sounds like the beginnings of a balmy night of summer romance. But this could be Madeira any night of the year, and if you throw in the world's largest fireworks festival (certified by the *Guinness Book of World Records*), you've got yourself a mid-Atlantic New Year's Eve to remember. More easily accessible than the Azores, Madeira has a

Lanzarote

reputation for being a bit of a party spot, never more so than on 31 December, when the mother of all pyrotechnical displays is launched from boats moored offshore (the exact location changes from year to year). Midwinter nights don't get any hotter than this.

**Stay** If ocean views and palm trees are your thing, then the Eden Mar (+351 291 709700, www.edenmar.co.uk), overlooking Funchal's Porto Bay, is well worth a look. The hotel is a self-contained resort, boasting a spa, tennis courts and a pair of well-rounded swimming pools. Don't book in if you want to see something of the island – blissing out is a real hazard.

**Getting there** Tap Portugal flies from London Heathrow to Funchal.

### Lanzarote
**Average high in January**
17 degrees
The most easterly of the Canary Islands may be the nearest thing we have to a holiday on Mars, and a damn sight warmer too. Known as the 'islands of eternal spring', local thermometers never record

anything less than T-shirt temperatures, and the volcanic topography looks permanently parched, which does wonders for a psyche mired in the British winter. Timinfaya National Park is the place to see these extraordinary islands at their most untouched, though Lanzarote is not short on rugged, red shorelines – perfect for a spot of exploring if the beach is still a tad too nippy.

**Stay** Heredad Kamezi (+34 928 51 8624, www.heredad kamezi.com) hotel prides itself on the personalised service guests receive at each of its private villas – buildings so pristinely whitewashed that they look like they belong in a traditional Greek village.

**Getting there** Ryanair flies to Lanzarote from Stansted, EasyJet from Gatwick.

### Center Parcs
**Average high in January** 29.5 degrees
Get away from it all – all the way to balmy Wiltshire, where the Subtropical Swimming Paradise buildings at Longleat Forest Center Parcs record the warmest midwinter temperatures on our list (the sun has nothing to do with it, obviously). The idea of spending your holiday savings for a long weekend under glass in the freezing south-west might not appeal to everyone, but for families

Center Parcs

it's not to be sniffed at – quality spa time for mum and dad, while the kids get their fill of energy-draining exercise under the supervision of someone less irritable.

**Stay** Center Parcs Longleat Forest (08448 267723, www.centerparcs.co.uk), an artificial village set in 400 acres of very real woodland, complete with its own train.

**Getting there** Train from Waterloo to Warminster – a three-mile taxi ride from Center Parcs.

### Cadiz

**Average high in January** 16 degrees

Settled some 3,000 years ago by the Phoenicians, Cadiz is thought to be the oldest city in Western Europe, so while midday temperatures often reach the 20s, it's the history buffs who really build up a sweat. However, if stone forts, ancient city walls and Andalusian architecture leave you cold, book your tickets for mid-to-late February, when the Cadiz Carnival is in full swing. There's no need for a hotel then, either – most people just rock up with a sleeping bag and kip on the public beach, which may be as far as you can stagger if you've been indulging in the local speciality. You'd be a fool to leave the so-called Sherry Triangle without visiting some of the *bodegas*, many of which are grouped around nearby Jerez. For €12, visitors can take a guided tour of the oldest sherry *bodega* in the area, the **Bodegas Fundador Pedro Domecq** (+34 956 151 500, www.bodegasfundadorpedrodomecq.com), including tasting and tapas. We suggest you take the train back.

**Stay** Hotel Los Jandalos Vistahermosa (+34 956 87 34 11, www.vistahermosa.jandalos.com) is a cosy inner-city boutique with its own spa, decked out in local wood furnishings, ideal for anyone who fancies more comfort than the aforementioned sleeping bag on a beach.

IN SEARCH OF WINTER SUN

Cadiz

Madeira

**Getting there** Cheap flights are available with Ryanair from Stansted to Jerez, which lies a 40-minute train journey north-east of Cadiz.

## Beirut
**Average high in January** 17 degrees
Few places can boast beach in the morning and pistes in the afternoon (unless you're talking about artificial Dubai), and it is on this premise that Beirut has built a roaring winter tourist trade. Whether the morning–afternoon trick can actually be done is a matter of debate and strategic planning – it'd make more sense to plan a day for each, keeping a third day aside purely for eating. A shawarma kebab from a street stall is a must, but if you want to try Lebanese fare at its best, Abdel Wahab (+961 1 200550), in Beirut's Achrafieh area, gets our vote every time.
**Stay** Casa d'Or Hotel (+961 1 746400, www.casadorhotel. com) in the Hamra district is a friendly if not overly handsome hotel, well located for the fashionable shopping district.

**Getting there** BMI and Middle East Airlines fly direct to Beirut from Heathrow.

## The Algarve
**Average high in January** 16 degrees
The Algarve is as synonymous with blistering, moaning Brits and crowded beaches as Benidorm, but there are still pockets that retain some character. A new fully waymarked footpath/bike path, the Via Algarviana (www.via-algarviana.org), will help you burn off the Christmas puds and show you something of the region's native vegetation and topography. If you hire a car, the neighbouring Alentejo region is dotted with prehistoric ruins, including very early examples of megalithic standing stones and neolithic cave paintings. While winter rains can be heavy in the north of the Algarve, the south enjoys year-round UV action, so bronzing on the beach is not out of the question if the history gets too much.
**Stay** The front is full of tower blocks and blingy resorts, but inland, and just 15 kilometres from Faro Airport, the 20 apartments of the Quinta dos Amigos (+351 289 395 269, www.quintadosamigos.com) are small, cosy and comfortable.
**Getting there** EasyJet flies from Gatwick to Faro.

## Cairo
**Average high in January** 19 degrees
Visiting Egypt may not seem like a quick in and out, but Cairo makes for an ideal long weekend (and we'd defy anyone to spend longer there without being driven round the bend). The Egyptian Museum is a dream day out for wannabe Indiana Joneses both young and old, and quite why the Pyramids and Sphinx haven't become the subject of a TV game show in which participants try and get away without being thoroughly fleeced is anyone's guess, but it's an experience not to be missed either way. Temperatures are just right for a few hours by the pool on your last day.
**Stay** It's worth scraping together the pennies to splurge on the Mena House Oberoi (+800 1234 0101, www.oberoi hotels.com), where you'll find yourself woken up each morning with the Great Pyramid tapping you on the shoulder.
**Getting there** London to Cairo direct with Egyptair.

Marrakech

Es Saadi Palace & Villas, Marrakech

# Cairo

Tahrir Square put Cairo squarely on the news map, and will hopefully have alerted European travellers to the Egyptian capital's potential as a fascinating historical, political and cultural destination. And not before time. While 'Sharm' and the Red Sea have proven popular with package holidaymakers and divers, we tend to think of Cairo as one of those grand old cities people used to visit. But, as well as the now iconic main square, there is much to see, from the wonders of the Museum of Egyptian Antiquities to the crumbling splendour of Downtown's Parisian-style boulevards to the opulent hotels on the banks of the Nile, where children living in deep poverty wash themselves every day. Mushroom-shaped Islamic spires share the skyline with the spikes of a million satellite dishes, and, on random taxi drives, you may well spy the ghostly forms of the pyramids of Giza in the distance. It's not every weekend you get to see a Wonder of the World.

## Fast facts

**Telephone country code** +20
**Journey time** Flight 5 hours
**Festivals & events** Flora Festival (January, www.floraegyptfair.com); Pharaoh's Rally (October, www.rallydespharaons.it); Sphinx Festival (December, www.sphinxfestival.com)
**Good for** culture, history

Great Pyramid of Giza

## SEE & DO

Before anything, visit the **Museum of Egyptian Antiquities** (Tahrir Square, Downtown, 2 2579 6974, www.egyptianmuseumcairo.org) for a breathtaking insight into Egypt's spectacular, 5,000-year history. Since its opening in 1902, the museum appears little changed, the darkened chambers of the neo-classical building filled to bursting with dusty glass cabinets and half-hidden statues piled into the corners. The ground floor is given over to statues and larger objects, while the upstairs houses jewellery, smaller pieces and the golden treasures of Tutankhamun's tomb, as well as thousands of other pharaonic artefacts. Labels are few and far between: this is less a place for learning, and more a sublime cornucopia of some of the greatest treasures in the world. Trying to see everything is futile: instead, abandon any sense of organisation and just go exploring. You'll suddenly realise you've spent several hours immersed in the staggering collection of 120,000 pieces.

Next visit the source. The **Great Pyramid of Giza**, only 11 kilometres from central Cairo, once rose up proudly in the desert but now sits in a suburb to the west of the city. Going very early in the morning will save you from the overwhelming desert heat, and is also one of the few things you can do in Cairo before noon. From central Cairo, just jump on the metro and take Line 2 to Giza, where you can get a taxi to take you the eight kilometres to the Pyramids. Expect to pay no more than LE33 (about £3.50) for the taxi ride. Alternatively, take buses 900 or 997 (although the numbers are written in Arabic) from the central bus station behind the Egyptian Museum in Tahrir Square. This will only cost you 50 piastres (about 5p) and is an adventure in itself: the dilapidated buses wind around Cairo's neighbourhoods, the hidden parts of the city that are rarely visited by tourists. Once you get there, you'll see the three Pyramids including the Great Pyramid – the oldest and largest, built in 2560 BC. You can pay extra to enter the pyramid via the **Robbers' Tunnel**, which was dug by workmen employed by Caliph al-Ma'mun in around AD 820. You can easily navigate the area around the Sphinx and pyramids on foot, or if you prefer you can buy a camel ride for about LE50 (£5) from one of the many touts near the entrance.

With all the ancient history on offer, it's no wonder young Cairene artists feel their modern-day efforts are often overshadowed. But Egyptian contemporary art is stimulating, witty and politically informed. Head to one of the many new contemporary galleries to get a glimpse of the revolutionary spirit that overthrew Hosni Mubarak in the revolution of 2011. The **Townhouse Gallery** (10 Nabrawy Street, 2 576 8086, www.thetownhousegallery.com), in the Downtown area, is a converted factory and holds public lectures, film screenings and theatre performances, as well as six exhibitions of contemporary Egyptian art a year. **El Sawy Culturewheel** (26th of July Street, 2 736 8881, www.culturewheel.com) in Zamalek – a green island in the centre of the Nile – is another place to experience Cairo's lively arts scene. Check its website's events calendar and take your pick from art exhibitions, talks and music performances, from Mozart recitals to Egyptian heavy metal.

Coptic Cairo is the oldest part of the city and is a good area to amble around, owing to the low traffic levels, narrow alleyways and number of early churches, mosques and synagogues. The most famous is the '**Hanging Church**', located above a gatehouse in the ancient **Roman Babylon Fortress**. Take the metro from Tahrir Square to Mar Girgis, which is located directly beside Babylon Fortress. Cairo is big, busy and can get very hot – temperatures in August can reach 40 degrees centigrade – and this is one of the reasons why the favourite activity of many Egyptians is to sit and observe the chaos from a roadside coffee shop, smoking a flavoured shisha pipe and drinking hot, sweet tea. Take a cue from the locals and spend a couple of hours in the afternoon just watching the world go by. These roadside cafés are called *ahwas* by the locals and are easy to spot by their plastic chairs and blissed-out patrons. Just pull up a seat and order a tea and shisha of your choice.

## EAT & DRINK

The best Egyptian food is not fancy or expensive. Some of the most delicious things to eat – such as the wholewheat flatbread, a staple of the Egyptian diet – cost less than a metro ticket. Flat, round *eish* bread (meaning 'life') is sold from donkey-drawn carts all over the city, especially in the warren-like streets of Downtown, and costs just 5 piastres a piece. Make like a local and eat them with *tahina*, *baba ghanouj* and *tameyya* (like falafel, but made with fava beans rather than chickpeas) at one of the hundreds of cafés that line Cairo's streets. For a feel of old colonial Egypt, head to **Café Riche** (17 Talaat Harb Street, Downtown, 2 392 9793, which opened in 1908 and is steeped in revolutionary history; it's the place where plotters of the 1919 revolution gathered to make plans. Now, it mainly caters to expat journalists and tourists, but it's a comfortable spot to sit and refuel in the hotter parts of the afternoon. For a cheap and cheerful bite, head to **Gad**, a popular restaurant chain that offers unbeatable value for money. There are dozens of branches around the city (look out for the red neon sign) and all have a takeaway service downstairs, while upstairs is reserved for sit-down diners. There is a democratic feel to these eateries, with young teenagers wolfing down plates of chargrilled poussins or lamb kofte, and television screens showing the football (an unrivalled Egyptian passion). A bottle of water is provided with every meal, as is a basket of hot flatbreads, meaning you'll never leave hungry.

Popular with Cairo's young professionals, the **Greek Club** (28 Mahmoud Bassyouni Street, Downtown, 2 575 0822) is an old social club right above Groppi (*see below*) with a vintage flavour. The terrace, which opens in the summer, is the preferred hangout of Cairo's intellectual liberal leftists, with Greek and Egyptian dishes on offer, as well as imported spirits. Main courses such as grilled lamb, Greek salads and calamari cost less than a fiver. After your meal, wander the bustling night markets and wrap up with an ice-cream from **Groppi** (Midan Talaat Harb), once Egypt's most famous tea house and pâtisserie and a throwback to Cairo's early 20th-century heyday as a hotspot for Mediterranean socialites. If you want more sweet things, buy some freshly baked biscuits from one of the many bakeries in Downtown, which put out their wares from about 4pm. If you are lucky, you'll be invited inside to pick a few buttery, sugar-drenched *Khak el Aid* biscuits straight from the baking tray.

Cairo's bar-restaurant of the moment is **Indigo** (Second Floor, First Mall, 35 El Giza Street, Giza, 2 3570 0121, www.firstmallcairo.com), a slick affair with lounge-style banquettes that does glamorous cocktails and an exquisitely executed menu taking in Spanish, Vietnamese and Malaysian influences. It's not cheap, though, so expect a London-style bill at the end of your night here. For an equally sumptuous (if not quite so glitzy) dinner, head to **Abou El-Sid** in Zamelek (157 26th of July Street, 2 735 9640, www.abou elsid.com). It's behind unmarked iron doors and serves traditional Egyptian meals – stuffed pigeon is a speciality.

## SHOP

**Khan el Khalili** is the market in Cairo's Islamic quarter, a warren of stalls and shops selling everything from perfume and dried fruit to Egyptian antiques (think 19th-century cigarette cases rather than Ancient Egyptian papyrus). Leather, cotton and jewellery are often of a high quality, but check that the workmanship is up to scratch before parting with your Egyptian pounds. Flex your haggling muscles – it's expected.

Heliopolis, a green, airy suburb of Cairo close to the airport, is home to **Korba**, a shopping district with Andalucian-style architecture and plenty of fashionable shops. The newly opened comics and collectibles store, **Kryptonite** (2 El Sobky Street, Heliopolis, 2 218 8700) is a one-stop geek shop filled with both Egyptian and Western graphic novels and comic books, from *Superman* to cool local lefty magazine *TokTok*.

Groppi

**Villa Belle Epoque**

The market at **Midan Korba** – in the heart of Korba – is rarely visited by tourists, and boasts a fascinating array of goods, from watches to gorgeous Egyptian cotton clothing. For one-off gifts, **TAO Gallery** (136, Flat 3, 26th of July Street, Zamalek, 2 735 0480) sells an assortment of handmade items for reasonable prices: hand-bound pigskin notebooks for LE50 (£5), jewellery, silk scarves and intricately decorated hammered silver bowls. Another place for browsing is **L'Orientaliste** (15 Kasr El Nil Street, Downtown, 2 575 3418, www.orientalecairo.com), which has been trading in rare books since the 1930s. Today, its collections of antiquarian books, lithographs, postcards and maps (some of them dating back to the 16th century) tempt book-lovers from around the world. Pick up some antique postcards for a cheap souvenir.

## STAY

Cairo is not short of fancy hotels. If you don't have a lot of time, plump for the **Sofitel El Gezirah** on the banks of the Nile (3 El Thawra Council Street, Zamalek, 2 736 3640, www.sofitel.com), which has its own internationally imported Buddha-Bar outpost – conforming to the same design aesthetic as its branches in Paris, Monte Carlo and Prague – where the young and hip of Cairo come to play. Sip cocktails on Le Deck, the hotel's floating chill-out bar on the Nile.

For a boutique bolthole, you'll find none better than 13-room **Villa Belle Epoque** (Road 13, Villa 63, 2 2358 0265, www.villabelleepoque.com) in the Nile-side suburb of Maadi. A world away from the chaos of modern Cairo, it's decorated with hand-picked antiques that suit the 1920s building. The hotel garden's swimming pool is surrounded by fragrant mimosa flowers and palm trees and you can breakfast on eggs, fruit, flatbreads, Egyptian curd cheese and honey on your private balcony, while shaded by drooping fruit trees.

If your budget is modest, a private room at a well-equipped hostel such as **King Tut Hostel** (37 Talaat Harb Street, Downtown, 10 029 1918, www.kingtuthostel.com) will provide everything you need for a fantastic stay. Friendly and centrally located, you can book an en-suite double room (with air-conditioning and satellite TV) for about LE150 (about £15). Staff will also pick you up from the airport and provide breakfast at no extra cost.

Note: many of the high-end hotels allow non-guests to use the pools for a small daytime fee; you can dine at **Atlas Zamalek Hotel**'s (20 Gamaet Al-Dewal Al-Arabia Street, 2 334 6723, www.atlaszamalek.com) poolside restaurant for a charge of LE60 (about £6) and get free access to the pool.

## GETTING THERE & AROUND

It takes just five hours to fly from Heathrow to Cairo International Airport. Egyptair and BMI both fly there, as does slightly pricier British Airways.

October to May is the best time for visitors unused to the blistering heat of an Egyptian summer. Ramadan falls on a different month every year (in summer for the past couple of years) and is best avoided – lots of businesses close for the duration, and the fasting hours of daytime can make it tricky to eat out.

Crossing Cairo is best done by taxi. Both the old taxis and the new white cars (with working meters) work out fairly cheap (as long as you aren't being ripped off), but try to agree on a price before you get in. A taxi from the airport to central Cairo shouldn't cost more than LE50 (about £5). The metro is clean, fast and cheap: one-way tickets cost LE1 (10p) and can be bought from the station. Make sure you observe the carriage seating plan: men cannot use two of the four carriages as they are reserved for women only. These are clearly marked and failure to comply will result in a hefty fine. Public buses are also cheap, but often confusing for tourists as most of the signage is in Arabic only.

Tourists, especially lone women, attract attention and this can be perturbing. If you find yourself being followed, it can help to confront the person involved. Policemen are notoriously ineffective at dealing with accusations of harassment. A useful website is www.harrassmap.org, with an interactive map of 'hotspots' of harassment, as well as suggested places of safety to head to if you're a victim of it.

# New York City

'When it's three o'clock in New York, it's still 1938 in London,' Bette Midler once said. Taken with the requisite mountain of salt, there's some truth to her quip. While New York may not be ahead of every curve, it moves fast and dares you to keep up. It's bold, brash and unapologetic about being – in the eyes of its fiercely proud citizenry – the greatest city on earth. For a visitor, there's something reassuring about a city so sure of itself; at every step, it's easy to feel like you're in the midst of something important, even if you don't quite know what it is.

While iconic sights such as the Statue of Liberty and Central Park are reliably awe-inspiring for first-timers, the past decade has seen the city continue to evolve. You can't pass a fire station without seeing tributes to the terrorist attacks that rocked the city a decade ago, and a beautiful new memorial at Ground Zero provides a tranquil place to consider the still-unclear legacy of 9/11. Many areas that used to be industrial and unsavoury have been rejuvenated by buzzy restaurants, shops and bars. And across the river, Brooklyn has blossomed into a bona fide cultural force, providing a foil to Manhattan's glitz with a creative DIY movement that manifests itself in everything from warehouse parties to artisanally roasted coffee.

With five boroughs and endlessly diverse neighbourhoods, New York is really a panoply of cities in one. Pick what you want it to be, and, nine times out of ten, it'll make you wonder why your imagination was so flaccid.

Rockefeller Center

## Fast facts

**International code** +1
**Journey time** Flight 7-8 hours
**Festivals & events** Midsummer Night Swing (June/July, www.lincolncenter.org); The ING New York City Marathon (November, www.nycmarathon.org); New York Comedy Festival (November, www.nycomedyfestival.com); Macy's Thanksgiving Day Parade (November, www.social.macys.com/parade2011); the lighting of the Rockefeller Center Christmas Tree (November, www.rockefellercenter.com)
**Good for** Culture, food, history, nightlife, shopping

## SEE & DO

Post-millenial NYC has been indelibly altered by the attacks on the World Trade Center, and the newly opened **9/11 Memorial** (enter at Albany and Greenwich Streets; 212 312 8800) offers a moving tribute to the victims. Two massive reflecting pools occupy the footprint of each of the Twin Towers; waterfalls cascade into the serene waters of the seemingly bottomless basins, and the names of those killed in 2001, as well as in the 1993 attack on the World Trade Center, are inscribed in bronze panels around the perimeter of each pool. Entrance is free, but timed reservations are required via www.911memorial.org. An on-site museum is set to open in 2012.

Though the grid-bucking Downtown streets and the outer boroughs can get tricky, New York is easily traversed by foot. One of the best places for an urban ramble is along the **High Line** (www.thehighline.org), an elevated train track that runs from the Meatpacking District up the west side

Brooklyn Flea

Standard Hotel

toward Midtown, meandering past Chelsea's gallery district along the way. The industrial relic has been reimagined as New York's first elevated park, offering commanding river views, as well as public art installations and landscaped pathways.

Another iconic stroll is along the mile-long **Brooklyn Bridge**. There's more reason than ever to make it all the way across these days, thanks to the redevelopment of **Brooklyn Bridge Park** (www.brooklynbridge parknyc.org). The waterfont area – featuring piers, lawns and tree-lined paths – makes a fine place to spend an afternoon on the other side of the river, taking advantage of free Wi-Fi, soaking up views of the Manhattan skyline, and taking a whirl on Jane's Carousel, a vintage 1922 spinner that's been restored inside an elegant glass structure (it took about 25

years to refurbish the 48 hand-painted horses, scenery panels and crests).

Culture vultures can run themselves ragged racing through the halls of the **Met** (1000 Fifth Avenue, at 82nd Street, 212 535 7710, www.metmuseum.org), the **Guggenheim** (1071 Fifth Avenue, at 89th Street, 212 423 3500, www.guggenheim.org) and other world-class museums. But don't miss the revamped **New-York Historical Society** (170 Central Park West, between 76th and 77th Streets, 212 873 3400, www.nyhistory.org), which reopened in November 2011. The much-anticipated upgrades include a children's museum, a multimedia film detailing the city's development, and new exhibitions such as 'Revolution! The Atlantic World Reborn', which explores the ties between the American, Haitian and French revolutions in the 18th century.

High Line Park

Apollo Theater

Chrysler Building

Santos Party House

## EAT & DRINK

New York's famous foodstuffs are the street-cart hot dog, the pizza slice and the bagel. It's hard to wander a block without bumping into at least one of the three, but food-lovers shouldn't stop there. From Michelin-starred haute-dining temples (Per Se, Eleven Madison Park) to diverse ethnic enclaves such as Flushing (home to the best cheap Chinese food), the city is endlessly rewarding for diners – other culinary capitals have great nosh, but no place embraces the theatre of restaurants quite like New York.

To crack the scene, know that New Yorkers have a cultish devotion to chefs, who enjoy rock-star status among the town's legions of gastro-groupies. Leading the pack is David Chang, whose hypercool **Momofuku Ssäm Bar** (207 Second Avenue, at 13th Street, 212 254 3500), which opened in 2006, continues to define the city's melting-pot eating habits. Tuck into local charcuterie, veal sweetbread

with Thai chillies and addictive pork-belly steamed bun, then shout your inevitable plaudits over the noisy rock 'n' roll soundtrack. Afterwards, pop into the restaurant's adjoining **Milk Bar** (at no.215) to sample delightfully lowbrow treats – like birthday-cake truffles and cornflake-marshmallow cookies – from pastry savant Christina Tosi.

Gordon Ramsay may have fallen from favour in the Big Apple, but chef April Bloomfield hasn't let the side down. You can't go wrong with any of the Birmingham-born toque's perpetually mobbed eateries. Hit the **Spotted Pig** (314 W 11th Street, at Greenwich Street, 212 620 0393, www.thespottedpig.com) for a roquefort-cloaked burger and other gastropubby fare; the **Breslin Bar & Restaurant**

Momofuku Ssam Bar

(Ace Hotel, 16 W 29th Street, at Broadway, 212 679 1939, www.thebreslin.com) for lamb-belly scrumpets and decadent guinea-hen terrines; and the **John Dory Oyster Bar** (Ace Hotel, 1196 Broadway, at 29th Street, 212 792 9000, www.thejohndory.com) for perfectly shucked bivalves and revelatory seafood dishes.

**Eataly** (200 Fifth Avenue, between 23rd and 24th Streets, 212 229 2560, www.eatalyny.com) is Harrods food hall on steroids: a 42,500-square-foot temple to Italian gastronomy with a dizzying array of comestibles (salumi, focaccia, gelato, oh my!), as well as six on-site restaurants, including a rooftop brewpub offering hand-crafted pints and impeccable sausage platters. Grab a glass of Barbera from the central piazza bar and commence grazing.

Craft beer and cocktails currently dominate the boozy zeitgeist. At **Rattle N Hum** (14 E 33rd Street, between Fifth and Madison Avenues, 212 481 1586, www.rattlenhumbarnyc.com), 40 taps and two casks will get you up to speed on boundary-pushing brews from across the USA, including locally made standouts (Sixpoint, Greenport Harbor) and aggressively hoppy IPAs from the West Coast. Belly up to the bar at either **PDT** (113 St Marks Place, between First Avenue and Avenue A, 212 614 0386) and **Little Branch** (20 Seventh Avenue South, at Leroy Street, 212 929 4360) for top-flight cocktails, both classic and new-school (order the bacon-infused Benton's Old-Fashioned at PDT). Or you can sod the fancy-pants drinks and nurse a whiskey and Budweiser at an old-school dive – go to the sawdust-covered **McSorley's Ale House** (15 E 7th Street, between Second and Third Avenues, 212 473 9148) for the tourist-friendly version, or try **Subway Inn** (143 E 60th Street, between Lexington and Third Avenues, 212 223 8929) and **Holiday Cocktail Lounge** (75 St Marks Place, between First and Second Avenues, 212 777 9637).

# Hello, Brooklyn!

Brooklyn Bridge Park

Hop across the river to sample Brooklyn's youthful cool.

**EAT** Locavore clubhouse **Roberta's** (261 Moore Street, between Bogart and White Streets, Bushwick, 718 417 1118, www.robertaspizza.com) offers excellent wood-fired pizzas, handmade pastas and other seasonally inspired dishes from über-talented chef Carlo Mirarchi.

**SHOP** At the bustling **Brooklyn Flea** (www.brooklyn flea.com) you'll find hundreds of indie vendors selling vintage clothing, artisanal grilled cheese sandwiches, and much more. Locations vary.

**STAY** In addition to a 40-foot backyard pool and a roof-deck with a raw bar, the boutique **Hotel Williamsburg** (160 N 12th Street, between Bedford Avenue and Berry Street, Williamsburg, 888 867 6767, www.hwbrooklyn.com) tips its hat to the surrounding 'hood with trendy details, such as a signature beer made by nearby Brooklyn Brewery, and local-skewed LP collections to play on in-room turntables.

**PARTY** The **Brooklyn Bowl** (61 Wythe Avenue, between N 11th and 12th Streets, Williamsburg, 718 963 3369, www.brooklynbowl.com) bowling alley and live music venue is a temple to Brooklyn, with local beers on tap and Coney Island-inspired decor. Check out the concert line-up, or head there on a Thursday for the regular DJ set by DJ Questlove of the Roots.

## NIGHTLIFE & MUSIC

Getting past the velvet rope can be tough at the high-octane hotspots in the boîte-heavy Meatpacking District. Our best advice is to dress the part, pad your wallet, and get there early. A less expensive (though no less rowdy) night out can be had by skipping the velvet-rope scene and party-hopping your way around more late-night 'hoods like the East Village and Williamsburg. The streets of the Lower East Side swarm with youthful revellers on weekends; you might start at the contemporary art gallery-cum-nightspot **Gallery Bar** (120 Orchard Street, at Delancey Street, 212 529 2266), before descending to the subterranean **Dark Room** (165 Ludlow Street, at Stanton Street, 212 353 0536) for first-rate DJs and dancing.

Music-lovers are spoiled for choice when it comes to catching gigs. See big-name acts at historic venues such as Harlem's **Apollo Theater** (53 W 125th Street, between Adam Clayton Powell Jr Boulevard (Seventh Avenue) and Frederick Douglass Boulevard (Eighth Avenue), and the **Beacon Theater** (2124 Broadway, at 74th Street), or at Midtown spots such as **BB King Blues Club** (237 W 42nd Street, between Seventh and Eighth Avenues) and the **Best Buy Theater** (515 Broadway, at 44th Street). Downtown rock clubs such as **Santos Party House** (96 Lafayette Street, at Walker Street) and the **Bowery Ballroom** (6 Delancey Street, between Bowery and Chrystie Streets) are seething with young, attractive crowds seeking out new music. Meanwhile, the bohemian West Village is still the place to find world-class jazz acts, at pedigreed haunts such as **Blue Note** (131 W 3rd Street, at Sixth Avenue) and **Smalls** (83 W 10th Street, between Seventh Avenue South and W 4th Street).

Pick up a copy of *Time Out New York* magazine for weekly concert listings.

## SHOP

The transatlantic shopping spree is a time-honoured tradition for card-carrying shopaholics, who hop the pond with the single-minded goal of pillaging NYC's retail wonderland. But while the hordes plunder the sales at mega department stores such as Macy's and fight through Canal Street for touristy knick-knacks, you'll want to get off the beaten track to nab the best finds.

Big-brand shops (Abercrombie & Fitch, Uniqlo, J Crew) line Broadway in Soho. But you'll find more unusual garms at the meticulously curated boutique **Opening Ceremony** (35 Howard Street, between Broadway and Lafayette Street, 212 219 2688, www.openingceremony.us). Owners Carol Lim and Humberto Leon showcase American designers alongside brands from other countries. Of particular note are the exclusive collaborations.

Another burgeoning shopping area can be found in the **Meatpacking District**. Dominated by the wholesale

---

### Cultural baggage

**Book** *Appetite City: A Culinary History of New York* (William Grimes, 2009)
**Film** *Manhattan* (Woody Allen, 1979)
**Music** 'No Sleep Till Brooklyn' (Beastie Boys, 1986)

---

meat industry in the early 20th century – and later, during the 1990s, notorious as a stomping ground for transsexual prostitutes – the area has now been colonised by fashionistas who soldier along cobbled streets in their Manolo Blahniks. It's here that you'll find the consumer playground of *Sex and the City* fame, with high-end labels, such as Diane von Furstenberg, slinging their wares out of fancy storefronts.

The best place to pick up quirky, high-quality gifts is the **MoMA Design Store** (81 Spring Street, at Crosby Street, 212 767 1050, www.momastore.org). The museum's stand-alone retail arm assembles an impressive array of contemporary furnishings and design-mag goodies, including sculptural vases, clocks, kitchenware and gadgets.

## STAY

The respectable 'medium' rooms at the hipster-baiting **Ace Hotel** chainlet (20 W 29th Street, between Fifth and Sixth Avenues, 646 214 5742) are outfitted with vintage furniture and original art; even cheaper are the snug bunk-bed set-ups. You won't want to spend too much time sleeping, though, as the Ace – founded in Seattle by a pair of DJs – is home to two white-hot restaurants, a Stumptown café brewing locally roasted coffee, and one of the city's buzziest lobbies.

The Brits behind Yo! Sushi (and the Japanese-inspired sleeping 'cabins' at Heathrow) recently opened the futuristic Midtown West **Yotel** (570 Tenth Avenue, at 42nd Street, 646 449 7700, www.yotel.com). Prices are kept in check by compact rooms, with smart tweaks to help you maximise the space: motorised beds fold up futon-style when you're not kipping, and a 20-foot robot will stash excess baggage for you in a lobby locker. For more room – and a private hot tub – upgrade to 'first class'.

If you tend to follow the downtown flock instead of the tourist trail, André Balazs's trendy Meatpacking District high-rise the **Standard** (848 Washington Street, at W 13th Street, 212 645 4646, www.standardhotels.com) offers a non-stop party: guests can grab a steak at the Standard Grill, mingle with boisterous locals in the biergarten, and sip champers in a giant jacuzzi at Le Bain nightclub. Floor-to-ceiling windows cash in on views of either the Hudson River or a Midtown cityscape, and 'peekaboo' bathrooms are fitted with Japanese-style tubs.

## GETTING THERE & AROUND

British Airways, US Airways, Virgin Atlantic and Delta all offer direct flights from London, arriving at JFK, La Guardia or Newark airports. These and other airlines also operate indirect flights from other major UK airports, including a BA service from London City. Direct flights start from approximately £350 return.

New York's yellow cabs are rarely in short supply, except during rush hour and bad weather. New Yorkers generally tell cab drivers cross streets rather than actual addresses.

The MTA runs the subway and bus lines. Far cleaner and safer than it was 20 years ago, the subway system is one of the world's largest and cheapest, with a flat fare of $2.25. Trains run around the clock. Stations are most often named after the street on which they're located. White and blue MTA buses are the best way to travel crosstown and a pleasant way to travel up- or downtown, as long as you're not in a hurry. They have a digital destination sign on the front, along with a route number preceded by a letter (M for Manhattan).

# Abu Dhabi

In the 40 years since being named the capital city of the newly formed United Arab Emirates, this sometime modest pearl-diving outpost has been transformed beyond recognition. Gone are the Bedouin tents and free-roaming camels of yore, replaced by stratosphere-bothering tower blocks and gas-guzzling SUVs, while the million-strong population is mostly expat. The oil boom has seen world-class restaurants and opulent beach clubs plonked on practically every corner, but the tourism industry is still relatively small in Abu Dhabi, making it less a millionaire's playground and more a black-doored members' club. There's still a sense that this is a city that's yet to sell out, and that both locals and regular visitors would prefer to keep it this way. Beyond the urban bling are experiences of old Arabia for those determined to find them, like shopping for spices in Souk Qaryat Al Beri, or bashing dunes and smoking grape shisha in the city's sandy outskirts. Abu Dhabi's Middle Eastern charm is still robust enough to retain its authenticity – something that's virtually disappeared from all-but-Westernised neighbour Dubai. So while it's every bit the 21st-century metropolis, leave your preconceptions about Abu Dhabi at the baggage carousel – they're probably way off the mark.

## Fast facts

**Country dialling code** +971
**Journey time** Flight 7 hours
**Festivals & events** WOMAD (April, www.womad abudhabi.ae) brings three days of world music and multicultural shenanigans to the public beach. Loud, lively and, best of all, free; Abu Dhabi Film Festival (October, www.abudhabifilmfestival.ae) – your only chance to see uncensored movies on the UAE's big screens, with tickets just Dhs25 per screening; Yasalam (November, www.yasalam.ae) – the programme of events that runs alongside the city's Formula One weekend.
**Good for** Culture, shopping

## SEE & DO

By far the most awe-inspiring spot in the city, **Sheikh Zayed Grand Mosque** (www.szgmc.ae/en) is a gleaming monument to the UAE's cherished founder and, with capacity for 40,000 worshippers, one of the largest mosques in the world. Visitors of all faiths are welcome, with free tours taking place daily at 10am, 11am and 4.30pm. However, bear in mind that those deemed to be dressed immodestly will be turned away, and that the mosque is closed to tourists on Friday mornings and certain Islamic holidays.

For more frivolous kicks, head to **Ferrari World** on **Yas Island** (www.ferrariworldabudhabi.com). Not only is it the world's largest indoor theme park, it's also home to the fastest rollercoaster on earth – Formula Rossa is a 150mph beast capable of reducing burly men to gibbering wrecks. Stomach-churners aside, it's also a great day out for families, with plenty of kid-friendly attractions, classic car museums and some decent restaurants. While the park is fairly quiet for most of the year, booking ahead is advisable if visiting when the Formula One circus rolls into town in November.

If you can stand the heat, a bike ride along the Corniche – the city's seafront promenade – provides an excellent antidote to the honking horns and high-rises of downtown.

**Sheikh Zayed Grand Mosque**

Ask your taxi driver to drop you at Hiltonia beach club, then follow the footpath for five minutes until you see the **Byky** stand (www.q8byky.com). From here, steeds can be hired for Dhs20 an hour – ample time to complete the seven-mile round trip, even factoring in a couple of stops to soak up the local colour. And given that the Corniche is one of the buzziest social hubs in the city, there's plenty of it, with everyone from traditionally garbed local folk to sunset-chasing amateur photographers and expat capoeira clubs mingling amid the coffee shops and beachside cafés.

Also well worth looking into is a half-day desert safari with **Emirates Adventures** (www.eatours.ae). After you've been picked up from your hotel, you'll be driven an hour or so out of the city and treated to a spot of dune bashing – the noble art of hurling a 4x4 off colossal mountains of sand. Following a stop to take photos of the sunset, the tour moves on to an open-air desert encampment, where, after a barbecue dinner, there's the chance to get involved with belly dancing, shisha and – for an extra cost – sandboarding and quad biking.

If you'd rather see the city from the water, jet skis can be hired from **Hiltonia beach club** (+971 2 681 1900). The views of the skyline (not to mention the feeling of being in an American cop show from the 1980s) justify the expense. For slightly more sophisticated aquatic action, head to **Al Forsan** sports resort (www.alforsan.com) in **Khalifa City A**. Opened in 2010, the complex has the most modern water sports facilities in the UAE, and features two purpose-built, cable-drawn wakeboarding lakes.

## EAT & DRINK

Don't go out of your way trying to find authentic Emirati cuisine in Abu Dhabi because, unless you're staying with a local family, it's simply not there. The staple grub for most is Lebanese, with low-key, cedar tree-emblazoned outlets never further than 200 metres apart, and all eager to fill your belly with houmous, tabbouleh and shish tawook. Charmingly ramshackle **Automatic in Al Markaziyah** (Hamdan Street, behind Al Mariah Mall, +971 2 677 9782) is a good example and a great place to try a shawarma – the ubiquitous UAE street snack consisting of a sprinkling of spit-roasted meat, fries, pickles and garlic sauce wrapped in Lebanese bread. Simple, filling and a good deal more elegant than the great British kebab.

**Marco Pierre White Steakhouse & Grill**

**Ferrari World**

At the classier end of the scale, recent years have seen Japanese cuisine take a stranglehold of Abu Dhabi's fine-dining scene, and fierce competition has resulted in some exceptional restaurants. None are better than **Toki** at **Hilton Abu Dhabi** (Corniche, near Khaleej Al Arabi Street, +971 2 681 4151), where the stern-looking chap behind the sushi bar works industriously to deliver tightly packed makis and the freshest sashimi in the city. It's not cheap, but worth every last dirham.

For finer dining, the **Marco Pierre White Steakhouse & Grill** at **Fairmont Bab Al Bahr** (Bain Al Jessrain, +971 2 654 3333, www.fairmont.com/babalbahr) is unbeatable. Service and food – simple, artfully presented steaks and classic sides – are both impeccable and, though they're far from cheap, those richly marbled wagyu tenderloins must surely be among the finest cuts of cow on the planet. The dessert menu is equally decadent, featuring rich, buttery takes on classic English puddings.

Contrary to popular belief, drinking alcohol is permitted in the UAE – providing you quaff within a licensed hotel. While most head there for its modern Chinese nosh, **Hakkasan** at **Emirates Palace** (*see below*) is also home to the best-stocked bar in the city, as well as a cocktail list made famous by the franchise's London flagship. At the other end of town, monochrome-styled **Pearls & Caviar** at the **Shangri-La Qaryat Al Beri** (Bain Al Jessrain, +971 2 509 8888) is the perfect place to sip in the cooler months; its open-air deck treats party folk to incredible views across Maqtaa Creek to the perma-glowing Sheikh Zayed Grand Mosque. **Cho Gao**, a South-east Asian-themed bar at **Crowne Plaza** (Hamdan Street, near Najda Street, +971 2 621 0000), is also worth investigating. Not only is it the only non-smoking bar in the city, but, with classy dark wood booths and softly glowing lanterns, it tends to attract a more discerning drinker than some of the murkier, expat-ruled downtown pubs.

## STAY

Luxury is everywhere in Abu Dhabi, with the city home to more than 20 five-star hotels and another five expected to open by the end of 2012. Though more architecturally conservative than the mind-boggling structures of Dubai, the city remains the setting for a massive game of one-upmanship between hospitality firms and, while prices are high as a result, so are standards. Constructed at a cost of £1.9 billion, **Emirates Palace** (Ras Al Akhdar, +971 2 690 9000) is the flashiest of them all, and was the most expensive hotel ever built when it

**Emirates Palace**

**Fairmont Bab Al Bahr**

opened in 2005. Though it's since been surpassed, its size, splendour and ostentatious Arabian decor have lost none of their jaw-slackening power. Should your £400-a-night room leave you with change, you'll be pleased to hear that the premises also include a Versace store and – we're not having you on here – an ATM that dispenses gold bars.

For slightly less extravagance, there's the **Fairmont Bab Al Bahr** (Bain Al Jessrain, +971 2 654 3333) – the pick of a cluster of hotels that opened in time for the city's inaugural Formula One Grand Prix in 2009. You'll notice the boutiquey vibe the second you step into the huge lobby; a feeling that's carried into each of the 369 guest rooms and five restaurants – all of which are excellent.

Though there are no hostels in the city, Abu Dhabi does sport a few options for budget travellers, with **Holiday Inn** (Muroor, +971 2 657 4888) the best of the bunch. Opened just two years ago, it's a shade or two more glamorous than the chain name implies, featuring a decent rooftop pool and a cracking Italian restaurant. **Park Rotana** (next to Sheikh Khalifa Park, +971 2 657 3333) is the cheapest five-star hotel in town, and, while it's a good Dhs30 taxi ride from downtown, is well placed for Sheikh Zayed Grand Mosque.

## GETTING THERE & AROUND

Etihad Airways offers direct flights to Abu Dhabi, while those willing to stop over in Bahrain can fly with Gulf Air for a slightly cheaper fare. Outside the airport, look for a silver taxi (politely decline if you're offered an older white taxi or a black airport taxi, since the former are unmetered and the latter fiercely expensive), which will take you downtown within half an hour for around Dhs50 (£8).

While a subway system is promised within the next decade, for now the city's public transport system is limited to a few, overcrowded buses. They only cost Dhs1 per journey, but as taxis are so cheap and plentiful (and the prospect of waiting at a bus stop in 45°C heat unthinkable), you might want to treat yourself to a more relaxing cab journey. Lone female travellers are advised to always take a seat in the back, and mention their husband as soon as possible should the chap at the wheel strike up a conversation – which he inevitably will.

# Sci-fi City: Abu Dhabi's Future Projects

### Guggenheim Abu Dhabi
If a threatened artist boycott (based around allegations that the gallery's Subcontinental construction workers are being exploited) is averted, this massive, Frank Gehry-designed modern art museum stands to make Abu Dhabi a world-leading arts hub by late 2013.
*www.guggenheim.org/abu-dhabi*

### Yas Water Park
Opening the world's biggest water park in the middle of the desert is unlikely to impress the green brigade, but with 40 attractions planned and over £100 million invested, tourism in the UAE is set to be bigger than ever. Due to open in 2012.
*www.yasisland.ae*

### Zayed National Museum
Currently little more than a construction site, Saadiyat Island is set to become the new cultural district, with this new museum as its centrepiece. Named after the UAE's beloved founding father, and designed by Foster + Partners, it's slated for a 2013 opening.
*www.zayednationalmuseum.ae*

### Masdar City
A bold attempt to make amends for the city's carbon-spewing ways, this walled-off commercial/residential district will be powered purely by renewable energy. While some sections are already open to the public, completion is due some time between 2020 and 2025.
*www.masdarcity.ae/en*

# Beirut

Beirut is the wild child of the Middle East. A heady mix of chaos and contradictions, the Lebanese capital's charms can be overwhelming for the first-time visitor but, once seduced, you'll be left craving the city's warm-hearted hospitality, riveting history, houmous and hedonism. A former Phoenician port, the city rests at the bottom of the Lebanese mountain range, jutting out into the eastern end of the Mediterranean. The older generation still clings to Beirut's 1960s heyday, when the yacht-sprinkled coastline became a playground for the international jetset, drawn to its pavement cafés, cosmopolitan culture and endless joie de vivre. The party was cut short in 1975. Militias forced the sunbathing movie stars out and Beirut was torn in half as one of the 20th century's bloodiest civil conflicts put the city in a stranglehold for the next 15 years. Since then, the road to recovery has been rocky. But while sectarian tensions continue to simmer, over the last few years a rapid regeneration has shrugged off its war-smeared reputation. Boutique hotels, contemporary art galleries and a lifetime's worth of bars and restaurants have given the city a fresh lick of paint, and a steady trickle of tourists have been welcomed with open arms. Now, after a revolution-filled year in the Middle East, it's with a typically Lebanese sense of mocking pride that Beirut is enjoying the limelight as one of the most stable destinations in the region. No longer a well-kept secret, Beirut is the ultimate alternative to a Euro-city break, boasting a unique Middle Eastern and Mediterranean spirit.

## Fast facts

**Country dialling code** +961
**Journey time** Flight 5 hours
**Festivals & events** Lebanon Mountain Trail Association Thru-Walk (April, www.lebanontrail.org) – join hikers on an annual month-long trek along 440 kilometres of mountains and vistas – or just sign up for a weekend; Fête de la Musique (June) – held during the summer solstice, this worldwide music festival is a chance to see Beirut's streets traffic-free and full of diverse local acts; Vinifest (October, www. vinifestlebanon.com) – find your favourite tipple from Lebanon's vineyards at this annual wine festival
**Good for** Culture, food, nightlife

## SEE & DO

Roughly half the size of Wales, Lebanon is a small country with a big history. Archaeology-lovers will lap up the **National Museum of Beirut**'s antiquities (www.beirutnationalmuseum.com), but Beirut's real sights are its 20th-century landmarks. Take advantage of the warm climate and absorb the city's architecture by foot. Tracing the path in and around the city's former Green Line, which divided East and West during the civil war, you'll find crumbling Ottoman mansions, bullet-scarred French Mandate-era apartments and contemporary structures standing side by side. Catch sight of the Dome, an egg-shaped husk next to the massive golden-hued Mohammed Al-Amin Mosque on **Martyrs' Square**, and the former sniper stronghold Holiday Inn while you still can; cranes dominate Beirut's skyline, indicating the

Mohammed Al-Amin Mosque

new high-rises that will soon – for better or for worse – make up most of the city's real estate.

Despite the influx of designer stores and occasional music festival, Downtown's cookie-cutter streets, rebuilt over the flattened city centre, still feel a tad eerie, so jump in a *servees* to the livelier neighbourhoods of Hamra and Achrafieh. The shared taxis are anecdote-worthy experiences; watch with dismay as chain-smoking drivers blast Arabic oldies and zig-zag their death-defying way through Beirut's kamikaze traffic.

At sunset, join the fishermen, joggers and loved-up teenagers for a stroll along the **Corniche**, a pedestrian boulevard that wraps itself around the coastline. The brave can hire a bike from **Beirut By Bike** (Graham Street, Ein El Mreyse, 961 1 365524, www.beirutbybike. com) – but beware of the crazy local drivers – and cycle up to **Pigeon Rock** (essentially, a doughnut-shaped rock

planted in the sea but also one of Beirut's most picturesque spots) before puffing on a *narguileh* at a seaside café.

Although Beirut's museums and sightseeing spots can be a little underwhelming compared to Lebanon's rich layers of history, the city's long list of art galleries offers a much more satisfying culture fix. **Beirut Exhibition Center** (01-962000 ext 2883, www.beirutexhibitioncenter.com) and **Beirut Art Center** (www.beirutartcenter.org) are dedicated warehouse-sized spaces, while smaller, independent white cubes, such as the **Running Horse** (www.therunninghorseart.com), give a flavour of the region's vibrant art scene.

Experience the other side of Beirut by spending a night in **Shatila**. The Children and Youth Center (CYC) runs a small guesthouse in the Palestinian refugee camp (www.cycshatila.org/guesthouse), and short stays cost roughly £7 a night.

## EAT & DRINK

When Israel broke the Guinness World Record for the world's largest amount of houmous in 2010, the situation escalated into a game of gastronomic one-upmanship, a 'houmous war' in which the two countries exercised their political tensions by vying to create the biggest and best amount of houmous known to man. Needless to say, the Lebanese take their food seriously – your options here are countless and the portions generous.

While you could survive a weekend on street food alone – a *manouche* (a type of Lebanese pizza) filled with thyme, cheese or meat, or fruit cocktails spilling with sweet avocado and *ashta* (Lebanese cream) – no trip to Beirut is complete without surrounding yourself with plates piled high with meze. **Abdel Wahab** (51 Abdel Wahab El Inglizi Street, Monot, +961 1 200550, www.ghiaholding.com) and former Yasser Arafat-haunt **Barometre** (Blue Building, Makhoul Street, Hamra, +961 3 678998) are old favourites, while **Le Chef**'s (Gouraud Street, Gemmayzeh, +961 1 445373) charisma and cheap prices have been keeping Beirut's bellies full for decades.

Head to **Souk el Tayeb** (Beirut Souks, Trablos Street, Downtown, 01 442664, www.soukeltayeb.com) on Saturday morning, a farmers' market devoted to Lebanon's traditional and organic agriculture. Farmers from all over Lebanon gather to share their produce here; pick up a freshly squeezed pomegranate juice or take home jars of delicious local *labneh* (local strained yoghurt that has a consistency between yoghurt and cheese) and fig jam. The market's sister restaurant, **Tawlet** (Chalhoub Building, Nahr Street, Mar Mikhael, +961 1 448129, www.tawlet.com), is the best place to sample a home-cooked Lebanese lunch, where every day a different cook or producer takes over the kitchen with the culinary secrets of their area.

Beirut's substantial Armenian community is also an excuse to savour specialities from the region, such as kebab in cherry sauce and dinky sparrows in pomegranate syrup. Try **Al Mayass** (Trabaud Street, Achrafieh, +961 1 215046, www.almayass.com) for fantastic Armenian dishes via Aleppo, and a moustached troubadour thrown in for free. Alternatively, jump in a *servees* to the 'Little Armenia' quarter of **Bourj Hammoud** for a cheap fix of *basterma* (highly seasoned dried cured beef) and garlicky street snacks, from stalls that are often open 24 hours a day.

For further culinary spots, visit www.timeoutbeirut.com.

## NIGHTLIFE

During the summer, the capital's pulsating beach resorts and glitzy rooftop clubs – many of which have a sweeping panorama of the surrounding mountains and Mediterranean – have won the city the somewhat turgid title of 'party capital of the Middle East'. But Beirut's real nightlife attraction can be found year-round at street level, by hopping between hip hole-in-the-wall bars, Hamra's legendary leftist watering holes and even a Charlie Chaplin-themed speakeasy (**Chaplins**, Mar Mikhael Street, Mar Mikhael, +961 3 286977). There's always a new bar to try out, and a night spent on **Gouraud Street** in Gemmayzeh, the city's steadfast nightlife strip, or **Makdessi Street** in Hamra can often feel like a wild goose chase, but that's just part of the fun.

**BarThreeSixty**

Avoid the tackier establishments (they're easy to spot) and start the night with a few bottles of lightweight local beer, Almaza, and a 'dou dou' shot – Beirut's vodka, lemon juice, Tabasco and olive-laced speciality – at **Dany's** (78th Street, Hamra, +961 3 904547), **Demo** (Libanon Street, off Gouraud Street, Gemmayzeh, +961 3 958504) or **Torino** (rue Gouraud, Gemmayzeh) alongside Beirut's fun-loving artsy crowd. Then see where the trail of bar snacks takes you – at weekends there's often a party or alternative club night happening just around the corner, or try out the industrial-style bar at ambitious new concert hall **DRM** (Democratic Republic of Music, Sourati Street, Hamra, +961 1 752 202, www.drmlebanon.com).

More classy, and pricey, cocktails can be found while enjoying the views from boutique hotel Le Gray's (*see right*) **BarThreeSixty**, and at **Centrale** (Mar Maroun Street, Saifi, +961 1 575858, www.centralerestaurant.com). Or in **Momo At The Souks** (Beirut Jewellery Souks, Downtown, + 961 76 700 407, www.momobeirut.com), which also does a champagne-fuelled brunch on Sunday.

## SHOP

Escape Downtown's expensive boutiques to **Mar Mikhael**. Independent bookstores and fashion and furniture designers have started to gentrify the residential/industrial area's former greasy garages, but the invasion is a happy one. Ageing mechanics, butchers and a man who only sells bananas – decades ahead of Europe's mono-boutique trend – now share the streets with trendier shopping options, such as arts and culture concept store **Plan Bey** (Geara Building, Armenia Street, Mar Mikhael, +961 1 444110).

**Beirut Souks** (Downtown, +961 1 973 418), an open-air shopping mall built on the site of Beirut's traditional souk,

### Cultural baggage

**Book** *Beirut* (Samir Kassir, 2010)
**Film** *West Beyrouth* (Ziad Doueiri, 1998)
**Album** *Houdou Nisbi* (Ziad Rahbani, 2007)

Plan Bey

Centrale

raised a few begrudging comments from locals when it opened in 2009, but an afternoon spent wandering through the high-street stores and newly opened big-name brands is pleasant enough. Pop in to nearby **Elie Saab** and **Zuhair Murad**, known for their red-carpet gowns and pure Lebanese glamour. On the other end of the spectrum, **Starch Boutique** (www.starchfoundation.org) showcases a fresh crop of young design talent every year, and is the best place to pick up one-off, contemporary clothing. Round off with a coffee-cardamom macaron from **Ladurée** (+961 1 992 922), a flavour created by the Parisian pastry and tea house in tribute to Beirut.

If you're craving a more typical souk experience, then travel to the coastal cities of **Tripoli** and **Saida**, known for their centuries-old soap factories and other traditional goods. For gifts, a box of sugary baklava or a bottle of Lebanese wine from the country's vineyards make for suitable Beiruti souvenirs.

## STAY

The Orientalist-inspired decor and spectacular terrace at **Hotel Albergo** (137 Abdel Wahab El Inglizi Street, +961 1 339 797, www.albergobeirut.com) and **Le Gray**'s contemporary luxury (Martyrs' Square, +961 1 971 111, www.campbellgrayhotels.com/le-gray-beirut) offer five-star boutique stays worthy of their hefty price tags. More modest accommodation can be found at **Saifi Urban Gardens** (Pasteur Street, Gemayze, +961 1 562 509, www.saifigardens.com); hostel-like rooms are supplemented by a café and rooftop bar that are also a hit with locals, as well as an Arabic language school.

## GETTING THERE & AROUND

BMI and MEA both operate surprisingly short (five-hour) flights direct from London Heathrow to Beirut International Airport.

Once in town, one of the best ways to get around – and also one of the best local experiences – is to hop into a *servees*, the informal community 'service' taxis that are shared by several people at once. Be sure to negotiate a price for your journey as you get going.

BEIRUT

DRM

# Further Reference

## Useful UK websites

**BBC Coast**
www.bbc.co.uk/coast

**BCU Surf**
www.bcusurf.org.uk

**Campaign for the Protection of Rural England**
www.cpre.org.uk

**Classic Sailing**
www.classic-sailing.co.uk

**Cornwall Sailing School**
www.paddleandsail.com

**Doors Open Days**
www.doorsopendays.org.uk

**English Heritage**
www.english-heritage.org.uk

**Enjoy England**
www.enjoyengland.com

**Enjoy Scotland**
www.enjoy-scotland.co.uk

**Good Beach Guide**
www.goodbeachguide.co.uk

**Good Pub Guide**
www.thegoodpubguide.co.uk

**Heritage Open Days**
www.heritageopendays.org.uk

**Lidos in the UK**
www.lidos.org.uk

**Met Office**
www.metoffice.gov.uk

**National Gardens Scheme**
www.ngs.org.uk

**National Parks**
www.nationalparks.gov.uk

**National Rail**
www.nationalrail.co.uk

**National Trails**
www.nationaltrail.co.uk

**National Trust**
www.nationaltrust.org.uk

**Natural England**
www.naturalengland.org.uk

**Ordnance Survey**
www.ordnancesurvey.co.uk

**Ramblers Association**
www.ramblers.org.uk

**River & Lake Swimming Association**
www.river-swimming.co.uk

**Royal Yachting Association**
www.rya.org.uk

**Sustrans**
www.sustrans.org.uk

**The Trainline**
www.thetrainline.com

**UK Camping & Caravanning Directory**
http://camping.uk-directory.com

**UK Campsites**
www.ukcampsite.co.uk

**UK Climbing**
www.ukclimbing.com

**UK Golf**
www.uk-golfguide.com

**UK World Heritage**
www.ukworldheritage.org.uk

**Visit Britain**
www.visitbritain.com

**Walking Britain**
www.walkingbritain.co.uk

**Walking Routes**
www.walking-routes.co.uk

**Wild About Britain**
www.wildaboutbritain.co.uk

**Wild Swimming**
www.wildswimming.com

**Woodland Trust**
www.british-trees.com

## Tourist boards

**Abu Dhabi**
www.visitabudhabi.ae

**Amsterdam**
www.holland.com

**Avignon**
www.avignon-tourisme.com

**Barcelona**
www.barcelonaturisme.com

**Beirut**
www.lebanon-tourism.gov.lb

**Bergerac**
www.pays-de-bergerac.com

**Berlin**
www.visitberlin.de

**Brussels**
www.visitflanders.co.uk

**Cairo**
www.egypt.travel

**Cologne**
www.koelntourismus.de

**Copenhagen**
www.visitcopenhagen.com

**Fès**
www.visitmorocco.com

**Florence**
www.firenzeturismo.it

**Granada**
www.turgranada.es

**Hamburg**
www.hamburg-tourism.de

**Helsinki**
www.visithelsinki.fi

**Iceland**
www.visiticeland.com

**Istanbul**
www.istanbul.com

**Leichtenstein**
www.tourismus.li

**Lisbon**
www.visitlisboa.com

**Luxembourg**
www.lcto.lu

**Madrid**
www.esmadrid.com

**Marrakech**
www.visitmorocco.com

**Milan**
http://ciaomilano.it

**New York City**
www.iloveny.com

**Nice**
www.nicetourism.com

**Normandy**
www.normandie-tourisme.fr

**Palermo**
www.palermotourism.com

**Palma**
www.illesbalears.es

**Paris**
http://en.parisinfo.com

**Porto**
www.visitportugal.com

**St Petersburg**
www.visitrussia.org.uk

**Stockholm**
www.visitstockholm.com

**Valencia**
www.turisvalencia.es

**Vienna**
www.austria.info

## Travel/Booking websites
**Expedia**
www.expedia.co.uk

**Hotel Link**
www.hotellink.co.uk

**lastminute.com**
www.lastminute.com

**Opodo**
www.opodo.co.uk

**Travel Intelligence**
www.travelintelligence.net

**Travelocity**
www.travelocity.co.uk

## Disabled travellers
**Tourism for All**
0303 303 0146,
www.tourismforall.org.uk

**Wheelchair travel & Access mini buses**
01483 233640, www.wheelchair-travel.co.uk

## Holiday home companies
**Best of Suffolk**
01728 638962,
www.bestofsuffolk.co.uk

**The Big Domain**
01237 426777,
www.thebigdomain.com

**Boutique Boltholes**
www.boutiqueboltholes.co.uk

**Cottages4you**
0845 268 0763,
www.cottages4you.co.uk

**Duchy of Cornwall Holiday Cottages**
01579 346473, www.duchyof
cornwallholidaycottages.co.uk

**Lake Lovers**
01539 488855, www.lakelovers.co.uk

**Landmark Trust**
01628 825925,
www.landmarktrust.org.uk

**The Little Domain**
01326 240028,
www.thelittledomain.com

**National Trust Cottages**
0844 800 2070,
www.nationaltrustcottages.co.uk

**North Devon Holiday Homes**
01271 376322,
www.northdevonholidays.co.uk

**Superior Cottages**
www.superiorcottages.co.uk

**Toad Hall Cottages**
01548 853089,
www.toadhallcottages.co.uk

**Unique Home Stays**
www.uniquehomestays.com

## Hotel chains
**Best Western**
www.bestwestern.com

**Britannia Hotels**
www.britanniahotels.com

**City Inn**
www.cityinn.com

**Exclusive Hotels**
www.exclusivehotels.com

**Golden Tulip**
www.goldentulip.com

**Hilton**
www.hilton.com

**Hotel du Vin**
www.hotelduvin.com

**Ibis Hotels**
www.ibishotels.com

**Intercontinental Hotels Group**
www.ichotelsgroup.com

**Macdonald Hotels & Resorts**
www.macdonaldhotels.co.uk

**Malmaison**
www.malmaison.com

**Marriott**
www.marriott.com

**my hotel**
www.myhotels.com

**Novotel**
www.novotel.com

**Premier Inn**
www.premiertravelinn.com

**Radisson**
www.radisson.com

**Travelodge**
www.travelodge.com

**Von Essen**
www.vonessenhotels.co.uk

## Airlines
**Aer Lingus**
0871 718 2020,
www.aerlingus.com

**American Airlines**
0800 433 7300,
www.americanairlines.co.uk

**bmi**
0844 848 4888, www.flybmi.com

**British Airways**
0844 493 0787,
www.britishairways.com

**easyjet**
www.easyjet.co.uk

**Flybe**
0871 700 2000,
www.flybe.com

**Ryanair**
0871 246 0000, www.ryanair.com

**Vigin Atlantic**
0844 209 7310, www.virgin-
atlantic.com

## Ferries
**Cairnryan (Scotland)–Larne
(Northern Ireland)**
P&O (0871 664 2121, www.po
ferries.com) sail from Cairnryan.

**Dover–Calais/Boulogne/
Dunkerque**
P&O (0871 664 2121, www.po
ferries.com) and Norfolk Line (0871
574 7235, www.norfolkline.com)
sail from Dover.

**Harwich–Esbjerg (Denmark)/
Hook of Holland (The Netherlands)**
Stena Lines (0844 770 7070,
www.stenalines.co.uk) and DFDS
Seaways (0871 522 9955, www.dfds
seaways.co.uk) sail from Harwich.

**Hull–Zeebrugge (Belgium)/
Rotterdam (The Netherlands)**
P&O (0871 664 2121,
www.poferries.com) sail from Hull.

**Newcastle–Amsterdam
(The Netherlands)**
DFDS Seaways (0871 522 9955,
www.dfds.co.uk) sails from
Newcastle.

**Newhaven–Dieppe (France)**
LD Lines (0844 576 8836,
www.ldlines.co.uk) sail from
Newhaven.

**Plymouth–Roscoff (France)/
Santander (Spain)**
Brittany Ferries (0871 244 0744,
www.brittany-ferries.co.uk) sail
from Plymouth.

**Poole–St Malo (France)**Condor
Ferries (0845 609 1024, www.
condorferries.co.uk) sail from Poole.

**Portsmouth–St Malo (France)/
Cherbourg (France)/Le Havre
(France)/Caen (France)/
Bilbao (Spain)**
Brittany Ferries (0871 244 0744,
www.brittany-ferries.co.uk) sails to
Caen, Cherbourg, St Malo & Bilbao.
Condor Ferries (0845 609 1024,
www.condorferries.co.uk) sails to
Cherbourg. LD Lines (0844 576
8836, www.ldlines.co.uk).

**Troon–Larne (Northern Ireland)**
P&O (0871 664 2121, www.po
ferries.com) sails from Troon.

**Weymouth–St Malo (France)**
Condor Ferries (0845 609 1024,
www.condorferries.co.uk) sails
from Weymouth.

## Cars and driving
When driving to or on the Continent,
you should take the following
documents with you: Driving licence
(full and valid) – an International
Driving Permit, if required by the
country you're visiting. Photographic
British driving licences will be accepted
by EU countries, but if you have an
older type of licence it's best to get
an International Driving Permit;
Vehicle registration document; Motor
insurance certificate You must display
a GB sticker if your number plate does
not state your country of origin. The
new EU number plates obviates this
but outside the EU the GB sticker
remains necessary; a warning triangle
(to display in case of breakdown) is
compulsory in many countries. Take
one with you; reflective jackets are
also compulsory if you break down
in many European countries.
   A first-aid kit, fire extinguisher and
spare bulbs are all good pieces of
kit to take with you.
   Before leaving, adjust your
headlights so that when driving on the
right oncoming drivers are not dazzled.
   It's also wise to take out breakdown
cover. The AA (www.theaa.com), RAC
(www.rac.co.uk) and other motoring
organisations provide cover through
most of Europe.

### Hire-car companies
**Alamo**
0871 384 1086, www.alamo.co.uk

**Avis**
0844 581 0147, www.avis.co.uk

**Budget**
www.budget.co.uk

**Easycar**
www.easycar.com

**Europcar**
0871 384 1087, www.europcar.co.uk

**Hertz**
0870 844 8844, www.hertz.co.uk

**Holiday Autos**
0871 472 5229,
www.holidayautos.co.uk

**Thrifty**
01494 751500, www.thrifty.co.uk

## Coaches
**National Express**
0871 781 8178,
www.nationalexpress.com

## Train information
**Eurostar**
Eurostar House, Waterloo Station,
London, SE1 8SE, 01233 777879,
www.eurostar.com

**Eurotunnel**
08705 35 35 35, www.eurotunnel.com

**National Rail Enquiries**
08457 48 49 50,
www.nationalrail.co.uk

**St Pancras International**
Pancras Road, London, NW1 2QP
020 7843 7688, www.stpancras.com

## Buying tickets
Below are some useful websites for
buying ticket, and most of them also
have real, live people available at the
other end of a telephone line if it all
gets too complicated.

**www.bahn.de**
The site for German railways:
generally acknowledged as the best
for working out routes and timetables.

**www.raileurope.co.uk**
Comprehensive booking service for
European rail travel, InterRail and
offical UK agent for SNCF, the French
railway operator; charges same
rates as SNCF and other European
agencies, subject to currency
exchange rates.

**www.eurostar.com**
Fast booking and offers for Paris and other French destinations, Brussels and Belgium, and The Netherlands.

**www.thalys.com**
The site for the high-speed train service linking France, Belgium, The Netherlands and Germany.

**www.voyages-sncf.com**
France-based trains and travel.

**www.seat61.com**
The man to go to for independent advice on rail travel.

**www.europeanrail.com**
An independent rail company, good for advice on tours and unusual routes. Charges £5 for a quote which is refunded if you purchase a ticket.

**www.internationalrail.com**
A rail specialist. Contact for tours and tickets.

**www.interrailnet.com**
Official pan-European site for InterRail passes.

**www.renfe.com**
Spanish railways site – English-language version.

## Telephone dialling codes

When dialling from the UK, use 00 followed by these codes:

## Good for

### Beaches

### Countryside

### Culture

### Food

# Notes

# Advertisers' Index

Please refer to relevant sections for addresses/telephone numbers

ADVERTISERS' INDEX